D0915431

PAUL METCALF

PAUL METCALF

COLLECTED WORKS · VOLUME ONE · 1956-1976

COFFEE HOUSE PRESS :: MINNEAPOLIS

MIDDLEBURY COLLEGE LIBRARY

Will West, copyright © 1956, 1973 by Paul Metcalf. *Genoa*, copyright © 1965 by Paul Metcalf. *Patagoni*, copyright © 1971 by Paul Metcalf. *Middle Passage*, copyright © 1976 by Paul Metcalf. *Apalache*, copyright © 1976 by Paul Metcalf. Introduction copyright © 1996 by Guy Davenport.

Dustjacket photograph by Jonathan Williams.

Will West, Genoa, Patagoni, and *The Middle Passage* were first published by The Jargon Society. *Will West* was later reprinted by The Bookstore Press. *Apalache* was first published by The Turtle Island Foundation. To Jonathan Williams, and to Bob and Eileen Callahan, adventurous, idealistic editor/publishers, the author and Coffee House Press extend thanks & respect.

This project was made possible by major funding from the Lannan Foundation. Additional support has been provided by the Minnesota State Arts Board, through an appropriation by the Minnesota State Legislature and a grant from the National Endowment for the Arts; the Lila Wallace-Reader's Digest Fund; The McKnight Foundation; Target Stores, Dayton's, and Mervyn's by the Dayton Hudson Foundation; General Mills Foundation; St. Paul Companies; Honeywell Foundation; Star Tribune/Cowles Media Company; The James R. Thorpe Foundation; Beverly J. and John A. Rollwagen Fund of The Minneapolis Foundation; and The Andrew W. Mellon Foundation.

Coffee House Press books are available to the trade through our primary distributor, Consortium Book Sales & Distribution, 1045 Westgate Drive, Saint Paul, MN 55114. For personal orders, catalogs, or other information, write to: Coffee House Press, 27 North Fourth Street, Suite 400, Minneapolis, MN 55401.

Library of Congress CIP Data
Metcalf, Paul C.
   [Works. 1996]
   Collected works, 1956-1976 / Paul Metcalf.
   v. <1> CM.
   Contents: v. 1. Will West
   ISBN 1-56689-050-0 (HC: V. 1)
   1. Title.
PS3563.E83   1996   96-2777
818'.5409—DC20   CIP

10   9   8   7   6   5   4   3   2   1

CONTENTS

INTRODUCTION

There was an evening not all that long ago when Paul Metcalf gave a reading at the University of Kentucky. In my twenty-seven years there I brought in all manner of strange creators of imaginative works: Stan Brakhage, Jonas Mekas, Louis Zukofsky, Bucky Fuller, Ronald Johnson, Jonathan Williams. Early on in this enterprise I learned that the audiences would vary wildly. The high sheriff of Fayette County joined the hundreds who came to see Jack Smith's film *Flaming Creatures* (banned at the time in New York), and large contingents of faculty, students, and the community came to hear Eudora Welty and Fuller. The English department rarely showed any interest, having not heard of most of my imported geniuses. Zukofsky proved to be particularly confusing, as the administration from whom I had to beg money understood him to be a lady pianist. Metcalf was wholly unknown, so unknown, in fact, that a sporting colleague in Romantic poetry who had the evening free ventured to give this Metcalf a dog's chance "and see what you modernists are up to." Paul, looking very Dutch, affable, and intelligent, read *Willie's Throw*, a collage that moves back and forth between a description of a famous peg by Mays and the kinesiology of throwing. The effect is something like hearing in concert a sportscaster, Willie Mays's own voice, and Aristotle explaining the physiology of Myron's discus thrower. We are at the Olympics in ancient Greece, at the Polo Grounds; we are watching a slow-motion film of the throw; we are in an ode of Pindar celebrating an athlete; we are in an Ivesian harmony of the vernacular, the scientific, and the lyric.

My scholarly colleague had never heard anything like it. He was amazed. He was surprised both by his pleasure and by the beauty of this intricate and powerful poem (as he heard it).

Every page of Paul Metcalf is a score for the voice. Or, as the truth is, for the imagination. For each page is a careful construct of voices, written voices for the most part, found in other texts by a searcher with eyes far sharper than ours, and infinitely more diligent in their search. "Whatever I am as a writer," Borges said, "I know that I am a great reader." Paul Metcalf is as great a reader. Borges's reading became a bottomless source for his stories, essays, and poems. Metcalf's reading is to find things which he puts together in patterns. Such was the working method of Plutarch, Montaigne, Burton, all of whose books are new contexts for other voices. It was Borges who showed us in his "Pierre Menard" that identical pages, one written by Cervantes, one rewritten in our time by Pierre Menard, are quite different.

Metcalf's quoted passages are different because they are now in a new field of force. We had never before seen a Greek discuss thrower on the Elean plain, a naked display of skill and strength, and Willie Mays in centerfield, "one continuous muscle" winding into a spring that hurls a ball, both at once, together in our imagination.

Metcalf's first published book, *Will West* (about a native American baseball player who must, like his ancestors, flee westward) is an alternating of original narrative and quoted history. Metcalf's method is not quite yet in place; neither is it new (O. Henry, of all people, once used it). The temptation is to read the narrative and skim the history, though readers who have learned to appreciate Metcalf read the history with attention and skim the narrative. The title contains a mystery: there was a real Will West, black, in Leavenworth in 1903, whose identical twin was sent to Leavenworth for an identical crime. Photographs of the two seem to be two prints from the same negative. They did not acknowledge each other. They were Will West and Will West.

The two Will Wests have, apparently, nothing to do with Paul's. Yet his next book, perhaps his masterpiece (it must vie with *Waters of Potowmack* and *Patagoni* for the distinction), *Genoa,* is about two brothers who are so different as to raise into sharp relief what we know of genetics, nature, and nurture. *Genoa,* Metcalf's most complex work and his last use of the novel as a form, is a study of Melville (Metcalf's great-grandfather), Columbus, biological monsters (the fictional narrator is a doctor), the second world war, and the kidnapping in 1953 of the child Bobby Greenlease by Bonnie Brown Heady and Carl Austin Mills in St. Louis.

Genoa is built: it is an architecture of analogies, similitudes, and Melvillean metaphors. It proceeds with a whale's vision, eyes at right angles to each other and with a ton of forehead to obviate a stereoptical view. And yet a whale must see as one thing what its disparate eyes focus on. So Metcalf, with one eye on Melville and the other on Columbus, one on healing and one on a sadistic murder, one on sanity and one on schizophrenia, and on and on, leaves us to feel, if not always see, the identity of different things. The smallest of animals is the spermatozoon, big-headed and with a lively tail; the largest of animals is the sperm whale. A galaxy, like the DNA molecule, is a spiral.

The boy Paul Metcalf remembers the discovery (by Raymond M. Weaver) of the manuscript of *Billy Budd* in the family attic. The Metcalfs were reluctant to allow scholars to inspect Melville's papers, and Paul's grandmother wouldn't have the name mentioned. Melville had died forgotten as an author, and considered by his family to have been a failure and a black sheep.

So Metcalf grew up watching his strange great-grandfather change from a scribbler of adventure stories to our greatest author. Metcalf was befriended by Charles Olson when he was thirteen; they remained friends for the rest of Olson's life. It is clear that Olson's *Call Me Ishmael*, the most imaginative of books about Melville, gave Paul the purchase he needed to look great-grandad in the eye. Other instigations must include William Carlos Williams's *Paterson*, with its imagery of spirals, birth, monsters (and the monstrosity of genius) and its use of other texts as an integral part of the poem. Also Williams's *In the American Grain*, and probably Hart Crane's *The Bridge*. There are as yet only rudimentary studies of *Genoa;* the exposition of its miraculous unity and resonating polyphony will establish Metcalf as a master of modern American writing.

He has notoriously and scandalously been at the periphery. This is partly due to his modesty and reticence, and to the fate of his books with publishers. He has been lucky to have many of his works designed and printed by Jonathan Williams at the Jargon Society. Jargon is one of the finest and most discriminating of American presses, publishing Olson and Zukofsky, for instance. Jargon, however, has never solved the problem of distribution. It is a paradoxical fusion of fine printing and samizdat diffusion. North Point Press went bankrupt soon after publishing *Waters of Potowmack;* this is not cause and effect. North Point failed because, as the *New York Times* said, it published only good writing.

Metcalf would never again write a work as densely intricate as *Genoa.* He opened out his method, using two or three themes in bold patterns. In *U.S. Dept. of the Interior,* the subject is migraine and earthquakes, analogs of each other, with surprising image rhymes between nerves and water courses, neural and geological events, geography and human anatomy.

In *Patagoni* (pre-conquest American cultures and Henry Ford's machine that is the conquistador of all our lives), this analogy of earth and body reaches its fullest expression. The New World is a man—like Olson's Maximus, Joyce's Finnegan, Blake's Albion—whose torso is North America and whose creative loins and legs are South America. Alaska is a newly raised right arm: the last frontier. This is a primitive idea—primal, totemistic, mythical. Williams had made Paterson both a city and a man. A city is an organism. All aggregates display a macrocosmic resemblance to each of its parts. An atom is a tiny solar system. Melville's most daring tropes are analogies Shakespearean in their leaps.

Science accumulates its information by noting differences: there is a zebra that's actually a white horse with black stripes. Poets think in likenesses. Metcalf is a poet working in images and signs. To the scientific mind, Columbus and Melville are two very different men four centuries apart. Yes, says Paul Metcalf, but listen and look, they were practically brothers. They understood space the same way; they hated limits and walls. They did not understand land, only water. Metcalf's collaged textures are ultimately derived from Pound's ideogrammatic method in *The Cantos,* where images in a field of force make a complex sign, just as the radicals in a Chinese character add up in a kind of poetic arithmetic to a meaning. Each of Metcalf's books is an ideogram. Whereas Pound's (and perhaps even Olson's) ideograms are, at least in the early cantos, resolvable enough to bear titles ("The Moral Splendor of John Adams," "Confucian Ethics," "The Hell of Usury"), Metcalf's remain a vibrant suspension. How hawks and forest fires sit together in a nest of affinities *(Firebird)* eludes linear reason. What Poe and Booth *(Both)* have in common occupies a geometry of the imagination hitherto unknown. We can follow the strategies and energies of books like *I-57* (the highway across Illinois, and "I, Paul Metcalf, age 57") with its terrifying contrast of madness and sanity, or *Mountaineers Are Always Free* (the motto of West Virginia), which amounts to ironic history at its sharpest.

Patagoni may be Metcalf's most congenial book: like *I-57,* it is a travel book, with Metcalf's own urbane, clear, and witty voice. And it is in *Patagoni* that we see Paul's place in an area of American writing that is undeservedly not well-known: the historical and cultural studies of Carl Sauer, the anthropology of Jaime de Angulo.

Whatever the public's problems with Metcalf's intensely imaginative works, there are the histories *(Apalache, Waters of Potowmack),* which for sheer scope and vividness of information ought to be read. In many places, Paul evokes the landing of the early explorers in, as they thought, a paradise—Chesapeake Bay completely covered with ducks, forests as old as time, meadows that, as might be, were Heaven—and the accounts he has found are justifiably unparaphrased, eloquently whole from the past (it is a comfort to see how badly George Washington spelled). *Waters of Potowmack* chronicles the valley and tributaries of that river from its discovery up to its industrialization and pollution, the Revolution and the Civil War, the arrival of the slaves, daily life on the plantations. The pace Metcalf sets for this history is majestically slow and includes kinds of history (road building, country life, hideous scenes of Civil War battles, local gossip) that you would have to get otherwise from many different books, old newspapers, and archives.

Pervading all of Metcalf's work is a tragic sense of the past, of a grief for how far wrong we've gone, how uselessly bloody our past has been, how ignorant we are of that past, and how inscrutibly strange our biological nature is. He has no Polynesia to gaze at in vision like Melville on his piazza. He has something better: a sense of wonder that has led him to inquire minutely and insatiably into the history of the New World and to trace its unsuspected patterns that stir us into wonder, too.   —Guy Davenport

AUTHOR'S NOTE

Early in the development of this project, I sat down with Allan Kornblum, the gifted editor at Coffee House Press, to determine the sequence in which the books should be published. Without hesitation, we agreed that the order should be chronological; that the reader might discover them pretty much as I did, as they were written: reader and writer witness to an author's developement, as partners.

These books depend heavily on research, the mining of the work of those who have explored the terrritory before. The question arises: how should these sources be acknowledged?

As a young writer, in *Will West*, I ignored the issue. There is no bibliography. In the second book, *Genoa*, I came to terms with the fact that the method I was developing was both creative and scholarly, a fact that must be recognized. I was, and am, averse to attaching little burrs at the bottom of each page, referring to notes at the back; this would have broken the flow, the rhythms. Instead, I began including a formal bibliography, at the end of the work; a simplified version in *Genoa*, which became more sophisticated in later works.

The reader should be cautioned that these bibliographies are not to be considered exhaustive. In most cases, many other books were consulted, their materials failing to adjust to the disciplines of my particular work.

The development of this perhaps idiosyncratic approach to bibliography is another aspect of this particular writer's growth and career.

—Paul Metcalf

for Nancy

WILL WEST

ONE

WILL STOOD on the mound, waiting, his feet planted apart. The two numerals sewn in thick maroon to the back of his shirt felt heavy. Number 19. Across his chest, in shorter maroon, armpit to collarbone to armpit, were six letters: R E B E L S. His gray flannel uniform was trimmed in maroon, and heavy maroon socks rose above his ankles, almost to the droop of his pants on his shins. He was hot, sweating under the four banks of lights, under the flannel uniform, the cotton underwear, sweating hard. His feet were tight in the black, spiked shoes. But his arm felt loose and rubbery.

"G'wan! G'wan! Pitch to him!"

The crowd was landing on him. Two or three thousand, perhaps. There were some Indian calls. But he waited. Under the visor of his cap, his quiet eyes looked down the trail, the path of red smooth dirt that led from the mound through the infield grass to home plate. He waited, without motion, and watched for the sign.

The catcher was waiting, too. Standing, not crouching. Will was in trouble. The eighth inning, a run already in and the lead gone. Men on the bases. The crowd, the home crowd, whooping it up. The catcher stood in front of the plate, looking around, hollering orders to the infield, his mask held in his hand. He was fat, and the chest protector made him look fatter. He gestured with the mask to the first baseman and then the third baseman, and they punched their gloves and danced a few steps in response to orders they couldn't possibly hear. It was a good ritual, holding up the game, and the crowd loved it. A fat catcher, when there's no more baseball left in him, can still get by as an actor.

This was the bush. The game was rough and simple, not machine-like, as in the majors. These boys had played baseball since they could walk. Played it until their legs gave out, or they couldn't fight off the extra flesh any more; until their arms turned from rubber to glass. . . .

Will was motionless, waiting. The catcher glowered around the infield, then turned toward the mound, and stepped forward. But Will didn't come down to meet him, so he stopped and turned toward the plate. The man in blue, short and stocky, was waiting, jaw thrust forward, hands clasped behind his back. The catcher went back to his position, and the crowd yelled, raucous. He turned to face Will, and put on his mask. Slowly, he let down his weight, went into a crouch, and lifted the bottom flap of the body protector. In front of the gray flannel stretched tight around his bottom, he lowered three fingers, and gave the sign.

Will moved, lifted one leg, drew his feet together. The banks of lights over the first and third base stands flooded directly upon him, and he was aware of the others, over the bleachers, pouring on his back. Shifting his weight to one foot, he began smoothing and re-arranging the loose earth of the mound with the toe cleats of the other. A slow, softshoe dance, with his glove hand on his hip, and his pitching hand holding the ball loosely at his side; his head declined, his figure arrogantly modest and indifferent. A pebble here, a pile of dirt there: building, smoothing, leveling the surface. The earth mound, he thought, surrounded by a forest of grass, the trails through the forest, and beyond, the howling wilds . . . turning, swirling, curving, the toe of the shoe. . . .

They're starting the Indian calls again not because they have anything against me but because that's the easiest handle to put on me because that's what I am an Indian a Cherokee Indian. Smoky they call me in the papers partly in derision because my fastball isn't very fast and partly because that's where I come from the Qualla Boundary the Cherokee Reservation in the Great Smoky Mountains of Western North Carolina. The Great Smokies where the summers are cool not hot like here in the low country not the tropical miasmic cloud of heat that hangs low over the land six months of the year that even the ocean can't dispel that spreads to the first row of dunes on the beach the heat that I live in all summer to pitch for this low country town. In the dugout to the left sit the home players in their white uniforms lined on the bench like dummies or like puppets with their arms and legs moved by strings from above. Their faces hidden from the lights against the concrete backwall are as ruddy as mine and motionless watching me waiting for me. The grandstands are full and even the white-coated coke sellers turn to look. On the right beyond the grandstand are the negro faces drawn together and isolated from the others. So I've got to pitch. Men on bases. The lead gone. And the sign. . . .

Will stopped sweeping the dirt with his foot and looked up. His eyes went down the trail and the catcher gave the sign again. Three fingers. A slow outside curve that drops in, cuts the outside corner. The crowd was howling now, many of them on their feet. Behind him, the shortstop and second baseman chanted encouragement. The fingers of his pitching hand flexed around the ball . . . but something in him would not begin. Again, his head went down, and the toe cut little paths in the surface of the mound. . . .

Because I'm an Indian and sometimes they question me when I get into a bus question which race I'm to sit with. Smoky Will. Smoky Will West Cherokee Indian pitcher. Full-blooded but not quite there was that fake Irishman that Scotchman who went to live in Ireland for a while and got himself called Scotch-Irish the one who came across the Atlantic water in a sailing ship landed at Baltimore or maybe up the river at Philadelphia but whichever it was cut out across across Pennsylvania which was still wild country got to the Alleghanies the Appalachian range and liked the natural flow of those north-south valleys he was a hill man a Scotch highlander with tight lips a thin face an eagle's nose and watery blue eyes he knew the north mountains the rough unyielding rocks but his blood needed warming so he turned south. Got himself a coonskin cap and put a feather in it a buckskin jacket and pants with leather trimming just like an Indian a rifle and powder horn and a horse to carry his belongings carry the trinkets and likker he bought to trade to the Indians for skins yes that was before the Removal and there were still Indians in the mountains they'd been pushed back but they were strong in the mountains just the Indians and the traders and the poachers. Maybe he drank at that spring on the edge of Indian country

that the traders all consider unlucky they said if you drink at that spring
on your way in you won't come out for weeks you'll go on a rootintootin
bender get yourself an Indian girl or maybe two or three get drunk and
then get drunker and just stay right on drunk. Maybe he drank at that
spring. I don't know. But in any case he got in and he stayed in. Smoky
Will West has that Scotchman in his blood.

The yelling had a different tone: angry, derisive. He had overplayed
the delay. When he looked up, the man in blue had stepped in front
of the plate and was approaching, walking up the trail toward the
mound. He was short, with heavy shoulders, a large head, and large
blue eyes. He stopped halfway, and gestured.

"Play ball!" he yelled.

He turned and walked back in short steps, head and shoulders
erect, to his position.

Will had watched him, had made no acknowledgement. He
watched him retreat down the path. Then he took his position on
the rubber. His muscles moved slowly, they didn't want to try. He
poised himself, his hands held before him with ball and glove against
the letters across his chest. He could take no wind-up, there were
men on base. He glanced at first. Both players were dancing ner-
vously, but they were different: the baserunner sporting like a clown,
putting on a show; the fielder really nervous, his feet lifting lightly,
the motion springing from the pit of his stomach, almost uncontrol-
lable. Will's eyes swept across his chest, over the white ball clutched
in his dark glove, and out to third base. The runner in his white uni-
form, his face pallid in the full flood of lights, looked like a phantom
against the negro bleachers. The fielder made a flurry toward the
base, and the runner responded with a flurry. Just a form, Will
thought. They're not really trying. He turned toward home. The bat-
ter waited, his bat held back off his shoulder. The catcher was raised
part way out of his crouch; he thrust his mitt forward, as though
pushing something away from him: challenging Will. Over his
shoulder, like a sun resting on the shoulder of a mountain before lift-
ing into the sky, was the large head of the man in blue.

The crowd yelled in unabated anger. Will thought of Chief Ben-
der, the great Indian pitcher, of a trick he'd pull when things were

going rough, when the crowd got on him. He'd step off the mound and amble toward the stands. 'Listen,' he'd say; 'I'm running things here. If you don't like it, why don't you go back where you came from?' And he thought of Ol' Bobo's remark: 'My stuff was good, they were just hitting it.'

He lifted his arms over his head in the stretch, the ball held in the glove. His muscles felt loose and rubbery and good. The sweat drenching his body and his clothes helped him, he thought. They wouldn't get a loud foul off me, if I could bring myself to try. . . .

He lowered his arms into the final pose. Again the quick, almost surreptitious glance at first and third. In each case, the runner gave him a little flurry. His arm jerked back and the muscle felt free and powerful all the way. As his body wheeled in support of the arm, he could see the white-flanneled runner on third faking for home. A deep breath seemed to catch in his throat, to dry it suddenly, at the nadir of his backward motion. . . .

It is those of us who cannot untangle ourselves from the past that are really dangerous in the present because we are only partly here our eyes are blind because our appetites are turned inward or backward chewing on the cold remnants of our inheritance of our facts of our history to try to find who we are what we are where we came from what is the ground we stand on to whom does it belong and did it belong. We are dangerous because when we come out of the past we are rich with its energies and poorly experienced in the business of daily living and we hurl ourselves across the present with the blind fierceness of a martyr or a convert defending our damage to the defenseless with a language they cannot understand a language created from false concepts of time of history of past present and future. In the end we will bring to the world nothing useful and although we may find what we have been and even what we are nevertheless for all our search the heavy helpless stumbling of men born in quicksand we will never know what we have done.

As his arm swung forward in a half sidearm motion, the length and weight of his body following it, pivoting on his left leg, the breath charged from him, and his throat felt hot. He was aware all the way of the free grip of his hand on the surface of the ball, of the healthy feeling of the muscles in his arm. He felt capable, 'right.' His wrist flicked, as his hand reached the end of its forward penetration, and his fingers spread: the ball went spinning from them. His right foot struck the forward slope of the mound, and his weight came to rest heavily. His throwing hand, completing its arc, swung back and forth loosely, hanging as though the arm had broken. He waited.

In the moment the ball spun from the cup of his hand, Will knew two things. First that the pitch was good. It would do what it was supposed to: float outside, and then break, cut in at the last minute, catch the outside corner. The speed, the delivery, the aim were right. And second, that the batter wouldn't be fooled. Caught in the fever of the rally, he'd set himself, was going to swing at the first pitch, good or bad. It was a good pitch, but it was the wrong one to call. 'My stuff was good, they were just hitting it.'

He waited, the hand swinging slowly, and watched the batter swing, watched him reach outside to get it on the end of the bat. In the last instant, the ball cut in, as it had been told, and struck the bat on the fattest, the healthiest part of the wood. The batter swung clean, pulled the pitch to left field. In the instant of the 'crack,' the angry, individual yelling of the crowd, the dissonance of separate voices sank into an ocean of enthusiasm. Will watched the white pellet disappear like a shooting star over his right shoulder. He drew himself up, brought his feet together on the surface of the mound, and waited, hands on hips, head declined. He looked up only casually to watch the fielding of the ball, watch the white-flanneled figures fading around the third base corner, waved on by their coach. It was a solid smash, close to the foul line, good for a double or triple. The runner on third was in of course, and the man from first came all the way around and scored. The play, when it was finally made, was at the plate, and the batter came into third, radiant with motion and confidence, for a stand-up triple. Will looked down and began again the idle smoothing and rearranging of loose earth on the surface of the mound.

The crowd was tumultuous. Individual voices were beginning to emerge out of the hum. Indian calls, riding on the crest of the noise, came to Will's ears. He didn't look up, but waited, the toe-spike scraping over the dirt.

He didn't need to look up, he knew what was happening. The ball had not been returned to him, was held by the catcher. The catcher, perhaps a couple of infielders were approaching. From the dugout came an older man, a man with a uniform like his own, but with no number on the back: the Manager.

Something in him broke. Looking up abruptly, he stepped off the mound and headed toward the dugout. He didn't wait to be approached, to submit to the ritual of having the ball withheld from him, of being patted on the back to warm his confidence and keep it warm for his next effort, the next time he would pitch. Stepping off the mound, he violated form, and wrote his own exit.

The manager had approached halfway, and stopped on the base path. Will glanced at him only briefly, at his surprised offended eyes, and walked past him without a word. Under a shower of derisive calls, he stepped into the dugout. He turned to the water fountain and drank deeply, let the water play over his face and into his mouth and throat. . . .

That is the last time I will stand on the mound will stand in the center under the four banks of lights. One day in the dead of winter when the ground is hard and the sky is gray and the parks are empty I will come down from the mountains to this or another field and I will walk out on the grass and up the path from home to the pitcher's mound and I will stand alone on the height of the earth and perhaps it will snow. I will face the black bare stands the boarded windows of the press box the empty dugouts the gray numberless lights darkly racked against the sky and I will let the snowflakes fall on my head and shoulders and off the backs of my empty hands. I will stand alone in the snow. . . .

TWO

WILL WENT east,
 to where red dirt turns to pluff,
 and pluff to white, finegrain
 sand,

Sand and ocean.
Sand, sun and ocean,
 and unhorizoned clouds reaching high,

High, above the water—Will looked
 into a blind horizon.

Damn the gulls, with their embracing wings!
 damn
 the heron, curlew, kite and rail—
 merganser, grebe and gallinule!!

God damn the tern and nigger goose!

The weather turns upon the weather
—midsummer handspring—
 and the ocean bakes a fish.
The sun is fat.

Turning to the land, Will discovered, across the sweep of beach, an approaching silhouette. The figure, despite distortions of lighting, was clearly that of a girl. She was walking up the beach away from town, planning to pass him, apparently, several yards in shore, toward the dunes. She followed a straight course, moving with athletic grace. He continued to watch her as she passed out of the distorted sunlight, came into her own substance and color. Her hair, dark brown, fell loosely across her shoulders. Her legs were long, slender at the calf, filling out within proportion at the groin and hips. She was tanned, but not too much, and wore a two-piece bathing suit, white. Her eyes, as he could make them out, were the color of her hair, and she had no make-up. Her breasts were firm.

Palmettos, rattling in a slow wind,
    draw back, back
    from winds of violence.

Sea oats fondle the air,
    and sand,
     singing a high song,
Stings the crust of sand.

      Will's foot
        is still,
     While water warms his toes,

     And on Will's back,
       the eastward back,
         sweat grows.

Dry sand fell from his feet and ankles as he ran across the hard beach, swinging in an arc to approach on the far side, the shore side. She kept her eyes forward and he saw only the flowing, richly curled hair on the back and sides of her head until he caught up with her and fell into her stride, his arm brushing against hers. Then she turned to him. She started to smile, but her face became suddenly serious and composed.

Now she knows she knows that I am an Indian not a stocky white youth burned in the sun but an Indian. This is the body these are the cheekbones the straight nose color not of the sun but of the man the body that played Indian ball game a mixture of football soccer lacrosse boxing wrestling played with sticks a hard ball no padding no shoes on a bare enormous stony field. . . .

The tide was low, and a wide hollow lay in their path, ridged by the action of earlier waves, holding at its center a pool of captive ocean. At the far end, through a single outlet, the water flowed gradually outward. A jellyfish hovered near the outlet.

> *History is not made by fish,*
>   *not by the bass,*
>   *the mullet or the cat,*
>
> *Not by the rugged-shelled oyster, or*
>   *the jellyfish,*
>   *holding off the tide,*
>
> *Not by the stingaree!!*

At the water's edge, a broad sand bar curled into the ocean, standing just above the wave surface. The breakers parted in approaching and lapped at its edges. Large gray gulls were gathered on it, and some took to flight, lifting themselves ponderously, drawing their legs to their bodies as they rose watchfully above sand and water. Those remaining on the sand crowded to the edge of the ocean, flapping their wings between flight and arrest, until Will and the girl had passed. Among the dunes, the palmettos became fewer and shorter, more wind destroyed.

Will stopped suddenly, feet spread apart, and held the girl, his right arm gripping her waist, lifting her so that her toes barely touched the sand. With his left arm, he drew her shoulders toward him; she held him back, pressing both palms against his chest, and they became motionless, locked together.

> From Will's crotch,
>   apex of the sand-leg man,
>   her legs descend
>
> A plumb line
> to the white,
>   white sand.

Will's arm is stone,
    and the man
     —man and girl—
        are
    carved of sand,

Old figures cut against
    salt,
    high gull,
       and wind.

Face to face, their eyes met, head on. Hers were dark and large and
sober, framed in a tan face; they held Will's gaze steadily.

I to I,
    thought of time,
       and out of time,
  of tide,
       and beyond tide,

    Red, and sun-fertile white
    girl, girl, girl, girl,
    the anger of nothing.

Although Will held her gaze, the edges of his vision nevertheless
"pulled in" the surrounding landscape—the soft, dissolving curves,
north and southward, of the beach.

And if the land be a map,
    or the map a terrain,
And if a man be given,
    or if a man uncover

What is the land, and
    What is the form of the man?
If the map, of itself,
Be a form, a plan for

the discovery of land,

What brings the land,
What brings the form of the man,

into relief?

As suddenly as he had stopped her, she broke and headed for the dunes. For a moment, he watched her, motionless. Then he started after her. The soft sand approaching the dunes slowed her: she leaned forward, propelling herself from the hips, swinging her arms awkwardly like a young gull struggling to learn flight. At the edge of the dunes he came up to her and caught her hand in his. They were panting and sweating as they trudged over the top and made their way among the dunes, up and down, around the patches of grass and briers. The wind descended to a whisper, and the air became sticky. Climbing to one of the higher points, they found a shady hollow directly behind it, and they jumped and skidded into the lowest part. Sitting down, facing oppositely, their hips touching, they swung their upper bodies in front of each other, and embraced hotly.

There was no wind, and the sun was relentless.

Through grasses, snarling
    the earth, and
Briers,

Comes a murmur,
    captive:
    a murmur of wind.

Sweat,
    sweat and sea air

Separating, rising, they stood back from one another. Will's trunks, and the two pieces of the girl's white bathing suit, fell to the sand. For a moment they faced each other, naked in the hot sun and dampness, in the still air. With the exposure of the parts of her body hitherto covered, the girl gave a striped appearance—tan and white and tan and white and tan.

She made a gesture as though to run, a flurry, laughing a little, and he met it, halting her by implication. Again they hesitated, watching.

> The whirlpool at
>   the end of each breast
> Draws her life
>   into heavy, unwhirling air,
>
> and to the hardness of the man.

As they came together he held her around the waist, and she leaned back, pressing against him. Then she came forward and dropped abruptly to one knee.

He lunged upon her, grasping her shoulders as she started to rise. Her legs passed between his, her knees bending, her breasts rising and spreading before him. Letting him support her, she dropped her head back so that the ends of her hair touched the sand.

> Among grass,
>   briers,
> Sea oats,
>   and salt,
> The hair falls,
>   entangled
>
> A true tangent
>   to the earth.

His hands upon her shoulders, his legs dividing across her abdomen, he leaned over her and kissed her. Panting, he lifted his head and let her down slowly to the sand. He stepped back a moment, and then lowered himself and approached.

Kissing her thigh and groin, he continued across the gentle rounding of her abdomen until he reached her breasts—as he had moved, earlier, from the water's edge across the modulated surface of the beach, to the dunes.

As I have moved every autumn since I have played baseball over the level piney loam of the low country across the gently rolling sandhill

*uplands the lifting cotton and peach fields of the Piedmont the foothills
the sharp friendly slopes of the Blue Ridge and into the Great Smoky
Mountains . . . as every invader has ever moved from the water's edge
the source across the gentleness and pushed climbed fought his way into
the heart of the desirable land. . . .*

He drew himself up the dampness of her body. Sweat poured from
them both, mingling and dropping to the sand. They were breath-
ing audibly, their lungs plunging at the bottom of each breath into
collapse, to expand again suddenly, gasping.

>It is without movement
>>that one begins,

>Without labor,
>>the one searching out
>>>the other,

>As the fish swims,
>>without movement.
>>>*Blood falls from the hills,*
>>>*The quiet spear*

>>>>*is a Spaniard*
>>>>*or a Frenchman.*

>>>*Homes are fired.*
>>*Men gather meat from*
>>>*the trees,*
>>>>*and chestnuts in*
>>>>>*the streams,*
>>*The deer is without a mountain.*

>>*The heart of*
>>>*the little squirrel*
>>*Is wrapped in the skin of*
>>>*the bear, and*

The moon falls into the river.
The little boy without feet

runs
to the middle of the sun.

A dead man watches fire
burn out the sumac
on his groin.

The river is a pumpkin.

Sweat rolled over them, their bodies were salty and wet as though they were lying at the ocean's edge among the waves. Their eyes were watering, closed.

The sun burned intensely on Will's back. Lifting himself gently he moved to the sand. She drew his head to her side, and shielded his eyes from the sun. In a moment, he was asleep.

* * * *

When he opened his eyes, she was leaning over him, watching him. Her head, set exactly against the sun, shielding it from his eyes, seemed darker; the whites of her eyes stood out as though from negro flesh, and her hair was almost black against the brilliant sky. Her face was intent and good-humored, the lips parted slightly as before.

Stretching himself, scarcely moving, he pushed the sleep out of his muscles, as though pushing it down his arms and legs and out of his body. He raised one knee. She leaned back, touched it, ran her fingers lightly down his thigh to his hip. Shoving his elbows behind him, he raised himself, and looked down on her. She turned, resting her other cheek on his lifted chest, and their eyes met.

Hers are still watering her face warm with love and sorrow and uncertainty and fulfillment and perhaps fear her mind is divided like the tans and whites of her body divided because she wants to talk to me to secure herself with words but more than that she wants to remain silent . . . we are both renegades outcasts I cannot guess her reasons but she must know mine she must know why it is that I swim at this end of the beach this far from town and perhaps there is a certain justice in it perhaps it is right I have no claim to the beach perhaps a Santee a Yemassee an Edisto yes but did Cherokee ever hold sway east of the middle waters of the rivers. . . .

He smiled, and laughed, and gave her a gentle slap on the back. Raising herself, laughing, she sat back on her heels, her shoulders straight, her palms spread on her forelegs, so that save for the shape of her breasts she looked like a child.

Scrambling to his feet, he started out of the hollow, stretching his arm to her. She hesitated a moment, and then took his hand. They charged into the soft, steep sand on the bank of the dune, their knees pumping until they came to the top.

Still holding hands, they headed toward the ocean, walking, half running around the grass and briers, through the hollows and over the dunes. At the head of the beach, before descending to the flatness, they paused again. There was no one in sight. They remained still, gazing at the sky, the horizon clouds, the methodic rows of low breakers creeping in from the ocean. Warm ocean wind curled around them, cooling them only with its motion. Will looked down on her, on the tan legs, midriff, shoulders, arms and face, separated by two bands of white.

For an instant, she leaned her head against his shoulder.

Stepping forward, they broke the handclasp as they plunged down the face of the dune to the level of the beach. She ran as hard as she could, and Will held his pace to hers, running a few feet apart from her. As they reached the line of high tides the sand became hard packed, and the bottoms of their feet slapped against it.

The water was warm, scarcely cooler than the air. Will approached her and they ran close together, splashing each other's legs as their feet struck the foam. They ran through the first low breakers and on out. Will moved faster now, went beyond her. At the first breaker of size, he dove in, passed through it, and swam a few feet under water, close to the sand.

When he came to the surface he turned, tossing the hair from his face, to see her dive in awkwardly and sit down. Catching the crest of another breaker, he rode it in, returned to her. She was laughing helplessly, splashing the water with her hands; her hair hung in wet curls against her cheeks. With both hands Will pushed back the hair, then slipped his arms under shoulders and legs and picked her up. She laughed and kicked, holding firm to his neck as he turned and faced the ocean.

Walking steadily, he carried her away from the beach. At each breaker he paused and set himself, one foot diagonally behind the other, his knees flexed; he lifted her body and she buried her face in his as the wave broke. They became covered with foam as he carried her further and further, walking, pausing, setting himself, and walking again. Between breakers his eyes were set upon the dim horizon, where ocean melted into sky. She laughed like a child.

When he could carry her no further, he let her down. Her arms clung to his neck, and she clasped her legs around his. They kissed, and he held her tightly to him. They were beyond the area of the breakers; as each wave approached he gave a little spring with his feet and they floated up with it together, descending slowly on the water.

Finding that she could stand, she let herself down and they faced each other, sideways to the waves, still holding hands, floating up and descending as before. . . .

The tide was still going out and they found themselves carried away from the beach. Separating, they started swimming in. They swam easily, close together, watching each other. She still laughed occasionally, and gulped water, but she kept pace with him. Among the breakers they started to ride on the crests, moving more rapidly. He was more skillful than she and came to the shallow breakers earlier; he sat among them and waited until she floated in. Coming together they embraced, resting as the water broke over their legs and hips.

> Waters pour two ways
>   to a joining, and
> Turn the matter.

Warmness, channeled,
   Streams upon them,

Upon the embracing,

   and old warmth,
   old exhaustion,
Gulfing out of endings,

   stirs.

She kissed him, grasped him firmly by an ear, by a lock of his hair. They slipped, lost balance, went under water, and came up spluttering. Breaking suddenly, she stood up and ran from him. She was laughing, exhausted. He rose and chased her, running parallel to the beach. She cut toward the ocean and he followed her. When he caught up with her, they were in the middle breakers; the water came up to his waist, and almost to her breasts. Facing the ocean, he caught her wrist, and swung her around. He lunged upon her, his legs spreading over her, and she fell back. Her head went under the ocean.

Reaching under her shoulders, he lifted her: and she came up gasping. She had swallowed deeply, and her eyes were bloodshot, the whites of them broadly exposed. Mucus and ocean poured from her nostrils. As he drew her toward him her breasts seemed to sink against her chest, and she pushed against him with real force, against his chest, neck and face. Her fingers caught in his throat; he released her suddenly and slapped her. He slapped her again.

That is an energy gathering in me without release for many years since I was a youth and lived on the reservation played the Indian ball game the energy of striking an opponent with my hand or with the stick shoving him to the ground and fighting hitting wrestling him to give up the ball then to capture it and run an energy nowhere opened in the later game. . . .

Her knees wavered and she reached toward his shoulders for support, gasping.

This is the decision the void the place where time stops the choice before an act enters the deadmarch. . . .

Stepping back, he caught her hands in his. Facing the ocean, the eastern horizon, he watched her cough, struggling to approach, and held her off. They were between breakers.

> The ocean,
>   foaming,
>
>   voided by clean land . . .

Stepping back again, he let her fall, and she went down on one knee, her face dipping in and out of the water. He lunged upon her like a dog, and turned her body under his. She struggled, her knees striking his back, her fingernails digging into his arms and chest; but he discovered her throat and pressed it with both hands, under the water. Letting her do to him what damage she could, he drew his fingers tighter and tighter.

Her motion grew slower, more lethargic. Her legs were almost floating. Gradually her body became taut, her hips pushing upward against the arch of his legs, her head turned back so that it almost touched the sand.

> As the head turned before,
> To the earth,
>   a tangent,
>
> Formed by her hair:
>
> This was the beginning.

> *and with this*
> *I reclaim myself,*
>
> *Recover what is*
>   *in the conch,*
>   *the gull and tern,*
>   *the long coastal sky,*

Draw back from horizons,
  from back breeze
    over marsh grass.

Come up from sand and briers,
Down from wing of curlew,

Out of mullet.
  clam shell, and
    frond of palmetto.

My parts fly back to my limbs.

Lifting himself, he jumped back from her.

It is as though she were a fish a porpoise a white whale belly-upward and dead. . . .

Her body turned over and over in the breakers, always at the surface. Her hair, following the motion, encircled her head so that her face was largely hidden; her breast and stomach and hips pushed forward on the thrust of each wave.

Jumping back further, he moved backward toward the beach, not taking his eyes from her. The tide was still retreating, slowly pulling her away from him, and there was a cross tide, carrying her up the beach.

Turning away for the first time, Will surveyed the land. After only a moment, he turned again to the ocean, and had to look more than once to find her. The body turned up, white and tan, in the foaming of a breaker, and then disappeared under the surface.

Facing the beach, the land, the continent, Will ran out of the ocean, to the hard sand. Bending forward, he ran hard, as he had not run in years, never in baseball; as he had not run since his youth. He ran toward the dunes, and the land beyond.

THREE

WILL LAY on his side on the cot, smoking quietly. His mother, who was a full-blooded Cherokee (the Scotchman had been on the father's side), sat by the table, by the oil lamp, weaving a basket. Strips of cane lay on her broad lap, and she wove them in and out among the vertical strips already attached to the base. She was a large woman, with heavy arms; she worked with great concentration, her brows knit, her eyes never lifting. Will watched her, watched her coarse fingers manipulate the cane at an unchanging pace.

He had not told her yet why he had come home. She would wait, she would not press him. The night was clear, fresh with mountain coolness; taking the air into his lungs, he felt as though he had not breathed in months. The cabin was much as he had remembered it, as it had been with only few changes since his childhood, since he could first remember. He lay still, puffing the pipe that he kept here at home, his "winter" pipe.

Lifting his eyes, he looked into her face, and it seemed also without change, seemed only to weather slowly, like the hewn logs of the cabin. She lived alone the better part of the year, but made no objection. There was a small allotment of land, farmed by relatives, and she kept chickens and a cow. She made baskets and small rugs for the tourist shops, to occupy herself. Will had sent her money from his checks now and then, but she never asked for it. Her wants appeared to be satisfied.

He could not get over the feeling, however, watching her stolid, concentrated, unexpressive face, that she must be lonely. Unlike most Indian women, she made friends poorly, and was not sociable. She avoided the dances, and the jovial obscenities that accompanied them, not because she disapproved, but because it was hard for her to join in—she had never learned how. Will's father was long dead, and a twin brother, the only other child, had died in infancy. Save for Will, she was alone in the world, and he was with her only a short portion of the year. There was one other force in her life: the church. She had been converted, and was a devout Baptist. Perhaps this was enough.

Watching her, he realized that if he was the only person close to her, the reverse was also true: she was still the only one close to him.

Perhaps when I was born my grandmother a thin leathery old woman known by many to be a witch was the midwife she stood behind my mother and held up her arms while my mother kneeled on the floor and the medicine man after giving her a decoction of the bark of the slippery elm to make the birth easier examined his beads to determine the future of the child. I was placed in a fresh deerskin and nursed on the plentiful milk of my mother's breasts together with my brother or perhaps as twins we were not raised to be normal children but witches for twenty-four days we were secluded from all visitors and denied the mother's milk but fed on connahaynee being corn parboiled beaten with a mortar and pestle returned to the pot boiled with beans and kept in a large earthen jar and at the end of twenty-four days my mother drank a decoction of the bark of the smooth sumac to make her milk flow abundantly and we were given the breast confirmed as witches. But something went wrong because my brother is dead and whatever else I can do I cannot fly through the air tunnel through the ground prepare and spoil food without touching it divine others' thoughts or walk upon sunbeams. I have wondered about my twin brother the other half of the burden of the womb what kind he was what he might have been they say he was fond of our grandmother and she of him that he used to pick up things pretty stones a flower even a dead bird and bring them to her perhaps I dominated the breast and he felt left out perhaps like the Snake Boy he left the cabin one morning without breakfast went into the woods and was gone all day returned in the evening with a pair of deer horns and went to a hut where his grandmother was waiting for him he told her he must be alone all night and she left but at daybreak she went to the hut and no boy was there but an immense green serpent with horns on its head still with human legs instead of a serpent tail. It spoke to her told her to leave and she went away and when the sun was well up it began to crawl out but it was not free of the hut until full noon it made a terrible hissing noise striking through the air like a vibrant wind reverberant and omnipresent and the people fled as it crawled among the cabins leaving a broad trail behind it until it came to the river to a deep bend in the river where it plunged in and went under the water and was never seen again. Except perhaps the grandmother who was a witch and who grieved over her grandson she went down to the river and plunged in and perhaps she saw him again. One day a man fishing saw the grandmother sitting on a large rock in the river looking as she had always looked but when she caught sight of him she jumped into the water where the Snake Boy her grandson had plunged and she was gone . . .

Will's eyes returned to his mother's hands, to the quick, restful motions of her fingers with the strips of cane . . .

As a boy I might have watched those hands dig clay from the bank of the river saw it fired in the open smoked with crushed corn cobs molded by hand decorated with paddles polished with smooth stones into pottery of chestnut-burr of frog bird fish or man. You wore beads pendants ear-ornaments and gorgets of animal teeth of bird bone of stone of pearls from the mussel of copper traded from the northern Indians of conch or other marine shells traded from Indians from the gulf or from the great eastern ocean. With my father made arrowheads and spearheads of flint and of the antler of the deer made bows of locust and strings of the entrails of the bear blowguns of bamboo pipes of steatite and awls of bone. Gathered horse chestnuts and roots pounded them into a powder spread the powder over a lake or pond stirred it with a pole until the fish drugged by the powder floated to the surface and were gathered in baskets covered overnight against the putrefaction of the moon. I might have become an eagle hunter . . .

Will's eyes closed, but he was not asleep.

. . . called to the village in late fall or winter I would set out for the mountains engage in a vigil of prayer and fasting for four days then I

would hunt and kill a deer place the body in an exposed position con-
ceal myself and sing in an undertone to attract an eagle. When the
eagle appeared I would shoot it emerge from concealment and stand
over the bird say a prayer to it asserting that it was not a Cherokee
that had killed it but a Spaniard! thus averting the vengeance of the
eagle spirits. I would leave the bird and return to the village announc-
ing that a snowbird had fallen thus again to mislead the eagles. Four
days later when the parasites had deserted the eagle feathers the village
hunters would go into the mountains they would strip the feathers and
wrap them in a fresh deer skin leave the body of the deer as a sacrifice
to the eagles and return to the village. The feathers would be hung in
a small hut by the dance ground a dish of venison and corn set before
them to satisfy their hunger also the body of a scarlet tanager. The eagle
dance would be held that night and the principal chiefs would wear
the feathers. . . .

He opened his eyes. His mother had not changed. If she had looked
at him, raised her eyes to him while his were closed, he would not
know it. Save for the swishing of the strips of cane, the cabin was
quiet, so that the one sound became a commotion, filled the room
with the warmth of another person, of human activity. Will lifted
himself partway and looked about.

The cabin was simply furnished, but it was comfortable and
clean. His mother slept in the other room, on a bed that had been
carved by his father before their wedding. In this room, in addition
to the cot where Will slept, where he was resting now, there were
two chairs and a table, and a wood stove for heat. An alcove in back,
partly cut off, contained the kitchen. The floor was covered with
worn linoleum. Decorations on the wall were few, and except for
the religious calendar on the back of the door, they never changed
from year to year. There was a small blanket that his mother had
woven long ago; a bunch of dried gourds hanging in the corner; an
old photograph of his mother and father together; and a newspaper
reproduction of an etching of the Woolworth Building. A fishing
pole stood in one corner, and a broom in another. Over the door, a
rusty gun with the works broken hung on two nails. He stared at the
gun for some moments.

Will became restless. Putting down the pipe, he swung his feet to the floor and stood up.

"I'll go out for a minute."

"All right."

He turned his back to her, opened the door. The swishing of the cane stopped for just a moment, and then picked up again. He didn't look back but closed the door after him, went down the steps and into the yard.

A tall cedar stood in one corner, its shape darker than the mountain and the sky. The night was clear, and the sky everywhere within the rim of mountains was filled with stars. Standing in the middle of the yard, he opened his shirt, let the cool air circulate over his chest, stomach and back.

He looked down the steep hillside, to the lights of other cabins. The sounds of dancing, chanting and drumming came to him from somewhere. A social affair, he thought; or perhaps practicing for the Indian Fair. He pictured the room: small, filled with people, smoke and heat, the old folks watching the young or maybe dancing themselves, enjoying the conviviality, the excessive warmth closeted from the mountains. Beyond the cabins, in the valley bottom by the river, there was a clearing where Will had played the Indian ball game as a youth. It was still a rough game, as he had played it, but not as in the old days. . . .

For ten days we would eat moderately abstain from women inure ourselves to hardship by cold plunges in the stream the night before the game we would fast and watch all night submit to scarification our skins scratched by seven splinters of turkey bone set in a frame of quill the ball ground was five hundred yards long the ball of scraped deer skin moistened stuffed with deers hair sewed with deer sinews goals marked with branches were set up at either end the object being to drive the ball through the opponent's goal the ball must be picked up by the racket and not by the hand but anything else was allowed the umpires were not called umpires but drivers. There were twelve goals to a game and if the twelve were not achieved by sunset we would fast watch another night and play the next day or as many days as might be necessary fasting and watching the intervening nights. . . .

By the ball field and spotted among the cabins on the mountainside were patches of ripening corn.

Somewhere a whippoorwill was calling. *Waguli!! Waguli!*

Will looked up at the mountains, at the familiar shapes and contours.

This is my home the rolling hills are my support the rim of mountains delimiting the sky the area of stars that I see is the exterior limit of my outward world. In these hills I was born and here I have lived longer than I or the dead generations before me can remember land despite what has happened to it cannot be bought cannot be owned but only poached on leased and occupied temporarily released with death like wealth which will be buried and destroyed with its owner . . .

He turned again toward the cabin, and paused. Through the glass window, he could see the deep-yellow dimness cast by the shaded oil lamp over the walls of the room, like the pleasant flame of candlelight.

I must tell her. Why else did I come back where they will look for me I must tell her why I have come home and why I must leave. I should be on the road now they will find me here but I will wait I will spend the night and get up before dawn I will go to her bed and tell her in darkness and leave at once and I will not have to see her face. . . .

He paused again on the step. The night air circulating within his shirt was almost chilly. It is a sin, he thought with a smile, to sweat unnecessarily in summer.

When he opened the door, his mother didn't look up but went on weaving the strips of cane. He stepped into the room, closed the door.

The basket was almost finished. He realized that she had worked on it only to protect herself from him, to avoid the words that must be spoken. Standing before her, partly facing her, his hands in his pockets, he felt the pressure of their presences struggling to approach and avoid, denied access through tongue and eye, filling the air of the bare cabin. He shifted away, sat down on the cot. Again he watched her hands.

"Why don't you go to bed, Mama," he said. "We'll talk in the morning."

She finished weaving the strip of cane, and then stopped. The room was silent.

"You work too hard," he said, laughing.

She looked up, smiled at him, and their eyes met.

"It's good to be home," he went on encouragingly.

She smiled, looked down at the basket, holding it between her hands.

"It's good to have you, Will."

She set the unfinished basket and the strips of cane on the table; leaning over, she squinted under the shade of the lamp, and turned the flame low. She rose, started toward the kitchen, and paused.

"You have enough blankets?"

"Sure, Mama."

She went into the kitchen, and Will could hear her washing. He kicked off his shoes and stretched out on top of the blankets. In a moment, he heard the back door close as she went out. Lifting his arm, he shaded his eyes from the lamp, and closed them. . . .

After mother's milk there is connahaynee corn is still the basic food of the Indian. In the beginning there were Kanati The Lucky Hunter and Selu The Corn Kanati brought in game and Selu washed it in the stream they had a son and the son played with a strange boy who came from the blood of the game that Selu washed in the stream Kanati Selu The Son and The Wild Boy. Selu went into a little cabin and shut the door the boys pushed out a chink of clay between the logs and watched her she stood before an empty basket she rubbed her belly and the basket was half full of corn she rubbed her armpits and the basket was full with beans The Son and The Wild Boy said we must kill her for she is a witch. Later when she saw them she looked at them and said so you know and you must kill me well when I am dead you will drag my body over the ground and sit up and watch all night wherever you drag my body corn will spring up and will be ripe before morning The Son and The Wild Boy killed her with clubs they cut off her head and put it on a stick on the house top so that Kanati would know when he returned from hunting. They dragged her body over the ground as she

had told them and they watched through the night the green shoots
sprang up and in the morning there was corn. . . .

He heard the door close, and in a moment his mother was standing
by the table, watching him. He lowered his arm.

"Do you want the light?"

"No. Blow it out."

She blew across the top of the globe, cupping her hand on the
other side of it, and the flame went out. The room was in darkness.
He heard the floorboards creak as she moved toward the door of her
room.

"Good night."

"Good night, Mama. Sleep well."

She went into her room and closed the door.

From habit Will put his arm over his eyes again, and closed them
as though to sleep. But he was uneasy. He knew that he must sleep
now if he was to waken early. He could not tell when he might sleep
again. He lay still, tried to compose himself, but his mind moved
restlessly. . . .

I must fast three days drink a consecrated mixture of herbs and roots I
must not rest except at night must not kill game must abstain from
women a pouch at my belt filled with parched corn will be my only food
. . . there is the old gun over the door but the works are broken . . . the
story tells the hunters not the deer the bear wild boar or buffalo flesh to
be washed in the stream but Nunyunuwi who follows the smell of
human flesh the hunters turn to the man of great medicine who says
seven! seven who menstruate shall be staggered unclothed in the path
where Nunyunuwi comes! Nunyunuwi sees the seven naked bleeding
and at the seventh oh child you are in a bad state (a virgin who has
just begun to bleed) Nunyunuwi falls in vomit of blood the hunters the
husbands build a great fire over Nunyunuwi who burns and crackles
in late darkness from the unwashed flesh the unwashed blood the can-
nibal is smoke . . . Utlunta the Spear-finger may still wander in the
mountains a woman monster with powers over stone she could lift
great rocks and join them without mortar her skin was of rock that no
weapon could wound or penetrate the stony forefinger of her right hand

*was of bone like an awl or a spearhead and she sang a pretty song
about human liver for this was her food she would stab a hunter with
the spear-finger. . . .*

He tossed about restlessly, his arm still over his eyes.

*I must sleep I must sleep but if I cannot perhaps I had better go now
they will come for me during the night they will think that I have come
home to see my mother to eat a home-cooked meal sleep in my own cot
in the cabin among the old mountains. . . .*

Lowering his arm, he listened. There was no sound from his moth-
er's room. She has said her prayers and is in bed, he thought. He
swung his feet to the floor, slipped them into his shoes, and waited.
Among the old mountains, the night was quiet. He heard the voice
of the whippoorwill.

Waguli! Waguli!

Restless as he was, it was hard for him to get up. He moved silent-
ly to his mother's door and listened. He could hear her breathing,
but not the deep, regular breathing of sleep. He opened the door a
little.

"Mama."

She turned over in bed. "Yes?"

He pushed the door open, and went in. His eyes were becoming
accustomed to the darkness, and in the dim starlight coming
through the window he made out the shape of her head on the pil-
low. He stood at the foot of the bed.

"Mama . . ." He hesitated, and there was a pause.

"What is it, Will?" Her voice was deep, without anxiety, and it
thrust deeply into him. She has gone under me, he thought; what-
ever am I going to say, she has framed it so that it will be easier to
say; impossible not to say.

"We had better talk now," he said, and he found his own voice
more settled, from the tone of hers. "I cannot stay long." He felt a
resolute hardness beginning to form in him.

"All right." She turned again, so that she lay on her back.

He approached, sat on the edge of the bed, looked down at her
featureless face. Her hair was straight and black, but it had fallen

loosely on the pillow in waving forms, framing her head. He looked away, looked down at his hands.

"I'm not going to play baseball any more," he said. There was silence.

"I've quit the team." Still, she said nothing, but waited for him.

"And now I've got to go. I can't stay any longer. I've got to leave, tonight." He looked up, and for the first time he was able to see the glint of her eyes. "I may not see you again."

She turned away, gazed through the window at the starlight. There was a long silence. As though it were an object whose approach he could watch, a sound to be seen rather than heard, he became aware of gentle sobbing, like the breaking of low waves on the beach. Her heavy arm came from under the covers, and without waiting for it he leaned toward her, let her hand settle on the back of his neck. He put his head beside hers on the pillow. . . .

When the warrior is taken prisoner he is tied by a long grape vine to a stake a firebrand is placed on the stake the warrior sings recounts his triumphs in battle while the women who are called Pretty Women rush at him with lighted brands. . . . The warrior fights back and when his tender parts become burned the women pause pour cold water over him to allow him to recover then they start again if he is brave he resists defies boasts sings to the end. When he falls they scalp him ampu-tate all exterior parts the women singing with joy during the torture while the men watch. What she is beginning to offer me what I am submitting to willingly what I have come home at the risk of my life to receive from her hands is scarcely more sufferable. . . .

Withdrawing her other arm from the covers, she placed a hand on either side of his head and lifted it, held it above hers. She stared into his eyes, and he into hers.

"What have you done, Will?"

"I have killed . . ." She held him, the sobs withheld. He had not finished, and she would not release him until he had.

"I killed a woman."

She held him a moment longer, then her hands dropped, and his head wavered a moment, discovered its own support. Her broad arms lay loosely on the covers, and she turned again to the starlight. Her breath came shortly: she was almost gasping. Suddenly, she cast an arm around his neck and drew him toward her again, so that his face was buried against hers. . . .

Now I have crossed her twice taken from her the sole survivor of her love and motherhood and committed the bitterest violence in her constellation of meekness the Christian belief thou shalt not kill. As nearly as any force of and within life can approach her destruction I have approached it now. . . .

Held tight against his mother's face, he thought back, bitterly and sadly, to the church of his youth. He remembered the part-singing of hymns by the Indian voices, and he remembered the look of open, profound sadness that the hymns, sung in Cherokee tongue, brought to the faces of Indian women. He remembered holding his mother's hand or dress, standing beside her, a mountain of strength and sadness. He remembered hating the sadness in her eyes, hating the hymns.

He held himself against her face, made no effort to struggle against the firm grip of her arm. She wept heavily, bitterly.

She does not blame me that would be easy to accept an anger from which we would both recover but she blames herself. She is remembering Will, the intractable aberrant child, and recognizes in me as she has many times before her own nature remote and difficult of access. We are of one nature the seed is the same we have become different only as an accident of exterior event.

Tears poured from her eyes, struggled for passage between their cheeks. When he felt them on his face, salty and burning, he lifted himself, gently but forcefully. Again their eyes met. He watched her broad, ruddy face swollen with tears, her high cheekbones, the disheveled hair on the pillow, the eyes narrowed and scarcely open.

The resoluteness that had begun to form earlier became harder within him. One of the tears from her face slipped down his own cheek and into the corner of his mouth. He closed his lips, drew them together.

*Except for the word for salt and the word for water the Cherokee
tongue is a lipless tongue spoken with the lips parted not clapping
together not breaking into fractions the flow of thought but allowing
it like the constant pouring of the streams and rivers the changeless
motion out of the Smokies out of the great underworld whose only
access is at the streams' heads. But in the word salt and the word water
in salt water the lips draw together and become tight as tight and nar-
row as the lips of the blue-eyed Scotchman. . . .*

"I must go," he said. His mother said nothing, but her weeping
became gentler.

*Tsulkalu the Slant-Eyed Giant came into the village and took a young
virgin for wife he never showed himself but came after dark to lie with
the girl and left before dawn he left meat for the girl and her mother
and the mother was glad. One night he reached into the stream where
the girl had bathed at the unclean time of month and he brought forth
a baby daughter Tsulkalu took his wife and child and left for the
mountains the girl's brother followed them and found places where
there had been a childbirth and where the children had played he came
to a cave in the mountains where many people were dancing his sister
came out and spoke to him. Tsulkalu did not come, but he promised to
appear in the village if the people would fast for seven days and seven
nights the people gathered in the council house but there was a stranger
with them who slipped out at night and broke the fast at the end of the
seventh night the people heard a roar approaching from the mountains
like thunder or a rock slide the roar became louder and louder the
stranger screamed and run out of the council house the sound stopped.
Then it started again and slowly disappeared into the mountains and
Tsulkalu was never seen. . . .*

He withdrew from her, still sitting on the bed.

"I'm going into the mountains," he said; "and across them. I'll
head west."

"You'll need food . . ."

"Don't worry."

". . . and money . . ."

"I have some . . ."

"The loose brick in the chimney . . . I've saved the money you sent me."

"No, Mama. . . ."

"Take it!" Her tone was deep again, informed with tragedy, subverting and holding their whole relation. She turned away from him, gazed again at the starlight.

"All right."

A light flashed across the window. She must have seen it, but she made no motion. Will sprang to his feet.

He went to the other room, to a front window. A disc of light was approaching over the rough ground of the yard. He could not see the flashlight or the figure that held it; only the bright circle following the path to the cabin. In three leaps he was across the cabin and into the kitchen, to a back window. Another circle was fixed on the grass, white, motionless. He turned, slowly, walked back to the front room. He made no motion for the loose brick in the chimney. Instead, he went to the cot, picked up his jacket, and held it over his arm. He remained still.

His mother continued to sob softly. Like the persistence of the waves, he thought. There was muffled conversation outdoors, and the light swept once across the front of the cabin; Will was out of range as it flashed through the window. Footsteps approached, and there was heavy knocking on the door. Then silence. Will was motionless.

"Come on out, Smoky."

Separated from him by the logs of the cabin, the words were muffled, inchoate. There was a pause.

"You'd better come, boy. We know you're there."

The voice was paternal, harsh only with the nature of its purpose, not of the man. Again there was silence, and a long pause. Even the sobbing of Will's mother had quieted. The door was kicked open, swung into the room, and the flashlight, backed by two figures, entered the opening. Will was at one side, and a moment passed before the light discovered him.

"All right, boy."

FOUR

At a fork in the path he stopped, caught his breath. His clothes were still wet in the night air, clinging to him, making him cold while he was still sweating. His shoulder throbbed regularly, the pain becoming more intense where the bullet lodged in it. He had no idea how long he'd been walking. He looked at the sky, recalled that he had once been able to tell time by the appearance of the stars, but had forgotten. Breathing more easily, he turned to the path that followed the stream, and went forward.

Again he walked and climbed for a long time, moving at a steady pace. The pain spread into his chest and partway down his arm. The area felt as though it were swelling. At a point where the path touched the edge of the stream, he stopped, was still, recovering his breath. For the first time, he looked at the wound. The jacket must have been thrown open at the time, for the bullet had escaped it, but had torn a hole in his shirt. Streaks of blood, partly dried, had gone down the arm and front of the shirt. He realized that he couldn't repair the hole, but would have to wash out the blood, and the wound should be washed and covered. He must find a place where he could stop for the night and sleep, where he could build a fire to keep warm, and dry his clothes. His mind, accelerated in the pace of his flight, had to be caught and slowed, like his breathing: since the shooting, he had formed no useful plan.

He looked at the sky again. The pattern of stars, largely hidden by the pines, was of no help. He knew however that he was well into the mountains, and he guessed the hour at after midnight. Lowering his eyes, he discovered and immediately remembered a low ridge, descending from the higher mountains, diverting the flow of the stream around its point as it fell to an end. He recalled the far side, the western side of the ridge, and realized that it offered a safe location for a fire and for the night. Matches were in his jacket pocket; they were safe and dry. Firewood could be found.

His head felt cloudy, and he thought he would become dizzy; but he remained still, and recovered himself. He knew that he was feverish. Taking off his jacket, putting it on the ground, he carefully removed the shirt. Shreds of it were caught in the dried blood, and the wound started to bleed again as he tore it away.

He soaked the shirt in the stream, and spread it over a bare rock. With sand from the edge of the water he scrubbed the stains, holding the shirt with the hand of the wounded arm. After the second rinse, the blood was gone and a faint yellow stain remained: it was the best he could do. Carrying the shirt and jacket, he made his way along the edge of the stream and around the bend.

The far side of the ridge was sheer rock, like a cliff. A short distance from the stream there was an indentation where the rock was partly hollowed. It was not a cave, but the cliff beetled overhead and gave protection: the light of a fire would not be seen from the east.

Spreading the shirt on a rock, he went out for firewood. With dry leaves and pine needles for kindling, he built a fire and ignited it, crouched before it, helped the flames to catch, and felt their first warmth. The night air was cold, and penetrated as soon as he stopped moving. The wounded arm hung limply at his side.

His head clouded again and he felt the approaching vertigo. He stood up, tried to secure himself, collect his balance, realized that he would have to dress the wound quickly if it were to be done, for he needed rest. Walking uncertainly, guiding himself along the cliff, he returned to the stream and crouched at the edge, shivering with cold and fever.

He soaked his handkerchief in the water, and began to wash the wound. It was swollen and the pain was intense. . . .

The stream the mountain stream emerging at its head from the underworld is purifying and health-giving its flow is eternal and is therefore sacred as the source of life its waters on the wound are not a specific but they are the best I can do. To be right I should sing the formula in the middle of the rocks in the middle of the earth in the middle of the woods in the middle of the water and I would say now then! in the center you are staying Brown Dog now you have come to let your path down you have come to halt in the middle of the spot where the blood is spouting now it has become your saliva relief has been caused at once now then! and I would chew on the bark of the hickory and through a hollow buzzard quill cut off at both ends I would blow the hickory and saliva upon the wound if a buzzard quill were not available the hollow stalk of the Gerardia would suffice but the buzzard in his foulness has great power over the foulness of infection. In addition I would pluck a ginseng root in the woods dropping a bead in the hole in payment for it and the ginseng would cure the vertigo I would make a poultice of the bark of the Tag Alder to soothe the swelling and a decoction of Wild Cherry bark boiled over the fire and drunk as tea would reduce my fever. But if I am feverish if I am sick there may be more than the wound as a cause the animals and insects that wittingly or unwittingly I have abused are striking the illness into me or I am longing for association with the departed with the spirit of some beloved my father or my brother who has gone to the Darkening Land in the West and who longs for me as I for him who exerts himself upon me to cause me through illness and death to join him mooning over the dead is not healthy. . . .

When the wound was clean he rinsed the handkerchief, soaked it again, and folded it double. He draped it over his shoulder so that it rested against the opening. The bleeding had stopped.

He returned, chattering with cold and fever, and added wood to the fire, sat as close to it as he could. Arranging his jacket as a pillow, he lay down, moving carefully so as not to disturb the handkerchief. His body ached with fatigue, and his shoulder became numb.

With the rock rising around him, the fire sheltering him from the night, he felt truly as though he were in a cave.

The Cherokee are people who live in caves the original Chalaqué the word used by the Choctaws the Indians of the Gulf Coast who met De Soto in Florida and who told him of us called us Chalaqué the people who come out of caves . . .

His eyes closed, and at once visions of the shooting, and all that led up to it flashed into his mind. He recalled leaving the cabin, and walking single file down the road, toward the officers' car. He recalled jerking the gun out of the holster of the man in front of him, and shooting while he scrambled over the road bank. He recalled the groaning, cursing figures lying on the road, the flashlights departed from their hands. His head began to twist back and forth, slowly, on the jacket, like the body of the wounded officer rolling in the gravel. His lips were dry, his mouth open. He became delirious with fever. . . .

I am dreaming I am dreaming if I dream of birds I will go insane if I dream of wrestling with a fat woman or having sexual relations with my mother I will be stricken with rheumatism will be unable to move through the mountains if I dream of bees and wasps I will go blind. If I dream I have a vision of the Darkening Land in the West it will mean that I am about to die the medicine man will attempt the cure for apoplexy and failing in that my family will serve me a square meal as square as I can eat to carry me on my journey death being a movement in space not in time no other preparations will be made lest they betray anxiety and when I die a relative will straighten the legs the arms place the hands on the abdomen tie a white kerchief around the head and chin to hold the lips together a friend not a relative will wash the body dress it in fine clothes given for the purpose and the body will be kept in the house for several days to be viewed by family and friends will be watched over at night protected against witches against Utlunta the Spear-finger who might steal the fresh-dead liver or against the Raven Mocker. The grave will be dug the body will be placed in the coffin will be avoided by medicine men and pregnant women whose business is life and not death the friends and family will pass in a circle around the coffin for a last look at the face and the coffin will be covered will be lowered into the grave with the head inclining westward toward the Darkening Land the grave will be filled and the burial finished. Seven days after death a dance will be held to speed the dead to divert the immediate relatives unlimber them freshen them with the feeling of life. . . .

He slept. He must have slept. Once during the night, during the darkness, he awoke. The fire had burned low and he was chilly, but his head was clear. The fever had burned partly out of him, and the

throbbing in his shoulder had changed to a dull, steady ache. The
woods, the mountains were silent. He lay still, looked up, past the
overhanging rock, through the pine tops to the sky. . . .

*The hunters were camping in the mountains one night when they saw
two lights moving along a distant ridge they watched and wondered
they saw them the next night and the next on the third morning they
crossed to the ridge they found two creatures round and large with fine
gray fur and little heads like those of terrapins when the breeze played
upon the fur showers of sparks flew out the hunters kept them several
days at night they would grow bright and shine by day they were balls
of gray fur except when the wind stirred and the sparks flew out they
were quiet and no one thought of their trying to escape but on the sev-
enth night they rose from the ground like balls of fire above the tree tops
climbing higher and higher until they were only bright points the
hunters then knew they were stars . . .*

Again he slept. When he woke, the birds were singing, and the gray
dawn had crept over the ridge into the valley. The pines were
motionless in the still air.

The fire had gone out and he was stiff with cold, with the clotted
pain in his shoulder. He lay still for a moment, not shivering, but
afraid to move. The night came back to him: confession, capture,
shooting and escape; delirium and dreams, expulsion of fever.

*All that is in back of me if not in the lowlands at least in the foothills
to the east parted from me by the impenetrable rock at my back. I bear
the wound of it in my shoulder and the tears of my mother in my heart
but rock is harder the rock is a shell projecting me westward and
although I have not crossed the highest ridge the divide between east
and west I am facing it I will cross it and descend westward I will fol-
low the half-blood Sequoyah who tamed the wild animal of language
who wrote the word who crossed the Great River in search of his
Cherokee brother to teach him the word went west and then south into
Mexico. . . .*

Pulling back his arms, he lifted himself slowly. His muscles were
strained and rigid, cracking like old leather, and the early, sharp

pains of the bullet wound revived, shooting down his arm and side. The handkerchief on his shoulder had dried, was stuck to the wound. He walked slowly to the stream and poured water on the handkerchief until it came loose. Then he soaked it and replaced it as before. He returned and built a fire. There was still no sunlight, only the gray chilly dawn. The leaves ignited quickly and the flames came up; he crouched before them, hungry for warmth. His shirt was dry, and he held it to the flames for a moment, then slipped it carefully over his wounded shoulder and put it on. He put on the jacket, and felt warmer.

Taking his wallet from his jacket, he removed all the contents except money. One by one he slipped the various cards and papers into the fire: social security, driver's license, draft card, certificate of award from a Rotary Club for being a twenty-game winner . . .

This is the end this is the finish never again will I look to the east . . .

He stood up, still gazing at the fire. The woods were loud and confused with birdsong. Stepping forward, he trampled on the fire, lifting his feet only slightly, shuffling through it until it was out. He stepped back and watched to make sure that no sparks were left; then he turned and headed for the stream.

I am hungry it will be a long time before I will dare approach a highway to buy beg or even steal food first I must get across the ridge and into Tennessee but I am hungry I must have something before then perhaps soup from the roots of the greenbrier bear rib barbecued on a hickory stick served with poke leaf and rattlesnake meat also chestnut bread and wild honey spicewood tea to drink and for dessert opossum grapes or persimmons with hickory nuts. But not like Tsali and the others I am a fugitive in the mountains there are no nuts or acorns in summer I will have only berries and bark. . . .

He forded the stream and moved away from it, headed diagonally up the wall of the valley. The going was rough, almost impossible through a tangle of undergrowth, the rhododendron and laurel, but he drove himself forward at an unchanging pace, as he had the night before. The shoulder throbbed in every movement of flesh.

The sun came up, striking his back as he retreated from it. He stopped at a waterfall, to drink; the grass was thick and damp, and maidenhair ferns were uncurling. Nearby he found blackberries, and he picked them and ate.

He pushed on. The sun was getting hot, and he took off his jacket, tied it around his waist. He began to hear an occasional car or truck, and knew that he was approaching the highway. He would have to cross it. Climbing steeply, he caught a glimpse of it, of the cut in the rock where it passed. He waited beside a tree while a heavy tractor-trailer swung around the curve, heading downward to North Carolina. Coming closer, he had to crawl on hands and knees; the bank was steep. At the edge of the paving, he ducked behind shrubbery as a car approached. He watched it pass: a new car filled with tourists and laden on top, sides, and back with luggage, camping equipment, fishing rods, camera tripods, etc. When it had gone, he lay still and listened. There was no other sound. Scrambling to the pavement, he ran across and ducked into the thick woods on the other side. He was out of sight.

Still he climbed, moving toward the ridge, toward a remote part of the mountains. He followed the stream beds where possible, to avoid the impenetrable tangles of undergrowth. Crossing a well-marked path, coming to it suddenly, without warning, he paused, listened, but there was no sound: he hastened into the woods beyond.

The sun climbed steadily, as though in extension of his own climbing. His shirt and handkerchief became drenched in sweat, but he didn't slow down or pause. So long as he climbed, so long as the ridge lay ahead of him, he was not tired.

In the high exposed areas, many of the pines were dead and rotting away, victims of blight. Some were still standing, the branches jagged and naked, others had fallen, the great trunks lying gray and without bark on the mountainsides. Will climbed over or crawled under them, staying as much as possible under the living trees.

As the morning grew older the birds retired and the woods became quiet. Only the junco fluttered persistently in the mountain ash.

At midday with the sun overhead, he reached the crest, the border of North Carolina and Tennessee, the divide between eastern and western Appalachian slopes, between Atlantic and Mississippi waters. There was a small clearing, an outcropping of rock. He approached, staying under the trees to avoid the sweeping eyes of binoculars, and looked out. A wide view of mountains met his eyes, of the Balsam range and others to the east and south. In the blue smoke of midday they seemed like soft waves, motionless and floating. Forested whorls, star whirls, and trowel scoops, gigantic and gentle, altered the surface. Cradled among them was Fontana Lake, the waters of the Little Tennessee dammed and impounded. As he gazed at it, at the sparkling blue, Will suddenly became tired. His legs ached, his shoulder pained him, and his eyes filled with tears of fatigue. He thought he would become ill again if he could not eat and rest. . . .

In the wildest depths of the Great Smokies lies the enchanted lake of Atagahi no one has seen it for the way is so difficult that only the animals can approach should a hunter come near he would know of it by the whirring of thousands of wild ducks and pigeons but he would not see it without praying and fasting and watching through the night floating lilies grow in its purple waters it is fed by springs spouting from the high cliffs around it Atagahi is the medicine lake of the birds and animals when a bear is wounded by the hunters he makes his way through the woods to the lake and plunges in when he comes out upon the other side the wounds are healed for this reason the animals keep the lake invisible to the hunters. . . .

Turning from the lake and mountains, Will entered the woods and crossed the ridge, moving west.

FIVE

and the noble hidalgos sold their estates gave up their incomes from land and church crowded into Seville to join Hernando De Soto fresh from the conquest of Peru now Governor of the Island of Cuba and Adelantado of Florida possessed of a fortune in Inca gold to be traded for the conquest of Florida. There was not space on the ships some gentlemen were left on the docks their luggage around them their goods and estates sold six hundred were chosen by the Governor and more than two hundred of the finest Spanish horses great festivities were held the trumpets sounded artillery blasted as the seven ships sailed out of the harbor. The fleet paused in the Canary Islands for bread and wine and meat and sailed out again arrived in Santiago de Cuba where the party divided some traveled by land others by sea to the port of Havana. Two months the Governor spent in final preparations in settling the affairs of his island arranging a home for his bride the Donna Isabella on a Sunday in the warm Caribbean spring the fleet set sail once more quitting the Island for the vast indeterminate continent known only as Florida. For twelve days the ships sailed the blue waters of the Gulf and on Friday the Thirtieth Day of May in the Year of Our Lord Fifteen Hundred and Thirty-Nine the first landing was made on the banks of a river in celebration whereof the place was named Puerto del Espiritu Santo. . . .

"My name's Ferd. Hop in."

Will was standing on u.s. 80, west of Jackson, Mississippi, when a truck slowed for him. He ran to catch up with it, and he was out of breath. When the driver put out his hand to him, accompanying the greeting, Will grasped it like a handle to pull himself up. The driver responded, gripping firmly and pulling. The muscle in the wounded shoulder wrenched as Will swung into the cab, and sharp pains went down his arm. He settled back in his seat and closed the door with his left hand.

"Where you bound?"

"West," said Will. He was still breathing hard, his arm resting limply in his lap. "Texas."

"Good. I'm heading for Dallas."

The driver glanced in the mirror and then concentrated on the road, as he started forward. It was a heavy truck, with extra gears and a roaring, grinding motor. The effort of acceleration suggested a full load. Will shifted his feet among a mass of tools, jacks, rags, etc. Over the windshield, and on the side and back walls between the windows, were snapshots of girls; a small calendar featuring a nude; a couple of kewpie dolls; and business cards of various drive-ins, restaurants, garages, etc.

Will glanced at Ferd. He was a slender, blue-eyed man of perhaps thirty, his face tense and alert. His eyes remained fixed on the road. Will turned away and looked out the window.

"Cigarette?"

When he looked back, Ferd was holding the pack, offering them.

"Thanks."

"Light one for me."

Will took two from the pack, waited for the matches that followed. He lit the cigarettes, his right hand trembling a little, and handed one to Ferd, together with the matches.

The first drag of smoke felt good and Will inhaled deeply, blowing it out with force. He leaned back, resting his head on the worn leather, and inhaled again. The cab became filled with the pleasant smoke. Ferd held his cigarette tightly between his lips, smoking without removing it.

"My name's Joe," Will said.

Ferd nodded without turning, and they drove on.

The Indians approached playing flutes as a sign of peaceful intentions the Cacique spoke VERY HIGH POWERFUL AND GOOD MASTER the things that seldom happen bring astonishment think then what must be the effect on me and mine the sight of you and your people whom we have at no time seen astride the fierce brutes your horses entering with such speed and fury into my country that we had no tidings of your coming things so altogether new as to strike awe and terror to our hearts which it was not nature to resist so that we should receive you with the sobriety due to so kingly and famous a lord trusting to your greatness and personal qualities I hope no fault will be found in me and that I shall rather receive favors of which one is that with my person my country and my vassals you will do as with your own things and another that you tell me who you are whence you come whither you go and what it is you seek that I may the better serve you. De Soto thanked him and replied that he was the child of the Sun that he came from the land of the Sun that he was traveling in search of treasure he erected a great wooden cross on the mound in the town yard told the Indians it was put there to commemorate the suffering of Christ who was God and man that He had created the skies and the earth and had suffered for the salvation of all and therefore they should revere that sign and they the Indians showed by their manner that they would. Whereupon as in every territory the Spaniards crossed the Cacique was taken prisoner slaves were demanded put in chains and iron collars to carry the burdens trinkets and mirrors were traded to the men for their women and the Christians lived off the crops and stores of the land beat the maize with mortar and pestle sifted it through their coats of armor baked it in clay dishes over fires after the manner of Indians. Throughout the summer they pushed through the wilds and tangles of the Florida peninsula changing Cacique and slaves and women at the border of each territory the Indians soon learned to give them false promises of gold and maize in the land beyond in order to be rid of them. . . .

Ferd pushed the truck into high gear and set it at a steady fifty miles an hour. The highway passed over rolling hills and level farmland, and the speedometer never varied more than a mile or two either side of fifty. He flicked his head sharply, and the ashes from his cigarette fell between the spokes of the steering wheel to the floor.

Will continued to lean back, his head on the leather, his eyes lazily watching the road. The cigarette, that had at first relieved his hunger and exhaustion, now intensified them. He let it burn down by itself, and threw it out the window.

For twelve days he had slept only an hour or two at a time, in woods and fields, beside streams. He had lived on corn and other vegetables taken at night from fields and gardens and eaten raw, and what few berries he could find in the woods. He had not been cold, it was summer, and he was out of the mountains; but he had walked and walked, day and night, had walked through his shoes and was wearing a pair that he had taken from the feet of a drunk he had found asleep in a ditch. Until now he had hitch-hiked only occasionally, for short rides on back roads. This was the first time he had dared a main highway. He was gambling on a long haul, and apparently had won. Always, as he walked or rode, or tried to sleep, there was the dull ache in his shoulder. He had spent some of his little cash at a general store for needle and thread, and had sewed the bullet hole in his shirt. But he still wore the jacket, although it was late morning and the day was hot and humid.

The roar of the motor became a steady drone. He could feel himself becoming drowsy, beginning to sink, as though into the enormous emptiness of his stomach. He held his eyes open with an effort. If I grit my teeth, he thought; imagine that the air filtering between them is a thin solid, that I am holding myself to it like an acrobat hanging by his teeth; or like a drowning man, struggling to hold mouth and nose above the surface....

. . . *Until in one town still in the peninsula of Florida the Indians planned an attack to release the captured Cacique but the Spaniards attacked first drove the Indians into a lake the Indians swam out beyond range of the crossbow and harquebus refused to surrender darkness fell the Indians were treading deep water in the middle of the lake some swam in silently waterlilies covering their heads and tried to scramble out but De Soto's cavalry encircling the lake discovered them plunged into the water to the horses' breasts drove the Indians back to the middle of the lake some surrendered exhausted and cold but at dawn twelve were still treading water others swam out and brought them in for their endurance they were tied to a stake and shot ...*

"Do you see that one?"

Ferd was pointing to one of the snapshots over the windshield. Will stirred himself and looked at head and shoulders of a pretty girl, with hard, vigorous face.

"Used to be my girlfriend." He turned quickly to Will, and his blue eye winked. "Small town in Georgia. That was when I was hauling hardware out of Augusta. Used to run down to spend the night." Again he turned quickly, his face bright with pleasure.

"Nine brothers and thirteen sisters," he went on, shouting above the drone of the motor. "One of them had epilepsy. Some in the navy, three in marines, a couple of WACS. One worked a carnival, another studying to be a sky pilot. Some of the girls married off and left town, didn't even know where they were. And could she fight! Umh!"

He leaned over the steering wheel, gripping it strenuously for emphasis.

"First time we went out she blacked my eyes. Next time, we were fooling around in the front parlor and she hit me with a solid brass lamp!"

Felled pines across the stream bound them with withes fought off the Indians as they crossed and entered the town that the Indians had burned before flight this being Wednesday of Saint Francis. . . .

"But I tamed her. Man, I tamed her!" He sat back, spreading his elbows. "One of her brothers that was away in service had a guitar that he kept home, and that's one box I can really play. I used to take her back by the barbecue and play for her, and she'd sing. Sometimes we'd both sing, with me on the harmony. We'd eat hamburgers on cornbread—did you ever try it? Singing like that, eating outdoors on a summer night, twanging the guitar real slow, she'd go all soft. After that it was easy. I'd take her out to a cabin, or maybe we'd go up to Augusta, to a hotel. She was really built, you can't tell from that." He shook his hand deprecatingly at the photograph.

Maize pumpkin bean and plum with rabbit opossum turkey and partridge the autumn harvest of a continent and the Spaniards pushed northward and eastward until they reached Cofitachiqui the name of a town a territory and of the lovely Cacica who ruled them. The town lay across a river and the Cacica came out to greet the Spaniards she was carried in a litter to the water's edge stepped into a magnificent canoe reclined in the stern on mats and cushions under an awning while her vassals paddled her across the stream accompanied by her ret-inue of consorts in lesser canoes. She greeted De Soto took a string of pearls from her throat with her own hands dropped them over his head her men ferried the Christians across the river and she gave them dec-orated deer skins and cloaks of thread made from the bark of the mul-berry tree others of white gray vermilion and yellow feathers she gave them turkeys to eat noting their interest in pearls she graciously led them to a sepulchre from which they took several hundred pounds. So fine the pearls so abundant the food so generous the Cacica many of the men wanted to settle to divide the land among themselves but De Soto remembered the Andes the Inca the gold. He took the lovely lady pris-oner obtained slaves and pushed northwestward to the great moun-tains. . . .

"That was right after the war, when hardware was scarce. Fellow with a truck could make a good living, provided he could find it. I got in with this operator in Augusta, strictly black market. I was hauling back up to Asheville and around there. That's my home."

He turned to the window and spat out the cigarette, that had burned almost to his lips. He was silent for a while, his eyes bright and alert as he watched the road.

"When hardware began to get easy I had to give it up. It was then my luck started going sour. I'd just bought a new semi—tractor-trailer, you know?—and she was a beauty. Brand new, all aluminum. Cost me two hundred and fifty for the tags alone. Had to mortgage the house to get her. Here."

He took down another snapshot and put it into Will's hands. It showed a young woman seated on the porch of a house, holding a baby in her arms.

"That's the wife. Finest little chick in the world. I wouldn't take a purty for her. And you see that kid? He's four years old now. Smart as a whip. Last Christmas I gave him a jigsaw puzzle, a map of the country, with a piece for every state, you know? The wife said it was too smart for him, I should have saved it. Well, I didn't give him a bit of help, I just set it down on the floor in front of him and damned if he didn't figure it all out by himself. Now he can put it together in five minutes. What I mean, smart. We got another one

on the way now. That's the house, you can see a little of it there, the
one that's got the mortgage on it."

Will nodded and handed him the snapshot. He replaced it over
the windshield.

"I got a deal going between Asheville and Atlanta, with this new
semi. Two or three trips a week, regular. Nice business. Well, one
morning, it was winter, and I set out of Asheville about four or five
o'clock, loaded down with beer. I got out beyond the mountains the
other side of the Gap. It's nice and straight going up, you know, but
down the other side it's just one hairpin after another. It was day-
light by then, but raining and foggy, and I was driving with lights. I
got on one of them turns and the brakes give out. The pedal went
down to the floor like I was stepping on air. Brand-new truck, did-
n't have two thousand on her by then! I wrenched that wheel one
way and the other, curled back and forth like a damn snake. I cut
into the bank on the inside, took a chunk out of it, and heaved back
on the road. I made the curve all right, but I wasn't stopped, not by
a long shot. I wasn't hardly slowed. There was a straight piece
ahead, not long, but straight down, with another hairpin at the end.
I snaked her back and forth and I could feel that beer swinging
behind me like I was swinging the whole mountain by the tail. I
shoved her out of gear and jammed her into second, nearly broke
my arm. That slowed her some, but not enough. By the time I got
to the hairpin I knew we couldn't make it. She was going to pitch
off and I was going to pitch with her. I opened the door and half
hung on it, watching. My foot was still sitting on that damn fool
brake pedal out of habit, and I was snaking the wheel. The bank was
so steep that it wasn't until we come right up on it that I could see
over. Cleared all the way, not a tree or nothing, two or three hun-
dred feet down to the streambed. Right at the edge of the road,
when the front wheels took off, I jumped clear. It wasn't until I was
half out of the truck and I couldn't have done nothing about it
nohow that I saw where I was heading—a hunk of rock sticking up
straight out of the bushes. I missed it all except my right leg and
that got smashed against it and tore up all to pieces. Holes and
gashes and bones sticking out. I mean, it was a mess!

"I didn't black out. I watched that tractor break loose and roll over

and over; I watched that pretty aluminum trailor shear open like it
was made out of paper. The two of them rolled down and I just lay
back and didn't look no more. And you know that damned white
trash, they must have smelled it for six counties around: they start-
ed coming out of the woods and picking up the beer bottles that
wasn't broke. . . ."

*. . . But they arrived in the mountains of the Chalaque in late spring
and there was little maize because the winter stores were gone and the
summer crops had not come in nevertheless they ate dogs. The captive
Cacica Cofitachiqui led them a merry chase in search of gold through the
blue-hazed ridges and smoke-blue mountains and quietly escaped tak-
ing with her a box of the finest pearls and a handsome Negro slave to
share the doeskin mats to idle the hours of night down by the river. . . .*

"I didn't lay there long. The bank was all tore up where we'd gone
off, and the truck was lit up like a forest fire. Couple of fellows in a
pickup stopped and I hollered to them. They came over and picked
me up, carried me into their truck, with the leg dangling like a half
butchered ham, and them afraid to touch it. They hauled me into a
clinic in this small town, the trap bouncing like a buckboard, me
stretched out in back. The doctor wasn't there, it was too early, and
the nurse didn't much know what to do. I was talking wild, I guess,
and cussing, and she got kind of hysterical and pumped me full of
dope to cut the edge out of my tongue. The doctor came and I still
hadn't gone out. He looked at the leg and then he gave me a look
that told me he was fixing to use the hatchet. I sat up and cussed
him out something awful, told him I'd as soon let him have my
neck. He talked back and I just talked louder. God knows what I
said but I pitched him a mean fit. They packed me into an ambu-
lance and headed for Asheville and me still babbling and carrying
on. Somewhere on the road I blacked out, and I didn't know noth-
ing for a day and a night. . . ."

*Southward and westward the Spaniards turned moving down the
southern passes of the mountains to the level land the rivers pouring to
the Gulf of New Spain they came to Taszaluza where a giant Cacique*

sat in a litter attended by his chiefs by a slave who fanned the flies from him he watched the Spaniards put on a show jousting running the horses and said nothing when De Soto demanded food and slaves he replied that he was accustomed to having others serve him and was put in chains. He sent word to Mauvila another of his towns to gather the warriors and told his captors their desires would be satisfied in Mauvila the Spaniards carried him thence a stockaded town stakes driven in the ground interlaced with withes covered inside and out with clay De Soto and others entered by way of graciousness and were entertained by women who danced for them and the attack began. The Spaniards were wounded but save only a priest and a friar they escaped the stockade in the confusion the slaves bearing the Christian possessions entered struck off their iron collars and joined the attack. The wounded Governor re-formed the cavalry approached the stockade the fighting was bitter and bloody slowly hour after hour the horsemen came closer until brands thrown over the wall fired the huts and the Christians entered the last confusion fighting within the stockade choked with thatch of huts in smoke and flame and the rampage of horses with Indians dead and burned and wounded fighting falling and clustering was bloodiest of all the mounted Spaniards shot and slashed and fired until the natives were exterminated until the last warrior hung himself from a tree to escape surrender. The Spaniards withdrew to the open field beyond the smoldering huts and lay down to nurse their wounds to count their losses. Indians lay dead by thousands the Spaniards had lost perhaps a hundred with hundreds wounded many of the best horses killed and wounded. All the possessions the clothes the pearls of Cofitachiqui were lost. The priest and friar trapped within the village had been rescued were safe this was a blessing but the ornaments for the saying of mass the sacramental cups the molds for making wafers the wine were gone. Worst of all worse than the loss of cloak horse or brother the precious wheat flour cherished from Spain was destroyed henceforth the Christians would partake of His body with no wine with wafers crudely fashioned of the profane maize. The fighters bemoaned their fate dressed their wounds with fat from the bodies of the dead Indians. . . .

"When I come to I was in a ward in the hospital. I cussed out the first nurse I saw until she told me I still had my leg. She told me I hadn't ought to have had it, that any other doctor in Buncombe County would have whacked it off, but this fellow I happened to get was a wizard and he'd put it back together again. They still didn't know, they'd have to wait until the bones set. So there was nothing for me to do but lay there week after week, counting up my debts and watching the pus pour out of the holes."

Ferd paused, and Will turned to the window, looked over the level Mississippi farmland, negro and white, spreading northward. The weather was hot and oppressive, and a bank of dark clouds threatened over them. Ferd remained silent, and Will became disturbed. He realized that he had come to depend on the driver's story to support the exhausted thread of his own conciousness. . . .

"The leg doesn't bother you now?" he asked.

"Not a bit," Ferd replied at once, as though he had been waiting for Will to ask him. "I get a twinge now and then, but I can do just about anything with it I could before. The bones set just as pretty as you could wish, and they stuck me full of penicillin until it was coming out of my ears. That dried up the pus and closed the holes. After six weeks I crawled out on crutches. It took another month at home, just laying around doing nothing. Cigarette?"

"I'll light one for you."

Will performed the service for Ferd and handed him the lighted cigarette.

"Thanks. So there I was. Debts on the house, the doc, and the hospital. And no truck. Time that wreck stopped burning, they hauled it out and sold it for junk. Had to bulldoze a road down there to get it out. The insurance paid off, but the finance company got most of that. So I put myself in hock again and bought this trap. I figured if I didn't have some kind of truck, I never would get out of the hole."

He turned to emphasize the point with an inquiring look, and Will nodded. Again there was silence, as Ferd gazed at the road. Will could feel himself sinking, drowsily.

"What are you hauling?" he asked, shifting his position.

"Peaches. Spartanburg County. But this truck don't set right.

She's loaded up heavy, she ought to ride good, but she don't. You know, after you've drove a semi, a beauty like the one I tore up, none of these regular jobs set right."

Ferd bounced gently in the seat, worked his hands and arms against the wheel, moved his head and chest back and forth. He treated the truck as though it were an animal, able to receive and respond to infusions from his own centers; approached it with extramechanical energy, drawn from the deepest resources, the resources from which men control cards and dice. He was 'riding' it.

Crouching over the wheel, he shook his head in exasperation.

"She don't set right . . ."

One month the Spaniards rested and recovered then drew away northwestward winter came with snow and cold in Chicaca the Indians filtered through the guard attacked at night fired the huts where the Spaniards slept men unclothed and beasts unharnessed ran and trampled in confusion the Spaniards could not find arms and saddles De Soto alone mounted his horse killed an Indian then twisted and fell the girth had not been fastened had the attack been pressed the Spaniards would have been annihilated but it was dark the Indians were confused they thought the wild chaotic horses were cavalry in attack they fled. The town was in cinders many were without clothes polar winds swept unhindered down the center of a continent the men tried to sleep by fires but one side burned while the other froze. Spring came a forge was set up harness saddles and weapons were made and repaired the Indians attacked again and the Spaniards placed foot soldiers in the front to spare the precious cavalry the Indians were driven off and the party pushed westward . . .

Will turned again to the window, gazed passively at the truck farms. The land was mostly level, with some rolling hills, and it was good land. Even the small negro mule farms with tumbling unpainted shacks seemed to produce well. Few trees survived, save in the towns where the highway might become, for a few moments, an avenue shaded with water oaks and Spanish moss. Beyond Will's view, to the northward, were the old Chickasaw country, and Yoknapatawpha County.

The truck passed over a river and Will lifted himself, gazed over the edge of the bridge at the turgid, slow-moving waters, reflecting the lowering clouds overhead . . .

The United States Government provided flatboats the John Cox the Sliger Blue Buck Rainbow Squeezer and Moll Thompson on the Hiwassee River for those Indians who could be cajoled bribed corrupted into leaving their homes in the Old Smokies and going West four hundred and fifty came out of their cabins lived in barracks by the river while they waited bought dainties whiskey and trinkets sold their western land claims to speculators before departure the measles broke out the flatboats floated down the Hiwassee a young lieutenant from West Point in command down the Tennessee through the Suck the Boiling-Pot the Skillet the Frying Pan measles raged through young and old but mostly young the government provided salt pork and white bread and no medicine at every stop the Indians went ashore to cut wood for coffins the whiskey vendors came on board at Waterloo Alabama the delay was long while the soldiers ploughed the Waterloo whores under way again one of the keelboats went down sixty-seven Cherokee rescued their belongings lost down the Tennessee the Ohio the Mississippi to the Whiskey Capitol of the emigration Fort Smith up the Arkansas but the water was low food put ashore but the boats would not float Indians put ashore but no wagons could be found the measles abated but it was hot country in the hot season fever season in the poisonous filth of the boat and shore camps cholera broke out the Indians scattered to the woods made their fires miles apart in terror of one another the doctor taken on in Alabama was dead in a week the young lieutenant with what he had learned at West Point was alone to hunt doctors food wagons to feed and cure four hundred Indians a doctor came left in horror food was scarce the farmers would not sell their wagons it was planting time no one would approach no one but horse thieves the lieutenant's horse was stolen he made his rounds over miles of woods on foot became ill stayed on his feet threw off the fever whites and half-breeds who had lost beloveds were weeping and wailing the Indians were silent digging graves wagons and teams were found for food and belongings infants and dying the rest marched on foot bloody and blistering to Indian Territory . . .

"Candy?" The truck went over a bump as it passed off the bridge onto the land, and nausea stirred in the enormous emptiness of Will's stomach. He turned to see Ferd offering him a chocolate bar, already opened.

"Thanks," he said, his voice breaking. His hands trembled as he took the bar, broke it in two, and returned half.

Ferd held his piece a moment and gazed at Will, his eyes blue and bright and hard.

"You don't look like you've et in a month," he said.

Will laughed gently and held his eyes down. He was almost in tears. Ferd watched him a moment longer, and then turned to the road and chewed his candy. The truck droned on at a steady fifty.

The first sensation of chocolate and almond passed over Will's tongue was one of ineffable sweetness, a sweetness so long desired, so long unadmitted, as to be almost unbearable. He sucked on a corner of the bar like a baby, broke off only little pieces at a time, not so much to savor the taste but out of fear, fear the sweetness and the enjoyment of it would overwhelm him. Only slowly did he dare open himself to it.

"Thanks," he said again, his eyes damp and warm, gazing at the road.

Biting a larger piece, he sat back and closed his eyes, let the chocolate rest on his tongue, and melt. For some time he was still. Once he looked up, but the sun had broken through for a moment, and the bright reflection from the highway hurt his eyes. He closed them again. The drone of the motor, the gentle shaking of the truck, the consummate sweetness carried him, like an unwilled body floating in the waves, into sleep. . . .

De Soto and the Spaniards came to a great river the largest they had seen they named it Rio Grande and some suggested it might even be larger than the Danube camp was set up and the men cut timber to make pirogues for a crossing Indians appeared in canopied barges and canoes parting the waters of the Great River like an armada of galleys the warriors painted and feathered in ochre and vermilion discharged arrows and retreated thirty days the Spaniards labored the pirogues were towed upstream that the landing would be opposite camp the crossing was made

men and horses ferried across the Great River the pirogues were
destroyed but the nails saved for future use. Westward the Christians
faced captured a town took skins of the deer buffalo bear and wildcat
made clothing for themselves and armor for the horses still westward
harried by rebellious Indians bed clothing made from buffalo skins and
winter came on the barren western plains with no maize slowly the
numbers of men and horses diminished De Soto turned back toward the
Great River for winter quarters but could not reach it passed the cold
months in Autiamque learned from the Indians to trap rabbits. The
interpreter died the Christians could not make themselves understood got
wrong directions retraced their steps and wandered as spring came the
rivers flooded men walked in swamps or swam dragging the horses
finally reached the Great River scouts departed to search for the ocean but
they could not pass the swamps the bogs the canebrakes and scrubs they
returned and still men and horses diminished in numbers. De Soto sent
word to the Cacique saying that he was the Child of the Sun and all men
came to him to pay him tribute and in token of love and obedience the
Cacique must come and bring him food and the Cacique replied as to
what you say of your being the son of the Sun if you will cause him to
dry up the Great River I will believe you as to the rest it is not my cus-
tom to visit anyone but rather all of whom I have ever heard have come
to visit me to serve and obey me and pay me tribute whether voluntar-
ily or by force if you desire to see me come where I am if for peace I will
receive you with special goodwill if for war I will await you in my town
but neither for you nor for any man will I set back one foot whereupon
De Soto became despondent ill with fever kept the cavalry mounted day
and night returned to a smaller town surprised killed and routed the
Indians and with this lift to his waning reputation he sickened named
Luis Moscoso Captain-General and died. . . .

Will stirred, opened his eyes. He was aware of deep sweetness and
relaxation penetrating his body and limbs; of rest and relaxation
barely initiated, richly and dreamily anticipated. Even the ache in
his shoulder was encircled with a delicious tingling. The sun had
gone in and the clouds were darker, more threatening than before.
He didn't move, afraid to break the trance. Closing his eyes, he let
the sound and motion of the truck restore him to sleep . . .

*De Soto was buried at night the death hidden from the Indians who
had been told he was immortal but the Indians missed him discovered
the grave the body was taken up carried at night in a canoe and
dropped in the Great River still the Indians asked for him Moscoso
said he had ascended into the heavens as he had many times before and
would return the Cacique sent two Indians to be beheaded that they
might join the Governor in the heavens and serve him and Moscoso
cursed their heathen practices. De Soto's property was distributed on
credit to be paid for out of gold and silver yet to be discovered and
again the Spaniards turned westward many were glad De Soto was
dead he had driven them onward into Florida but they were anxious
to reach New Spain by way of land and get out of Florida they had
had enough all but one who stayed behind with his Indian concubine
for fear of losing her in payment of gambling debts still the Indians
attacked and men and horses slowly diminished in numbers. As before
the towns became thin the maize scarce winter was coming westward
lay only desert and wild homeless Indians who lived as the Spaniards
said like Arabs again the Christians turned headed for the Great River
where the soil nourished by abundant waters produced quantities of
maize they would build brigantines and in the spring would sail down
the river and out of the continent of Florida forever Moscoso wanted
only to reach a place where for once he could get his full measure of
sleep. Back to the river they struggled through towns they had already
devastated what little food remained the Indians had hidden reaching
the river they found no maize the Indians in fear of them had not
planted in driving cold and rain through flooded waters and north
wind carrying their sick they came to Aminoya where old stores of
maize were found and the harried Christians camped for the winter.*
. . .

Will opened his eyes and was still for a moment, uncomprehending.
The world seemed to have closed upon him. The cab was hot and
tight, filled with smoke; both windows were shut. The drone of the
motor was buried in the sound of thunder and of a torrential rain
that tumbled out of the clouds, rain falling not in drops but in
globes, graying the air, clattering against glass and steel. The wind-
shield wiper arched back and forth, useless and persistent.

Ferd was crouching over the wheel, smoking, driving much slower. From time to time he rubbed the windshield with his sleeve. Seeing Will awake he turned to him, moving only his head, and smiled, the hard lines of his mouth drawing back, the cigarette trembling in the corner.

"I guess you ain't slept in a month, neither," he said.

Will laughed a little and sat up.

"I feel better."

Kicking among the junk on the floor he found a rag moderately clean and picked it up, wiped the full width of the windshield. Ferd nodded his thanks.

"This'll quit arter a while. It's a river rain. Delta rain. Comes down in tubs and then quits and the sun comes out and it'll be hotter than ever."

Will opened his window a crack for air. A little rain came in and felt good on his face.

"Man, I hate this weather," Ferd continued. "Don't see how they stand it. My home's the mountains. I guess once you lived up there you can't never get used to this low country. Know what I do first thing when I get back up yonder? Stop by a stream someplace and get a drink of water. Cool, fresh mountain water! Nothing like it!"

The rain let up a little and the wiper began to make headway with the floods on the windshield. Thunder threatened remotely, withdrawing. Will ate some more of his candy bar.

"How long was I out?" he asked.

"Not long. Half hour, maybe. But you slept good."

Ferd was concentrating on the road, stepping up his speed.

Through the window Will made out changes in the countryside.

The level farmland was gone, had given way to short broken hills, bluff hills, many of them wooded. The highway rolled and turned and passed through deep cuts. We must be near the river, Will thought.

The rain exhausted itself abruptly, and almost at once the sun came out. It was not a pure sun but filtered through clouds, glaring. Steam rose from the truck and highway, and isolated showers, tiny spray drops glistening in the sunlight, drifted and fell erratically. Will and Ferd opened their windows, let the hot wet air drive the smoke from the cab. Ferd sat up straight and resumed his original speed, where the road permitted.

They drove in silence for a short while. Will was aware that Ferd was glancing calculatingly at the snapshots over the windshield. He couldn't seem to make up his mind. Suddenly his arm shot out and he pointed to the one at the end, directly in front of Will.

"See that one?"

Will looked at head, shoulders, and well-developed figure of a young girl. She had a posed smile, and a self-willed face.

"Take her down and look at her."

Will took the snapshot from its place and held it before him.

"How old would you say she was?"

"About eighteen," Will guessed.

"Thirteen when that was took. She's fifteen now. Been getting the curse since she was ten."

He paused, glancing back and forth between picture and road. Then he turned wholly to the road, gripping the wheel.

"Jailbait," he barked, between tight-drawn lips.

Will continued to look at the picture.

"You know, there ain't nothing about that gal but what you see right there." He spoke tensely. "What I mean, just to look at and put into bed. That's all. She's the orneriest brat this side of the river. Lives alone with her aunt, down the road from us. The old woman works all day to support her and then comes home and cooks dinner, cleans the house, does the washing, the ironing, and the dishes and then like as not sets down and makes a dress for her. That one just sets around after school and suns herself. Weekends she'll go to the drive-in or the square dance, flirt with the married men, fool around with other gals' fellows. Their house ain't half finished but she's got to have a hunk of her aunt's dough to go to town every week, take dancing lessons, buy candy and new clothes and go to the movies. Sometimes I guess the old woman figures it an investment. But she's going to get a shock someday: if the kid ever does strike it rich her aunt will be somebody she ain't never heard of. And you know there ain't nothing you can tell her. She tells my wife jokes and the wife comes home and tells me and you'd think she just come out of the stable. What I mean, she knows it all. If my little woman knew I even had that picture up here she'd cut my throat."

He turned to the window and spat out the cigarette butt.

"Man, there ain't nothing to recommend her. Nothing but what she's got under that sweater."

He was silent for a while, watching the road. His eyes for the first time lost their brightness. Unconsciously he slowed the truck, and the motor became quieter.

"But you know, it's a funny thing," he went on. "I know all that. Knew it the first time I met the kid. It don't take long to find out what folks are up to, just the way they act is enough. She's a bitch. There ain't nothing she's ever done or most likely ever will do that'll make me change her out of the damnedest bitch in forty-eight states. But you know what? That kid's got me. Silly, ain't it? It's the truth. Deep down plum inside me, I've been took. There ain't a thing nasty enough you can say about her in front of me: but if she'd have me I'd crawl into the hay with her tomorrow. I'd do just about anything she wanted to name so's I could have her just once. I'd sleep with her right in her own home or just whatever place she wanted to pick out. I'd work sixteen hours a day seven days a week just to spend a half hour at night with her, and her out flirting around the rest of the time. I'd go plum to hell and sit there twenty years if I thought she'd be in my bed when I got back."

He sat soberly at the wheel, still driving slowly. The sun suddenly vanished and the clouds threatened again. The hills became dark and the luminosity vanished from the highway. Fresh thunder rumbled ahead of them.

"Do you know what she thinks of me?" Ferd asked, speaking with more confidence. "Nothing. Plain dirt nothing. I could drop this truck into the Mississippi River and she wouldn't care if I never come up. Let me tell you something else. The first time I got to know this kid she set her sights for me. Didn't give a damn about me and still don't, just wanted to break me down, get me on her list. She started flirting right out in broad daylight. Just a kid, you know. The wife and I used to laugh about it, she was so damn flat-footed. Then something happened. All of a sudden something sprung in me. All this flirting and swishing her hips and coming over to say hello in a bathing suit and worrying her plunging neckline all over the kitchen began to take. I couldn't tell you what happened or even when it happened. It's like she was building up this charge against me, just a little bit every day, piling it up and piling it up. At first it didn't look like much and I laughed at it; then I quit paying heed because it went on just the same all the time. Until one day I turned around and I just couldn't stand it no more, the charge had got too big, and the lightning struck. Only it wasn't like that because it just happened, I didn't know nothing about it. From then on, didn't matter what we was before, leastways as far as I was concerned, we were stuck."

Lightning flashed across the highway and the rain burst upon them, pouring in great floods as before. Thunder roared overhead. They rolled up the windows quickly, and Will replaced the photograph over the windshield. Ferd glanced at it as he saw it restored.

"Now she's got me on the hook she just gives me the light treatment." He was leaning toward Will, talking louder, almost shouting to drown out the rain. "Keep me irritated, keep me coming. Maybe she's been to town and bought herself a new playsuit. She's got to come over and show us how the halter snaps in back and the elastic in it is too tight and makes a line in front and how the skirt swirls up when she turns around and the tights are nothing but a little old netting and you can see her white panties underneath riding up to her hips. Once or twice she's let me get close to her. Put my arm on her shoulder, or sneak a kiss."

Will began to withdraw slowly to the far side of the seat. There was a strange sensation in the cab. The windows were shut up tight, the air was hot and close, the windshield began to fog again. The drone of the motor, the pelting of the rain, the rumbling of thunder intensified the sense of enclosure, of being in a compartment, insufferably tight, projected through nameless atmosphere. The sound of Ferd's voice became almost unbearable. The words, the vowels seemed to form into physical objects as they left his mouth, roaring and echoing back and forth in the cab, striking the steel and glass in response to the raindrops on the outside. Will felt as though his head were swelling, as though it nearly filled the space of the cab, and the heat of the motor, the reverberations, the suddenly intolerable presence of Ferd existed in a space encompassed by his own physical being.

"Once we was playing cards, me and her and the wife. I put my hand on her knee, under the table, and started to move up. She caught it between her legs and squeezed them together, held it there. That's as close as I ever got. Or ever will get, I reckon. She don't have to let me get no closer. Just keep me swinging, like a fish she's got all hooked up and she's just too damn lazy to pull into the boat."

Will opened the window a crack. His chest was heaving; he was breathing hard. The hills were thickly wooded with a variety of trees. Suddenly the space opened and they came to a network of interlocking roads: the entrance to Vicksburg National Military Park . . .

The river flows through soft alluvial mud intersected for twenty miles on either side by a web a maze of interlocking and obstructed bayous the banks overgrown with a wild jungle tangle the intervening spaces sunken in swamps it is the crookedest big river in the world also the orneriest changing or refusing to change its course at will this was the problem that faced Grant the river that must be opened to New Orleans to cut off Confederate supplies isolate the Rebels from their granary in the West open now to St. Louis to Cairo to Memphis but at Vicksburg the bluff hills rise two hundred feet the highest and strongest point on the river terraced and fortified with entrenched batteries so that no ships could pass. Vicksburg the Hill City protected south and west by the river north by the fortifications at Hayne's Bluff could only be attacked in the rear in the tail that is from the east Grant approached from the north moving slowly to keep open his supplies food forage and ammunition via railroad and river but the rail lines were broken by raids stores destroyed and Grant retreated he approached from the west tried to dig a canal in the peninsula opposite Vicksburg so the fleet could by-pass the batteries but the river refused to stay out of the work finally flooded the operation the soldiers had to withdraw or be drowned Grant tried to open a passage through the bayous but the Rebels felled trees across them in all his efforts he had failed with his northern soldiers suffering the terrors not only of the terrain but of the climate the pestilential fevers the drinking water on which the

*Confederates thrived. Grant crossed the river above Vicksburg to the
western shore made corduroy roads moved southward through swamps
bogs canebrakes over bayous to the river below Vicksburg some of the
fleet protected by gunboats moving at night without lights ran the bat-
teries at Vicksburg the Confederates fired houses to illuminate the river
but the ships passed brought supplies to Grant below the city and fer-
ried his army across the river back to the eastern shore forty-three thou-
sand men ready to strike. The supply line past Vicksburg was difficult
he must move fast subdue Jackson and Vicksburg reopen securer lines
from the north when Washington heard of his plans they were prompt-
ly countermanded but Grant had left before the order arrived holding
his army together with none to protect the rear he broke from his only
source of supplies the river the men carried five days' rations foraging
parties went out at night to scavenge on the land find corn and poul-
try on the plantations feinting north at Vicksburg the army moved
northeast to Jackson a maneuver without precedent in modern war-
fare an army moving as a unit cut off by its own volition from sup-
plies and sources a man projected willfully into alien country to which
he has not been invited subject constantly to destruction depending on
mobility subsisting on the food scavenged from day to day off the diffi-
cult resistant land. Grant routed the Confederate Army at Jackson left
the city devastated the railroads destroyed for twenty miles in all direc-
tions turned and headed west over the main route toward the bluff
hills to strike Vicksburg the fortress on the river from the east routed
the Rebels at Champion's Hill captured the batteries at Hayne's Bluff
above the city opened supply lines to the north via the river and the
men rejoicing to quit the plantation diet of chicken turkey and corn-
bread return to hardtack and bacon attacked the fortified eastern lines
of Vicksburg. . . .*

The rain slackened, and stopped abruptly, as before. The sun
remained hidden but spread a dull glare over the land. Will opened
his window, breathed deeply, more easily.

Ferd was silent, morose, opening his window absently. He drove
with mechanical caution as the highway passed through the park,
under the Memorial Arch and into the city of Vicksburg.

... *but the Rebels had dug in repulsed the Federals in two days of bloody attacks three thousand dead and wounded lay between the close lines the Federals dug in for a siege neither side would yield to bury the dead the fighting went on it was late May under a burning sun the corpses stank the stench climbing the fortified hills to the noses of the Rebels fearing an epidemic they called an armistice and the dead were buried while officers of two sides conversed and joked exchanging views regarding the siege trading news for smokes. The work done the men returned to their entrenchments the siege began the Federals supplied by the river to the north poured shrapnel mortar and Parrott shells grape shot canister grenades and musketry into the city the residents dug caves in the hillsides cavediggers were in demand brought good wages the ladies would go to Sky Parlor Hill or stand on their verandas to watch the fireworks when the shattering iron came too close they retired to their caves learned to cook eat sleep in them troglodytes lying sitting or crouching in darkness listening to the rattle of musketry the distant whistling of a shell coming closer screaming rushing waiting for the explosion wondering then the electric shock the sickening jolting the shaking cave supports the sifting dirt people who have crawled back into caves into the earth longing for the thrill and privilege of once more standing erect. Unfed dogs wandered in the streets and the Rebels stayed in the trenches day and night sun and rain unable to stand or sleep their rations brought to them the stocks were low half rations quarter rations then a biscuit a day hunger and then scurvy a cow a horse an ox wandering to the hills for grass killed by wandering shrapnel went into the hands of speculators rats were eaten the soldiers rejoiced when fresh-dead mule came on the rations the wounded caught between the lines were left to rot and die moaning rolling slowly back and forth begging for a drink of fresh water the Federals worked at night digging closer trenches mining exploding Confederate lines so close were the lines that insults jokes and wisecracks brother to brother shared the air with shrapnel more guns and men came down the river to Grant an armistice was called the silence in the caves the trenches the shelled streets and homes was awful. Starved and overpowered the city surrendered on the fourth day of July opened itself to the east while the soldiers wept the invaders entered and in the words of Abraham Lincoln the Father of Waters rolled unvexed to the sea. ...*

Near the center of Vicksburg Ferd took a left turn, following the
highway markers, and it was not long before Will had his first view
of the river. They were driving southward, parallel to it, and the
great bridge that they would cross from Mississippi to Louisiana
loomed ahead, built high over the river, but mightier in its length
over the broadness of the river than in its height. The sun broke
through again and the clouds began to dispel: the city became blan-
keted with heat. Will watched the low, even flow of the river, as
Ferd drove on in silence. . . .

*The forge was set up the iron collars the slave chains were gathered also the
iron in ammunition all were melted down beaten into nails timber was
felled a Portuguese who had learned to saw lumber as a slave in Fez
taught the art to four Biscayan carpenters who hewed the planks and ribs
a Genoese and Sardinian caulked with oakum from henequen also with
flax with ravelings from the Indian shawls the cooper became sick almost
died but recovered labored while still sick made two half hogsheads for
water the Indians brought fish for food also shawls for sails and watched
the work. The river began to rise the town was encircled the cavalry
became useless the Indians outnumbered the Christians hut still they
brought fish and shawls and ropes cables were made from mulberry bark
anchors from stirrups the river rose covered the ground in March and the
work stopped rafts were made strewn with boughs for the horses the men
lived in the lofts of their huts traveled in canoes and still the Indians came
to look at the ships. Moscoso had an Indian captured tortured he revealed
a plot of attack when thirty Indians came with fish Moscoso cut off their
right hands sent them back others came their right hands and noses were
cut off Moscoso boasted to the Caciques that they could not have so much
warlike thought that he did not know about in advance the plot was bro-
ken but the Indians were starving for want of the maize the Spaniards
had taken they came begging thin and weak Moscoso forbade feeding them
but they were so pitiful many of the men gave them maize on the sly in
return for work on the ships. In June the brigantines and pirogues were
finished it pleased God for the river to rise again and the ships were float-
ed into deep water twenty-two of the finest horses were put on board the
rest killed the meat jerked along with that of the hogs and put on board
early in July four years after the first landing in Puerto del Espiritu Santo*

the Christians their numbers reduced by half their ships without slaves or gold pushed into the tide of the Great River the waters flooding through the continent of Florida washing the body of the Adelantado De Soto and headed for the open waters beyond . . .

Will kept his eyes on the oceanic expanse of the river and on the great bridge looming ahead. It became easy to imagine that the truck was stationary, rolling on a treadmill, while the bridge moved, changing perspective, jockeying and disciplining its length into position to pass under the wheels of the truck. The very size of the bridge lent itself to this illusion.

"Reckon I'll give 'em up," Ferd said abruptly. "All of 'em. Quit fooling around. If that kid comes over and starts throwing herself in my face I'll just go out back, start fooling with the truck. Give her the cold shoulder."

He took out his cigarettes and lit one for himself, absently. As he was about to put them away he remembered Will, and offered them.

"Thanks," said Will, accepting.

"After all, I got the cutest little wife in the world. I got a fine kid and another one on the way. I'll just quit fooling with all these others and stick to home. Stay out of trouble."

He raised himself, crouched a moment over the wheel, and sat back in a more confident posture.

"Fellow's only got one life. If you wreck that they ain't going to hand out another. Reckon I'll play it straight. I'm going to get that house paid off, then I'm going to trade in this hunk of junk, buy me another semi like the one I tore up. She'll be as good or better."

He nodded authoritatively to himself.

"Arter all, a fellow can't hope to get out of debt when he's got his mind on other things . . ."

Indians escorted them in canoes a short distance then retreated the Christians put ashore for the night set out in the morning they came to an empty town helped themselves to maize and stopped to shell it Indians attacked and were driven off. The Christians set out again were followed through the day by Indians in canoes stopped for the

night in an open field and the Indians fled but the next day they were
followed by more than a hundred Indian canoes spread in formation
across the breadth of the Great River a curtain on the flood waters
rushing the Christians from the continent some of the canoes detached
themselves paddled downstream to attack and the pirogues moved
upstream to meet them but the brigantines could not follow in hand-
to-hand fighting the pirogues capsized the Spaniards in their iron
armor sank to the bottom. The ships stayed on the river through the
night next day the fleet of canoes still followed they attacked the brig-
antines one at a time from one ship to another the Spaniards without
armor were easy targets dropped their oars scurried to the bottom
boards the ship began to swing crazily until the steersman guarded by
one armored shielded Christian took his oar the Spaniards found their
sleeping mats withstood the arrows they hung them around the brig-
antines returned to their oars but the Indians lofted their arrows
arched them into the sky and they fell over the mats and into the ships.
Through the day the night and into the next day the attacks continued
the war cries screaming across the waters so the Spaniards could not
rest when a ship lagged the Indians clustered upon it until the oarsmen
strained themselves and regained the others at a border of territories
the warriors retreated and warriors of the new territory took up the
chase thus the chain of attack was unbroken as in the earlier days the
chain of slaves had been unbroken. The horses slowed the ships their
pirogues were easy prey the Spaniards stopped to slaughter them the
last of the Spanish cavalry the great beast that had carried the Chris-
tians over body of land and Indian the meat was jerked and taken
aboard and at last after days of harrying warfare the Indians retreat-
ed and were not replaced by others the men rested on their oars float-
ed peacefully under the summer sun down the broadening river. At the
very mouth with the open welcoming waters spreading before them
they put onto the sandy shore and once more Indians appeared rushed
in to attack and withdraw beyond range of the crossbow the Spaniards
helpless without horses retired to their ships and left the shore left the
brown waters muddy with the land that had driven them out the land
that had given them nothing but hardship hunger and warfare had
destroyed their equipment their clothes the ornaments of their belief
and left them to live like the Indians who inhabited it the land that

save for a mighty arterial flooding stream might have swallowed and destroyed them. They quit the brown waters without regret and entered the blue. . . .

The truck started across the bridge. Will looked to the north, toward the city, the junction of the Yazoo Canal and the river at the point of De Soto Island.

    This is the first of my borders, he thought. The river that splits a nation. I have left the East behind. The rock cave in the Smokies where I spent the first night has projected me this far across the land: I have wandered and scavenged and begged my way to the Mississippi, and I have not turned. This river is the first of my borders. Now there is more land and another border, another river, dividing land and people, a river that bears the name once given to these waters: the Rio Grande. . . .

Following the coast the Spaniards set out for New Spain some were blown out to sea ran out of water but they made land and beached the ships a south wind came up the brigantines were almost wrecked but water was taken on and the voyage begun again high winds were followed by a calm mosquitos appeared the sails were black with them the men's faces and bodies swollen in welts the ships parted and came together fair weather returned and the Christians put ashore to hold service on the beach by way of thanks. Sailing under fair skies they came at last to the Rio de Panico where they put ashore discovered Christian Indians who told them of a Christian town the men rejoiced went wild on the beach fell to their knees kissed the sand they were like children rabid with joy after four and one half bitter years without conquest or gold crowding to a land where the Cross the Holy Spirit the Virgin were worshiped a land of their own kind. . . .

GENOA

A TELLING OF WONDERS

HEADWATERS

ONE

CITY OF INDIANAPOLIS, a cold spring day, late. Blackberry winter, my father called it—after some warm days, some affluence of sunshine, a sudden crackling blast of cold, rain edged with sleet, low, almost formless clouds scudding across the level land.

> "When ocean clouds over inland hills
> Sweep storming . . ."

Thus Herman Melville put it, thinking, perhaps of Pittsfield. Here there are no hills—only the squared-out city. Further south, toward the Ohio, Crawford County, where Mother's family, the Stoneciphers, came from, there are hills—hills and valleys, woods and caves.

But here I turn a square corner, and the old house comes into view, the house that used to be country and now is city, that has not moved, but in remaining still has allowed our fellow Americans to sweep around it, to put up suburban dwellings in what used to be the cornfield, so that it now stands, as it ever was, but with the largeness of land lopped off; the house in which I was born and raised, on the land that we farmed; house and land that we lost, or that I thought we had lost, but that unknown to the rest of us remained, during the years of depression, in the arthritic grip of my mother, so that when I married and gave evidence of settling down, it fell into my lap, a gift—the land gone, but the rough old house, of timbers pegged and nailed before the Civil War, the house my father was born in, and his father before him, standing strong.

My father's name was Paul B. Mills—he would never tell us what the B. stood for—we would guess and joke about it, Carl and I, but he remained passive and humorless—nor did my mother offer help, either condone or criticize our curiosity, and to this day I don't know if she ever discovered what it was—but there was the strange look from him one day when out of a clear blue, I had been thinking of other matters, I suddenly said "Bunyan—my father is Paul Bunyan," and again he neither affirmed nor denied, just for a moment the queer look—but there it was, on the birth certificate that showed up after his death, and the shock, perhaps greater than the accident of his death and those who died with him, the funeral, the relatives, the shock when I read it, the spelling of it: "Paul Bunion Mills."

Making the right angle turn I am now "running up into the wind's eye," as Melville said it—the only approach to a storm. Elbows digging into ribs hold an overcoat tight around me, and I lean forward, letting the rain and sleet beat against my face, so that forehead, cheeks, nose and chin, and the lines incised into my face, become a mask, at once me and not me, alive . . .

> "During the Cambrian, Ordovician, and most of the Silurian periods, Indiana was submerged beneath the seas. In the later Silurian, a mighty upheaval began; eventually most of the continent was uplifted and the great interior seas slowly receded. This was not a violent or sudden process; the earth rose only an inch, perhaps, in a century or more."

> "In the Mississippian and Pennsylvanian epochs of the Carboniferous period, Indiana was steadily elevated; at the close of the Mississippian the whole region was above sea level. During the Pennsylvanian, a period of millions of years, Indiana was probably a rank, lush swamp—populated by amphibious creatures, and covered with fern-like plants growing in vast luxuriance."

> "In the Pleistocene about five-sixths of the whole region—all except what is now south central Indiana—was at one time or another under a massive layer of ice, sometimes 2,000 feet thick."

and

The Miami, original Indian inhabitants of Indiana, lived on wild game and fowl, corn, tubers, roots and dogs. As late as 1812, the Miami burned their war captives, but the practice of cooking and eating them, which had once been very popular, ceased around 1789.

Passing the suburban houses, homogenized so that one might be another, I approach the old farm house down the road, anachronistic and stubborn; but for this, the regularity would be complete.

Complete, that is, but for one other factor, rendering irregular all that I reach through my eyes: with every step I lean off balance, off center, and back again, the prairie landscape ragging down with every leftward thrust:

Klumpfuss. Pied bot. Reel foot. Or, from the medical book: "Talipes equinovalgus, or 'rocker foot,' with some syndactilism." I have clubfoot.

From Melville, MARDI:

> *"Averse to the barbarous custom of destroying at birth all infants not symmetrically formed; but equally desirous of removing from their sight those unfortunate beings; the islanders of a neighboring group had long ago established an asylum for cripples; where they lived, subject to their own regulations; ruled by a king of their own election; in short, formed a distinct class of beings by themselves.*
> *One only restriction was placed upon them: on no account must they quit the isle assigned them. And to the surrounding islanders, so unpleasant the sight of a distorted mortal, that a stranger landing at Hooloomooloo, was deemed a prodigy. Wherefore, respecting any knowledge of aught beyond them, the cripples were well nigh as isolated, as if Hooloomooloo was the only terra firma extant.*
> *Dwelling in a community of their own, these unfortunates, who otherwise had remained few in number, increased and multiplied greatly. Nor did successive generations improve in symmetry upon those preceding them.*
> *Soon, we drew nigh the isle.*
> *Heaped up, and jagged with rocks; and, here and there, covered*

with dwarfed, twisted thickets, it seemed a fit place for its denizens. Landing, we were surrounded by a heterogeneous mob; and thus escorted, took our way inland, toward the abode of their lord, King Yoky.

What a scene!

Here, helping himself along with two crotched roots, hobbled a dwarf without legs; another stalked before, one arm fixed in the air, like a lightning rod; a third, more active than any, seal-like, flirted a pair of flippers, and went skipping along; a fourth hopped on a solitary pin, at every bound, spinning around like a top, to gaze; while still another, furnished with feelers or fins, rolled himself up in a ball, bowling over the ground in advance."

The sleet cuts into my eyes, and I incise deeper the lines among the features, steel myself to the weather. Limping, steady-gaited, I turn into the path, past the frosted jonquils, leading to the door. The heavy latch responds.

"Oh, Daddy, Daddy—close the door, quick!" Only one of my three children turns, the youngest, Jenifer. And quickly her back is to me again, like the others.

As I stand just inside the closed door, shaking the weather from me, there is, first, the warmth of the house—central heating and therefore without source, simply a presence—then the second warmth, radiant from a source, and it is this that draws the family, as I felt drawn, as a child, to the black wood range, back in the kitchen: the family, now, the children, attentive to the glowing vacuum tube: the television. Taking off my coat, watching the hunched heads, the shoulders, the little backsides perched on stools, I think, for a moment,

> *(of Maria Melville, Herman Melville's mother, who, it is reliably reported, would require her eight children to sit on little stools around her bed, motionless, while she took her daily nap, that she might keep track of them)*

of the weird business, soon after we got the TV, of the electronic particles that hit the screen one night, and then kept recurring—I was in the kitchen, and the children came running, said there was a woman's face interfering with the cowboys—I recognized her from the show the night before—she stayed for a while, went away, and kept coming back—the service man tried to explain her, the local station, even the network people—none could give an answer, they had to take out the set, put in a new one.

Stepping into the kitchen, I reach at once for the oven

BECAUSE MY WIFE WORKS. I don't make enough money at General Motors to support the family—and it is this—this mystery, that my classmates at medical school are now making twenty, forty, fifty thousand a year, and I, possessing the same sheepskin, Doctor of Medicine, and with a school record better actually than most of theirs, but the sheepskin is furled, in the attic, and I am unshingled, I cannot, will not practice, and this is mysterious to me

and so Linda works, going on the second shift at GM, already at her machine before I leave the first, and we have dates on the weekends. She cooks dinner before leaving home, puts it in the Frigidaire in warm weather, in the oven in cold, leaves the kids in care of the vacuum tube,

and I reach for the oven.

Now, there is a kind of ceremony about this, that I like. I, Michael Mills, presiding over the kitchen, the living room, the children, the house and grounds—a great chief, chef (of a meal already cooked), *un jefe grande*—Opening the oven door, lifting out the meatloaf and setting it on the stove, I stand for a moment, rubbing the five o'clock stubble on the mandible, listening to the sounds of home (cowboy bullets) from the next room, and thinking

of Ushant, the old tar in WHITE-JACKET *who survived the massacre of the beards—one of the people, merely, he held the hair of his chin, grimly, against the officers*

*and of Melville's own—"no soft silken beard, but tight curled like the
horse hair breaking out of old upholstered chairs, firm and wiry to the
grasp, and squarely chopped."*

and thinking, too, as the warm air from the open oven fills the
room, of

*Melville's daughter, Fanny, reporting him to be unhandy with tools, of
no use around the house,*

*and thinking that, as common sailor on many a ship, he must have
learned a certain handiness—but this he would not employ, to benefit*
THE BARK OF DOMESTIC FELICITY . . .

and passing the meatloaf to the table, and the beans and the pota-
toes, from the top of the stove, there is a momentary recall, a plea-
surable memory in the glands and the blood, of the three occasions
when the children were born—I took leave from work and kept
house while Linda was in the hospital, and each day, after cleaning,
washing, making beds and taking in the milk, there was the cere-
mony of cooking dinner—made truly ceremonial, made ritual by
the fact that, for a week, I grew a helluva ragged beard, and, as I
cooked each evening, drank a glass of white port wine and smoked
a black, child-destroying, outsize cigar

> *"Now, the leaf called tobacco is of diverse species and sorts. Not
> to dwell upon vile Shag, Pig-tail, Plug, Nail-rod, Negro-head,
> Cavendish, and misnamed Lady's twist . . ."*

Knowing better than to call the children before the commercials are
over, I sit at the table and wait, warm and reminiscent. Then—we
might have pickles, milk for the children, butter for beans and pota-
toes, and—a glance through the window at the steady dripping rain,
the thick atmosphere—and

"ale must be drank in a fog and a drizzle."

These from the Frigidaire to the table, and a swallow of ale inside; turning the bottle in my hand, and then staring at the jar of pickles, and my hand goes off the bottle and into my pocket, drawing forth a fragment of paper, before I think the connection. Shard of an old shopping list:

> pickles
> &
> popsicles

and a scribbling on the back, that I must have copied or added,

> Pick-L-Joy
> &
> Popsie Pete
> "enclose the wrapper
>> with twenty-five cents
> and you will
>> receive two ball point pens"

The cowboy bullets have changed to talking cereal boxes, and I begin to serve the plates. In a moment, the children come to the table, and we have jokes, laughter, squabbles, scattered information, questions, jumping up and sitting down, a few tears, and—only casually and incidentally—the business of eating. Still, for all that,

a better temper than prevailed in the Melville household, where Herman would harangue his wife and two daughters (this was after the sons were gone) on matters that had no interest for them, and they would roll their eyes, and sigh, and wait, or there would be outbursts of temper, sarcasm

"Daddy, are we going to have a dessert tonight? A popsicle?"

There is an experience that I must try to understand, and it has to do with awareness, with a point in time and perhaps also in space where the awareness may be fixed, a time-space location, such as, say, a whale-ship, or perhaps what a cosmologist means when he says—

with his stage the universe—"A fundamental observer partakes of the motion of the substratum, that is, he is located on a fundamental particle." Or, in my own terms, there is Carl, my brother, and the picture that flashes is Carl laughing, holding a book and laughing, and, at once, the illusion of hugeness, an illusion fostered, perhaps, by contrast with my own small frame, but shared nonetheless by others who also reported it, and it came not from height, for he was only five foot eight, but perhaps from a way of using himself, arrogant and careless, from a general stockiness of build, from a sultanic gluteus maximus, and, most of all, from the monstrous, out-shapen head that heaved and rolled with his mood, upon his shoulders. And it is all there, in this picture that flashed up from some back corner of my brain: the hugeness, a little of what Pliny meant when he said that "nature creates monsters for the purpose of astonishing us and amusing herself," and of the meaning of the word "Teratology," the medical term for the Science of Malformations and Monstrosities, from the Greek "teratologia," meaning "a telling of wonders." It is in the way his body and head shift, shake, and revolve, as he laughs, as though composed of epicenters, randomly contiguous, with no single center, the parts loose, accidentally associated; it is in his hands, which are large hands, but again not as large as they appear from the way he uses them, the manner he has of holding the book, possessing it loosely, embracing it so as altogether to smother it, and at the same time letting it go loosely from his fingers, holding it at no single point, seeming to extend some of the casual humanity through his extremities into the very binding and paper, so that the pages flutter with the fierceness of the wings of a bird trapped, as he loses his place and finds it again, and quotes, from WHITE-JACKET:

> *"I love an indefinite, infinite background—a vast, heaving, rolling, mysterious rear."*

And again the burst of laughter, the explosion and reshaping of his body, the unplanned and weirdly incomplete arcs described by his head, the book squeezed and relinquished in one gesture. And as I hold this picture in my brain, this momentary recall—or as I am held by it—and add to it, bring alongside it, the fact, the datum: Carl is dead, killed by gases released into a pan beneath his chair in the death chamber at Jefferson City, Missouri—this, his execution, being the last in a series of events as strangely associated as everything in his life, and which I still do not understand; when these—the image of him laughing, quoting, and the fact of his execution—are brought together, there is this experience, the fixing of my awareness at some time-space point that I am unable to identify, a seizure of elation

"My memory is a life beyond birth . . ."

Melville, in MARDI. And there is this: the time-space point is not limited to my own lifespan, nor to the surfaces of the earth that I have traveled—nor are these areas excluded. My body feels dull, the blood slows, sensation withdraws from the extremities and consciousness, toward the trunk, and the meatloaf sits in ale, undigested in my stomach.

There is, after this, an illumination, an area of local bodily sensation, random and ephemeral, one following another, as a corollary, perhaps, an inscrutable hint, to the time-space fix itself—an intense warmth just above the heart, then something, an alertness, say, in the cells of the thigh; an ache in the shoulder, answered in a vertebra, and back again to the shoulder . . . and in the club, in the high, thick-soled boot, a tingling

"Daddy! Daddy!"

It is Jenifer, and her voice conveys alarm. I localize myself, search out the condition that she has discovered, and realize that, for some moments, I have been gazing at her, altogether oblivious to her. I glance for a moment at the room, open the senses: the old woodwork painted white, the warm air, the food smells. Turning to Jenifer—a smile, a word, a gesture, and she is restored. The dinner begins to move once more.

But eating I recall the medical student, interning in obstetrics, who made a custom of talking to newborn infants, presenting simple requests such as "open your eyes," "raise your right hand," or the like, and claimed remarkable results—the nurses liked to have him around, said he could quiet the most irritated or soothe the most feverish child;—pursuing his research, he developed a strange look, began to study philosophy and religion, and left medicine abruptly for divinity school.

One of the greatest pleasures of this house is the presence in it of the old chimney. In a fit of modernizing, Mother once wanted to cover it with wallboard, but I protested, successfully. A great mass of stone and mortar, it centers and roots the house; and, although all the fireplaces except the one in the livingroom have been sealed, portions of it appear, the stonework obtruding, refusing to be hidden, in nearly every room. Sitting at the table, now, observing the corner of it that appears in the kitchen, the sealed flue opening before which the old black cookstove used to sit, I am reminded of Melville's I AND MY CHIMNEY—and of the engineers, when we put in the furnace, telling me that the old chimney couldn't be used, a new one would have to be built, the flue wouldn't work—and of how I argued and persisted, with the result that now the stones impart flue heat—heat that would otherwise be wasted—to every room of the house, and even the long, narrow attic, running the length of the house, the attic where I keep my desk and books, the husbanding of Melville and medicine, history and archeology, even the attic is made livable, on a stormy spring night, by virtue of heat radiant from the old stones.

The children have begun the nightly chore of cleaning up the table and washing the dishes—spreading the job, fluctuant between dishwater and television. The day's manifest obligations having been met, it is not difficult for me to ascend the two flights to the attic—the heavy foot following the light, and then leading it—to meet, to face, to examine, perhaps, some of the other obligations, such as

Item: a Post-mortem: to understand my brother Carl

and

Item: for the living, myself and others, to discover what it is to heal, and why, as a doctor, I will not.

TWO

"Save the prairie-hen, sometimes startled from its lurking-place in the rank grass; and, in their migratory season, pigeons, high overhead on the wing, in dense multitudes eclipsing the day like a passing storm-cloud; save these—there being no wide woods with their underwood—birds were strangely few.

"Blank stillness would for hours reign unbroken on this prairie. 'It is the bed of a dried-up sea,' said the companionless sailor— no geologist—to himself, musing at twilight upon the fixed undulations of that immense alluvial expanse bounded only by the horizon, and missing there the stir that, to alert eyes and ears, animates at all times the apparent solitudes of the deep.

"But a scene quite at variance with one's antecedents may yet prove suggestive of them. Hooped round by a level rim, the prairie was to John Marr a reminder of ocean.

"With some of his former shipmates, chums on certain cruises, he had contrived, prior to this last and more remote removal, to keep up a little correspondence at odd intervals. But from tidings of anybody of any sort he, in common with the other settlers, was now cut off; quite cut off, except from such news as might be conveyed over the grassy billows by the last-arrived prairie-schooner —the vernacular term, in those parts and times, for the emigrant wagon arched high over with sail-cloth, and voyaging across the vast champaign. There was no reachable post-office as yet; not even the rude little receptive box with lid and leather hinges, set up at convenient intervals on a stout stake along some solitary green way, affording a perch for birds, and which, later in the unremitting advance of the frontier, would perhaps decay into a mossy monument, attesting yet another successive over-leaped limit of civilized life; a life which in America can today hardly be said to have any western bound but the ocean that washes Asia. Throughout these plains, now in places overpopu-

lous with towns overopulent; sweeping plains, elsewhere fenced off in every direction into flourishing farms—pale townsmen and hale farmers alike, in part, the descendants of the first sallow settlers; a region that half a century ago produced little for the sustenance of man; but to-day launching its superabundant wheat-harvest on the world;—of this prairie, now everywhere intersected with wire and rail, hardly can it be said that at the period here written of there was so much as a traceable road. To the long-distance traveller the oak-groves, wide apart, and varying in compass and form; these, with recent settlements, yet more widely separate, offered some landmarks; but otherwise he steered by the sun. In early midsummer, even going but from one log-encampment to the next, a journey it might be of hours or good part of a day, travel was much like navigation. In some more enriched depressions between the long, green, graduated swells, smooth as those of ocean becalmed receiving and subduing to its own tranquility the voluminous surge raised by some far-off hurricane of days previous, here one would catch the first indication of advancing strangers either in the distance, as a far sail at sea, by the glistening white canvas of the wagon, the wagon itself wading through the rank vegetation and hidden by it, or, failing that, when near to, in the ears of the team, peeking, if not above the tall tiger-lilies, yet above the yet taller grass.

"Luxuriant, this wilderness; but, to its denizen, a friend left behind anywhere in the world seemed not alone absent to sight, but an absentee from existence.

"Though John Marr's shipmates could not all have departed life, yet as subjects of meditation they were like phantoms of the dead. As the growing sense of his environment threw him more and more upon retrospective musings, these phantoms, next to those of his wife and child, became spiritual companions, losing something of their first indistinctness and putting on at last a dim semblance of mute life; and they were lit by that aureola circling over any object of the affections in the past for reunion with which an imaginative heart passionately yearns."

Melville.

The dark oak rafters, forming the main roof gable of the house, are pitched low, so that there is only a narrow corridor, running east and west, of standing room, and this is flanked on either side by low-roofed shadows, filled with trunks, old furniture, magazines, and the like, things that Mother—though she survives in the nursing home downtown and knows she will never leave it—will not allow us to dispose of. Against the rock chimney is a makeshift desk—an old door, laid flat on crates—and running the length of this are the books—books that I have bought, found, begged throughout my life, ever since the morning when Carl and I were playing in a haunted house, and we broke into what appeared to be a secret closet, discovered a small decanter of medicated sherry, the remnants of a whalebone corset, and an old copy of TYPEE. We rescued the whalebone from the rotted cloth, drank the sherry, and spent the rest of the day devouring what the bookworms had left of TYPEE.

Reaching the desk, I sit before it for a moment, uncritical, with perception undiminished, searching a balance.

> *(Melville,* WHITE-JACKET, *called to observe a flogging: "... balanced myself on my best centre."*

There are the titles, the feel of an old binding: MARDI, for example, an early edition, in two volumes, dark brown, maroon, and black, the backing ribbed, and inside, the marbled end-papers, and the Preface:

> *"Not long ago, having published two narratives of voyages in the Pacific, which, in many quarters, were received with incredulity, the thought occurred to me, of indeed writing a romance of Polynesian adventure, and publishing it as such; to see whether, the fiction might not, possibly be received for a verity: in some degree the reverse of my previous experience."*

Then, GRAY'S ANATOMY, Goss, Twenty-fifth Edition; and a disreputable copy of THE HOOSIER SCHOOLMASTER, by Edward Eggleston. A thin, modern English book, COSMOLOGY, by H. Bondi; THE SEARCH FOR ATLANTIS, by Edwin Bjorkman; and a copy of NATURAL HISTORY, March, 1952, including an article,

SHRUNKEN HEADS. A TEXTBOOK OF EMBRYOLOGY, by Jordon
and Kindred; also, JOURNAL OF MORPHOLOGY, Volume XLX, 1908,
containing A STUDY OF THE CAUSES UNDERLYING THE ORIGIN
OF HUMAN MONSTERS.

Glancing upward, at the eight-inch rafters casting regular shadows
across each other and across the roof boards, down the length of the
attic, I am reminded

> *of the forecastle of the* Julia *in* OMOO, *planted "right in the
> bows, or, as sailors say, in the very eyes of the ship . . ."*

> *"All over, the ship was in a most dilapidated condition; but in
> the forecastle it looked like the hollow of an old tree going to
> decay. In every direction the wood was damp and discoloured,
> and here and there soft and porous. Moreover, it was hacked and
> hewed without mercy, the cook frequently helping himself to
> splinters for kindling-wood from the bitts and beams."*

> *and there was "that gloomy hole where we burrowed like rab-
> bits," in* REDBURN *. . . as well as*

> *The Gunner in* WHITE-JACKET— *". . . among all the persons
> and things on board that puzzled me, and filled me most with
> strange emotions of doubt, misgivings, and mystery, was the
> gunner—a short, square, grim man, his hair and beard grizzled
> and singed, as if with gunpowder. His skin was of a flecky
> brown, like the stained barrel of a fowling-piece, and his hollow
> eyes burned in his head like blue-lights. He it was who had
> access to many of those mysterious vaults I have spoken of. Often
> he might be seen groping his way into them . . ."*

and

> *". . . he was, withal, a very cross, bitter, illnatured, inflamma-
> ble little old man. So, too, were all the members of the gunner's
> gang; including the two gunner's mates, and all the quarter-
> gunners. Every one of them had the same dark brown complex-
> ion; all their faces looked like smoked hams. They were continu-*

*ally grumbling and growling about the batteries; running in
and out among the guns; driving the sailors away from them;
and cursing and swearing as if all their consciences had been
powder-singed and made callous by their calling. Indeed they
were a most unpleasant set of men; especially Priming, the
nasal-voiced gunner's mate, with the harelip; and Cylinder, his
stuttering coadjutor, with the clubbed foot."*

The wind rises, screaming faintly, intensely, against the north side,
and the old house creaks.

"The hemlock shakes in the rafter, the oak in the driving keel."

and, in a letter, he (Melville)

*"I have a sort of sea-feeling here in the country, now that the
ground is covered with snow. I look out of my window in the
morning when I rise as I would out of a port-hole of a ship in
the Atlantic. My room seems a ship's cabin; & at nights when I
wake up & hear the wind shrieking, I almost fancy there is too
much sail in the house, & I had better go on the roof and rig in
the chimney."*

and again, at another season,

*"In summer, too, Canute-like: sitting here, one is often remind-
ed of the sea. For not only do long ground-swells roll the slant-
ing grain, and little wavelets of the grass ripple over upon the
low piazza, as their beach, and the blown down of dandelions
is wafted like the spray, and the purple of the mountains is just
the purple of the billows, and a still August noon broods upon
the deep meadows, as a calm upon the Line; but the vastness and
the lonesomeness are so oceanic, and the silence and the sameness,
too, that the first peep of a strange house, rising beyond the trees,
is for all the world like spying, on the Barbary coast, an
unknown sail."*

Glancing again at the rafters, I think of my great-grandfather, who
built this house with his own hands: Hammond Mills, a Yankee,
born in New York City, who went upriver to Albany, and then west

to Ohio and Indiana—a serious, hard-working man, whose favorite saying, his philosophy, perhaps, was handed down carefully from generation to generation, with the old furniture:

"The Mind is to the Body as the Whole Man is to the Earth."

> (*and there is Melville,* MARDI: *"We have had vast developments of parts of men: but none of manly wholes."*

Hammond Mills built this house, acquired the land, and farmed it. His first-born son, by the law of primogeniture, inherited and continued farming, passing on in turn to his first-born son: my father; and

Father married a Stonecipher, poor white, southerner. Her people came over from England as bond servants, landed somewhere on the coast, say Charleston, worked out their time and then worked gradually inland, keeping the mountains to the west until Boone had shown the way; then moving through the Gap, to the Ohio, down as far as *Injeanny,* where they settled in Brown and Crawford counties, started little hill farms, and hung on when many of the others continued west to Pike County, Missouri, and thence to California, as Pikers . . .

Greasy Creek, Gnaw Bone, and Shake Rag Hollow—the hills, ridges, knolls, and bluffs to the north of the river—this is where the Stoneciphers dug in—farming, hunting, brawling, making likker—and later, in the flatboat era, moving down the Ohio and the Wabash, "half alligator and half horse, with a tech of wildcat" . . . but always, back to the farm, the root.

The folklore, too, came with the Stoneciphers:

Cut fence rails in the light of the moon, butcher before the full moon if the meat is to fry hard. Soap is to be made in the light of the moon, and stirred one way by one person. A waning moon is good for shingling, because it pulls the shingles flat.

and

A girl should never marry until she can pick clothes out of boiling water with her fingers, and if she sits on a table she will never marry. If a person kills a toad, his cow will give bloody milk.

And there was other folklore, too. Mother, hard-working, proud of the little cleanliness and respectability she could muster for us, quick with the flat of her hand when Carl or I misused the language, nevertheless used one word for all occasions, a word as old as words, ancient Anglo-Saxon association of four letters: *shit.* I have seen her dressed in her one good dress, serving tea for the preacher and his wife, and the word would come out, hang there in the middle of the room, unadorned and unexplained: and Mother would continue pouring.

After Father died, Carl left school, and, for a while, worked as a lumberjack in the Pacific Northwest; Mother was nearly frantic, he was gone for months and months, without sending word. Finally there was a postcard, undated and unsigned, but in his handwriting:

> *Drink gin after cutting oak;*
> *bourbon follows pine.*

This was all, for more than a year. He came home one day, "to get more winter clothes," as he said. He had joined an archeological expedition, persuading some college men of his erudition in Indian lore: in a few days—after delivering a lecture to Mother and me on the origins of American civilization—he was off to Alaska and the Aleutians,

"to dig boneyards in the Rat Islands."

Again, there was no word for months. Then there began to arrive, not cards or letters, but weird objects, drawings, fragments of stone and bone. A piece of steatite, apparently carved by Carl himself, in the shape of a killer whale; a section of human skull, occipital, huge, larger than Carl's own; a carving of an Indian woman, seated, with a symmetrical opening in her abdomen in which appeared a face, with a pair of huge, fierce eyes.

He was back again after several months, with more wild objects—
and stories, in which, as Melville said, "fact and fancy, halfway
meeting, interpenetrate, and form one seamless whole."

There was the shrunken human head, from the headwaters of the Ama-
zon, which he admitted to having won from a fellow archeologist in a
poker game;

his story of a day's work carrying human remains from the cave where
they were discovered, across the rocky, treacherous terrain, in a rain-
storm, racing against the tide, to the boat—the description, with ges-
tures, of picking up a bag of bones, the feeling of holding it in his arms,
of having to hurry, with great delicacy, over the wet rocks, cradling the
empty, formless treasures; and

the obscure tale of cannibalism, told when Carl was drunk, part of which
seemed to take place a thousand years ago and involve Indians, and part
of which took place just recently and involved Carl—something to do
with eating a human being, genitals and extremities first, then the inter-
nal organs, flesh of the trunk, the neck, and finally the head—but the
eyes! (and here Carl's eyes became wild) he couldn't eat the eyes!—or he
did eat them and couldn't forget them, they haunted him, went straight
to the brain, clinging to the lobes like barnacles to a ship's hull . . . and the
feeling of holding only the skull in his hand, the eyes gone . . .

Olson:

> "Herman Melville was born in New York, August 1, 1819, and on the
> 12th of that month the ESSEX, a well-found whaler of 238 tons, sailed
> from Nantucket with George Pollard, Jr. as captain, Owen Chase
> and Matthew Joy mates, 6 of her complement of 20 men Negroes,
> bound for the Pacific Ocean, victualled and provided for two years
> and a half.
>
> "A year and three months later, on November 20, 1820, just south
> of the equator in longitude 119 West, this ship on a calm day, with the
> sun at east, was struck head on twice by a bull whale, a spermaceti
> about 85 feet long, and with her bows stove in, filled and sank.
>
> Her twenty men set out in three open whaleboats for the coast of
> South America 2000 miles away. They had bread (200 lb. a boat),

water (65 gallons), and some Galapagos turtles. Although they were at the time no great distance from Tahiti, they were ignorant of the temper of the natives and feared cannibalism."

and

"The three boats, with the seventeen men divided among them, moved under the sun across ocean together until the 12th of January when, during the night, the one under the command of Owen Chase, First Mate, became separated from the other two.

"Already one of the seventeen had died, Matthew Joy, Second Mate. He had been buried January 10th. When Charles Shorter, Negro, out of the same boat as Joy, died on January 23rd, his body was shared among the men of that boat and the Captain's, and eaten. Two days more and Lawson Thomas, Negro, died and was eaten. The bodies were roasted to dryness by means of fires kindled on the ballast sand at the bottom of the boats."

Thus, Herman Melville was born . . .

"*. . . which joyous event occured at 1/2 past 11 last night—our dear Maria displayed her accustomed fortitude in the hour of peril, & is as well as circumstances & the intense heat will admit—while the little Stranger has good lungs, sleeps well & feeds kindly, he is in truth a chopping Boy—*"

But there is more to this, to the birth of Herman: what is it about *legs* that so possessed the later man? Age twenty-one, the father dead, the family without funds, Herman, unpaid for a year's teaching, and unemployed, shipped on a whaler for the Pacific, and thus broke away from home; but reaching the Marquesas, he again broke away, deserting ship on the island of Nukahiva, and thus doubly escaped, twice radically changed his world; and, at the entrance to the valley of Typee,

"*I began to feel symptoms which I at once attributed to the exposure of the preceding night. Cold shiverings and a burning fever succeeded one another at intervals, while one of my legs was swelled to such a degree, and pained me so acutely, that I half suspected I had been bitten by some venomous reptile . . ."*

And subsequently, the leg swelled and pained him whenever he thought or acted to escape from the Typees, subsiding when he was content with his life there: the leg saying to him—or he to himself—*I cannot move.*

Again, in Omoo, confined to the stocks in the Calabooza Beretanee (British Jail):

> *"How the rest managed, I know not; but, for my own part, I found it very hard to get asleep. The consciousness of having one's foot pinned; and the impossibility of getting it anywhere else than just where it was, was most distressing.*

> *"But this was not all: there was no way of lying but straight on your back; unless, to be sure, one's limb went round and round in the ankle, like a swivel. Upon getting into a sort of doze, it was no wonder this uneasy posture gave me the nightmare. Under the delusion that I was about some gymnastics or other, I gave my unfortunate member such a twitch, that I started up with the idea that some one was dragging the stocks away."*

Or, in White-Jacket, the amputation performed by Dr. Cuticle:

> *". . . and then the top-man seemed parted in twain at the hip, as the leg slowly slid into the arms of the pale, gaunt man in the shroud, who at once made away with it, and tucked it out of sight under one of the guns."*

> **(Note: how Melville hated doctors!**

And in Moby-Dick, there is Captain Peleg (Pegleg) addressing young Ishmael:

> *"Dost see that leg?—I'll take that leg away from thy stern . . .'"*

And Ahab:

"So powerfully did the whole grim aspect of Ahab affect me, and the livid brand which streaked it, that for the first few moments I hardly noted that not a little of this overbearing grimness was owing to the barbaric white leg upon which he partly stood. It had previously come to me that this ivory leg had at sea been fashioned from the polished bone of the sperm whale's jaw. 'Aye, he was dismasted off Japan,' said the old Gay-Head Indian once; 'but like his dismasted craft, he shipped another mast without coming home for it. He has a quiver of 'em.'"

and

"His three boats stove around him, and oars and men both whirling in the eddies; one captain, seizing the lineknife from his broken prow, had dashed at the whale, as an Arkansas duellist at his foe, blindly seeking with a six-inch blade to reach the fathom-deep life of the whale. That captain was Ahab. And then it was, that suddenly sweeping his sickle-shaped lower jaw beneath him, Moby-Dick had reaped away Ahab's leg, as a mower a blade of grass in the field."

August 1, 1819, New York City, a hot, dark night: Maria Melville, Herman's mother, has, for the third time, gone down into the valley, and Herman, still unborn, struggling in the Dardanelles, the Narrows of a white woman, and perhaps, like the baby whales, "still spiritually feasting upon some unearthly reminiscence"—Herman dies, to the extent that all life, all vitality retreats trunkward from one leg:—and then the "chopping Boy" is born.

". . . deep memories yield no epitaphs." And yet, somewhere lies the thought: one must die to be born.

Pierre:

"And here it may be randomly suggested . . . whether some things men think they do not know, are not for all that thoroughly comprehended by them; and yet, so to speak, though contained in themselves, are kept a secret from themselves? The idea of Death seems such a thing."

ISRAEL POTTER:

> *"It was not the pang of hunger then, but a nightmare originating in his mysterious incarceration, which appalled him. All through the long hours of this particular night, the sense of being masoned up in the wall, grew, and grew, and grew upon him . . . he stretched his two arms sideways, and felt as if coffined at not being able to extend them straight out, on opposite sides, for the narrowness of the cell . . . He mutely raved in the darkness."*

WHITE-JACKET:

> *"Just then the ship gave another sudden jerk, and, head foremost, I pitched from the yard. I knew where I was, from the rush of the air by my ears, but all else was a nightmare . . .*
>
> *"As I gushed into the sea, a thunder-boom sounded in my ear; my soul seemed flying from my mouth. The feeling of death flooded over me with the billows . . .*
>
> *"For one instant an agonizing revulsion came over me as I found myself utterly sinking. Next moment the force of my fall was expended; and there I hung, vibrating in the mid-deep. What wild sounds then rang in my ear! One was a soft moaning, as of low waves on the beach; the other wild and heartlessly jubilant, as of the sea in the height of a tempest . . . The life-and-death poise soon passed; and then I found myself slowly ascending, and caught a dim glimmering of light."*

Perhaps on that hot night in August, 1819, the unborn Herman lingered like Queequeg in his coffin,

> *(a rehearsal of death that was all the cure the savage needed . . .*
>
> *(the same coffin, the death-box—unhinged from the sunken whaler—on which Ishmael ultimately survived . . .*

And we have this: the great, white, humped monster, that dismasted Ahab:

"Judge, then, to what pitches of inflamed, distracted fury the minds of his more desperate hunters were impelled, when amid the chips of chewed boats, and the sinking limbs of torn comrades, they swam out of the white curds of the whale's direful wrath into the serene, exasperating sunlight, that smiled on, as if at a birth . . ."

There is again a split, a division of awareness, as earlier, at the dinner table, and for some time I am still, aware of my stillness, aware of my surroundings, of the nineteenth-century attic whose dark, sloping lines seem an extension of frontal and parietal bones of the skull itself—aware that my attention is wandering, or perhaps fixed but inaccessible, and aware that this condition must be allowed to play itself out . . .

There being division, I am able to observe myself, to be at once within and without, and an exploration occurs, inwardly derived, over the surfaces, the topography of face and head, and downward over my body; I gain the sense of being different, of causing this difference in myself, of altering the outwardness of myself. I discover that flesh and muscle, perhaps even bone, and certainly cartilage, are potentially alterable, according as the plan is laid down. And the plan itself may shift and change: I may be this Michael or that, Stonecipher or Mills—Western Man or Indian, sea-dog or lubber, large-headed or small, living then or now; and even such outrageous fables as that of converting Ulysses' men into swine become not unreasonable, when we understand that the men must have experienced some swinish designs within themselves, to which Circe had access . . .

Certainly, the study of Man : Literature is the study of Man : Anatomy . . . when it ceases to be, books become merely literary.

(Melville: "I rejoice in my spine."

Leaning back in the chair, my body straight out, I let the awareness sweep, as a tide, through my trunk, down my legs and into my feet.

Ahab: ". . . I'll order a complete man after a desirable pattern. Imprimus, fifty feet high in his socks; then, chest modelled after the Thames Tunnel; then, legs with roots to 'em, to stay in one place . . ."

and, with the carpenter,

"Look ye, carpenter, I dare say thou callest thyself a right good workmanlike workman, eh? Well, then, will it speak thoroughly well for thy work, if, when I come to mount this leg thou makest, I shall nevertheless feel another leg in the same identical place with it; that is, carpenter, my old lost leg; the flesh and blood one, I mean. Canst thou not drive that old Adam away?

"Truly, sir, I begin to understand somewhat now. Yes, I have heard something curious on that score, sir; how that a dismasted man never entirely loses the feeling of his old spar, but it will be still pricking him at times. May I humbly ask if it be really so, sir?

"It is, man. Look, put thy live leg here in the place where mine was; so, now, here is only one distinct leg to the eye, yet two to the soul. Where thou feelest tingling life; there, exactly there, to a hair, do I. Is't a riddle?

"I should humbly call it a poser, sir.

"Hiss, then. How dost thou know that some entire, living, thinking thing may not be invisibly and uninterpenetratingly standing precisely where thou now standest; aye, and standing there in thy spite? In thy most solitary hours, then, dost thou not fear eavesdroppers?"

A sudden fury lashes me, a desire to mutilate myself, to amputate the great, round, ugly globe of a clubfoot—to make it *not me.* As in MARDI, in the chapter Dedicated To The College Of Physicians And Surgeons,

"In Polynesia, every man is his own barber and surgeon, cutting off his beard or arm, as occasion demands. No unusual thing, for the warriors . . . to saw off their own limbs, desperately wounded in battle . . ."

and

> "The wound was then scorched, and held over the smoke of the fire, till all signs of blood vanished. From that day forward it healed, and troubled Samoa but little.
>
> "But shall the sequel be told? How that, superstitiously averse to burying in the sea the dead limb of a body yet living; since in that case Samoa held, that he must very soon drown and follow it; and how, that equally dreading to keep the thing near him, he at last hung it aloft from the topmast-stay; where yet it was suspended, bandaged over and over in cerements . . .
>
> "Now, which was Samoa? The dead arm swinging high as Haman? Or the living trunk below? Was the arm severed from the body, or the body from the arm? The residual part of Samoa was alive, and therefore we say it was he. But which of the writhing sections of a ten times severed worm, is the worm proper?"

The fury lingers, contorting, aggravating . . .

> "Small reason was there to doubt, then, that ever since that almost fatal encounter, Ahab had cherished a wild vindictiveness against the whale, all the more fell for that in his frantic morbidness he at last came to identify with him, not only all his bodily woes, but all his intellectual and spiritual exasperations. The White Whale swam before him as the monomaniac incarnation of all those malicious agencies which some deep men feel eating in them, till they are left living on with half a heart and half a lung."

and there was the woman in the mental hospital, brought onto the platform in the lecture hall to demonstrate for the medical students, of which I was one:—she suffered with a compulsion to strip her ragged clothes, and over and over to lash herself . . .

The anger quiets a little, becoming sardonic, and then wrying into a smile. Again, there is Ahab:

> ". . . for this hunt, my malady becomes my most desired health."

And Melville himself, reading of a writer whose work was presumed to be influenced by his illness, makes a marginal comment:

> "So is every one influenced—the robust, the weak, all constitutions—by the very fibre of the flesh, & chalk of the bone. We are what we were made."

THREE

Rising, I turn from the desk, and begin to walk, without aim, but confined by the structure of the attic itself. I think again of the infant Melville, held motionless through a brain-caking hiatus, before his delivery; and then of myself, and of the medical data regarding Talipes:

The notion that heredity may not be a factor; that, more likely, clubfoot results from the maintenance of a strained position in the uterus, or entanglement with the cord, or interlocking of the feet . . .

And further:

> "Equinus—*The heel cord and the posterior structures of the leg are contracted, holding the foot in plantarflection. The arch of the foot is abnormally elevated into cavus and weight is borne on the ball of the foot. In infancy, correction may be accomplished by successive plasters gradually* forcing the foot into dorsiflexion. *It is extremely important that the cavus, or high arch, be corrected before the cord is lengthened. It may be necessary to sever the contracted structures on the sole of the foot. These consist principally of the plantar fascia and short toe flexors. These structures may be divided subcutaneously. After the cavus deformity has been completely corrected, the* heel cord *may be* lengthened *by tenotomy or successive plaster."*

"Valgus—In early infancy, the foot should be manipulated daily by the mother, twisting it into a position of adduction and inversion. A light aluminum splint *should be* worn day and night *to maintain correction. . . . After care consists in the wearing of a* Thomas heel *and special exercises to develop the anticus, posticus and toe flexors."*

I have observed these operations and manipulations, performed on others; but in my own case, things being as they were, none of this was done.

The westward end of the attic, farthest removed from the chimney, is cold, and I hear the rain against the side of the house. I turn, and amble back to the desk.

"I was struck with the singular position he maintained. Upon each side of the Pequod's quarter deck, and pretty close to the mizzen shrouds, there was an auger hole, bored about half an inch or so, into the plank. His bone leg steadied in that hole; one arm elevated, and holding by a shroud; Captain Ahab stood erect, looking straight out beyond the ship's ever-pitching prow. There was an infinity of firmest fortitude, a determinate, unsurrenderable willfulness, in the fixed and fearless, forward dedication of that glance."

But my foot finds no auger holes, and if bare, would roll like a globe on the old planks.

Reaching the desk, I sit down, body straight out as before, head tilted back . . .

"But that night, in particular, a strange (and ever since inexplicable) thing occurred to me. Starting from a brief standing sleep, I was horribly conscious of something fatally wrong. The jawbone tiller smote my side, which leaned against it; in my ears was the low hum of sails, just beginning to shake in the wind; I thought my eyes were open; I was half conscious of putting my

fingers to the lids and mechanically stretching them still further
apart. But, in spite of all this, I could see no compass before me to
steer by; though it seemed but a minute since I had been watch-
ing the card, by the steady binnacle lamp illuminating it. Noth-
ing seemed before me but a jet gloom, now and then made ghast-
ly by flashes of redness. Uppermost was the impression, that
whatever swift, rushing thing I stood on was not so much bound
to any haven ahead as rushing from all havens astern. A stark,
bewildered feeling, as of death, came over me. Convulsively my
hands grasped the tiller, but with the crazy conceit that the tiller
was, somehow, in some enchanted way, inverted. My God! what
is the matter with me? thought I. Lo! in my brief sleep I had
turned myself about, and was fronting the ship's stern, with my
back to her prow and the compass."

My eyes suddenly grow dim. I am, in effect, under water, my vision
snuffing out like candle flames. I am rigid, but alive, aware.

There is a sense of motion, barely perceptible, yet abrupt; motion
neither within nor around me, but something of both . . .

like the cadaverous man in the mental hospital, haggard with sleeplessness,
who fixed a rigid grip on his bedposts every night, "to keep from slipping
away" . . .

Or Melville in OMOO, feet in the stocks, waking with the notion of being
dragged . . .

Or perhaps like an old sea captain, comfortably resting in his home ashore,
startled by the thought of the house pitching . . .

"It is not probable that this monomania in him took its instant
rise at the precise time of his bodily dismemberment. Then, in
darting at the monster, knife in hand, he had but given loose to
a sudden, passionate, corporal animosity; and when he received
the stroke that tore him, he probably but felt the agonizing bod-
ily laceration, but nothing more. Yet, when by this collision
forced to turn towards home, and for long months of days and

weeks, Ahab and anguish lay stretched together in one ham-mock, rounding in mid winter that dreary, howling Patagon-ian Cape; then it was, that his torn body and gashed soul bled into one another . . ."

I am covered from head to foot, unable to move, a small boy, stand-ing upright; I taste dirt on my lips. There is a moment of amnesia, and, separate from this, the knowledge that the bottoms of my feet hurt, and the lower spine and back of the head have been jolted. Then, the recognition, the discovery: I have fallen, with arms pinned to my body, into the empty post-hole, around the edges of which I had a moment before been playing.

With this recognition comes the experience: I had wandered from Carl, discovered the freshly dug holes along the edge of the field, had inspected them one after another, skipping over them, leaning into them, dropping pebbles in, and finally, reaching the last and loneliest, farthest from the house, had slipped on the clubfoot, and, as in burial of a sailor died at sea, had slid beneath the surface and out of sight.

The modified sensations linger in my body, still rigid in the chair, as more of the emotion comes back: the desolation and helplessness, the abandonment; the stopping of time, and, in its place, a circular expansion of sensation, a vortex in reverse, limitless in proportion to my physical confinement. Almost dizzy, I am not at first aware of the shadow that moves over my head, or even of my father's hands slipping under my arms to lift me out. It is only the merest chance that he decided to survey his day's digging, and heard my cries.

Worse than the accident itself were the cold pity I received, the as-sumption, without asking, that the "bad foot" was to blame, and my own knowledge that this and only this saved me from punishment. . . . There was, too, the nature of the accident, the ignominy of it; especially as it came soon after Carl's more dramatic tumble out of the haymow, twelve feet to the concrete floor of the barn . . .

(We had been playing in the hay, and when I ducked suddenly, he lunged past me and over the edge. I looked up and watched him fall: he landed flat on his back, his rump, shoulder blades and back of his head taking the blow; he appeared to bounce, the act of rising being continuous with that of falling, so that he was for a moment off the floor again, landing the second time on his feet, and emitting two single words,

"JESUS CHRIST!"

that my father claimed to have heard at the far end of the cornfield, half a mile away.

(He staggered for a moment, and shook himself—the motion originating in his buttocks, and rising loosely through his torso, until finally his great head rocked and shivered; then he glanced at me, and, for an instant, there was a queer smile, at once large-hearted and derisive, and a look in his eye that understood and conveyed more than he could speak. Then he raced for the ladder, and a moment later we were playing again in the hay, the accident ignored.

My body relaxes a little, releases itself, unwilling to participate further in the work of the mind. Other images, however, come flashing in . . .

I see Carl, age twelve, the time he found a bottle of gin, and got himself fabulously drunk. No longer able to stand, he suddenly discovered that he could roll the pupils of his eyes in little circles, and could control the motion: rolling them first one way then the other, clockwise and counterclockwise; then rolling one eye at a time, while the other was still; rolling both at once, each in a different direction; then reversing the directions. This gave him an idiotic satisfaction, and he continued until he passed out, going to sleep without ever lowering his eyelids, so that when he was snoring, I could still see the naked eyes, free of design and volition, meandering . . .

Now I see him swimming, going under the surface to take in a mouthful of water, then coming up, floating on his back, his body all belly and head in profile, while he spouts a great long stream of water, so that it seems he must have the whole lake in his head.

"But as the colossal skull embraces so very large a proportion of the entire extent of the skeleton . . ."

Melville, speaking of the sperm whale; and

"It does seem to me, that herein we see the rare virtue of a strong individual vitality, and the rare virtue of thick walls, and the rare virtue of interior spaciousness. Oh, man! admire and model thyself after the whale!"

and

"If you unload his skull of its spermy heaps and then take a rear view of its rear end, which is the high end, you will be struck by its resemblance to the human skull, beheld in the same situation, and from the same point of view. Indeed, place this reversed skull (scaled down to the human magnitude) among a plate of men's skulls, and you would involuntarily confound it with them . . ."

Now it is Carl coming at me, in mock fierceness, when we are roughhousing. He imitates a professional wrestler, ape-like, all arms and shoulders, with the illusion not only of having no neck, but of his head actually being sunk in his body—a round, weather-smooth rock wedged in a cleft between boulders.

"If you attentively regard almost any quadruped's spine, you will be struck with the resemblance of its vertebrae to a strung

necklace of dwarfed skulls, all bearing rudimental resemblance to the skull proper. It is a German conceit, that the vertebrae are absolutely undeveloped skulls. But the curious external resemblance, I take it the Germans were not the first men to perceive. A foreign friend once pointed it out to me, in the skeleton of a foe he had slain, and with the vertebrae of which he was inlaying, in a sort of basso relievo, the beaked prow of his canoe. Now, I consider that the phrenologists have omitted an important thing in not pushing their investigations from the cerebellum through the spinal canal. For I believe that much of a man's character will be found betokened in his backbone . . .

"Apply this spinal branch of phrenology to the Sperm Whale. His cranial cavity is continuous with the first neck-vertebra; and in that vertebra the bottom of the spinal canal will measure ten inches across, being eight in height, and of a triangular figure with the base downwards. As it passes through the remaining vertebrae the canal tapers in size, but for a considerable distance remains of large capacity. Now, of course, this canal is filled with much the same strangely fibrous substance—the spinal cord—as the brain; and directly communicates with the brain. And what is still more, for many feet after emerging from the brain's cavity, the spinal cord remains of an undecreasing girth, almost equal to that of the brain. Under all these circumstances, would it be unreasonable to survey and map out the whale's spine phrenologically? For, viewed in this light, the wonderful smallness of his brain proper is more than compensated by the wonderful comparative magnitude of his spinal cord."

Melville, and the leviathanic unconscious . . .

Carl the wrestler fades, and his huge head approaches, blocking the sun. There is a moment of terror before the image finds its frame . . . Carl is leaving for the summer, to work on an uncle's farm, and we are standing on the front steps, late afternoon. Mother is standing over us, insisting that, as brothers, we should kiss, full on the lips, before parting. She places a firm hand on the back of each neck. Carl acquiesces somberly, and his head approaches, a great purple shadow without features, a giant eggplant. I shrink from the contact, narrowing my mouth to an incision—and his kiss descends on me, a wet plum.

> *"It should not have been omitted that previous to completely stripping the body of the leviathan, he was beheaded. Now, the beheading of the Sperm Whale is a scientific anatomical feat, upon which experienced whale surgeons very much pride themselves: and not without reason.*
>
> *"Consider that the whale has nothing that can properly be called a neck; on the contrary, where his head and body seem to join, there, in that very place, is the thickest part of him. Remember, also, that the surgeon must operate from above, some eight or ten feet intervening between him and his subject, and that subject almost hidden in a discolored, rolling, and oftentimes tumultuous and bursting sea. Bear in mind, too, that under these untoward circumstances he has to cut many feet deep in the flesh; and in that subterraneous manner, without so much as getting one single peep into the ever-contracting gash thus made, he must skilfully steer clear of all adjacent, interdicted parts, and exactly divide the spine at a critical point hard by its insertion into the skull. Do you not marvel, then, at Stubb's boast, that he demanded but ten minutes to behead a sperm whale?*
>
> *"When first severed, the head is dropped astern and held there by a cable till the body is stripped. That done, if it belong to a small whale it is hoisted on deck to be deliberately disposed of. But, with a full grown leviathan this is impossible; for the sperm whale's head embraces nearly one third of his entire bulk, and completely to suspend such a burden as that, even by the immense tackles of a whaler, this were as vain a thing as to attempt weighing a Dutch barn in jeweller's scales."*

There is this about Carl: all the evidence indicates that he was conceived out of wedlock. There was the hasty wedding, and his birth in less than the full time thereafter. Mother's only comment was that he was a fast baby, but perhaps that's the way she wished to think of him. The only mystery to me is that she ever consented to conceive and bear another—myself—after the time she must have had in delivering Carl.

There was Tashtego, dipping sperm oil by the bucketful from the whale's head:

> "... but, on a sudden, as the eightieth or ninetieth bucket came suckingly up—my God! poor Tashtego—like the twin reciprocating bucket in a veritable well, dropped head-foremost down into this great Tun of Heidelburgh, and with a horrible oily gurgling, went clean out of sight!
>
> .   .   .   .
>
> " 'Stand clear of the tackle!' cried a voice like the bursting of a rocket.
>
> "Almost in the same instant, with a thunder-boom, the enormous mass dropped into the sea, like Niagara's Table-Rock into the whirlpool; the suddenly relieved hull rolled away from it, to far down her glittering copper; and all caught their breath, as half swinging—now over the sailors' heads and now over the water—Daggoo, through a thick mist of spray, was dimly beheld clinging to the pendulous tackles, while poor, buried-alive Tashtego was sinking utterly down to the bottom of the sea! But hardly had the blinding vapor cleared away, when a naked figure with a boarding sword in his hand, was for one swift moment seen hovering over the bulwarks. The next a loud splash announced that my brave Queequeg had dived to the rescue. One packed rush was made to the side, and every one counted every ripple, as moment followed moment, and no sign of either the sinker or the diver could be seen. Some hands now jumped into a boat alongside, and pushed a little off from the ship.
>
> "'Ha! ha!' cried Daggoo, all at once, from his now quiet, swinging perch overhead; and looking further off from the side, we saw an arm thrust upright from the blue waves; a sight strange to see, as an arm thrust forth from the grass over a grave.
>
> "'Both! both!—it is both!'—cried Daggoo again with a joyful shout; and soon after, Queequeg was seen striking out with

*one hand, and with the other clutching the long hair of the
Indian. Drawn into the waiting boat, they were quickly
brought to the deck; but Tashtego was long in coming to, and
Queequeg did not look very brisk.*

*"Now, how had this noble rescue been accomplished? Why,
diving after the slowly descending head, Queequeg with his keen
sword had made side lunges near its bottom, so as to scuttle a
large hole there; then dropping his sword, had thrust his long arm
far inwards and upwards, and so hauled out poor Tash by the
head. He averred, that upon first thrusting in for him, a leg was
presented; but well knowing that that was not as it ought to be,
and might occasion great trouble;—he had thrust back the leg,
and by a dexterous heave and toss, had wrought a somerset upon
the Indian; so that with the next trial, he came forth in the good
old way—head foremost. As for the great head itself, that was
doing as well as could be expected."*

As a boy, Carl went through a period of monumental hay fever
marked by no ordinary sneezes, but by explosions, one following
another in rapid succession so that they seemed continuous, his
eyes, nose, and mouth become fountains. I see him now as I came
upon him one day, where he had gone to isolate himself during an
attack, in an unused room of the house. Glancing at me, through
bloodshot, aqueous eyes, he turned, in sequence, to the four points
of the compass, saluting each with a shattering blast that doubled
him over, scattered spray to the walls, and brought his forehead
nearly to his feet. Subsiding a moment, shoulders and head hanging
to one side, he turned to me and spoke, the words running togeth-
er in his wet mouth:

"I must have the ocean in my head."

And there were allusions, legendary in the family—to a difficulty
immediately following his birth. The doctor diagnosed *Hydro-
cephalus Internus:*

"In *infants,* the most notable symptom is the progressive enlarge-
ment of the head. The fontanels remain open and are tense, and

often the sagittal suture fails to close . . . The bones of the skull are thin. The face of the child appears small because of the cranial enlargement and the bulging overhanging forehead. The hair is thin. The skin appears to be tightly stretched and the veins are prominent. The thin orbital plates are pushed downward, with displacement of the eyeballs, so that each iris and often a part of the pupil is covered by the lower lid, and the sclera is visible above. Optic neuritis, followed by optic atrophy, results from pressure of the distended third ventricle upon the chiasm. Strabismus is usually present. The child's head has a tendency to fall backward or to one side, and cannot be held erect. The extremities and trunk are thin and there is rigidity, especially of the abductor muscles. Late in the disease there is spasticity. Convulsions are caused by pressure on the cortex. If the child walks at all, it is with difficulty. Mental development is usually arrested and varying degrees of mental deficiency result, depending upon the amount of ventricular distortion and the severity of the pressure."

But the condition disappeared, as mysteriously as it had arrived, and the doctor could only assume that there had been a rupture or absorption of adhesions. This was the beginning—the headwaters, perhaps—of a series of unique medical phenomena that occurred throughout Carl's generally robust life.

Shifting in the chair, I get to my feet, stand up, and look down at the row of books: the medical books. I think again of my diploma, unframed, and of the back-breaking burden of dollars and hope— my own and my parents'—invested in my education. There is the sound of television and children from downstairs. Sitting again, leaning on my elbows, I recall a visit to a hospital ward, when the doctor, knowing me for a medical student, pointed out a crippled youth, and asked me, half-facetiously, what I would do for him:

> there was the face, the
> white-blue face, and the body,
> the young man, band leader,
> he had sleep-walked out a
> second-story window to be found

legs paralyzed
from the hips down,
hands stove,

and the eyes,
the pale blue watery
eyes . . .

they sent him home, and
he lives now, on a narrow board
of a bed, day and night,
smoking,

attended by a mother who
shuts the door . . .

What would I do:

to bring back,
to save,
to return,

a not very talented musician . . .

And there is Melville, in WHITE-JACKET:

*"Strange! that so many of those who would fain minister to our
own health should look so much like invalids themselves."*

And Carl, reading Melville:

*"In the case of a Sperm Whale the brains are accounted a fine
dish. The casket of the skull is broken into with an axe, and the
two plump, whitish lobes being withdrawn (precisely resem-
bling two large puddings), they are then mixed with flour, and
cooked into a most delectable mess . . ."*

And, again, the way he held the book, possessing it, as though the open halves of it were themselves two plump, whitish lobes . . . he smiled broadly, smacking his lips.

Letting my eyes close, and my arms hang over the sides of the chair—I experience motion once more,

not this time as the house pitching, the stocks dragging, but as a thing, familiar, expected; as a man might climb into his berth before his ship is underway, and then the motion, the departure, the gentle slipping away from the wharf, comes as a thing good and confirming.

Melville, regarding MARDI, in a letter:

> ". . . *proceeding in my narrative of facts, I began to feel an incurable distaste for the same; & a longing to plume my powers for a flight, & felt irked, cramped & fettered by plodding along with dull commonplaces,—So suddenly abandoning the thing altogether, I went to work heart & soul at a romance which is now in fair progress . . .*"

The illusion I have is of being split from head to toe, as in hemiplegia or an imperfect twinning process—with separate circulation on each side, the blood rushing furiously. There are no recalls, no flashing images, no digging in and rooting of the body—rather, the beginning of a journey such as I have never before taken

GENOA

ONE

THERE WAS THE MAN from Genoa, who went to sea at fourteen, and

> "I have been twenty-three years upon the sea without quitting it for any time long enough to be counted, and I saw all the East and West . . ."

A Man

> ". . . of a good size and looks, taller than the average and of sturdy limbs; the eyes lively and the other features of the face in good proportion; the hair very red; and the complexion somewhat flushed and freckled; a good speaker, cautious and of great talent and an elegant latinist and a most learned cosmographer, graceful when he wished, irate when he was crossed . . .":

Christopher Columbus.

The wind rises again, sifting through the cracks at the eaves, and I draw close to the old chimney. My head seems large, and my legs feel as though joined, wedge-shaped. I read

that twenty-five thousand years ago Cro-Magnon man invaded Europe, from unknown origins. He was tall, averaging above six feet, and had a large brain case, larger than any known man of the present. Settling in southern France, he pushed over the mountains, to the Spanish Peninsula. He worshipped bulls, and buried his dead facing west, the direction in which he migrated, moving, perhaps, all the way to the brink, the eaves of the unknown ocean, to Cabo de Sao Vicente, which Columbus called "the beginning of Europe."

Eastward on the map, there is Genoa, at the northernmost pitch of the Ligurian Sea, with land and water falling away southwestward,

just as, beyond Gibraltar, beyond the Pillars of Hercules, from Palos the ocean falls away from the land, again southwestward,

and farther eastward, there is Crete, progenitor of Greece . . . but

> *"'A man overboard!' I shouted at the top of my compass; and like lightning the cords slid through our blistering hands, and with a tremendous shock the boat bounded on the sea's back. One mad sheer and plunge, one terrible strain on the tackles as we sunk in the trough of the waves, tugged upon by the towing breaker, and our knives severed the tackle ropes—we hazarded not unhooking the blocks—our oars were out, and the good boat headed round, with prow to leeward."*

Melville in MARDI, with Jarl the Viking, stole a whaleboat and escaped the ARCTURIAN— ". . . and right into the darkness, and dead to leeward, we rowed and sailed . . ."

As earlier, with Toby, he had in fact jumped ship to the valley of the Typee, he now, in the same south seas, with northman as companion, fictively jumped ship into open waters, and

> *". . . West, West! Whitherward point Hope and prophet-fingers; whitherward, at sunset, kneel all worshipers of fire; whitherward in mid-ocean, the great whales turn to die . . ."*

sailed westward to fabulous Mardi

> (to be greeted as a white god from the east, as Columbus and his men were greeted in the Indies . . .

Melville, out of the known cosmos of the sperm whaler, leaped to the unknown . . .

> ". . . I've chartless voyaged. With compass and the lead, we had not found these Mardian Isles. Those who boldly launch, cast off all cables; and turning from the common breeze, that's fair for all, with their own breath, fill their own sails. Hug the shore, naught new is seen; and 'Land ho!' at last was sung, when a new world was sought.
>
> "But this new world here sought, is stranger far than his, who stretched his vans from Palos. It is the world of mind; wherein the wanderer may gaze round with more of wonder . . ."

To guarantee escape—a thousand miles at sea in an open boat were not enough—Melville cut off the father ship, the whaler from which he fled,

> "For of the stout Arcturian no word was ever heard, from the dark hour we pushed from her fated planks."

and thus made of himself an Ishmael—wanderer in space.

But for Melville, space and time are one . . .

> "Do you believe that you lived three thousand years ago? That you were at the taking of Tyre, were overwhelmed in Gomorrah? No. But for me, I was at the subsiding of the Deluge, and helped swab the ground, and build the first house. With the Israelites, I fainted in the wilderness; was in court, when Solomon outdid all the judges before him. I, it was, who . . . touched Isabella's heart, that she hearkened to Columbus."

I become aware now of a different sensation, and realize that it has been with me for some moments:

It is the sound of silence. Wind and rain have vanished, child and home noises from below are hushed. I have fallen into a void, have journeyed to beginnings earlier than I have yet discovered. I sit still, clamoring for a sound; my head feels huge, my body and legs are one.

"If therefore," as Einstein says, "a body is removed sufficiently far from all other masses of the universe its inertia must be reduced to zero."

And Bondi: "This in turn implies that it is possible to introduce an omnipresent cosmic time which has the property of measuring proper time . . ."

And further: "A separate time-reckoning belongs therefore to every natural phenomenon."

"The picture of the history of the universe . . ., then, was that for an infinite period in the distant past there was a completely homogeneous distribution of matter in equilibrium . . . until some event started off the expansion, which has been going on at an increasing pace ever since."

Stubb, in MOBY-DICK: *"I wonder, Flask, whether the world is anchored anywhere; if she is, she swings with an uncommon long cable . . ."*

And Melville, in a letter: ". . . & for me, I shall write such things as the Great Publisher of Mankind ordained ages before he published 'The World'—this planet, I mean . . .

Again, in MOBY-DICK: *"When I stand among these mighty Leviathan skeletons . . . I am, by a flood, borne back to that wondrous period, ere time itself can be said to have begun; for time began with man. Here Saturn's gray chaos rolls over me, and I obtain dim, shuddering glimpses into those Polar eternities; when wedged bastions of ice pressed hard upon what are now the Tropics; and in all the 25,000 miles of this world's circumference, not an inhabitable hand's breadth of land was visible."*

Rousing, shifting myself, I feel impelled to break through the silence. I find it an effort, muscular, involving sensation at once stiff and pliant in the inner ear, down the sides of the neck, and in the shoulders; and it is not until I rise to my feet and tap my fingers sharply on the desk, that I realize the silence has been altogether subjective—wind and rain have not ceased, the children are still below; I have been controlling these sounds, turning the volume down, as in functional deafness. Experimenting, I realize that the volume is still down, that I wish it to be that way. For an instant, hope and excitement flash through me, so that, in this moment, my two feet are equivalent and normal. This passes quickly. I sink into the chair, and the old sensations of deformity, actual and projected, overtake me, in the silence. I am at once clubfooted and footless.

Melville, describing a calm: "At first he is taken by surprise, never having dreamt of a state of existence where existence itself seems suspended. He shakes himself in his coat, to see whether it be empty or no. He closes his eyes, to test the reality of the glassy expanse. He fetches a deep breath, by way of experiment, and for the sake of witnessing the effect."

"The stillness of the calm is awful. His voice begins to grow strange and portentous. He feels it in him like something swallowed too big for the esophagus. It keeps up a sort of involuntary interior humming in him, like a live beetle. His cranium is a dome full of reverberations. The hollows of his very bones are as whispering galleries. He is afraid to speak loud, lest he be stunned . . ."

"But that morning, the two gray firmaments of sky and water seemed collapsed into a vague ellipsis . . . Every thing was fused into the calm: sky, air, water, and all. Not a fish was to be seen. The silence was that of a vacuum. No vitality lurked in the air. And this inert blending and brooding of all things seemed gray chaos in conception."

And there is Ahab, in MOBY-DICK: *". . . not the smallest atom stirs or lives on matter, but has its cunning duplicate in mind."*

An odor—the odor of sulphur—comes to me. I turn my head variously, but the odor persists. Powerful, sourceless, it pervades the attic. I reach for the medical book, and read that at one time there was a popular theory, disproved in 1668, that slime and decaying matter were capable of giving rise to living animals, and

that the human spermatozoon was discovered by Leeuwenhoek in 1677 . . .

It was believed, according to the theory of preformation, that fully formed human bodies existed in miniature in either the sperm or the ovum; all future generations were thought to be encased, one inside the sex cells of the other, and it was calculated that the egg of Eve must have contained two hundred thousand million human beings, concentrically arranged, and that when all these miniatures were released and unfolded, the human race would terminate.

> (There is the drawing (Hartsoeker, 1694) of a tiny human organism, crouched over, huge-headed, encased in a sperm cell. A dark star, four-pointed like a compass, covers his pate . . .

And there are the other drawings:

> The testicle, the ovary, the
> head of the sperm, in the
> shape of an egg . . .
>
> the uterus pear-shaped, the ovum,
> round, like a planet . . .
>
> the egg, the pear,
> the planet,
> with the flagellum for energy . . .

Glancing at the picture: "Human spermatozoon. Diagrammatic."

> and the text: "The head is oval or elliptical, but flattened, so that when viewed in profile it is pear-shaped."

I am aware again of internal sensation, and there is a sudden identification:

> "The human spermatozoon possesses a head, a neck, a connecting piece or body, and a tail."

It is this—the huge-headed and long-tailed sensation—that I have been experiencing for some time. Pliant as a creature out of myth, I am—nerve, blood and muscle—disciplined and reshapen. My head is black, the skull-bones inflated, retaining their thickness, but become enormous, cavernous, so that all of me is within the head, only the tail remaining outside: flagellant, spring-like . . .

Again there is motion, this time with awe and terror; for whatever my condition, the condition of thought and flesh, the reality in which I am formed and deformed, in which I am known to myself and to others—all is become mutable. I am monstrous, my head merges into the attic, the attic into blackness . . .

my breath comes rapidly, I am restless . . . flashing the pages before me, I stop at

the picture of the uterus and tubes—like the head of a longhorn steer, the ends of the horns exfoliating with fimbriae,

and the ovum, bursting from the follicle, to become momentarily free in the abdomen, out of all direct contact . . . communicating its condition, perhaps, by means of hormones, but nonetheless adrift, as in an open ocean . . .

> MOBY-DICK: *"All the yard-arms were tipped with a pallid fire; and touched at each tri-pointed lightning-rod-end with three tapering white flames, each of the three tall masts was silently burning in that sulphurous air . . ."*

> And Columbus, reported by Fernando: "On the same Saturday, in the night, was seen St. Elmo, with seven lighted tapers, at the top-mast. There was much rain and thunder. I mean to say that those lights were seen, which mariners affirm to be the body of St. Elmo, in beholding which they chaunted many litanies and orisons . . ."

The corpusants.

I am still for some moments, as though waiting for lightning—but there is none; only the steady hum of wind and rain, the muffled voices of children, vague sounds of the city in the distance—and the creaking of the television aerial, in the wind, straining the chimney brackets.

In Lisbon,—rank with bodega, wine in the wood, salt fish, tar, tal-
low, musk, and cinnamon—the sailors talk

of monsters in the western ocean, of gorgons and demons, succubi
and succubae, maleficent spirits and unclean devils, unspeakable
things that command the ocean currents—of cuttlefish and sea ser-
pents, of lobsters the tips of whose claws are fathoms asunder, of
sirens and bishop-fish, the Margyzr and Marmennil of the north,
goblins who visit the ship at night, singe hair, tie knots in ropes, tear
sails to shreds—of witches who raise tempests and gigantic water-
spouts that suck ships into the sky—of dragon, crocodile, griffin,
hippogrif, Cerberus, and Ammit

or Melville:

> *"Megalosaurus, iguanodon,*
> *Palaeotherium glypthaecon,*
> *   A Barnum-show raree;*
> *   The vomit of slimy and sludgey sea:*
> *Purposeless creatures, odd inchoate things*
> *Which splashed thro' morasses on fleshly wings;*
> *The cubs of Chaos, with eyes askance,*
> *Preposterous griffins that squint at Chance . . ."*

And the medical book:

> "At one time the human sperm cells were regarded as parasites, and
> under this misapprehension the name spermatozoa, or 'semen ani-
> mals,' was given to them."

Melville again:

> *"You must have plenty of sea-room to tell the Truth in; espe-*
> *cially when it seems to hare an aspect of newness, as America did*
> *in 1492, though it was then just as old, and perhaps older than*
> *Asia, only those sagacious philosophers, the common sailors, had*
> *never seen it before, swearing it was all water and moonshine*
> *there."*

The sailors talked of islands:

of Antilia, and the splendid mirages beyond Gomera; of the French and Portuguese Green Island, and the Irish O'Brasil;

of the great pines, of a kind unknown, cast ashore on the Azores by west and north-west winds—and the lemons, green branches, and other fruits washing upon the Canaries;

of Saint Brandon's, to be seen now and again from the Canaries, but always eluding discovery,

except by the Saint himself, who set out in search of islands possessing the delights of paradise, and finally landed,

found a dead giant in a sepulchre, revived him, conversed with him, found him docile, converted him, and permitted him to die again. The sailors talked of

> *"the desert islands inhabited by wild men with tails . . ."*

or of Atlantis, where the gods were born, and whose first king, Uranus, was given to prophecy . . .

discovered, perhaps, by Phoenicians blown west, and reported by Silenus (whose words are beyond question, as he was drunk at the time) to be "a mass of dry land, which in greatness was infinite and immeasurable, and it nourishes and maintains by virtue of its green meadow and pastures many great and mighty beasts. The men who inhabit this clime are more than twice the height of human stature . . ."

The shore was lofty and precipitous, with a vast, fertile plain lying inland, and great mountains to the north. The land abounded in all precious minerals, and cattle and elephants were plentiful.

> (modern excavations in southwest Spain have unearthed elephant tusks . . .

There was a canal, and a proud, barbaric city, with copper-clad walls, and a great temple to Poseidon, clad with silver, and a gigantic statue in gold.

And there was Scheria, home of Nausicaa and the Phaeacians, Ulysses' longest resting place before his return home—like Atlantis, it boasted a great city, and was located beyond the Pillars of Hercules.

And Tarshish, the port for which Jonah set sail from Joppa.

> *(Melville in Joppa: "No sleep last night—only resource to cut tobacco, and watch the six windows of my room, which is like a lighthouse—& hear the surf & wind . . . I have such a feeling in this lonely old Joppa, with the prospect of a long detention here, owing to the surf—that it is only by stern self-control & grim defiance that I continue to keep cool and patient."*

Joppa, the point of departure, the Palos, from which Jonah sought to escape, to Tarshish . . .

But perhaps Tarshish, Atlantis, and Scheria were all one: islands locked in the minds of those who dwelt in the internal sea . . .

perhaps they were all Cadiz: the barbaric western city beyond the Pillars, on the southwest shore of Spain (not far from Palos), where the Guadalquivir pours into "the real ocean," as the Egyptian priest called it; or, in the words of the Arabians, "the green sea of gloom" . . .

The Western Ocean.

> **In Lisbon, the sailors say: "He who sails beyond the Cape of No may return or not.**

> **"For many said: how is it possible to sail beyond a Cape which the navigators of Spain had set as the terminus and end of all navigation in those parts, as men who knew that the sea beyond was not navigable, not only because of the strong currents, but because it was very broken with so much boiling over of its waters that it sucked up all the ships."**

TWO

there was Marco Polo, talking of Cipango, from a jail cell in Genoa:

reporting it to be fifteen hundred miles east of Asia, to be reached by huge Chinese ships made of the fir tree, ships that sailed freely upon the ocean that washed the eastern shores of that continent . . .

> (and if Asia extended to the ocean, and Cipango were fifteen hundred miles east of Asia—to where did the ocean extend?

> *And Melville in Genoa: "Ramparts overhanging the open sea, arches thrown over ravines. Fine views of sections of town. Up & up. Galley-slave prison. Gratings commanding view of sea—infinite liberty."*

And Genoa itself:

> *"Janus, the first king of Italy, and descended from the Giants, founded Genoa on this spot in the time of Abraham; and Janus, Prince of Troy, skilled in astronomy, while sailing in search of a place wherein to dwell in healthfulness and security, came to the same Genoa founded by Janus, King of Italy and great-grand-son of Noah; and seeing that the sea and the encompassing hills seemed in all things convenient, he increased it in fame and greatness."*

Janus, Roman god,

doorkeeper of the firmament, presider over gates, the entrance upon and beginning of things . . .

Ianus geminus, faced front and back,

East and West . . .

I close my eyes, and there is again a sense of split, a jagged crease running the length of my forehead—only for a moment, and it is gone.

Genoa,

at the northernmost pitch of the Ligurian Sea, turning

southeast, to trade with the East, and

southwest, perhaps, through the Pillars of Hercules, to

the Terrestrial Paradise . . . (for many philosophers believe this will be found south of the equator, the torrid zone serving as a flaming sword to ward off invasion. They divide the globe into northern and southern hemispheres, the southern being the head, or better part, and the northern the feet, or lesser part (this being confirmed by the stars of the southern hemisphere, which shine with a larger and brighter aspect). The east, according to the philosophers, is to the right, and to the left, the west.)

In Genoa. in the year 1451, Susanna Columbus, wife to Domenico, gave birth to a son, Christopher . . .

> **"His parents were notable persons, one time rich . . .; at other times they must have been poor . . ."**

> *Allan Melvill, Herman's father, in a letter: "I have now to request in the most* urgent manner, *as equally involving my personal honor & the welfare of my Family, that you would favor me by* return of mail *with your Note to my Order at six months from 31st March, for Five Thousand Dollars . . ."*

At the age of fourteen, Columbus went to sea . . .

*Melville: "Sad disappointments in several plans which I had
sketched for my future life; the necessity of doing something for
myself, united to a naturally roving disposition, had now con-
spired within me, to send me to sea as a sailor."*

and

*". . . thought me an erring and a wilful boy, and perhaps I was;
but if I was, it had been a hard-hearted world and hard times
that had made me so. I had learned to think much and bitterly
before my time . . ."*

Domenico, Christopher's father, was a well-liked man, easily obtaining
property on credit . . .

*Allan Melvill: "I rec^d this morning with unutterable satisfac-
tion your most opportune & highly esteemed favour . . . with the
annexed two notes drawn by yourself . . . one for $2500—the
other for $2750—payable at the Bank of America . . ."*

But—a weaver by trade—he neglected his loom, took on sidelines:
cheese, wine, a tavern . . . so that Christopher, returning from a sea voy-
age, age nineteen, found himself responsible for his father's debts, and,
with his mariner's wages, secured the father's freedom from a Genoese
jail.

*Allan Melvill: ". . . my situation has become almost intolerable
for the want of $500 to discharge some urgent debts, and provide
necessaries for my Family . . . I may soon be prosecuted for my
last quarters Rent, & other demands which were unavoidably
left unpaid . . ."*

Christopher remained, throughout his life, mysterious regarding his ori-
gins, speaking of himself never as Genoese, but only as foreigner . . .

*Ahab, gazing at the corpusants: "Oh, thou magnanimous! Now I
do glory in my genealogy! . . . thou foundling fire, thou hermit
immemorial, thou too hast thy incommunicable riddle, thy unpar-
ticipated grief. Here again with haughty agony, I read my sire."*

Columbus and Melville—the paternity blasted . . .

> (perhaps Domenico and Allan should have practiced a custom of the Iberians and Caribs,
>
> (The Couvade,
>
> (the father taking to his bed for several days or weeks at the birth of a child, so as not to endanger the delicate affinity with the new-born . . .

Columbus:

> "Most exalted Sovereigns: At a very early age I entered upon the sea navigating, and I have continued doing so until today. The calling in itself inclines whoever follows it to desire to know the secrets of this world. Forty years are already passing which I have employed in this manner: I have traversed every region which up to the present time is navigated."
>
> "During this time I have seen, and in seeing, have studied all writings, cosmography, histories, chronicles, and philosophy and those relating to other arts, by means of which our Lord made me understand with a palpable hand, that it was practicable to navigate from here to the Indies and inspired me with a will for the execution of this navigation. And with this fire, I came to your Highnesses."

> *Melville, as Pierre: "A varied scope of reading, little suspected by his friends, and randomly acquired by a random but lynx-eyed mind . . .; this poured one considerable contributory stream into that bottomless spring of original thought which the occasion and time had caused to burst out in himself."*

Columbus:

> "It might be that your Highnesses and all the others who knew me, . . . either in secret or public would reprove me in divers manners, saying that I am not learned in letters and calling me a crazy sailor, a worldly man, etc."

"I say that the holy spirit works in Christians, Jews, Moors, and in all others of all sects, and not only in the wise but the ignorant: for in my time I have seen a villager who gave a better account of the heaven and the stars and their courses than others who expended money in learning of them."

And Melville—always a man of the fo'castle:

"... a whale-ship was my Yale College and my Harvard."

Christopher, who called himself "an ignorant man," was captain of his own ship and a corsair, at twenty-one. And

"... I saw all the East and West ..."

Once,

"It happened to me that King Reynal ... sent me to Tunis to seize the galleas Fernandina, and when I was already on the island of St. Peter in Sardinia, a settee informed me that the galleas was accompanied by two other ships and a carack, whereupon there was agitation among the men and they refused to sail on unless we returned first to Marseilles to pick up another ship and more men. Seeing that I could not force their hand without some artifice, I agreed to what they asked me, but, changing the bait of the magnetic needle, I spread sails at sunset, and the next morning, at dawn, we were within the cape of Carthagine while all had been certain that we were going to Marseilles."

MOBY-DICK: "Thrusting his head halfway into the binnacle, Ahab caught one glimpse of the compasses; his uplifted arm slowly fell; for a moment he almost seemed to stagger. Standing behind him Starbuck looked, and lo! the two compasses pointed East, and the 'Pequod' was as infallibly going West."

Fourteen hundred seventy-eight and -nine: Columbus in all probability sailed to the East, in the service of the House of Centurione. The course was through the Straits of Messina,

(Melville: "Coasts of Calabria & Sicily ahead at day break. Neared them at 10 o'clock . . . At 1 P.M. anchored in harbor of Messina . . . Rainy day.")

. . thence across the Ionian Sea to Taenarum, through the Cervi Channel north of Cythera, past the white columns of the Temple of Poseidon on Cape Sunium, through the difficult currents of the D'Oro channel to Cape Mastika and the island of Chios, due south of Lesbos.

Melville: "Sea less cross. At 12.M. pleasant, & made the coast of Greece, the Morea. Passed through the straits, & Cape Matapan."

Matapan being the Taenarum of Christopher . . .

Thus Columbus before the Indies, and Melville, after Polynesia . . . rubbing among the old islands . . .

And August the thirteenth, 1476, Columbus, on board a Genoese trading vessel, engaged in sea-battle with a Franco-Portuguese outfit: another ship locked with his, both caught fire, and both eventually went down. Columbus, in the open sea,

> *(Melville: "A bloody film was before my eyes, through which, ghost–like, passed and repassed my father, mother, and sisters. An unutterable nausea oppressed me; I was conscious of gasping; there seemed no breath in my body . . . I thought to myself, Great God! this is death!"*

. . . grasped an oar and, alternately swimming and resting, despite wounds, finally landed at Lagos, twenty miles from "the beginning of Europe," and not far from Cadiz and Palos.

> de Madariaga: "On August 13th, 1476, Christoforo Columbo, then just under twenty-five years of age, was in danger of death. He was near enough to death to be able to say that on that day he was reborn."

Melville, to Hawthorne: "My development has been all within a few years past. I am like one of those seeds taken out of the Egyptian Pyramids, which, after being three thousand years a seed & nothing but a seed, being planted in English soil, it developed itself, grew to greenness, and then fell to mould. So I. Until I was twenty-five, I had no development at all. From my twenty-fifth year I date my life."

I shift my position, turn to sit sideways, throwing one leg over the arm of the chair. The strange internal sensations are still with me, but are less terrifying, with greater possibility of change . . .

In Portugal, Columbus, Genoese Ishmael, married one Filipa Moniz Perestrello, of an old, established family, and thus took a step up the ladder, toward the court,

as Herman married, or was married perhaps, to Lizzie Shaw . . .

"Not the slightest hint has come down to us of the appearance or disposition of Columbus's only wife; Dona Felipa is as shadowy a figure as the Discoverer's mother."

But there was Beatriz,

whom he loved and did not marry . . . whose last name, despite all attempts by herself and family to suppress it, was Torquemada, and whose origin, therefore, was probably Jewish . . .

Christopher and Beatriz—joined, not in matrimony, but in blasted paternity—got a son, the illegitimate Ferdinand (who later claimed noble ancestry for his father),

as, in PIERRE, *Mr. Glendinning begat upon his French mistress a daughter, Isabel,*

(and perhaps, in Polynesia, Herman and Fayaway . . .

But in Portugal, with the help of Dona Felipa, Columbus gained the court:

"The King, as he observed this Christovao Colom to be a big talker and boastful in setting forth his accomplishments, and full of fancy and imagination with his Isle Cypango than certain whereof he spoke, gave him small credit. However, by strength of his importunity it was ordered that he confer with D. Diego Ortiz bishop of Ceuta and Master Roderigo and Master José, to whom the King had committed these matters of cosmography and discovery, and they all considered the words of Christovao Colom as vain, simply founded on imagination, or things like that Isle Cypango of Marco Polo . . ."

And so he left the court, left Portugal, left Dona Felipa . . .

became, in fact, the ideal unwed Ishmael, wanderer in the wilderness, of which Melville, long since returned from the seas, never stopped thinking . . .

> (Pasted to the inside of Melville's desk, discovered after his death: "Keep true to the dreams of thy youth."

Christopher, wed "to the magnanimity of the sea, which" as Melville says, "will permit no records" . . .

searching an insular paternity, left Portugal, for Spain

THREE

and Isabella,

who, like himself, was blue-eyed, fair-skinned, and red-haired . . .

He told her, perhaps, of the books he had been reading, such as the YMAGO MUNDI:

> "There is a spring in Paradise which waters the Garden of Delights and which splays into four rivers."
>
> "The Paradise on Earth is a pleasant place, situated in certain regions of the Orient, at a long distance by land and by sea from our inherited world. It rises so high that it touches the lunar sphere . . ."

> *(Melville,* BILLY BUDD*: "Who in the rainbow can draw the line where the violet tint ends and the orange tint begins? Distinctly we see the difference of the color, but where exactly does the first one visibly enter into the other? So with sanity and insanity."*

> ". . . and the water of the Deluge could not reach it . . . its altitude over the lowlands is incomparable . . . and it reaches the layers of calm air which lie on top of the zone of troubled air . . ."
>
> "From this lake, as from a main spring, there flow the four rivers of Paradise: Phison or Ganges; Gihon or Nile; Tigris and Euphrates . . ."

Certain it is that Melville performed an act original and radical to himself, in MOBY-DICK. In all his works hitherto, he had voyaged southward to Cape Horn, then westward to the Pacific, returning via that same essentially western route (the one exception being REDBURN, dealing not at all with the Pacific, nor with cosmographical man).

*"... the sight of many unclad, lovely island creatures, round the
Horn"*—that was the route to the Treasures: southward, the
Horn, and then west.

But in Moby-Dick, Melville turned upon himself and Western
Man, performing an act as violent as subsequent war and catastro-
phe—an act rich, perhaps, with revenge as Ahab's pursuit of the
whale: the *Pequod* turned and headed *back east*—a route Melville
himself never followed to the Pacific—eastward, via Good Hope,
the Indian Ocean, and

> *"By the straits of Sunda, chiefly, vessels bound to China from the
> west, emerge into the China seas."*

Thus, it was a return, a going back, a going back upward, perhaps . . .

like the Pacific salmon, who spend their lives in salt water, and then,
anadromous, run upward to the fresh, to the very individual source
waters, the headwaters, to spawn and die

> (developing, often, a humpback, hooked
> snout, and elongated jaw—becoming alto-
> gether monstrous, while in this pursuit . . .

> Columbus: "I always read that the world, land and water, was
> spherical . . . Now I observed so much divergence, that I began to
> hold different views about the world and I found that it was not
> round . . . but pear-shaped, round except where it has a nipple, for
> there it is taller, or as if one had a round ball and, on one side, it
> should be like a woman's breast, and this nipple part is the highest
> and closest to heaven . . ."

Columbus, ascending the mounting waters, "running upward" to the very
source point, "highest and closest to heaven . . ."

> *Genesis, the St. Jerome version: "But the Lord God in the begin-
> ning had planted a Paradise of Delight: in which he placed the*

man whom he had fashioned . . . And a river came out from the Place of Delight to water Paradise: which from thence is divided into four heads . . ."

Spanish cosmographers, however, were not impressed. In fourteen hundred ninety, they "judged his promises and offers were impossible and vain and worthy of rejection . . . they ridiculed his reasoning saying that they had tried so many times and had sent ships in search of the mainland and that it was all air and there was no reason in it . . ."

Lizzie Melville, Herman's wife, in a letter to her mother: "I suppose by this time you are deep in the 'fogs' of 'Mardi'—if the mist ever does clear away, I should like to know what it reveals . . ."

They further advised the Sovereigns "that it was not a proper object for their royal authority to favor an affair that rested on such weak foundations, and which appeared uncertain and impossible to any educated person, however little learning he might have."

But Columbus "had conceived in his heart the most certain confidence to find what he claimed he would, as if he had this world locked up in his trunk."

Later, in the Indies:
"We reached the latter island near a large mountain which seemed almost to reach heaven, and in the centre of that mountain there was a peak which was much higher than all the rest of the mountain, and from which many streams flowed in different directions, especially toward the direction in which we lay. At a distance of three leagues a waterfall appeared as large through as an ox, which precipitated itself from such a high point that it seemed to fall from heaven. It was at such a distance that there were many wagers on the ships, as some said that it was white rocks and others that it was water. As soon as they arrived nearer, the truth was learned, and it was the most wonderful thing in the world to see from what a high place it was precipitated and from what a small place such a large waterfall sprang."

And the *Pequod*, approaching the Straits of Sunda:

> *"Broad on both bows, at the distance of some two or three miles,*
> *and forming a great semi-circle, embracing one half of the level*
> *horizon, a continuous chain of whale-jets were up-playing and*
> *sparkling in the noonday air."*

Swinging my foot to the floor, I sit tense, crouched forward, straight in the chair. Huge-headed, I am one of millions, and there is a gateway, an opening, for which all of us have been alerted.

> *"As marching armies approaching an unfriendly defile in the*
> *mountains, accelerate their march, all eagerness to place that*
> *perilous passage in their rear, and once more expand in compar-*
> *ative security upon the plain; even so did this vast fleet of*
> *whales now seem hurrying forward through the straits; gradu-*
> *ally contracting the wings of their semicircle, and swimming on,*
> *in one solid, but still crescentic centre."*

From Nantucket, east,

to Good Hope, the Indian Ocean, the Straits of Sunda, and

> *". . . we glided between two whales into the innermost heart of*
> *the shoal, as if from some mountain torrent we had slid into a*
> *serene valley lake. Here the storms in the roaring glens between*
> *the outermost whales, were heard but not felt. In this central*
> *expanse the sea presented the smooth satin-like surface, called a*
> *sleek, produced by the subtle moisture thrown off by the whale in*
> *his more quiet moods. Yes, we were now in that enchanted calm*
> *which they say lurks at the heart of every commotion."*

> *"Keeping at the centre of the lake, we were occasionally visited*
> *by small tame cows and calves; the women and children of this*
> *routed host."*

> *"Some of the subtlest secrets of the seas seemed divulged to us in*
> *this enchanted pond. We saw young Leviathan amours in the*
> *deep."*

And Columbus, on the third voyage, sailing in the Gulf of Paria, observing the mangroves lining the shore, with tiny oysters clinging to their roots . . . the oyster shells open, to catch from the mangrove leaves the dewdrops that engender pearls . . .

Fourteen hundred and ninety, Isabella, rejecting the advice of her cosmographers, was hesitant. Perhaps, with insanity touching her mother and her daughter, rendering her thus bracketed

> *(as Melville, his father dying maniacal and his son a suicide, was similarly bracketed),*

she was just strange enough to listen . . .

Certainly, the natural direction for Spain's colonial expansion was Africa, in pursuit of the Moors. America was altogether irrelevant, distant, difficult, tempting, and ultimately untenable and ruinous. Thus, as Melville to Western Man, so Columbus to Spanish history, did more violence, perhaps, than all the wars that followed.

But as Albertus Magnus said of the Antipodes:

> *"Perhaps also some magnetic power in that region draws human stones even as the magnet draws iron."*

FOUR

And there was Michele de Cuneo, with his Carib slave: "Having taken her into my cabin, she being naked according to their custom, I conceived a desire to take pleasure. I wanted to put my desire into execution but she did not want it and treated me with her fingernails in such manner that I wished I had never begun. But seeing that (to tell you the end of it all), I took a rope and thrashed her well, for which she raised such unheard of screams that you would not have believed your ears. Finally we came to an agreement in such a manner that I can tell you that she seemed to have been brought up in a school of harlots."

And the letter to the Marquis of Mantua, announcing that vessels of the King of Spain "discovered certain islands, among others a very large island toward the Orient which had very great rivers and terrible mountains and a most fertile country inhabited by handsome men and women, but they all go naked, except that some wear a leaf of cotton over their genitals . . ."

Melville, in TYPEE:

". . . we found ourselves close in with the island the next morning, but as the bay we sought lay on its farther side, we were obliged to sail some distance along the shore, catching, as we proceeded, short glimpses of blooming valleys, deep glens, waterfalls, and waving groves, hidden here and there by projecting and rocky headlands, every moment opening to the view some new and startling scene of beauty."

"As they drew nearer, and I watched the rising and sinking of their forms, and beheld the uplifted right arm bearing above the water the girdle of tapa, and their long dark hair trailing beside them as they swam, I almost fancied they could be nothing else than so many mermaids . . ."

> (Columbus, First Voyage: "On the previous day, when the Admiral went to the Rio del Oro, he saw three mermaids, which rose well out of the sea . . .")

TYPEE: "We were still some distance from the beach, and under slow headway, when we sailed right into the midst of these swimming nymphs, and they boarded us at every quarter; many seizing hold of the chainplates and springing into the chains; others . . . wreathing their slender forms about the ropes . . . All of them at length succeeded in getting up the ship's side, where they clung dripping with the brine and glowing from the bath, their jet-black tresses streaming over their shoulders, and half-enveloping their otherwise naked forms. There they hung, sparkling with savage vivacity . . ."
"Our ship was now given up to every species of riot . . ."

But Columbus in Spain, fourteen eighty-five to ninety-two:

> "All this delay did not go without great anguish and grief for
> Cristóbal Colón, for ... he saw his life was flowing past wasted ...
> and above all because he saw how distrusted his truth and person
> were, which for generous persons it is known to be as painful and
> detestable as death."

Columbus waited.

FIVF

I am lifted from my chair, headlong. I stand, leaning over the desk,
my head whirling, consonant with the gusts of blackberry winter, of
the catbird storm. Decision crowds upon me, and, like one of the
sperm whales crowding for the Straits of Sunda, pursued by a Nan-
tucket madman who is in turn pursued by Malays, I push for a gate-
way, an entrance upon and beginning of things.

August 2nd, 1492,

ninth day of the Jewish Ab, The Father, when Jewry mourned the
destruction of Jerusalem . . . the exodus from Spain began. Three
hundred thousand funneled to the seaports, not far from "the
beginning of Europe."

> "Those who went to embark in El Puerto de Santa Maria
> and in Cadiz, as soon as they saw the sea, shouted and yelled,
> men and women, grown-ups and children, asking mercy of
> the Lord in their prayers, and they thought they would see
> some marvels from God and that they would have a road
> opened for them across the sea . . ."

But the Jews embarked and headed back east, into the internal sea, to the old haunts . . . and

on that day, Columbus ordered his men aboard three ships, before night-fall.

Perhaps, within himself, Christopher journeyed to the old haunts, herded himself into the tribe, to Esdras of the Apocrypha, to the earlier prophets, and to Genesis;

but it is not so much that Columbus may have been a Jew, or Melville at war with Christ, as it is that both men ran upward to the sources. Melville, an Ishmael, and Columbus, displaying an arrogance greater than Joan's, sought the prophets—men who, like the first king of Atlantis, imagined and predicted, and from whom, therefore, action flowed . . .

> (Columbus the navigator: "All people received their astronomy from the Jews."

August 3,

before daylight of a gray, calm day—a day so quiet that one would think time had stopped—three ships slipped from their moorings—the motion a thing good and confirming—and drifted down the Rio Tinto on the tide. Guided by the sweeps, with no wind, the ships altered their course to port, and entered the Rio Saltes, floating past the piney sand dunes, and spoke another ship, outward bound on the same tide, with a cargo of emigrant Jews

> (and the Pinta spoke the same ship on the return voyage of both, the one bound from the Levant, the other from the Indies . . .

Turning fifty degrees to starboard, the fleet crossed the bar, and

> "proceeded with a strong breeze until sunset, towards the south, for 60 miles, equal to 15 leagues . . ."

There was the letter from Paul Toscanelli, Florentine physician and philosopher (in those days, the one implied the other):

> "To Christopher Columbus, Paul the physician, greeting: I see your great and magnificent desire to go where the spices grow, and in reply to your letter I send you the copy of another letter which I wrote a long time ago . . . and I send you another seaman's chart . . . And although I know from my own knowledge that the world can be shown as it is in the form of a sphere, I have determined for greater facility and greater intelligence to show the said route by a chart similar to those which are made for navigation . . . straight to the west the commencement of the Indies is shown, and the islands and places where you can deviate towards the equinoctial line, and by how much space, that is to say, in how many leagues you can reach those most fertile places, filled with all kinds of spices and jewels and precious stones: and you must not wonder if I call the place where spices grow, *West,* because it is commonly said that they grow in the *East;* but whoever will navigate to the West will always find the said places in the West . . ."

But Columbus did not head "straight to the west," but

South and by West, for the Canaries, and, further, for the Terrestrial Paradise . . .

Monday August 6,

> "The rudder of the caravel *Pinta* became unshipped, and Martin Alonzo Pinzon, who was in command, believed or suspected that it was by contrivance of Gomes Rascon and Cristobal Quintero, to whom the caravel belonged, for they dreaded to go on that voyage. The Admiral says that, before they sailed, these men had been displaying a certain backwardness . . ."

Still standing, I step back from the desk, gaining my sea-legs. I am braced, with one hand on the chimney. The house arches and shudders—an inverted hull, with kelson aloft—against the weather.
and the human sperm enters a reservoir, low in oxygen—and thence to the

vas deferens, in the lowest, coolest scrotal area . . .

upward, then, through the spermatic cord, to globus minor and the seminal vesicle . . .

The Canaries: insular remnants, perhaps, of Atlantis—thence to Antillia, showing on Toscanelli's chart half-way to Cathay. Antillia: of which the Indies might be scattered remnants . . .

The ships were shaken down . . . there were no desertions at the Canaries. The voyage was begun . . .

Sunday September 9:

> **"On this day they lost sight of land; and many, fearful of not being able to return for a long time to see it, sighed and shed tears. But the admiral . . . when that day the sailors reckoned the distance 18 leagues, said he had counted only 15, having decided to lessen the record so that the crew would not think they were as far from Spain as in fact they were."**

So a great head shrinks the distance . . .

shrinks the very globe itself:—for it was only the bold and persistent acceptance of cosmographical errors in the mind of Columbus— shrinking the earth by a quarter, and juggling Cypango until it fell among the Virgin Islands—that made possible the discovery . . .

> (and in San Salvador, Columbus noted among the natives that "the whole forehead and head is very broad"—the result of artificially flattening the skulls of infants, by pressing them between boards.

Monday September 17:

> **Passing the true north, Columbus—making the "pilot's blessing"— marked the North Star, and noted that the needle now began pointing to the west of north, instead of to the customary east.**

"All the sailors feared greatly and all became very sad, and began to murmur under their breaths again, without making it known altogether to Christopher Columbus, seeing such a new thing, and one they had never seen or experienced, and there they feared they were in another world."

MOBY-DICK:—*"At first, the steel went round and round, quivering and vibrating at either end; but at last it settled to its place, when Ahab, who had been intently watching for this result, stepped frankly back from the binnacle, and pointing his stretched arm towards it, exclaimed,—'Look ye, for yourselves, if Ahab be not Lord of the level loadstone! . . .'*

"One after another they peered in, for nothing but their own eyes could persuade such ignorance as theirs, and one after another they slunk away."

Whale, boobie, sandpiper, dove, crab, and boatswain bird—all were signs of land . . . for hitherto none had sailed far enough to see such things other than close to land . . .

and there was sargasso weed, rumored to trap ships as in a web . . . detritus, perhaps, of Atlantis . . .

From the posterior, the vault of the vagina, the sperm's journey measures, perhaps, five inches. The cilia in the oviduct have an outward stroke, against the motion of the sperm . . .

(Columbus reported the usual course of the sargasso weed to be from west to east . . .

In addition, there are the folds and ridges, like waves, of the mucous membrane, and the powerful leukocytes, white monsters that attack the sperm.

"Forward progress of the human spermatozoon is at the rate of about 1.5 mm a minute which, in relation to their respective lengths, compares well with average swimming ability for man."

Driven by temperature and secretions, the sperm's action is a fight against time; for

"A spermatozoon is only fertile if it is capable of performing *powerful* movements."

Olson, on Melville: "He only rode his own space once—MOBY-DICK. He had to be wild or he was nothing in particular. He had to go fast, like an American . . ."

Thus, the spermatozoon, like the salmon, swimming "a spiral course upstream."

September 19:

". . . but as the land never appeared they presently believed nothing, concluding from those signs since they failed, that they were going through another world whence they would never return."

September 24:

". . . they said that it was a great madness and homicidal on their part, to venture their lives in following out the madness of a foreigner, who . . . had risked his life . . . and was deceiving so many people: especially as his proposition or dream had been contradicted by so many great and lettered men, and considered as vain and foolish: and that it was enough to excuse themselves from whatever might be done in the matter, that they had arrived where men had never dared to navigate, and that they were not obliged to go to the end of the world . . ."

"Some went further, saying, that if he persisted in going onward, that the best thing of all was to throw him into the sea some night, publishing that he had fallen in taking the position of the star with his quadrant or astrolabe . . ."

Ahab, in MOBY-DICK: *"Then gazing at his quadrant, and handling one after the other, its numerous cabalistical contrivances, he pondered again, and muttered: 'Foolish toy! babies' plaything of haughty Admirals, and Commodores, and Captains; the world brags of thee, of thy cunning and might; but what after all canst thou do, but tell the poor, pitiful point, where thou thyself happenest to be in this wide planet, and the hand that holds thee: no! not one jot more! Thou canst not tell where one drop of water or one grain of sand will be to-morrow noon; and yet with thy impotence thou insultest the sun! Science! Curse thee, thou vain toy; and cursed be all things that cast men's eyes aloft to that heaven, whose live vividness but scorches him, as these old eyes are even now scorched with thy light, O sun! Level by nature to this earth's horizon are the glances of man's eyes; not shot from the crown of his head, as if God had meant him to gaze on his firmament. Curse thee, thou quadrant!' dashing it to the deck, 'no longer will I guide my earthly way by thee; the level ship's compass, and the level dead-reckoning, by log and by line; these shall conduct me, and show me my place on the sea.'"*

And Columbus—greatest dead-reckoning navigator of all time, whose bearings may be followed and trusted today, whose faulty observations of the stars never interfered with his level look at sea, signs, and weather— Columbus

> "here says that he has had the quadrant hung up until he reaches land, to repair it . . ."

October 7, course changed from West to West-South-West, to follow the great flocks of birds overhead.

October 10:

> "Here the people could endure no longer. They complained of the length of the voyage. But the Admiral cheered them up in the best way he could, giving them good hopes of the advantages they might gain from it. He added that, however much they might complain, he had to go to the Indies, and that he would go on until he found them . . ."

Ahab: "'What is it, what nameless, inscrutable, unearthly thing is it; what cozening, hidden lord and master, and cruel, remorseless emperor commands me; that against all natural lov-

*ings and longings, I so keep pushing, and crowding, and jam-
ming myself on all the time . . . ?'"*

October 11:

> The crew of the *Pinta* picked up "a reed and a stick, and another
> stick carved, as it seemed, with iron tools and some grass which
> grows on land and a tablet of wood. They all breathed on seeing
> these signs and felt great joy."

October 11:

> ". . . the Admiral asked and admonished the men to keep a good
> look-out on the forecastle, and to watch well for land . . ."

> *"'It's a white whale, I say' resumed Ahab . . .: 'a white whale.
> Skin your eyes for him, men; look sharp for white water; if ye see
> but a bubble, sing out.'"*

> ". . . and to him who should first cry out that he saw land, he would
> give a silk doublet, besides the other rewards promised by the Sov-
> ereigns, which were 10,000 maravedis to him who should first see
> it."

> *"'Whosoever of ye raises me a white-headed whale with a wrin-
> kled brow and a crooked jaw; whosoever of ye raises me that
> white-headed whale, with three holes punctured in his star-
> board fluke—look ye, whosoever of ye raises me that same white
> whale, he shall have this gold ounce my boys!'"*

October 11, course changed again to West.

> > (As a traveler to unknown parts, Columbus was of
> > course expected to bring back tales of fish growing
> > on trees men with tails and headless people with
> > eyes in their bellies . . .

And there was the light, seen by Columbus—or so he says—two hours

before midnight on the Eleventh: ". . . like a little wax candle rising and falling." Be it the pine-knot torch of an Indian . . . sea worms, phosphorescent . . . or the jammed and crowded imaginings of Christopher . . . whatever it be, Columbus, on the strength of it, claimed his own doublet, and the Sovereigns' 10,000 maravedis . . .

> *Ahab: "'. . . the doubloon is mine, Fate reserved the doubloon for me. I only; none of ye could have raised the White Whale first. There she blows! . . .'"*

Like a great albuminous globe, monstrous beyond all proportion, the ovum looms ahead . . .

October 12:

> "At two hours after midnight the land was sighted . . ."

CHARYBDIS

ONE

AFTER ALASKA, Carl came back to Indianapolis, with a duffle bag of old clothes and odd relics . . . bits of bone from walrus, seal, and man, pieces of carved wood, various stones shaped by the ocean, or by Carl himself, or perhaps by long-dead Indians. He stayed (as always) only a short time . . . "just long enough to change my sox." Then he was off, apparently without funds (this is another story, where his money came from, where he got it, or whose it was—he never seemed to have any except just when he needed it, and then only just enough), heading east . . .

and the next we heard he was in Spain, flying a plane . . . seat of the pants flying, he said, no instruments, no time to learn (he had never flown before) . . . for the Loyalists.

Columbus:

> "this night the wind increased, and the waves were terrible, rising against each other and so shaking and straining the vessel that she would make no headway, and was in danger of being stove in."

The first return voyage:—as on all eastward voyages, the voyages of return, voyages back—opposite and contrary to those westward— he met dirty weather.

> "At sunrise the wind blew still harder, and the cross sea was terrific. They continued to show the closely reefed mainsail to enable her to rise from between the waves, or she would otherwise have been swamped."

For two days, on board the *Niña*, the officer of the watch scanned each on-coming wave, and gave quick orders to the helmsman, in order that the wave might be met at the best angle. All contact with the *Pinta* was lost, and no attempt was made to hold to a course.

"... no one expected to escape, holding themselves for lost, owing to the fearful weather ..."

"Here the Admiral writes of the causes that made him fear he would perish, and of others that gave him hope that God would work his salvation, in order that such news as he was bringing to the Sovereigns might not be lost. It seemed to him the strong desire he felt to bring such great news, and to show that all he had said and offered to discover had turned out true, suggested the fear that he would not be able to do so ..."

> *(Melville to Hawthorne: "... I am so pulled hither and thither by circumstances. The calm, the coolness, the silent grass-growing mood in which a man* ought *always to compose,—that, I fear, can seldom be mine.")*

"He says further that it gave him great sorrow to think of the two sons he had left at their studies in Cordova, who would be left ... without father ..., in a strange land; while the Sovereigns would not know of the services he had performed in this voyage, nor would they receive the prosperous news which would move them to help the orphans."

And Melville in Pittsfield, winter of 1851, writing MOBY-DICK: *his son Malcolm an infant, and Lizzie pregnant again: to Hawthorne: "Dollars damn me ..."*

"... that the Sovereigns might still have information, even if he perished in the storm, he took a parchment and wrote on it as good an account as he could of all he had discovered ... He rolled this parchment up in waxed cloth, fastened it very securely, ordered a large wooden barrel to be brought, and put it inside ... and so he ordered the barrel to be thrown into the sea."

Lizzie, reporting Herman: "Wrote White Whale or Moby Dick
under unfavorable circumstances—would sit at his desk all day
not eating anything till four or five oclock—then ride to the vil-
lage after dark . . ."

. . . heading for the conclusion, the disaster, the sinking of the
Pequod:

Melville, as Starbuck: ". . . may survive to hug his wife and
child again.—Oh Mary! Mary!—boy! boy! boy! . . . who can
tell to what unsounded deeps Starbuck's body this day week may
sink . . . !"

And Ahab, to Captain Gardiner of the Rachel *(who has begged*
him to join in searching for his lost son): "Captain Gardiner, I
will not do it. Even now I lose time. Good bye, good bye. God
bless ye, man, and may I forgive myself . . ."

Ahab to Starbuck: "I see my wife and my child in thine eye."

And: "About this time—yes, it is his noon nap now—the boy
vivaciously wakes; sits up in bed; and his mother tells him of me,
of cannibal old me . . ."

Pittsfield, 1851—the infant Malcolm; Lizzie, pregnant; and cannibal
old Melville, in the chase:

"At length the breathless hunter came so nigh his seemingly
unsuspecting prey, that his entire dazzling hump was distinct-
ly visible, sliding along the sea as if an isolated thing, and con-
tinually set in a revolving ring of finest, fleecy greenish foam.
He saw the vast involved wrinkles of the slightly projecting
head beyond."

From the medical book: "It is even assumed that the ovum itself has
a certain radiation designed to attract the spermatozoa."

(Ahab: ". . . the most vital stuff of vital fathers."

"As soon as the first spermatozoa have reached the ovum, they surround it and try to penetrate with their heads the outer membrane."

Starbuck: "Oh! my God! what is this that . . . leaves me so deadly calm, yet expectant,—fixed at the top of a shudder! Future things swim before me, as in empty outlines and skeletons; all the past is somehow grown dim. Mary, girl! thou fadest in pale glories behind me; boy! I seem to see but thy eyes grown wondrous blue."

Again, the wind hesitates, the children below are quiet. The sensation I have had of the attic as a ship, pitching upon the plain, is gone, and I tilt back in the chair, balancing on the back legs; my body is still, and numb,

and glancing upward, I notice the crossbeam, a tremendous piece of oak, hand-hewn, that divides the attic over my desk . . . something associated with it comes to mind, and in a moment I recall

the tornado

We had seen it coming from the front porch, and my father had herded us—Mother, Carl, and myself—into the basement, while he went first to the barn to secure a logging chain, and then returned to the house, and climbed (we could hear his footsteps, the chain clanking on the stairs behind him) to the attic . . . then there was silence, save for the rising wind. I was little then, easily held by the wrist, but Carl, whining and squirming, suddenly broke away, and before he could be reached he had jumped the steps three at a time and was gone . . . Mother screamed after him, but didn't follow: she tightened her grip on me, and let him go. The house fairly shook, we heard the barn roof lifting and settling in the pasture, some of the other outbuildings collapsing, and we thought for a moment that the roof of the house had been moved . . . After it was over, Father would say little, except to command Carl to what was left of the barn for punishment . . .

but Carl—the excitement of the storm mixed with the tears of his beating—couldn't wait to tell me what had happened: how Father had lifted planks, had secured one end of the chain to floor beams, the other to the cross-beam overhead; how the roof had started to lift, and the chain had held—but the second time, the chain had broken, and Father had grasped an end in each hand . . .

. . . when the roof lifted a third time, Father had spreadeagled himself, his feet off the floor, the whole superstructure held by his hands, arms, and shoulders . . .

> (Melville: "And prove that oak, and iron, and man/Are tough in fibre yet . . ."

The roof twisted slightly, and settled back in its old position . . .

. . . and after, Father had deliberately unfastened the chain, surveyed the broken link, restored the floor planks, and (although he had taken no notice of him, Carl had thought himself undiscovered) called to Carl, dragged him from his hiding place near the eaves, and marched him to the barn for a thrashing . . .

It was the Polar Front—meeting of Polar Continental and Tropical Maritime—that caused Columbus' dirty weather. The violent air masses, forming a circular motion . . .

> (Bondi, COSMOLOGY: "The nebulae show great similarity amongst themselves. They are probably all rotating and many of them show a spiral structure."

. . . create a hurricane, or perhaps tornado or waterspout, a sucking up . . .

But Columbus, first and always a navigator, fought it out . . .

and Melville, too, whose eye was level . . .

(". . . let me look into a human eye; it is better than to gaze upon God."

. . . went—not up—but sounding, into the whirlpool, the vortex . . .

. . . went down.

". . . resuming his horizontal attitude, Moby-Dick swam swiftly round and round the wrecked crew; sideways churning the water in his vengeful wake, as if lashing himself up to still another and more deadly assault. The sight of the splintered boat seemed to madden him . . . Meanwhile Ahab half smothered in the foam of the whale's insolent tail, and too much of a cripple to swim,—though he could still keep afloat, even in the heart of such a whirlpool as that; helpless Ahab's head was seen, like a tossed bubble . . ."

The vortex: ". . . whose centre had now become the old man's head."

TWO

Hur obed, the Phoenician sailors called it: *hole of perdition . . .*

Charybdis.

And on the second voyage, Columbus, sailing along the southern coast of Cuba, suddenly "entered a white sea, which was as white as milk, and as thick as the water in which tanners treat their skins." The colors changed—white, green, crystal-clear, to black—and the men recalled old Arabic tales of the Green Sea of Gloom, and endless shoals that fringed the edge of the world.

". . . there was no room to shoot up into the wind and anchor; nor was there holding ground . . ."

Carib Charybdis—such, perhaps, as Hart Crane—the ocean
already in his head—leaped into . . .

First voyage, return: "All night they were beating to windward, and
going as near as they could, so as to see some way to the island at
sunrise. That night the Admiral got a little rest, for he had not slept
nor been able to sleep since Wednesday, and he had lost the use of
his legs from long exposure to the wet and cold."

And elsewhere, contending with cannibals: "The barbarians, being
only three men with two women and a single Indian captive . . . per-
severed in seeking safety by swimming, in which art they are skilful.
At last they were captured and taken to the Admiral. One of them
was pierced through in seven places and his intestines protruded
from his wounds. Since it was believed that he could not be healed,
he was thrown into the sea. But emerging to the surface, with one
foot upraised, and with his left hand holding his intestines in their
place, he swam courageously towards the shore. This caused great
alarm to the Indians who were brought along as interpreters . . . The
Cannibal was therefore recaptured near the shore, bound hand and
foot more tightly, and again thrown headlong into the sea. This res-
olute barbarian swam still more eagerly towards the shore, till, tran-
spierced with many arrows, he at length expired."

Reaching Portugal, ". . . they were told that such a winter, with as
many storms, had never before been known, and that 25 ships had
been lost in Flanders . . ."

And on Española, at Navidad, a few Spaniards had been left behind,
the first colonists: "These, fighting bravely to the last, when they
could no longer withstand the attack of the thronged battalions of
their foes, were at length cut to pieces. The information conveyed . . .
was confirmed by the discovery of the dead bodies of ten Spaniards.
These bodies were emaciated and ghastly, covered with dust and
bespattered with blood, discoloured, and retaining still a fierce
aspect. They had lain now nearly three months neglected and
unburied under the open air."

MOBY-DICK: *"At length as the craft was cast to one side, and ran ranging along with the White Whale's flank, he seemed strangely oblivious of its advance—as the whale sometimes will—and Ahab was fairly within the smoky mountain mist, which, thrown off from the whale's spout, curled round his great Monadnock hump; he was even thus close to him; when, with body arched back, and both arms lengthwise high-lifted to the poise . . ."*

> (Melville, elsewhere: ". . . since all human affairs are subject to organic disorder, since they are created in and sustained by a sort of half-disciplined chaos, hence he who in great things seeks success must never wait for smooth water, which never was and never will be, but, with what straggling method he can, dash with all his derangements at his object . . .")

". . . he darted his fierce iron, and his far fiercer curse into the whale."

The medical book: "Once within the periphery of the ovum the sperm's head and neck detach from its tail which may be left wholly outside and in no case plays any part in the events to follow. The head next rotates 180° and proceeds toward the centre of the egg where the egg nucleus, having finished the maturative divisions, awaits it. During this journey the sperm head enlarges, becomes open-structured, and is converted into the *male pronucleus*."

The head enlarges, becomes open-structured . . . I tilt forward, the front legs of the chair striking the floor, and then turn to face the far end, the western end of the attic . . . turning, then, completely around, I face the desk again, and become dizzy . . .

> MOBY-DICK: *"And now, concentric circles seized the lone boat itself, and all its crew, and each floating oar, and every lance-pole, and spinning, animate and inanimate, all round and round in one vortex, carried the smallest chip of the Pequod out of sight."*

(Melville, elsewhere: ". . . in tremendous ex-
tremities human souls are like drowning men;
well enough they know they are in peril; well
enough they know the causes of that peril;—
nevertheless, the sea is the sea, and these drown-
ing men do drown."

To Hawthorne: "The Whale *is completed."*

THREE

But the waters came pouring in, rushing and filling:

"My dear Hawthorne, the atmospheric skepticisms steal into me
now, and make me doubtful of my sanity . . ."

and

". . . let us add Moby Dick to our blessing, and step from that.
Leviathan is not the biggest fish;—I have heard of Krakens."

(a sea-monster, mile and a half in circumfer-
ence, darkening the ocean with a black liquid,
and causing a gigantic whirlpool when it
sinks . . .

MOBY-DICK: *"Now small fowls flew screaming over the yet*
yawning gulf; a sullen white surf beat against its steep sides;
then all collapsed, and the great shroud of the sea rolled on as it
rolled five thousand years ago."

. . . rolled on over Herman Melville, his compatriots and descen-
dants, who breathed and wrote, thenceforth, from within the ocean.
But there was that which followed after the closing of the waters:
there was the family . . .

Lizzie, wife to Herman, and counterpole to Fayaway . . .

> (with Columbus—discoverer, beginner—the order was reversed: wife first, and then mistress . . .

. . . struggling to help by copying MARDI (whose fogs she could not penetrate), and

> *"My cold is very bad indeed, perhaps worse than it has ever been so early . . ."*

There was the bond:

Lizzie, whose mother died in delivering her, and who might have said to herself, "I killed my mother"; and who, having been thus abandoned, would have been strongly averse to abandoning Herman . . .

Lizzie, who, like Hart Crane, suffered from hay fever, and thus, wet-headed, mourned her mother . . .

and Herman, as Jonah, swallowed by a white monster—Herman, who might have said: "My mother killed me" . . .

> *(and Maria Melville, as Mrs. Glendinning: "I feel now as though I had borne the last of a swiftly to be extinguished race . . ."*

In any case—love, prestige, privation—they were established: Lizzie and Herman . . . Mr. & Mrs. Herman Melville . . . Mr. H. Melville, & wife.

And there were the children:
Mackey,
Stanny,
Bessie,
& Fanny,

hovering at the edge of the storm, the vortex, and

killed, crippled, or withered, according to the order of birth, to how near in time (the father's *space*) they came

to the eye of it.

Melville—as good a parent as, say, Columbus was an administrator—was more of a prophet:

> There was the letter to Mackey, 1860: "Whilst the sailors were aloft on one of the yards, the ship rolled and plunged terribly; and it blew with sleet and hail, and was very cold & biting. Well, all at once, Uncle Tom saw something falling through the air, and then heard a thump, and then,—looking before him, saw a poor sailor lying dead on the deck. He had fallen from the yard, and was killed instantly."

> (Mackey, you shall die violently . . .

> And the letter written by Stanny, as a little boy, to his grandmother: "Papa took me to the cattle show grounds to see the soldiers drill, but we did not see them, . . . it was too bad. But papa took me a ride all through the Cemetary."

> (Stanny, you shall die quietly . . .

> And the letter Melville wrote to Bessie, 1860: "Many [sea-birds] have followed the ship day after day . . . they were all over speckled—and they would sometimes, during a calm, keep behind the ship, fluttering about in the water, with a mighty cackling, and wherever anything was thrown overboard they would hurry to get it. But they would never light on the ship—they kept all the time flying or else resting themselves by floating on the water like ducks in a pond. These birds have no home, unless it is some wild rocks in the middle of the ocean."

> (Bessie, you shall be homeless . . .

And the children responded:

Mackey, age 18, young dog, fond of firearms, who slept with a pistol under his pillow—came home one night at 3 A.M., and failed to rise in the morning.

> *"Time went on and Herman advised Lizzie to let him sleep, be late at the office & take the consequences as a sort of punishment . . ."*

> *". . . in the evening, the door of the room was opened, and young Melville was found dead, lying on the bed, with a single-barrelled pistol firmly grasped in his right hand, and a pistol-shot wound in the right temple."*

> > *(Melville: "I wish you could have seen him as he lay in his last attitude, the ease of a gentle nature.")*

> *And the funeral: ". . . the young Volunteer Company to which Malcolm belonged & who had asked the privilege of being present & carrying the coffin from the house to the cars—filed in at one door from the hall & out at the other—each pausing for an instant to look at the face of their lost comrade. Cousin Helen says they were all so young & it was really a sadly beautiful sight—for the cold limbs of the dead wore the same garments as the strong active ones of the living—Cousin Lizzie—his almost heart broken Mother having dressed her eldest son in the new suit he had taken such pride & pleasure in wearing—Four superb wreaths and crosses of the choicest white flowers were placed on the coffin . . ."*

And after, the family pondered whether it was suicide or accident, not thinking that Mackey had held the pistol, and Mackey had pulled the trigger—

the only question being whether he had been conscious of his actions, of his motives.

And there was Stanny:

> *"My deafness has been a great trouble to me lately . . ."*

>> (What was he trying to drown out—the
>> brother's gunshot? . . . the family arguments?
>> . . . or:

> *Stanwix: "I fear it will give you but little pleasure to hear from
> one, who has been guilty of so many follies, and deaf to the coun-
> sel of older heads."*

> And: *"Stanwix is full of the desire to go to sea, & see something
> of this great world. He used to talk to me about it, but I always
> tried to talk him out of it. But now he seems so bent upon it, that
> Herman & Lizzie have given their consent, thinking that* one
> *voyage to China will cure him of the fancy."*

But it took more than one voyage to cure his father . . .

> *"What have you heard of Stanwix Melville from what point
> did he run away? & where was his place of destination? Poor
> Cousin Lizzie She will be almost broken hearted."*

A shadow of his father, even to the running away . . . or perhaps,
simply, escaping the disaster . . .

> *Later: "You know I left New York in April & went to a small
> town in Kansas, I staid there a few weeks, then I thought I
> could do better South so I came down through the Indian
> Nation, & then into Arkansas, I stopped at a number of towns
> on the Arkansas river till I came to the Mississippi, then down
> that river to Vicksburgh I staid there a few days, & then took
> the train to Jackson, from there by Railroad to New Orleans, I
> found that a lively city, but no work, so I thought I should like
> a trip to Central America, I went on a steamer to Havana,
> Cuba & from there to half a dozen or more ports on the Central
> America coast till I came to Limon Bay in Costa Rica."*

Columbus, fourth voyage, off Central America: "It was one continu-
al rain, thunder and lightning. The ships lay exposed to the weather,
with sails torn, and anchors, rigging, cables, boats and many of the
stores lost; the people exhausted . . . Other tempests I have seen, but
none that lasted so long or so grim as this. Many old hands whom we
looked on as stout fellows lost their courage. . . . I was sick and many
times lay at death's door, but gave orders from a dog-house that the
people clapped together for me on the poop deck."

Rounding Cabo Gracia á Dios, he was able to coast southward to
what is now called Limon Bay, in Costa Rica, where he anchored
and rested for ten days.

> *Stanny: "I walked from there on the beach with two other young
> fellows to Greytown in Nicaragua, one of the boys died on the
> beach, & we dug a grave in the sand by the sea, & buried him,
> & travelled on again, each of us not knowing who would have
> to bury the other before we got there, as we were both sick with
> the fever & ague."*

Columbus drifted down the coast, searching for a passage, a chan-
nel to the Red Sea . . .

> (Plato, describing Atlantis: ". . . and drove a canal
> through the zones of land three hundred feet in
> width, about a hundred feet deep, and about sixty
> miles in length. At the landward end of this water-
> way, which was capable of navigation by the largest
> vessels, they constructed a harbour. The two zones
> of land were cut by large canals, by which means a
> trireme, or three-decked galley, was able to pass
> from one sea-zone to another."

> *Stanny: "I went up the San Juan river to Lake Nicaragua about
> a hundred miles with a Naval surveying expedition going up to
> survey for a ship Canal . . .*

. . . searching for a canal, a short-cut, to avoid the rigors of the long
voyage . . .

(Melville, commenting on Emerson: "To one who has weathered Cape Horn as a common sailor what stuff all this is."

Stanny: ". . . from Greytown I shipped on a schooner for Aspinwall; after arriving in Aspinwall, I got wrecked there in that heavy gale of wind . . . and I lost all my clothes, & every thing I had, & was taken sick again with the fever, I went into the hospital there, & then came home on the Steamer Henry Chauncey, where I find the cold weather agrees with me much better, than the sun of the tropics.
Now I say New York forever."

Later: "I am happy to announce to you that this morning I went to work for a dentist, a Dr. Read; I went to his office on Saturday, & told him I wanted a place to work & perfect myself in the profession . . ."

MOBY-DICK: *"With a long, weary hoist the jaw is dragged on board, as if it were an anchor; and when the proper time comes—some few days after the other work—Queequeg, Dagoo, and Tashtego, being all accomplished dentists, are set to drawing teeth. With a keen cutting-spade, Queequeg lances the gums; then the jaw is lashed down to ringbolts, and a tackle being rigged from aloft, they drag out these teeth, as Michigan oxen drag stumps of old oaks out of wild wood-lands."*

And in MARDI, the cannibals wore teeth as ornaments, and hoarded them as money—teeth, like money, being the means of eating . . .

(Stanny: ". . . in a few years I will be independent of any man."

But: "I have encountered a serious obstacle which will prevent me from becoming a number one dentist, & that is I am too near sighted; I found it out as quick as I commenced operating in the mouth . . . I am going to sail Wednesday for San Francisco . . ."

Lizzie: "We have better news from Stanny—He is on a sheep-ranch in California . . ."

And: "I wanted to tell you that we are expecting Stanny home in a short time—A very favorable opening for his going back to his old business, mechanical *dentistry offered itself . . ."*

"Stanny begs me to thank you very much for all your kind wishes—he is very well now (with the exception of a little bowel trouble) . . ."

1875, departs for San Francisco, and

"There is a party of five or six of us that are going to start for the Black Hills country about the middle or last of January . . . I have made up my mind, this is a chance, & I may be lucky there, at any rate I can get miners wages which is more than I can make here . . . and I am going this winter if I die of starvation or get frozen to death on the road."

Lizzie: "I have been writing to Stanny . . . he has been sick poor fellow, and had to go in the hospital at Sacramento . . ."

"We hear constantly from Stanny—I wish I could say he is materially better . . ."

". . . a good deal worried about Stanny's health—his pulmonary troubles have been worse . . ."

and Melville, now age 66—whose own paternity had been blasted, who had been thrust loose in an earlier world—signs a letter to Stanny:

Good bye, & God bless you
Your affectionate Father
H. Melville.

A death notice:

MELVILLE—At San Francisco, Cal., 23ᵈ inst., Stanwix, son of Herman and Elizabeth S. Melville, in the 35th year of his age.

And there was Bessie, third-born, and oldest daughter:

thin, small, weak-voiced, but with a sharp tongue (she liked raw humor),

crippled with arthritis (they never saw such feet on one who could still walk), afraid of strong winds, afraid that she would be blown over . . .

lived with her mother, and then alone, an old maid (she didn't like little children, couldn't stand their little smelly drawers),

and when she died, quarts of black liquid—undigested food—were found in her system . . .

And finally, Fanny, last-born, furthest removed from the disaster,

who salvaged life and fertility (she married a man from Philadelphia, and gave birth to four daughters . . .

who nevertheless had her troubles (and blamed them all on her own father . . .

developed arthritis (she could be seen on the porch of her summer home, Edgartown—white-headed, her sweet, gentle face, white, she in a white dress—her leg out stiff, arthritic . . .

and died, finally, incontinent and placid, a baby—1935.

Thus the four children of Herman Melville:

The men:

one, dead by his own hand, and the other, wasted . . .

> *(Melville, as Pierre: "Lo! I leave corpses wher-*
> *ever I go!"*

And the women:

arthritic, motionless, holding against the down-rushing waters . . .

And hovering over all, moving, surviving, through the long term of Melville's life, and beyond—was Lizzie . . .

Shifting again, I glance, not upward, as at the crossbeam, but downward, between my legs, at the floor . . . and I recall (my arms and legs are tense, a little tired, as though strained) waiting in the basement, alone with Mother, during the tornado . . . the loneliness, the wanting to be with Carl, wanting to be, as he was, up in the rigging, in the storm, with Father—and having to wait, instead, in the darkness, in the grip that I was too young to break . . . lifting my eyes level again, I read

that the bride of Columbus in all probability did not survive five years of the marriage; and

> "Not the slightest hint has come down to us of the appearance or disposition of Columbus's only wife; Dona Felipa is as shadowy a figure as the Discoverer's mother."

> (About Melville's wife, and mother, a great
> deal is known . . .

Whether dead or still living, Dona Felipa was abandoned when Columbus left Portugal.

And on the first voyage, early in the return, Columbus set out to discover the island of *Matinino,* inhabited, as the Indians told him, only by women; for this might be Marco Polo's *Feminea* . . .

. . . but the ships were leaking, and the wind blew strong from the west: he changed his course for Spain.

Third voyage: ". . . at the lengthe an Eastsoutheaste wynde arose, and gave a prosperous blaste to his sayles." . . . the fleet coasted before the trades, through "El Golfo de las Damas," the Ladies' Sea . . .

And Mellville, late in life, in a letter: "But you do not know, perhaps, that I have already entered my eighth decade. After twenty years nearly, as an outdoor Customs House officer, I have latterly come into possession of unobstructed leisure, but only just as, in the course of nature, my vigor sensibly declines."

Columbus, on the third voyage, executed one of the most extraordinary feats of dead-reckoning navigation: Margarita (The Terrestrial Paradise) to Hispaniola . . .

and arriving, troubled with gout, found the colony disorganized, Roldan in rebellion . . . and instead of clean action, fighting and subduing Roldan, he negotiated, submitted to a set of humiliating agreements . . .

(Fanny, describing Melville, his later peacefulness: "He just didn't have the energy any more . . ."

. . . and later he was put in fetters (darbies, Melville called them) and sent back to Spain, on what proved to be the only eastward voyage, return voyage, accompanied by any sort of good weather . . .

(on shipboard, they offered to take off the fetters, but he refused, declared that he would wear them until he had the opportunity to kneel with them still on, before the Sovereigns. Ever after this, he guarded them jealously, kept them in his room, directed that they be interred with his body . . .
Melville, reading Homer, checks and underscores: "The work that I was born to do is done!"

After the Civil War, when Franco had won, Carl teamed with a Spanish family, four brothers and a sister: Rico, Rafael, Salomón, Diego, and Concha—old Spanish aristocrats (though they had been fighting, so Carl claimed, for the Loyalists). All wanted to get out of Spain (the Spaniards complained that no one spoke Spanish, it was all Russian and German), so they acquired a yacht and set sail for Cuba . . .

. . . where Carl lived for several years, becoming embroiled in one after another of the rebellions. One by one, three of the four brothers (Rico alone escaped) were destroyed, aligning themselves on different sides in the fighting . . . Carl carried with him a photo of Rafael, his shirt torn, his body spattered with blood, lying drenched in sunlight on the pavement, where he had fallen . . . it came out (when Carl was drunk) that they had been fighting on opposite sides, and that perhaps it had been Carl's own gun that had killed him . . .

We heard little of Concha, she was studying medicine, and was quiet, but she fought side by side with the men . . . and Carl seemed to be always where she was . . .

THE INDES

ONE

COLUMBUS, in the original capitulations—a set of outrageous demands imposed upon the Sovereigns, before undertaking the first voyage—refers to "the things requested and which Your Highnesses give and grant Don Cristóbal Colón, as some satisfaction for what he has discovered in the ocean seas, and of the voyage which now, with the help of God, he is to undertake through those seas in the service of Your Highnesses."

. . . the man from Genoa, at a time when the Indes existed only as spots in his own wild imaginings, referring to them as "what he *has* discovered" . . .

> (as the Azores were first pulled out
> of the ocean by Portuguese, in search of
> St. Brandon's . . .

There is a law of excess, of abundance, whereby a people must explore the ocean, in order to be competent on land . . .

> *(Melville: "You must have plenty of*
> *sea-room to tell the Truth in . . ."*

Men must put out space, and nations ships . . .

> *Columbus, reported by a contemporary: ". . . the said Admiral*
> *always went beyond the bounds of truth in reporting his own*
> *affairs."*

and TYPEE, *Melville's first book, was first rejected because "it was impossible that it could be true and therefore was without real value"* . . .

Columbus: "I hold it for certain that the waters of the sea move from east to west with the sky, and that in passing this track they hold a more rapid course, and have thus carried away large tracts of land, and that from hence has resulted this great number of islands; indeed these islands themselves afford an additional proof of it, for all of them, without exception, run lengthwise, from west to east . . ."

Sitting forward in my chair, I am aware of energy flows in my body—nerve sensations, something that feels like accelerated blood circulation—as though internal balances, relationships, centers of control have been disturbed. Pushing the chair back, I stand up, leaning forward slightly, my arms limp, and give the sensation full play . . . in the matter of balance, I am aware almost at once of the clubfoot: there is the old anger, the hatred, the desire to amputate the monstrous member . . .

Slumping in the chair, I let the anger rankle in me . . . my blood is warm, and begins to move more thickly . . .

As the anger diminishes, there is left the warmth, and again, the disturbance, the imbalance, and something erotic . . .

Columbus: "In Cariay and the neighboring country there are great enchanters of a very fearful character. They would have given the world to prevent my remaining there an hour. When I arrived they sent me immediately two girls very showily dressed; the eldest could not be more than eleven years of age, and the other seven, and both exhibited so much immodesty that more could not be expected from public women; they carried concealed about them a magic powder . . ."

Elsewhere: "They afterwards came to the ship's boats where we were, swimming and bringing us parrots, cotton threads in skeins, darts, and many other things . . ."

"Here the fish are so unlike ours that it is wonderful. Some are the shape of dories, and of the finest colors in the world, blue, yellow, red, and other tints, all painted in various ways, and the colors are so bright that there is not a man who would not be astonished, and would take great delight in seeing them."

". . . the women have very pretty bodies, and they were the first to bring what they had, especially things to eat, bread made of yams, and shrivelled quinces . . ."

Rising, pushing back the chair, I step to my left, leading with the club . . . but the stride is strange. There is something other than the old sensation of heel and ball, in the false boot, striking the floor: an over- or under-balance in a different direction . . . as though the right foot were clubbed, globular, and more monstrous than the left. I pause, and retreat, my hands reaching back for the arms of the chair . . . and am scarcely seated again before the third leg, the middle leg—clubbed in its own way—hardens and rises . . .

but this is not all: I am refreshed, my body renewed: remaining still, leaning back in the chair, I become aware of different locations, different sources from which motion might originate, from which my body might begin to move: shoulder, thigh, elbow, knee—random centers never before used, or neglected and atrophied . . . and as I consider each, fresh energy comes into me, and the old centered leg subsides . . .

Columbus:

"This said island of Juana is exceedingly fertile, as, indeed, are all the others; it is surrounded with many bays, spacious, very secure and surpassing any that I have ever seen; numerous large and healthful rivers intersect it, and it also contains many very lofty mountains. All these islands are very beautiful, and distinguished by a diversity of scenery; they are filled with a great variety of trees of immense height, and which I believe to retain their foliage in all seasons; for when I saw them they were as

verdant and luxuriant as they usually are in Spain in the month of May—some of them were blossoming, some bearing fruit, and all flourishing in the greatest perfection, according to their respective stages of growth, and the nature and quality of each: yet the islands are not so thickly wooded as to be impassable. The nightingale and various birds were singing in countless numbers, and that in November, the month in which I arrived there. There are, besides, in the same island of Juana, seven or eight kinds of palm trees, which, like all the other trees, herbs and fruits, considerably surpass ours in height and beauty. The pines, also, are very handsome, and there are very extensive fields and meadows, a variety of birds, different kinds of honey . . ."

". . . there are mountains of very great size and beauty, vast plains, groves, and very fruitful fields, admirably adapted for tillage, pasture and habitation. The convenience and excellence of the harbors in this island, so indispensable to the health of man, surpass anything that would be believed by one who had not seen it."

"The island of Española is preeminent in beauty and excellence, offering to the sight the most enchanting view of mountains, plains, rich fields for cultivation, and pastures for flocks of all sorts, with situations for towns and settlements. Its harbours are of such excellence that their description would not gain belief, and the like may be said of its abundance of large and fine rivers . . ."

"In all this district there are very high mountains which seem to reach the sky . . . and they are all green with trees. Between them there are very delicious valleys."

"He said that all he saw was so beautiful that his eyes could never tire of gazing on such loveliness, nor his ears of listening to the songs of birds."

and there was the review of Melville's MARDI: *"Wild similes, cloudy philosophy, all things turned topsy-turvy, until we seem to feel all earth melting away from beneath our feet, and nothing but Mardi remaining . . ."*

Dr. Chanca, reporting on the second voyage: "Thus, surely, their Highnesses the King and Queen may henceforth regard themselves as the most prosperous and wealthy sovereigns in the world; never yet, since the creation, has such a thing been seen or read of . . ."

TWO

Glancing at the books, reaching for my handkerchief to rearrange the dust among them, I become, for a moment, the pale Usher, at the very beginning of MOBY-DICK: ". . . Threadbare in coat, heart, body, and brain; I see him now. He was ever dusting his old lexicons and grammars, with a queer handkerchief, mockingly embellished with all the gay flags of all the known nations of the world. He loved to dust his old grammars; it somehow mildly reminded him of his mortality."

Musing for a moment, the dusty handkerchief in hand, my body relaxed, refreshed, waiting for something, I read that on a certain cruise away from Isabella, Columbus was constantly on duty, day and night, at one time going thirty-two days without sleep. He suddenly became ill, suffering a pestilential fever and a drowsiness or supreme stupor which totally deprived him of all his forces and senses, so that he was believed to be dying.

Melville, in a letter: "For my part, I love sleepy fellows, and the more ignorant the better. Damn your wideawake and knowing chaps. As for sleepiness, it is one of the noblest qualities of humanity. There is something sociable about it, too. Think of those sensible and sociable millions of good fellows all taking a good long snooze together, under the sod . . ."

Musing, still, I think of islands, of the meaning of islands . . .

. . . of the Aegean, the Indes, and Polynesia . . .

and the endings in islands: Antillia disintegrating, perhaps, into the Indes, and Atlantis, into the Canaries, Azores and Cape Verdes . . .

There was Melville, an old man, 104 East Twenty-Sixth Street: withdrawn into family, books, and private publications: lonely as Hunilla on the Encantadas, the enchanted islands: insular on Manhattan . . .

and Columbus, back in Spain, in Valladolid, shunted from the Court, alone, crippled with gout . . .

(from the medical book:

called in the old days the "Disease of Diana," because it afflicted hunters, gout is arthritic in type, resulting from imperfect excretion of uric acid. It occurs more often in spring and autumn—the seasons of change.

> "The disturbance of uric acid metabolism causes an over-saturation of urates in the blood . . . Crystalline deposits formed will . . . act as centers for further precipitation of the over-saturated fluids.
> In the bone-marrow below the endochondral junction, small deposits of urate crystals may be found . . ."

. . . the Indes, lost to Columbus now that they had become actual, were repossessed, precipitated once more from his imagination into the extremities of his body—the joints of his toes—as he had precipitated them before into the extremities of the known world: the islands, once more his, as crystals . . .

THREE

Beyond the attic is the wind, and beyond that, the sounds of the city, a general hum, a background, through which breaks the midnight whistle at General Motors, announcing the graveyard . . .

> *"Twelve o'clock! It is the natural centre, key-stone, and very heart of the day. At that hour, the sun has arrived at the top of his hill; and as he seems to hang poised there a while, before coming down on the other side, it is but reasonable to suppose that he is then stopping to dine . . ."*

Melville, describing the other twelve, the sunny one . . .

Linda will soon be home—she gets a ride in an old Plymouth, the back door hanging loose from the hinges, with some people who live beyond us, in what may still be described as country . . .

The wind turns the north corner, and whistles under the eaves . . . leaning back in the chair, stretching my limbs, I experience well-being, as though I had just dined . . . I reach for an inner pocket, and take out a fine cigar, given me yesterday by the superintendent at the plant. I prolong the ritual: removing the cellophane, sniffing the weed, and lighting up . . .

> *Las Casas: ". . . and having lighted one part of it, by the other they suck, absorb or receive that smoke inside with the breath, by which they become benumbed and almost drunk, and so it is said that they do not feel fatigue. These muskats, as we call them, they call tobacco."*

Withdrawing the cigar, holding it before me, I inspect it, the craftsmanship of it, and think of the Indian canoes, made of "very tall, large, long and odoriferous red cedars . . ."

Leaning forward again, the cigar now fixed in the corner of my mouth, I read

of dexter and sinister: the old words for right and left . . .

to the Greeks, whose gods resided in the north, the word for right also meant east, the word for left west . . .

and in Mayan mummification, white was associated with the north and the lungs, yellow with the south and the belly, red with the east and larger intestines, black with the west and the lesser intestines . . .

There was Columbus, making the "Pilot's blessing": arm raised, with flattened palm between the eyes, pointing at Polaris, the North Star . . . the arm then brought straight down to the compass card, to see if the needle varied . . .

. . . or telling time, by checking the rotation of the Guards, two brightest stars of the Dipper, around Polaris . . . the time being determined by where the principal Guard appeared on the chart: West Shoulder, East Arm, Line below West Arm, or East Shoulder . . .

As I sit here, facing east, crouching over the desk, north and south at my elbows, my back to the west, I read

(Columbus)

> ". . . that the world of which I speak is different from that in which the Romans, and Alexander, and the Greeks made mighty efforts with great armies to gain possession of."

Columbus, extending himself, stretching against the contractile tensions of the known world, became a world to himself,

exasperating his fellow-pilots, in any navigational dispute, because he invariably turned out *right*, even his errors, gross as they were, being more accurate than those of the others; and his unreasonable and least accurate presumptions had a way of meeting compensations, that made the results of these presumptions correct . . .

. . . proud and arrogant, demanding (second voyage) more honors than those by which he was already overwhelmed . . . suspicious and distrustful, breaking, one by one, with all his associates: Pinzon, Fonseca, Buil, Margarite, Aguado . . .

> (as Melville broke with Hawthorne,
> Duyckink . . .

. . . unable to understand the Spaniards, who clamored to join him on the second voyage out, and who must therefore (he thought) desire to establish a permanent colony in the Indes . . .

> (but who only wanted to get their rape, gold, slaves and the hell home to Spain, so that on the second voyage, return, the *Niña* and the *India,* each designed for a complement of 25 men, carried a total of 255 . . .

Stranded,

like Melville (whose family all made attempts to "bring him out of himself":

> *"I am as deeply impressed as you possibly can be of the necessity of Herman's getting away from Pitts. He is there solitary, without society, without exercise or occupation except that which is very likely to be injurious to him in over-straining his mind."*

> *Lizzie: "The fact is, that Herman, poor fellow, is in such a frightfully nervous state . . . that I am actually* afraid *to have any one here for fear that he will be upset entirely . . ."*

There is a commotion on the stairs, voices: one of them seems to be Linda, and I get the sense that she is going in two directions—her footsteps ascending (the old stairs creaking under her weight), while her voice goes down the stairwell, to one of the children.

I am confused, the midnight whistle has only just blown, Linda couldn't possibly be home . . . off-balance, I stumble as I get up, nearly tipping the chair,

pause to set the cigar carefully on the table-edge, and then go to the door . . .

"Michael . . ."

There is at once, as I open the door, before the word is spoken, the view, the perception (the door swinging darkly, from right to left)—what I see:

Linda, standing midway on the stairs, perhaps a little nearer the top, her feet close together, her body, her attention turned (as I had felt) in two directions: not twisted or unnatural, but, in the disposition of her feet, her hips, her shoulders, her head, a tendency of motion: partly upward, toward me, and partly down the stairs, toward Mike Jr., the oldest child,

who stands near the bottom, his motion or rather his stillness likewise tentative: ready to climb or withdraw, so that he seems peeking from behind himself. His right foot is advanced to the tread above, his head tilted slightly; and I guess at the look in his face, hidden within the oversized plastic space helmet (he insisted on getting the large one), which makes his head seem a great gray globe, nearly as large as his trunk, with vast space between the plastic and the boy. In his hand he holds (I remember the cereal boxtops collected and squirreled away on kitchen shelves until the necessary accompanying dimes and quarters could be accumulated) the cosmic atomic space gun, green, with concentric circles on the handle and the barrel—the gun pointed upward, not directly, but vaguely, toward his father.

"Michael, what have you been doing? What's the meaning of this?"

"What . . . ?" (still holding the door, my body erect, so that an iron-like firmness runs up from the clubfoot through the knee-joint, the hip, the shoulder, and down through the arm, to the brass knob) ". . . the meaning of what?"

"Michael . . ."

. . . and as she begins to speak, to act, moving her body, swinging her arm in a small arc (as large as the stairwell permits) I endeavor to sort out the feelings, the emotions that slam into me. There is her appearance: short, like myself, a little shorter than I, and getting stout, so that her stomach protrudes, just below the belt of her dress—protrudes further than her breasts; her feet small, her feet and legs that seem to go so well with any floor, pavement or ground on which she stands, so that however tired she may become, however sagging her posture, she seems to belong to and celebrate, be it in grace or in weariness, the act of standing; her arms, seeming to grow shorter as they gain more flesh; and her head, her face, not pretty now because she is complaining, but, in all its plainness (the blond-auburn curls hanging in disarray over the steel-rimmed glasses, and her eyes, blue, set wide apart, not angry, but simply committed to an act, a gesture, committed to and facing and participating in it) a great delicacy that, even now, as so often in the past, I find compelling . . .

> "Michael, every light in the house is burning, the children are in an uproar, the television going . . .

> *Mike Jr.* (gains confidence, takes a step up—the voice muffled): "Jenifer's crying!"

> *Linda:* "What have you been doing?"

and, not waiting for an answer,

> "I came home early, I had to tell the foreman I was ill, because I knew something was wrong, I just felt that things weren't right . . ."

and

> "I suppose we'll have to hire a sitter . . ."

Relaxing my hold on the doorknob, I shift balance to the other foot, take a step, gesture toward her,

> "Linda . . . I'm sorry . . . I didn't know . . ."

and before I say more she turns away from me, careful to reject what I have to say before I say it, and for this I feel no annoyance, neither at her failure nor mine, but only a great stupid sort of pity for both of us . . .

Linda (turns downstairs, her voice snapping): "Mike Jr.! Get down there! Get into your bed!"

. . . angry now, because she doesn't want to, will not, cannot face what is with me . . . The boy vanishes with the crack of her syllables, and

Linda (turning at the bottom of the stairs, her words pointed, not directly, but vaguely, toward me): "After all, the kids have to get up for school tomorrow, and you have to work . . ."

Without speaking, I start down the stairs, but again, quickly, she stops me:

"Never mind . . ." (her back turned toward me, her feet now on the floor below

and I: "Linda . . ."

then she, turning partly toward me again): "I'm home now . . ." (and closes the door at the bottom of the stairs).

Pausing, pivoting on the club, my hand on the rail, I stand in the near dark—the only light being that which spills, many times reflected and diminished, through the open doorway above.

For some moments, I am still.

Turning, then, completing the half-circle pivot, I glance at the stair treads above, and take a step upward, the right foot leading, the left dragging heavily behind . . .

> *(Melville: "But live & push—tho' we put one leg forward ten miles—it's no reason the other must lag behind—no, that must again distance the other—& so we go till we get the cramp . . ."*

Reaching the upper floor again, the old planks, I pause and look around, to recreate the dimensions of the attic. Walking to the desk, I am conscious of the act, the motions and sounds I make, as on a

voyage: the few steps across the boards, from the head of the stairs
to the desk. I pick up the cigar, draw on it, and stand for some
moments. I recall that

Columbus at first thought he had discovered India . . .

> *("They found a large nut of the kind belonging
> to India, great rats, and enormous crabs. He saw
> many birds, and there was a strong smell of
> musk . . ."*

. . . thereby lopping off, roughly, one-half the globe: a hemisphere
gone . . .

> *Melville, describing Hawthorne: "Still there is something lack-
> ing—a good deal lacking—to the plump sphericity of the man."*

FOUR

I have been holding my head still for some moments, and I experi-
ence something like a headache, but not quite the same . . . a wall
seems to run through the middle of my head, from front to back,
and all of me, the total "I," is cramped into one side, the right . . .

> *Melville, describing Ahab: "Threading its way out from among
> his gray hairs, and continuing right down his tawny scorched
> face and neck, till it disappeared in his clothing, you saw a slen-
> der rod-like mark, lividly whitish. It resembled that perpendic-
> ular seam sometimes made in the straight lofty trunk of a great
> tree, when the upper lightning tearingly darts down it, and
> without wrenching a single twig, peels and grooves out the bark
> from top to bottom, ere running off into the soil, leaving the tree
> still greenly alive, but branded. Whether that mark was born
> with him, or whether it was the scar left by some desperate
> wound, no one could certainly say."*

And elsewhere: "Seems to me some sort of equator cuts yon old man . . ."

And PIERRE: *". . . his body contorted, and one side drooping, as though that moment halfway down-stricken with a paralysis, and yet unconscious of the stroke."*

The vision in my left eye dims, all but disappears. I remain still, effectively blind in the left eye. Then, as suddenly as it vanished, the vision returns, starting from a central point and opening over the normal field. There remains something strange about it, however, not as before. I reach for the cigar, which I had placed on the edge of the desk, and am surprised when my hand goes beyond it. Reaching again, my hand this time falls short. There is emptiness in my stomach, and I realize what has happened: I have lost binocular vision—am unable to judge distances. It is only with the utmost care and concentration, now, that I am able to pick up the cigar.

Leaning back in the chair, smoking, I experiment with vision, let it do what it will . . . but there is no change . . . still the strange, two-dimensional sensation. I recall a time when Carl, late in life, experienced something similar, only apparently much worse. For a time he lost three-dimensional vision altogether, the world appearing to him as a flat plane.

MOBY-DICK: *"Now, from this peculiar sideways position of the whale's eyes, it is plain that he can never see an object which is exactly ahead, no more than he can one exactly astern. In a word, the position of the whale's eyes corresponds to that of a man's ears; and you may fancy, for yourself, how it would fare with you, did you sideways survey objects through your ears . . . you would have two backs, so to speak; but, at the same time, also, two fronts (side fronts): for what is it that makes the front of a man—what, indeed, but his eyes?"*

Not only this, but Carl's eyes—set wide apart in his head—seemed to focus and move independent of one another, to receive separate images, imperfectly blended.

"Moreover, while in most other animals that I can now think of, the eyes are so planted as imperceptibly to blend their visual power, so as to produce one picture and not two to the brain; the peculiar position of the whale's eyes, effectually divided as they are by many cubic feet of solid head, which towers between them like a great mountain separating two lakes in valleys; this, of course, must wholly separate the impressions which each independent organ imparts. The whale, therefore, must see one distinct picture on this side, and another distinct picture on that side; while all between must be profound darkness and nothingness to him."

He was expert in dissembling, in making his way among others without arousing suspicion. Only a few of us who knew him well, who knew what he was experiencing, could see him falter and waver, manipulate others into doing things for him that he was afraid he might fumble . . .

"It may be but an idle whim, but it has always seemed to me, that the extraordinary vacillations of movement displayed by some whales when beset by three or four boats; the timidity and liability to queer frights, so common to such whales; I think that all this indirectly proceeds from the helpless perplexity of volition, in which their divided and diametrically opposite powers of vision must involve them."

The condition of my own vision remains unchanged. Smoking quietly, musing over it, I think that in flattening the world,

as Columbus, at first, saw India for America,

> (and as others, much later, while living off the
> fat, still see only India

one loses the look of the land . . .

And it occurs that when the world comes in upon a man, it whirls in at the eyes: two vortices, gouging the outlook . . .

Melville in Cairo: ". . . multitudes of blind men—worst city in the world for them. Flies on the eyes at noon. Nature feeding on man."

And Columbus, fourth voyage, engaged with the natives at Belén:

Captain Diego Tristan went upstream to get fresh water, just before the caravels were to depart—his boat was attacked by Indians, and he was killed by a spear that went through his eye. Only one man of his company escaped. All the corpses floated downstream, covered with wounds, and with carrion crows circling over them, for Columbus and his men—their ships trapped by low water inside the bar—to see.

Melville and Columbus, men of vision:

". . . my eyes, which are tender as young sparrows."

". . . on my former voyage, when I discovered terra firma, I passed thirty-three days without natural rest, and was all that time deprived of sight . . ."

". . . like an owl I steal about by twilight, owing to the twilight of my eyes."

"There the eyes of the Admiral became very bad from not sleeping . . . he says that he found himself more fatigued here than when he discovered the island of Cuba . . . because his eyes were bloodshot . . ."

". . . my recovery from an acute attack of neuralgia in the eyes . . ."

". . . nor did they burst and bleed as they have done now."

". . . and I felt a queer feeling in my left eye, which, as sometimes is the case with people, was the weaker one; probably from being on the same side with the heart."

And there was the country fellow, a relative of Mother's (she tried to deny him because he was thought to be not right in his head—lived by himself in a little shack, did odd jobs, studied strange books at night although it was thought he couldn't read, had difficulty forming thoughts in his head and passing them as words under his hare lip—but there was the name, Stonecipher, and the relationship, some sort of cousin): I remember him trying to explain to me (he used to get up early in the morning and observe the wild animals, gather herbs in the woods to sell to the neighbor women for medicines) what it is about a baby's eyesight, how it takes days or weeks after birth for the infant's eyes to focus, and gain depth perception.

"He can't . . ."

(his great crude hand raised, the fingers spread, coming toward me, as though he were the infant, I the object to be seen, and his hand the agent of vision

". . . he can't MAKE THE OBJECT!"

(the fingers suddenly clutched, grasping air before my nose . . . revelation and delight in his face

and early one Sunday morning, when Carl and I were small boys, we went into Father's room, tried to get him to play with us. He was, or pretended to be asleep . . . we called, pulled, shoved, and jounced, with no effect. We were sitting on him, out of breath, when Carl cautiously approached his face, lifted one eyelid between thumb and forefinger, and peered in. Then he turned to me, the eyelid held open as evidence:

"He's still in there."

FIVE

Genoblast,

the bisexual nucleus of the impregnated ovum.

and, the anatomy book, diagram of cell division:

> "t. End of telophase. The daughter cells are connected by the ecto-
> plasmic stalk. The endoplasm has been completely divided by the
> constriction of the equatorial band. It has mixed with the interchro-
> mosomal (exnuclear) material. The compact daughter nuclei have
> begun to show clear areas and to enlarge. u. The daughter cells have
> moved in opposite directions and stretched the connecting stalk.
> The nuclei have larger clear areas and less visible chromosome mate-
> rial. v. The connecting stalk has been pulled into a thin strand by the
> migration of the daughter cells in opposite directions."

and

> "w. . . . The connecting stalk is broken."

Blastomere,

one of the segments into which the fertilized egg divides. And

Morula,

the mulberry mass, coral- or sponge-like, a mass of blastomeres . . . this hol-
lows into a shell, surrounding a central cavity, and is called a

Blastosphere,

> which "becomes adherent by its embryonic pole to the epithelial lin-
> ing of the uterus. There it flattens out somewhat and erodes and
> digests the underlying surface of the uterus."

(Isabel, in PIERRE: *"I pray for peace—for mo-*
tionlessness—for the feeling of myself, as of some
plant, absorbing life without seeking it . . ."

and for the next two weeks the invader attacks the host, destroying epithe-
lial tissue to make room for itself, and set up embryotrophic nutrition.

MOBY-DICK, *The Shark Massacre: "But in the foamy confu-*
sion of their mixed and struggling hosts, the marksmen could
not always hit their mark; and this brought about new revela-
tions of the incredible ferocity of the foe. They viciously snapped,
not only at each other's disembowelments, but like flexible bows,
bent round, and bit their own; till these entrails seemed swal-
lowed over and over again by the same mouth, to be oppositely
voided by the gaping wound."

And on the fourth voyage of Columbus, the men, having eaten all
their supply of meat, killed some sharks. In the stomach of one, they
found the head of another, a head that they had thrown back earli-
er into the sea, as being unfit to eat.

"The trophoblast proliferates rapidly, forms a network of branching
processes which cover the entire ovum, invade the maternal tissues
and open into the maternal blood vessels . . ."

(there was the Royal Order, granting
amnesty to all convicts who would colonize
the Indes . . .

(the new islands overrun with the undifferen-
tiated

(like the red, rushing growth that fills the
space of a wound:

(proud flesh

I shift position in the chair, my eyes having trouble with the type-face before me . . . trying by changing the fundamental balance of my body, of my spine, to alter what I see . . .

> "Parallel *neural folds* rise higher and higher, flanking the *neural groove,* and finally meet and fuse to form a closed tube which is the primordial brain . . ."

and there are the drawings in the medical book:

embryos, 4 to 10 weeks: the wide-set, bead-like eyes, the pig-snouts, the enormous double foreheads, grotesque, like the masks and carv-ings Carl acquired in Alaska . . .

> "The conclusion is that each organ not only originates from a definite embryonic area or primordium and from no other but also that it arises at a very definite moment which must be utilized then if ever."

and as I read this, the print, the black letters on white, come into sure focus. I reach to the ashtray—judging the distance with ease and pleasure—and put out the stump of my cigar.

I remain still, enjoying again a sense of refreshment, of well-being . . .

there is this about Columbus and Melville: both were blunt men, setting the written word on the page and letting it stand, not going back to correct their errors, not caring to be neat . . .

> (Melville: "It is impossible to talk or to write without apparently throwing oneself helpless-ly open . . ."

The orthography, the spelling of both was hurried, splashed with errors, and both men annotated, scattered postils, in whatever books they read: putting islands, fragments of themselves, at the extremes of the page . . .

There was the handwriting:

Columbus, the early Columbus, man of the ocean-sea and the Indes, confident, level, forward-flowing, the touch light, the form disciplined, not flamboyant (the tops of the consonants rising and curving like Mediterranean lateen sails), exuberant,

and later, as he grew old, writing to the Sovereigns to complain and beg, the words became cramped, the letters thick, the pen bore heavily on the page, the flowing lines conflicted, became eccentric . . .

And Melville: harder, more incised (the Yankee) and crabbed, but, like Christopher, leaning forward against restraints, and on a level line: level with the horizon . . .

Whereas Columbus, complaining and failing, jabbed the page, Melville (likewise failing) withdrew from it, the pen, the thought, the man scarcely forming the word . . .

And Columbus, a very old man, all hope and islands lost to him save only as gout, as crystals at the extremities of his body, permitted his two styles to flow together and become one . . .

> (always, however, the line remaining level . . . the only variation being, upon occasion, a moderate roll, the pen riding the page like a caravel coasting a gentle ground swell, among the Indes . . .

JOURNAL DOWN THE STRAITS

ONE

COLUMBUS: *"In the dead of night, while I was on deck, I heard an awful roaring that came from the south, toward the ship; I stopped to observe what it might be, and I saw the sea rolling from west to east like a mountain, as high as the ship, and approaching little by little; on the top of this rolling sea came a mighty wave roaring with a frightful noise, and with all this terrific uproar were other conflicting currents, producing, as I have already said, a sound as of breakers upon the rocks. To this day I have a vivid recollection of the dread I then felt, lest the ship might founder under the force of that tremendous sea . . ."*

and Las Casas: *". . . since the force of the water is very great at all times and particularly so in this season . . . which is the season of high water, . . . and since it wants naturally to get to the sea, and the sea with its great mass under the same natural impulse wants to break upon the land, and since this gulf is enclosed by the mainland on one side and on the other side by the island . . . and since it is very narrow for such a violent force of contrary waters, it must needs be that when they meet a terrific struggle takes place and a conflict most perilous for those that find themselves in that place."*

The house, the attic, are once more become a ship, but in a different sense, that of a ship struck at different points by contending waters, so that it shivers, the timbers work against one another, and the whole seems scarcely to move. I am still, and it is some moments before I realize that this sensation comes to me, not as from the timbers of the house, but as from those—the rafters, joists, sills, and sleepers—of my own frame . . . my bones being of oak, carved and pegged (the club left as a trademark, unwhittled)—an oaken frame somehow assaulted. I am cramped, unable to move . . .

> MOBY-DICK: *"For not only are whalemen as a body unexempt from that ignorance and superstitiousness hereditary to all sailors; but of all sailors, they are by all odds the most directly brought into contact with whatever is appallingly astonishing in the sea; face to face they not only eye its greatest marvels, but, hand to jaw, give battle to them. Alone, in such remotest waters, that though you sailed a thousand miles, and passed a thousand shores, you would not come to any chiselled hearthstone, or aught hospitable beneath that part of the sun; in such latitudes and longitudes, pursuing too such a calling as he does, the whaleman is wrapped by influences all tending to make his fancy pregnant with many a mighty birth."*

> *"But far beneath this wondrous world upon the surface, another and still stranger world met our eyes as we gazed over the side. For, suspended in those watery vaults, floated the forms of the nursing mothers of the whales, and those that by their enormous girth seemed shortly to become mothers."*

> *"One of those little infants, that from certain queer tokens seemed hardly a day old, might have measured some fourteen feet in length, and some six feet in girth. He was a little frisky; though as yet his body seemed scarce yet recovered from that irksome position it had so lately occupied . . . where, tail to head, and all ready for the final spring, the unborn whale lies bent like a Tartar's bow."*

Sitting cramped, I recall the maternity hospital where, three times, I have taken Linda to produce: the old building, crowded and outdated; the various corridors leading, like the spokes of a wheel, to the hub, the labor and delivery rooms—corridors filled with grunting, sweating, and sometimes screaming women; the labor room itself often hurriedly converted for a delivery—the building charged with haste and effort to cope with the mighty postwar tide of infants, rushing down the corridors, thrusting into the world.

Again, I am assaulted, the sensation this time largely in my head. There is a sense of separation, the skull, like a case, holding firm under attack, and the brains, separate, trapped within—struggling and pushing . . . I attempt to scream, but the action of throat muscles, as of all else, is suspended, and I am left with silence . . .

> *(Melville, describing the pyramids: "A feeling of awe & terror came over me. Dread of the Arabs. Offering to lead me into a sidehole. The Dust. Long arched way,—then down as in a coal shaft. Then as in mines, under the sea. (At one moment seeming in the Mammoth Cave. Subterranean gorges, & c.) The stooping & doubling . . ."*

Thrusting my body back full length in the chair, I try to break the enclosure, the cramp—but there is no change: each position, each arrangement of trunk, head, and limbs, becomes ultimate, a final one, from which my frame would become a thing made, without life.

Shifting again, unable to create Space, I try to reach with awareness alone, to grasp and control Time . . . and am reminded at once of childhood, when I slipped and fell into the posthole: alone at the end of the corn field, with earth all around me, rising to beyond the top of my head—there is again the dizziness, the volatile awareness, expanding in proportion to my confinement, and the loneliness, the waiting . . .

> MOBY-DICK: *"Leaning over in his hammock, Queequeg long regarded the coffin with an attentive eye. He then called for his harpoon, had the wooden stock drawn from it, and then had the iron part placed in the coffin along with one of the paddles of his boat. All by his own request, also, biscuits were then ranged*

around the sides within: a flask of fresh water was placed at the head, and a small bag of woody earth scraped up in the hold at the foot; and a piece of sail cloth being rolled up for a pillow, Queequeg now entreated to be lifted into his final bed, that he might make trial of its comforts, if any it had. He lay without moving a few minutes, then told one to go to his bag and bring out his little god, Yojo. Then crossing his arms on his breast with Yojo between, he called for the coffin lid (hatch he called it) to be placed over him. The head part turned over with a leather hinge, and there lay Queequeg in his coffin with little but his composed countenance in view. 'Rarmai' (it will do; it is easy), he murmured at last, and signed to be replaced in his hammock."

and BARTLEBY: *"The yard was entirely quiet. It was not accessible to the common prisoners. The surrounding walls, of amazing thickness, kept off all sounds behind them. The Egyptian character of the masonry weighed upon me with its gloom. But a soft imprisoned turf grew underfoot. The heart of the eternal pyramids, it seemed, wherein by some strange magic, through the clefts grass seed, dropped by birds, had sprung.*

"Strangely huddled at the base of the wall—his knees drawn up, and lying on his side, his head touching the cold stones—I saw the wasted Bartleby. But nothing stirred. I paused; then went close up to him; stooped over, and saw that his dim eyes were open; otherwise he seemed profoundly sleeping. Something prompted me to touch him. I felt his hand, when a tingling shiver ran up my arm and down my spine . . ."

and there was Navidad: first toehold, first bit of land secured and colonized, in the New World: the inhabitants, to a man, wiped out . . .

Waiting now, the very quality of it sinking in me, so that waiting becomes a kind of desperation, hopelessness, I remain huddled, cramped and desolate, as though dead . . .

TWO

Homer, THE ODYSSEY: "... a sea broke over him with such terrific fury that the raft reeled again, and he was carried overboard a long way off. He let go the helm, and the force of the hurricane was so great that it broke the mast half way up, and both sail and yard went over into the sea. For a long time Ulysses was under water, and it was all he could do to rise to the surface again ..."

and Leucothea, marine goddess, white goddess, "... rising like a seagull from the waves, took her seat upon the raft ..." and spoke to Ulysses:

"'... strip, leave your raft to drive before the wind, and swim to the Phaeacian coast where better luck awaits you. And here, take my veil and put it around your chest; it is enchanted, and you can come to no harm so long as you wear it. As soon as you touch land, throw it back as far as you can into the sea, and then go away again.' With these words she took off her veil and gave it to him. Then she dived down again like a sea-gull and vanished beneath the dark blue waters."

An enchanted veil ...

(The medical book:

("It is inferred that the human embryo ... forms an amnion cavity in its solid ectodermal mass."

("If the tough amnion fails to burst, the head is delivered enveloped in it and it is then known popularly as the 'caul.'"

The caul—an enchanted veil—presumed to bring luck, to prevent shipwreck, and to save from drowning ...

(there was the one advertised in the London Times—*May 8, 1848—the owner asking 6 guineas, the caul "having been afloat with its last owner forty years, through all the perils of a seaman's life, and the owner died at last in his bed, at the place of his birth."*

The pressure is growing, and my body, pushed tight against it, is now immovable; tremendous effort is exerted, at every point and plane of skin surface, to maintain the contact, and therefore any hope of identity. My skull, where the tension becomes greatest, is a fragile vault, in which I swim, helpless, as in an ocean.

I am aware of the clubfoot, of the five toes, and the flesh fusing them . . .

(the medical book:

("*Syndactylism:* . . . a common cause is adhesions of the fetus to the amnion."

There is an explosion, detonating somewhere in my head, and spreading with force and violence. The pressure collapses, and all sense of balance is gone, leaving me dizzy and ill. It is like shipwreck in a storm, the ship broken and scattered, the timbers—timbers of my skull—crashing against one another in gigantic waves. The structure—the partition between left and right sides in my head—is shattered, so that there is no longer an origin of direction, of motion, and I drift randomly, without form or shape . . .

(Moby-Dick: *". . . the breaking-up of the ice-bound stream of Time."*

and Cosmology: *"For then . . . we see that . . . all the nebulae were packed into a small region . . . years ago and moved away as though an explosion had taken place there, each with its own individual velocity . . ."*

". . . for an infinite period in the distant past there was a com-
pletely homogeneous distribution of matter in equilibrium . . .
until some event started off the expansion, which has been going
on at an increasing pace ever since."

At the zero point of creation, when all is infinite mass and zero size
. . . from this point—to one second—the distribution of elements
occurs . . .

Gaseous Nebulae, coalescing into small suns, the suns clustering
into galaxies,

The galaxies swirling, with angular momentum, in vortices,

> (like a hand swirled in water,

> (or like dust motes in an ever-expanding
> balloon . . .

particles in vortices,

subparticles in vortices,

planets . . .

My body, huddled before a makeshift desk—an old door lain flat on
crates—is relinquished, abandoned . . .

floating above it, above the ancient house and attic, above Indiana
and the broad continent, I am no longer Michael, but have become
everyone . . . no longer compact with pain, fear, anger and content-
ment, I am only aware . . .

aware of explosion and outflow, of letting go and spreading apart, of
vaporizing into widening space . . .

> *(*COSMOLOGY: *"In many ways we consider*
> *radiative energy to be 'lost' energy, picturing*
> *somehow space as an infinite receptacle, an*
> *almost perfect sink."*

No longer Michael, I am without borders . . . I glance down and see the city, the suburban row houses, hanging by television aerials from the atmosphere . . .

Turning from these, I drift, further and further from the land . . .

> *(Melville, in* PIERRE: *"Better might one be pushed off into the material spaces beyond the uttermost orbit of our sun, than once feel himself fairly afloat in himself!"*

Once again, I lose depth perception; the world beneath me, and the stars, are flat, without dimension. Further, I am unable to see through the center of the eye, the images reaching me only peripherally . . . I see only through the white. I am floating in space, without center or distance . . .

> (KINEMATIC RELATIVITY: *"Here it is sufficient to recall that 'space' is not a physical attribute of the universe, but is a mode of description of phenomena which is at the disposal of the observer . . ."*

Everything comes to me in gray, a perfect gray, perfect in its neatness: tiny dots, as though created by a pointillist, ranging from black through various grays to white. I might be peering at a movie or television screen, or, perhaps, through Mike Jr.'s space helmet . . . or the gray gauze of a churchman's eyes:

a membrane, imperfectly transparent, filtering and veiling all reality . . .

I find my hands, clenched like a baby's, rubbing clumsily at my cheeks, eyes, forehead . . .

> (the root of the word *caul* is the same as that for *hell* and *cellar:* a matter of hiding . . .

All at once, my fists hang away from my face. The gray, peripheral images vanish, and are replaced by an unvarying white . . .

MOBY-DICK: ". . . *there yet lurks an elusive something in the innermost idea of this hue, which strikes more of panic to the soul than that redness which affrights in blood.*"

"*This elusive quality it is, which causes the thought of whiteness, when divorced from more kindly associations, and coupled with any object terrible in itself, to heighten that terror to the furthest bounds. Witness the white bear of the poles, and the white shark of the tropics; what but their smooth, flaky whiteness makes them the transcendent horrors they are? That ghastly whiteness it is which imparts such an abhorrent mildness, even more loathsome than terrific, to the dumb bloating of their aspect.*"

"*What is it that in the Albino man so peculiarly repels and often shocks the eye, as that sometimes he is loathed by his own kith and kin! It is that whiteness that invests him, a thing expressed by the name he bears. The Albino is as well made as other men—has no substantive deformity—and yet this mere aspect of all pervading whiteness makes him more strangely hideous than the ugliest abortion. Why should this be so?*"

"*Nor, in some things, does the common, hereditary experience of all mankind fail to bear witness to the supernaturalism of this hue. It cannot well be doubted, that the one visible quality in the aspect of the dead which most appals the gazer, is the marble pallor lingering there . . .*"

Melville's bedroom, described by his granddaughter: "*The great mahogany desk, heavily bearing up four shelves of dull gilt and leather books; the high dim book-case; . . . the small black iron bed, covered with dark cretonne; the narrow iron grate . . .*"

and Lizzie's: "*That was a very different place—sunny, comfortable and familiar, with a sewing machine and a white bed like other people's.*"

Olson, describing Melville: "He made a white marriage."

> (but before that, before Lizzie, before the
> white, there was Fayaway, dark, on a green
> island . . .

I recall the many hospitals I have visited, studied, and worked in:
the floors, walls, and furniture in pastels, the colors, the force of
color, bleached out of them; the apparatus of laboratory, surgery,
and kitchen in chrome and steel; and everything else, whether inti-
mately or remotely pertaining to healing—the uniforms of nurse,
intern, attendant, and doctor, the sheets covering the sick and the
ceilings over the beds, the curtains, screens, towels, and bandages—
all drained and blanched, sterile and antiseptic—all white.

and there was Melville, possessed—like Ahab—by that "dark Hin-
doo half of nature"—and to all who surrounded him—to Lizzie, to
his sons and daughters, to the Gansevoorts and Melvilles—a poi-
son, potent and to be feared . . .

a sepsis.

White and vague, I am drifting, without space or time . . .

> (COSMOLOGY: ". . . *since the age of the universe
> (especially if its origin was catastrophic) cannot
> be less than the age of any part of it, however
> small."*

. . . disincarnate . . .

> *(Melville: "While there is life hereafter, there is
> despair. . ."*

Once again, the tiny dots of gray appear, shaping images of Indiana,
like the first image of the afternoon projected on a movie screen. I
see the row houses, the factories and stores of Indianapolis, all neat-
ly arranged and harmonized, a uniform gray . . .

. . . a vision of reality, filtered and orderly . . .

as an old sailor, retired ashore, makes a ship inside a bottle . . .

or a man makes a philosophy: life viewed through a caul.

I remember, in the psychiatric courses I took, studying the life of Freud, and discovering that the Viennese, father of modern psychology—the first to introduce modern man to the pear-shaped world from which he sprang—Freud was born with a caul . . .

Fusing with the amnion, becoming the amnion, turning all to gray and white, I am no longer Michael, but everyone—a particle in an explosion—all time and space—and therefore, nothing . . .

> *(Columbus: "The pilots . . . do not know the way to return thither; . . . they would be obliged to go on a voyage of discovery as much as if they had never been there before. There is a mode of reckoning derived from astronomy which is sure and safe, and a sufficient guide to any one who understands it. This resembles a prophetic vision."*

I look down at Michael, fixed in the chair—as the attic is fixed upon the house and the old house rooted in the soil—and the images suddenly vanish, whirling into one another. There is a different sensation—as though I had become sensitive to the spinning of the globe. I am aware again of my body, and feel myself sucked down, drawn into it. Within my skull all is gray chaos, whirling and dizzy, with no origin of direction or motion. The desk, the attic, the world are pitching and rolling, and I am ill . . .

. . . drawn into the body, I am drawn down with it: compacted and chaotic, beyond control, I begin strangely to move . . . I seem drowning, drawn to unknown bottoms . . . there is a monstrous, choking fear . . .

The medical book: "The amnion in the human develops probably by degeneration of the central portion of a lenticular enlargement of the cell mass . . ."

". . . but this has not yet been determined, even though of great significance in the production of monsters."

THREE

Melville, BENITO CERENO: *". . . when at sunrise, the deponent coming on deck, the negro Babo showed him a skeleton, which had been substituted for the ship's proper figure-head . . ."*

. . . the proper and original figurehead having been that of the discoverer, Christopher Columbus.

Thus Melville, after MOBY-DICK, after the sinking of the Pequod—sucked into the whirlpool, at the very bottom—yields the overwater discoverer . . . and

"Seguid vuestro jefe" . . . the leader, in this case, a skeleton . . .

My left leg—lying straight from the edge of the chair to the floor beneath the desk—seems to enlarge, the flesh prickly and fat . . . then it goes numb: all sensation vanishes . . .

and it occurs to me that, whereas in MOBY-DICK Melville fought his way upstream, like the Pacific salmon, to the original sources— in PIERRE, there was no need to return, no stream to ascend . . . the fight gone out of him, he remained still, and the past overwhelmed him . . . sinking, drowning, he pulled the world, his family, in over himself . . .

. . . the amniotic waters, closing over the eye of the vortex, over Melville's wreck . . .

Although in MOBY-DICK Melville reached deep into "the invisible spheres . . . formed in fright," he yet maintained freeboard, working from above the surface—if safe by only the few perilous inches of a whaleboat . . . but in PIERRE, the author, the story, the people of whom he wrote, all are one—gelatinous, subaquatic—the verbs become blobs of sound . . .

The absence of sensation in my left leg has become something positive, and yet I can't put words to it . . . the leg having passed into a condition remote from the rest of my body, untranslatable . . . I am aware only of its motionlessness, of its arrest not only in space but in time . . . being stopped itself, the leg stops the rest of me: my body stiffens, tenses, for or against what, I cannot tell

. . . a thought floats in, however, that I am struggling, by physical force, to prevent Melville from writing PIERRE . . .

> "For while still dreading your doom, you foreknow it. Yet how foreknow and dread in one breath . . . ?"

> Thus, PIERRE. And Melville—as Ahab, barely before the sinking of the Pequod—foreknew his doom: ". . . from all your furthest bounds, pour ye now in, ye bold billows of my whole foregone life . . . !"

I remember Carl, in St. Louis, after the war, after he had come back from nineteen months in a Japanese Prisoner-Of-War Camp: we were afraid of what had happened to his mind, and, for want of a better answer, I was trying to get him to a psychiatrist, to help him go over his experiences, untangle something of what he was, what had happened to him . . . I recall the look on his face when I made the suggestion: the features withdrawing, not from me, but from one another, shifting their arrangement, becoming without form; and the smile, part of his mouth spreading, as he said, "I ain't drowning, Mike boy . . ."

My leg is now dead, passed into a condition from which there is no recall. I become aware of the hip joint, the part that is still me. I cherish the separation, the feeling of identity going no further than the hip . . .

Ahab: ". . . it was Moby-Dick that dismasted me . . .

Moby-Dick . . . a great white monster, with "a hump like a snow-hill . . ."

not Leucothea, not a white and winged goddess, protectress, who gave Ulysses an enchanted veil . . .

but moving out from this, from the closed and friendly Mediterranean, from the near ocean shores,

moving out, as Columbus, across the Atlantic, and, through Melville, into the Pacific:

the white gull become a white whale, cast in monstrous, malignant revenge . . .

Melville, in the Pacific—the western extreme of American force— untethered, fatherless, the paternity blasted—turning—as Ahab— with vengeance and malice to match the monster's: turning and thrusting back to his own beginnings: to

Moby-Dick, the white monster: to Maria Gansevoort Melville . . .

(Lizzie's account of Herman: "A severe attack of what he called crick in the back laid him up at his Mothers in Gansevoort in March 1858—and he never regained his former vigor & strength."

The snow-hill hump, rumbling in the interior caverns of the sea book, bursts forth as the ultimate image in the book of the drowned—all of PIERRE perhaps being written as an excuse to expose it:

". . . in thy breasts, life for infants lodgeth not, but death-milk for thee and me!—The drug!' and tearing her bosom loose, he seized the secret vial nestling there."

Carl, some years ago, on one of his rare and random splurges of reading—invading the library, chewing his way through stacks of books—came up with a volume of Indian legends: there was one about a woman with a toothed vagina, who had killed many men by having intercourse with them—but the hero inserted sticks too hard for her to masticate, and thus knocked out the teeth . . . and there was another about the first woman in the world, whose vagina contained a carnivorous fish . . .

> *(Columbus, in the Boca de la Sierpe—mouth of the serpent—observed that the tides were much greater than anywhere else in the Indies, the current roaring like surf . . .*

Dead-legged, helpless and unwilling, I feel my body dragged down . . .

> *Melville, blubbering from beneath the ocean, announces* PIERRE *to a Hawthorne—not Nathaniel, but Sophia: "My Dear Lady, I shall not again send you a bowl of salt water. The next chalice I shall commend, will be a rural bowl of milk."*

> *From a contemporary review of* PIERRE: *"The sooner this author is put in a ward the better."*

FOUR

The interior of my head is an ocean, vast and unvarying, the watery horizon curving as with the curve of the globe. There is no island, no source of direction, or action. Floating, centerless, in this expanse, I am ready to drown . . .

But there is a sudden change: my left leg—or that which had been my left leg—comes back to me: I feel blood and warmth entering again, sweeping in waves from the hip, and with this, the rest of me, all of my body becomes charged with sensation . . .

There is also a difference: sinking in one ocean, I have risen to the surface of another—in a different hemisphere, or on the other side of the equator. The heart beats, the blood flows, the lungs inhale and discharge air—but all are radically altered. Reaching for the butt of the cigar resting in the ashtray, I am surprised to discover the gesture originating, not in my right hand, but in my left. My arm and shoulder, my whole left side, ache and feel uncomfortable—but this is not so strange as when I try to countermand the order, originate the gesture as I would normally, from the right. Plunging once more into the ocean, I attempt to force myself back, to force the gesture, and all gestures, to emerge and spring from the right: my body becomes rigid, all the machinery, all the moving parts, jammed . . .

> PIERRE: ". . . a sudden, unwonted, and all-pervading sensation seized him. He knew not where he was; he did not have any ordinary life-feeling at all. He could not see; though instinctively putting his hand to his eyes, he seemed to feel that the lids were open. Then he was sensible of a combined blindness, and vertigo, and staggering; before his eyes a million green meteors danced; he felt his foot tottering on the curb, he put out his hands, and knew no more for the time. When he came to himself he found that he was lying crosswise in the gutter, dabbled with mud and slime. He raised himself to try if he could stand; but the fit was entirely gone."

and Murray, commenting on this: "Although there is no record of Melville's having suffered an attack of syncope, there is verisimilitude in his description of Pierre's fainting. Furthermore, the time relation of Pierre's attack . . . would indicate that Melville himself had experienced syncope."

> (From the medical book: ". . . characterized by an abrupt onset, with uneasiness, weakness, restlessness, vague abdominal discomfort associated with moderate nausea, lightheadedness, blurring of vision, inability to walk, cold perspiration, collapse, unconsciousness, and sometimes a flaccid paralysis and mild convulsions . . .")

Melville, standing on a Pacific island—TYPEE—floating up to effervescent MARDI—charging, then, full force, back to the origin and beginning of things—the center of the whale-herd, east of the Straits of Sunda—and turning, to plunge . . .

> (from a letter, written before MOBY-DICK: "I love all men who dive. Any fish can swim near the surface, but it takes a great whale to go down stairs five miles or more . . ."

. . . plunge to the depths and bottom of the ocean, to drown, as PIERRE . . .

rising, then, struggling to disgorge the ocean from his lungs (and his head), to find another island, another origin of action,

through syncope: fainting—a small and imitation death—perhaps a drowning . . . in effect, saying to himself—and to any who would listen:

"I have to change centers, and I have to drown to do it."

Failed as an author—and as a Pittsfield farmer—failing now in health, to the extent that the family had him examined by Dr. Holmes in regard to his sanity—Melville set about in his own way to recenter: he took to writing verse . . .

"For poetry is not a thing of ink and rhyme, but of thought and act..." (Melville)

The joints, the motion-sources of my body, remain rigid, the bones and muscles forcing against one another. My tongue and eyelids are heavy, and

I recall a time when Carl came home for a visit—it was just before the war, and I was away in medical school: he was experiencing mysterious convulsions, and the doctors for some time withheld a diagnosis, uncertain of what term to use—although I knew they suspected a recurrence of hydrocephalus. Mother and I were sub-jected to the electroencephalograph, in search of genetic dysrhyth-mia—but the findings were negative. Carl experienced all the typi-cal preconvulsive phenomena—unexplained faints, attacks of giddi-ness, sleepiness, myoclonic jerks—and finally the diagnosis was made: acquired epilepsy . . .

> (the word meaning to "seize upon": as a drowning man would seize upon an island . . .

Perhaps because I was studying medicine—and was, as well, his brother—Carl sent me reports on his seizures . . . fragmentary let-ters, notes jotted on old pieces of wrapping paper, or the backs of prescriptions:

> "A touch of fear . . . great thickness and heaviness, moving to my tongue . . . last stage before the attack.
>
> "This time the aura was black, and the closing-in type . . .
>
> "It is always flashover, definite—like the stepping out of a warm room into the cold . . .
>
> "Have discovered I can induce the aura: driving the car, I put myself as someone in one of the other cars, then someone in another car, then another, and so forth—an overwhelmed-by-numbers bizzniss turns up, and right under (or after) that: the aura . . .

". . . a breeze . . . gateway to a fabulous world, everything maneu-
verable . . . like an explosion, reaching, spreading into widening
space, all white . . .

"As for question of the head and interpenetration . . . the effect is
gradual . . . as for shape, configuration, the same, but as for size, I
don't know . . .
"While I write this, I feel the approach of the aura. Realize that I
have walked past where it is stored . . . go back and contact it . . .
now it has me, full force . . . as long as I keep my eyes closed, it's
there . . . Feeling: it's all in my head, and I'm in and occupy very
little of it . . . all the world in there (or here) since my head is the
limit of the world . . . I am a little bigger than the rest of the uni-
verse . . . the feeling now persists even with eyes open: I make des-
perate efforts to get away from it . . .

"Thought, under attack: I must recap the birth of the universe . . ."

> (from the medical book: "A patient who invariably
> dislocated his right shoulder as he fell, explained
> this by saying that he would see a star before him
> for which he would reach . . ."

and Carl: "A dream: conjure up a chorus, with the director (thin-
faced) telling them to start the theme, god damnit, on the UP beat!
Chorus furious, marches on him, on the *strong* beat . . . feeling of
horror . . ."

> (the medical book: "The authors present the case of
> a woman aged 44 in whom extensive clinical inves-
> tigation failed to reveal an acquired cerebral lesion,
> but which represented a case of musicogenic epilep-
> sy. The patient experienced increases of blood pres-
> sure, heart rate, and respiration while listening to
> music. Fits could not be induced by pure tones,
> although the patient felt emotional to a tone of 512
> cycles which persisted and was varied in loudness.
> Different kinds of music were invariably followed
> by a fit within five minutes."

The period in which Carl had attacks lasted only a few months, terminating as abruptly as it started; and for this, the doctors had no explanation. Nor would Carl himself speak of it, then or thereafter . . .

Melville, collapsing the world of Pittsfield and the Pacific, salvaged the remains, hoarded them into 104 East 26th Street—fortunate to be taken on as outdoor customs inspector (badge #75), Port of New York, at a reward of $4 per diem (later reduced to $3.60). Reduced, circumscribed, and aging, he still thrashed . . .

From DANIEL ORME *(and perhaps he meant* DANIEL OR ME*): . . . his moodiness and mutterings, his strange freaks, starts, eccentric shrugs and grimaces . . ."*

and from a contemporary review of Melville's verse: "Mr. Melville has abundant force and fire . . . But he has written too rapidly to avoid great crudities. His poetry runs into the epileptic. His rhymes are fearful . . ."

FIVE

MOBY-DICK: *"But now that he had apparently made every preparation for death; now that his coffin was proved a good fit, Queequeg suddenly rallied; soon there seemed no need of the carpenter's box: and thereupon, when some expressed their delighted surprise, he, in substance, said, that the cause of his sudden convalescence was this;—at a critical moment, he had just recalled a little duty ashore, which he was leaving undone; and therefore had changed his mind about dying: he could not die yet, he averred. They asked him, then, whether to live or die was a matter of his own sovereign will and pleasure. He answered, certainly. In a word, it was Queequeg's conceit, that if a man*

made up his mind to live, mere sickness could not kill him: noth-
ing but a whale, or a gale, or some violent, ungovernable, unin-
telligent destroyer of that sort. "

I experience an abrupt relaxation, a lifting of tensions, and, with
this, a restoration of vision, so marked, the dark corners and recess-
es of the attic stand out so sharply—that I seem to have gained new
powers. Random motives, impulses to shift and rearrange limbs and
muscles, occur throughout my frame. I am restless, moving, want-
ing to move in ways I have never tried before . . .

Melville: "Let us speak, tho' we show all our faults and weak-
nesses,—for it is a sign of strength to be weak, to know it, and
out with it . . ."

Reviving within myself, I am aware also of external motion, motion
of my body as a whole, from the outside, and there are the two:
inside and outside, working with and against one another . . .

Stretched loosely in the chair, giving the sensations full play, I am
aware of fresh sources of energy opening in me, opening barely in
time to be poured into the increasing demands, both in action and
duration, that are to be made upon me . . .

Melville, after MOBY-DICK: *"Lord, when shall we be done*
growing? As long as we have anything more to do, we have
done nothing."

and Las Casas, describing Christopher, embarking on the
third voyage: ". . . wherefore it appeared to him that what he
already had done was not sufficient but that he must renew his
labors . . ."

I remember the three occasions—but especially the first—of
Linda's pregnancies . . . our watching and wondering as the end of
her term approached, what day or night it would be when we would
hurry to the hospital . . . the obvious pleasure with which she
allowed me to place my hand on her, to try to anticipate, as hus-

band, father, and doctor, the exact hour . . . her figure, short and
broad, so exquisitely designed for childbirth, carrying the weight
lower and lower, as the head approached the cervix, the ultimate
part of its pear-shaped world, until it seemed that the infant must
drop at any moment—in the kitchen, the bathroom, or on the bed
where he began . . .

> *Columbus: ". . . it is impossible to give a correct account of all our
> movements, because I was carried away by the current so many
> days without seeing land."*

> *and from the "Libretto": ". . . not very far from there they found
> a stream of water from east to west, so swift and impetuous that
> the Admiral says that never since he has sailed . . . has he been
> more afraid."*

I am shaken—head, ribs, and limbs—by a tremendous effort . . .

> *Columbus: "At this time the river forced a channel for itself, by
> which I managed, with great difficulty, to extricate . . ."*

> *and Las Casas: "Arriving at the said mouth . . . he found a great
> struggle between the fresh water striving to go out to the sea and
> the salt water of the sea striving to enter the gulf, and it was so
> strong and fearful, that it raised a great swell, like a very high
> hill, and with this, both waters made a noise and thundering,
> from east to west, very great and fearful, with currents of water,
> and after one came four great waves one after the other, which
> made contending currents; here they thought to perish . . ."*
>
> *"It pleased the goodness of God that from the same danger
> safety and deliverance came to them and the current of the fresh
> water overcame the current of the salt water and carried the
> ships safely out, and thus they were placed in security; because
> when God wills that one or many shall be kept alive, water is a
> remedy for them."*

THE ODYSSEY: "Here at last Ulysses' knees and strong hands failed him, for the sea had completely broken him. His body was all swollen, and his mouth and nostrils ran down like a river with sea water, so that he could neither breathe nor speak, and lay swooning from near exhaustion; presently, when he had got his breath and came to himself again, he took off the scarf that Leucothea had given him and threw it back into the salt stream of the river, whereon Leucothea received it into her hands from the wave that bore it towards her. Then he left the river, laid himself down among the rushes, and kissed the bounteous earth."

I am invaded by a great warmth, my entire skin surface tingling . . .

(Melville: ". . . as we mortals ourselves spring all naked and scabbardless into the world."

. . . and with it, an indescribable relief, satisfaction, and well-being. Reaching for the cigar butt, I lean back, stretch my legs, and light up again, relishing the warmth of the match flame, as it nearly burns my face. Drawing lungs full of smoke, I tilt my head against the back of the chair, and watch the clouds, floating in the yellow lamplight to the rafters. I recall the cigars I smoked and gave away at the plant on the occasions of Mike Jr.'s birth, our firstborn; and, with the tobacco smoke, I taste again the pleasure, the pride that I enjoyed at that time—pride such as a man might feel at the mouth of the Mississippi or Amazon, sharing in those waters that push back the ocean, the waters they are in the act of joining . . .

BATTLE PIECES
AND ASPECTS OF THE WAR

ONE

"It was on a bomber run *that Rico and I cracked up near a hospital in China—a small outpost hospital—and discovered that Concha was assigned to it. Christ, we didn't even know she was out of the states . . .*

"*We bailed out and no one was hurt except Rico, who had stayed behind to shoot out the bombsight and set the ship afire. He tore a shoulder pretty bad, but he clamped the cut himself. By twos and threes the Chinese took us to the hospital, where they assured us Concha would smuggle us back to HQ. Seems she'd been doing this for months . . .*

"*We arrived at the same time the Japs captured the hospital and surrounding town. Rico had cautioned us before we bailed out to destroy our insignia and not to admit to being officers, so the Japs would think us privates and not try to pump us. However, the Japs seem to base seniority on age, so Rico and I, not being in our twenties, were stuck—as well as a fifty-year-old sergeant, who they thought must be a general: he was tortured, and when he wouldn't talk—because he didn't know any-thing—they cut his head off, to scare the rest of us.*

"*Rico raged and cursed when he was tortured, but appeared more angry than hurt. I wish I could say as much for myself . . .*

"Concha, I guess, didn't know what to expect . . . she was only thinking of her patients. This was a general hospital, and among other things she had women in labor, and some who had just delivered. The Japs explained, through a Chinese doctor. that they were going to take over the hospital for billets . . .

"They started evacuating the patients at sword point. One of the privates threw a baby up and caught it through the belly on his bayonet; Concha didn't move, but when the C.O. laughed, she lost her head and struck him. It wasn't a ladylike slap, but, well, you know Concha—she just rifled one off the floor and planted it on him, and he went down for the count. It was beautiful . . . but we all knew she would suffer for it. At his command, they grabbed her, yanked her back and forth among them, until we couldn't always keep sight of her. When the crowd thinned out she was naked, her skin in ribbons, her long hair hanging down—and several handfuls trailed from many hands. Her knuckles were bleeding, her eyes flashed, her head was up and she was mad clear through. I was proud of her. She had given a good account, too, being outnumbered—had blacked several eyes, and quite a few men had lumps appearing on their jaws.

"The Chinese doctor groaned aloud when he heard the C.O. say that he would rape her first, and then the others could have her. He explained that she was in for a bad time, she was such a small woman . . .

"We were invited to watch, with our hands tied behind our backs. They threw her to the ground and when they twisted her legs behind her shoulders, and her hips came out of joint or broke, Rico yelled curses and tore at his bonds until his wrists were bleeding. The officer, of course, couldn't get into her and he seemed to be in a hurry. He gave a command and a soldier jammed his rifle barrel into her three or four times until he broke through . . . She blacked out at the first jab . . .

*"He raped her then . . . some of us declined the invitation to look
and closed our eyes and turned our heads—but they went
around our circle and cut off a few pairs of eyelids."*

(MOBY-DICK: "That unblinkingly vivid Japanese
sun . . ."

Carl . . . from notes made during and after his captivity, and secret-
ed in his duffle, until finally, in a backhanded gesture—placing
them where I and no one else would discover them—he let them
fall into my hands.

Early in the war, he had tried to enlist in the Air Force, but, for
some reason, had been turned down. Cabling Rico—the only sur-
vivor of the Spanish brothers—in Havana, he arranged to meet him
in England: he assumed the pose of some sort of civilian technician,
and managed to hitchhike on military craft, in a matter of only a
few hours, from Indianapolis to London. Together, Carl and Rico
enlisted in the RAF.

For months we heard nothing—until a card came from Concha: she
was trying to trace Rico through Carl, and Carl through me. I did-
n't know until years after, when I read Carl's notes, that, with my
reply, she had headed for London, and, with her medical training—
she had specialized in surgery—had been taken into the British
Army, and given an assignment in China.

There were others who made notes—the Chinese doctor, Concha's
adjutant, was one—and these I found with Carl's:

*"I once asked Concha where she had gained her knowledge and
technique in gunshot wounds (she was too young for the first
war) and she told me that she had had ample experience during
the various revolutions in Cuba. (In one of these, her father and
twin brothers were army officers, and she fought with the stu-
dents against them—as I believe she fought against her father
in Spain. When her father and Rico's twin were killed, she may
have suffered more than any of us realize . . .*

"Her surgery was remarkable, I've never seen anyone, even a man, more deft and sure. Her reactions were quick, her decisions rapid and accurate, her reflexes amazing. The Japs have ruined her hands, they now shake badly.

"Our captors could never be still for long; they chose projects and then suddenly dropped them for no apparent reason. When they attacked Carl, though, they stayed with the idea until it is a miracle he wasn't killed. They fought over him, dragged him around by his hair (his hands were bound together over his head) and all the time the whip never ceased lashing his back. His mouth was bleeding; blood came from his nose in spurts and bubbles. His knees were raw from being dragged back and forth over the sand and gravel; when one tired of the whip, another took over. They broke his teeth and ribs, and when he evacuated, they dragged him about in it. His pleading was pitiful, it was what might have been expected from a woman, in extreme pain and fear . . .

"When finally they tired of him, only Rico and I would touch him—the others turned away. We tried to clean him as best we could, but we had nothing to work with. Rico got some putrid water from a ditch, and we threw it over his buttocks. He was in a great deal of pain for some time—broken teeth and ribs, abrasions on his legs, his back practically flayed. And all the time he tried to explain himself, weeping and pleading incoherently. I don't know what I pitied more, his condition of mind or body. He finally fell into an exhausted sleep. I think Rico was disgusted with him, but he has a big heart and like me was more charitable, because we felt pity at having had to watch—and we were forced to watch. Neither of us, after all, knew how we would react in his position. The Japs are past masters at reducing human beings . . ."

(Melville—1850—admits the East on board:

"With a start all glared at dark Ahab, who was surrounded by five dusky phantoms that seemed fresh formed out of air."

"For me, I silently recalled the mysterious shadows I had seen creeping on board the Pequod during the dim Nantucket dawn . . .

". . . while the subordinate phantoms soon found their place among the crew, though still as it were somehow distinct from them, yet that hair-turbaned Fedallah remained a muffled mystery to the last . . . He has such a creature as civilized, domestic people in the temperate zone only see in their dreams, and that but dimly; but the like of whom now and then glide among the unchanging Asiatic communities, especially the Oriental isles to the east of the continent—those insulated, immemorial, unalterable countries, which even in these modern days, still preserve much of the ghostly aboriginalness of earth's primal generations . . ."

Carl:

" There was one tree in the yard and in it they hung by the wrists the women who were about to deliver; they tied strips of sheets between their legs, and left them hanging until they died. Those whose kids they had murdered just wandered around crying while their breasts swelled with milk, until some of them burst.

"They gave us nothing to drink and we were fed only salt pork, fish heads, and rice."

(Columbus—who had set out in search of Cipango—sends a message back to the Sovereigns:

". . . the greatest necessity we feel here at the present time is for wines and it is what we desire most to have . . . It is necessary that each time a caravel comes here, fresh meat shall be sent, and even more than that, lambs and little ewe lambs, more females than males, and some little yearling calves, male and female . . ."

Carl:

"Thirst became an agony, until one man went berserk and grabbed a Chinese woman and started sucking her breast. She screamed and fought at first, until she realized that the pressure in her breasts was being relieved, and in a moment each of us had a woman, or half of one . . .

"The Japs laughed and capered around . . . they weren't missing a trick. Mike, I wielded a whip on some of our own men, to save myself. I went down on my knees to those little brown bastards and did as they told me. I must have taken down a hundred of them . . ."

(Columbus:

"Thus, as I have already said, I saw no cannibals, nor did I hear of any, except in a certain island called Charis, which is the second from Española, on the side towards India, where dwell a people who are considered by the neighboring islanders as most ferocious: and these feed upon human flesh."

(and elsewhere:

"The boys that they take they castrate; as we cause castration; because they become fatter for eating; and the mature men also, when they take them they kill them and they eat them: and they eat the intestines fresh and the extreme members of the body . . ."

Carl:

"Believe me, Mike, it was the warm milk—the horror of those days and nights, and the affection I had for him. He had been through so much, and when they shot the aphrodisiac into him and we heard what they intended, the Chinese doctor groaned again.

"Night fell, and Rico had thrown his beaten body off Concha's a hundred times, and each time they threw him on her he promised her he wouldn't hurt her. She didn't appear to be afraid, even when some of the boys shouted at him to take her, that he couldn't fight that drug. He shook like the ague, and kept his jaws clamped tight; his eyes burned, and he was so close to breaking that we all wondered how he held out. The Japs finally tired of that game and went inside for chow, and Rick stumbled off by himself . . .

"It was dark, and when I found him he was lying on his back, his arms rigid at his sides, the bloody nail-less fingers clenched. I ran my hands over his sweat-slick body . . .

"I had to hold his hips with both arms, he pitched so violently . . . I could feel my mouth tearing and my jaws breaking . . ."

(Ishmael, in MOBY-DICK—embedded with a cannibal:

"I looked at the grand and glorious fellow . . ."

"Wild he was; a very sight of sights to see; yet I began to feel myself mysteriously drawn to him."

"For though I tried to move his arm—unlock his bridegroom clasp—yet, sleeping as he was, he still hugged me tightly, as though naught but death should part us . . ."

(Melville, elsewhere:

> *"The Anglo-Saxons—lacking grace*
> *To win the love of any race;*
> *Hated by myriads dispossessed*
> *. . . —the Indians East and West."*

(and

> *"Asia shall stop her at the least,*
> *That old inertness of the East."*

Carl:

*"Did you ever see a man die, Mike? The Japs made me beat
Curley—one of our own boys—to death, and I guess that's
when I really lost my mind: I can't help it, it was a wonderful
sensation . . . they had kicked in his face first, until we couldn't
understand a word he said, but he pleaded and whimpered, and
his wild, pain-racked eyes stared at me . . .*

*"Among the prisoners was a missionary family, who had a little
girl about ten years old, fat, blue-eyed and blonde. The Japs
thought it would hurt the parents more if they tortured the
child, so they decided to rape her. They used a sword point to
make her big enough . . . Dozens of them took her . . . she lay in
a pool of blood, cried all the time, and never lost consciousness.
We were all driven crazy—I doubt if any one had ever said an
unkind word to her in her life, she just didn't know what it was
all about.*

*"After chow the Japs came back and decided to have more game
with her. Rico didn't have a square inch of skin on him that
hadn't been torn or burned, and he couldn't get on his feet, but
he crawled over to her, spoke to her quietly, and put his hands—
burned and bleeding—on her neck. He put his head down on his
arms . . . and in seconds, she was dead. The Chinese doctor felt
her pulse, and then gently released Rico's hands . . .*

*" The Japs never could stand being frustrated, they almost killed
Rico for that gesture . . . I don't know how he survived it. Blood
trickled down his chin where he bit through his lip, and when
they left him, he shook uncontrollably . . ."*

TWO

When he was finally rescued—the town was relieved near the end of the war—Carl didn't return directly to Indianapolis. Wealthy with back pay, he went first to the Mayo Clinic, for plastic surgery and other repairs; then he rejoined Rico and Concha, and two or three others from the RAF—there was an ex-prizefighter, whose only name, so far as I could find out, was Meat-Nose. They collected others—a singer named Joey was one—and formed a dance band. One or two got jobs as test pilots, on the side, and together they rented a ramshackle old house on the coast of California, which they all shared.

Leaving Minnesota, Carl came first to Indianapolis, staying only overnight—his manner as affable, his personality and presence as broad, hazarded, and infrangible as it had ever been. When I asked him once, only vaguely, about the war, he leaned back in his chair— I thought he would fall, or the chair would break; he laughed heartily, his great head rocking as I had seen it so often before—and changed the subject.

But he left his notes for me—though I didn't find them until later. I don't know how he did it—I was with him when he unpacked his duffle—saw him take out the dirty clothes, the spare airplane parts, pieces of sheet music, photographs of friends and bartenders; trinkets and lucky charms, Indian relics and archeological fragments; a thumbed and tattered collection of pre-war comic books—the circulating library of the POW camp; and, at the bottom of the sack, down among the last of the comics, a book that he must have picked up in England, published by John Lehman of London: Melville, H.: THE CONFIDENCE-MAN.

Again, for a long time, we heard nothing. Then a letter came from Meat-Nose . . . he had heard that I was Carl's brother, and a doctor, and he was asking my help. He'd had a talk with Carl that he tape-recorded, without Carl knowing it, and he transcribed some of Carl's words and sent them to me:

"I don't expect you to understand, it's a feeling that can't be described. Joey is different . . . even after I'm through with him, the sensation of pleasure goes on and on and builds up until I'm drunk with it . . . nothing seems real, I'm above everything human, I see nothing but red streamers of blood widening out . . . For hours afterward I can see the kid's eyes wide with pain, his face twisted, and I can hear that voice everyone admires so beating in my ears, in my blood . . . after I'm home in bed, I can relive the whole thing . . .

"I know he's insane. I wish I could stop. I never felt this way with anyone before. There have been others who were afraid of me, but none like Joe. When he's panicked to the edge of madness, I think my veins will bust . . .

"When his voice is gone, and he can't manage to get on his knees without pulling himself up, I look at him, and I'm sad because he doesn't die. I tell him I hate him, I swear at him, and he tries to get to his knees and starts kissing my feet and looks at me with those wild eyes . . . Even after I've thrown down the whip I like to sink my fingers into his flesh and twist it. He begs me to stop, prays to me, swears he wants to make me happy—then he says that if the only way I can love him is to hurt him, then hurt him more.

"What in hell keeps him alive? How does anyone survive . . . ? I thought sometimes that I'd reached the end with him, and I've even considered taking him away like he begs me to . . . let his hair grow, dress him like a woman, take him where everyone will think he's my wife. I was about to make up my mind to do it, when he refused to let me cut him up so he'd look like a woman. Why in hell he wants to hang on to such a sorry mess of stuff as he has, I don't know, but the little bastard clings to it as though it were made of gold . . ."

THREE

The cigar gone, burned down beyond rekindling—the stump splayed in the ashtray—I close the books, and get to my feet. The suburbs, the city itself seem hushed . . . standing alone at the desk, I enjoy for a moment possession of myself, and of the attic, the form and structure of the house, and beyond, the city, the plains.

My joints are stiff, and I recall the bottle of ale, drunk earlier in the evening, downstairs in the old kitchen, when I was in a nineteenth-century mood—a little painful now . . .

The creak of the planks seems louder, as I move toward the stairs. Descending the dark stairwell, I tread softly.

The house is quiet, the lights out. Pausing a moment in the hallway, I can hear Linda's breathing. Then I pass down the second flight, and out the front door . . .

The air is chilled, but the wind is quiet . . . the blackberry winter, the catbird storm, subsiding as we push past midnight, into the early hours . . .

Returning to the kitchen, I think of eating—cold meatloaf, a piece of rye bread, another bottle of ale. There is an urge to turn on the television, hunt for some late show, a bit of fiction that will haul me into the screen, the eye of the thing. Hesitating between the two— refrigerator and TV—I am drawn both ways. Then I pass beyond them, move quietly to the stairs and climb again, both flights, moving swiftly through the dark, through the familiarity of many years in the old house. I climb once more to the attic.

FOUR

A card came from Carl, postmarked St. Louis. He said that he had left the coast for good, was in St. Louis, but gave no address.

Later I discovered that his departure, and the break-up of the band, was coincidental with the death, under mysterious circumstances, of the singer named Joey. Joey was a good sailor, had managed boats all his life—but he took a small catboat out when the storm warnings were up, headed the thing into the rain and wind . . . and, according to the Coast Guard, deliberately capsized her, turning downwind, and then coming about, so that she jibed. His body—what was left of it—was never found . . .

Why Carl came to St. Louis, in particular, I didn't know . . . although I found out later. I also found that he was not alone: he had brought Concha with him . . .

There followed a succession of weird illnesses, disconnected physical manifestations, and, as with the epilepsy, he took the trouble to report to me: random cards, postmarked St. Louis, giving the strict details, and no address.

He reported the appearance of a succession of shapes and markings in odd areas of his body—stars, crosses, and various abstractions, like microscopic cell life . . . One after another, or in groups, they appeared, and vanished . . .

> (MOBY-DICK: ". . . *the visible surface of the Sperm Whale is not the least among the many marvels he presents. Almost invariably it is all over obliquely crossed and recrossed with numberless straight marks in thick array.*"
>
> "*By my retentive memory of the hieroglyphics upon one Sperm Whale in particular, I was*

*much struck with a plate representing the old
Indian characters chiselled on the famous hiero-
glyphic palisades on the banks of the Upper Mis-
sissippi. Like those mystic rocks, too, the mystic-
marked whale remains undecipherable."*

These shapes and forms finally resolved into a set of mammary
rudiments—a mere suggestion of nipples, appearing in lines from
the crotch to the true breasts, to the armpits. They remained for
some time, and then disappeared.

Later, during the summer—with the intense heat beating up from
river, brick, and asphalt, as it can only in St. Louis—he reported
what appeared to be Elephantiasis of the Scrotum—the scrotum
swollen and hanging to his knees, the penis enveloped, with only an
invagination to indicate its presence. Whether he treated this con-
dition, or allowed it to pursue its course, in any case, he eventually
recovered.

Over a considerable period of time, he lost several teeth. Nothing
seemed to happen to them, they didn't decay or cause pain—they
simply fell out. And, in every empty socket—after an extended
delay—he grew a replacement; so that, by the time the process
ended, he had, to a large extent, a third set of teeth.

At one time, he developed an abdominal swelling, so marked and
painful it could not be ignored. For this, he went to the hospital, and
underwent surgery. The result was the removal of a teratoma, or
dermoid cyst—containing bits of skin, hair, nails, teeth, and tongue,
fully developed. The only explanation was the predatory conquest
by Carl, at some very early prenatal stage, of an unfortunate, com-
petitive twin. The lesser organism, attacked and overcome, had nev-
ertheless managed to place random cells within the folds and
envelopes of the conquering embryo; and these, now fully devel-
oped, had waited until Carl's full growth to present themselves.

Recovering from the operation, he became involved in a drunken
brawl. The trouble started in a tavern, spread to the sidewalk, and
eventually to the whole block, and Carl, resisting the police, turned

on an officer and attacked him. I never discovered the nature of the attack, but it put the officer in the hospital and Carl in jail.

Locked in solitary, in a cell remote from the others, Carl remained out of control, raving and screaming long after he was sober.

Then he suddenly became quiet. He began chatting with the guards, and, through them, sent messages to the other officers. In a short time, he was in a front office, having an interview . . . and a little after that, he was on the street, a free man, all charges dropped. He had simply conned his way out . . .

Once when I asked him about this, he laughed, put his arm on my shoulder, and quoted Melville, with appropriate flourish: ". . . men are jailors all; jailors of themselves."

. . . and added, matter-of-factly: "I liberated myself . . ."

For a while, Carl seemed to desert Concha, or at least two-time her. He took up with his final companion, a creature named Bonnie—fat, blowsy, alcoholic . . . she would sit in a rumpled bed, drunk, dirty, her stringy hair falling down, and quote Wordsworth and Keats . . . sneezing and weeping violently, lamenting that she suffered from "Rose Fever": unconsoled when Carl told her that Hart Crane, American poet, was similarly allergic . . .

Carl once bragged to me, confidentially, that he had accomplished intercourse with Bonnie twelve times during thirty hours . . .

Whatever else he did was mysterious . . . but the law was on his heels again—his position in St. Louis became untenable. Expecting to hear of his arrest, I was surprised to hear, instead, that he had committed himself to a private institution. It was a shrewd gesture: the police gradually lost interest in him, and yet, the commitment having been his own act, he was free to leave whenever the heat was off.

I tried very hard to locate him, but could find no trace—as usual, he had left no address. For many months, I knew nothing of him, and I began to feel that he was passing, or had already passed, into institutional oblivion.

FIVE

The New York Central train, westbound for St. Louis, rumbled out of the Indianapolis station, and I settled myself by the window, with little thought of sleep.

Slumping, I let my shoulder and the side of my head rest against the window. My bag was in the rack overhead, and in my pocket, my breast pocket, was the letter from Carl: I had, at long last, an address, and I was using it quickly, before it passed, like all the others, into obsolescence.

He had written of his discharge from the institution—and had taken the trouble to enclose a letter from the staff, proclaiming him cured. He announced, further, that he had opened a one-chair barbershop, in the old section of St. Louis, on 4th Street—and he went so far as to invite me to spend the weekend. Coming off the swing shift at midnight, I had packed my bag, and headed for the first train.

I thought of Carl as a barber, and wondered where and how he had learned this skill—or if he had taken the trouble to learn at all. My eyes closed, I became numbed, insulated, like the dim interior in which I was riding. I may have slept, I'm not sure; I had the sense, in any case, of entering and passing through something . . .

When I opened my eyes, there was gray in the sky. It was not dawn—just a dull, general lifting of the dark. We were in southern Illinois, the tracks slicing diagonally across flat, squared-off farm land. Snow remained on the ground, and occasional gusts of sleet and cold rain washed the outer glass.

I may have slept again. When I looked through the window, it was full day, though still overcast. But the land had changed, and I didn't quite understand how . . . the flatness was there, but there was a different tilt to it, a kind of flow, an imminence. Sitting up straight,

I bought coffee and a dry cheese sandwich from a vendor. As the hot, strong liquid went down my throat, I realized that we were approaching St. Louis, and the river . . .

All at once, I understood why Carl had come here, to St. Louis, of all places; why California had been only a stopping place, and this, the Mound City, had become his inevitable destination. I could see ahead, in the distance, some elevations of earth: I couldn't tell whether these were part of the original Indian mounds, or railroad embankments, or perhaps part of the levee system. In any case, the contour was low, level, and smooth; with the knowledge of the location of the city on the river, and the river's place in the face of the land, I realized that St. Louis was "home," the very eye and center of centripetal American geography, the land pouring in upon itself. I thought of China, and recalled that Carl's journey from there, from all that had happened there, was an eastward voyage, across half the globe; and, perhaps like Ishmael on board the *Pequod*, he was hunting back toward the beginnings of things; and, like the voyage of the *Pequod*,—or of any of the various caravels of Columbus that struck fierce weather returning from the Indies—perhaps Carl's eastward voyage, his voyage "home," was disastrous . . .

We entered East St. Louis, and the train slowed, as we passed through mile after mile of factory, tenement, dump, and slum, an abandoned industrial desolation . . .

Rising over the earth mounds, the tracks entered a bridge, and we approached the river. The cold rainy wind blew waves onto the surface—dark black and purple, the wind squalls rushing across it, here and there turning a white cap. Through the steel girders I watched the water as long as I could see it. When we reached the other side, I felt that we had passed over a great hump . . .

Leaving the train at Union Station, I headed for 4th St., and had little trouble finding Carl. Tucked in a corner, in an ancient loft building, it looked like a poor spot for business. But the shop was open, and he was busy.

The sign read CARL AUSTIN MILLS, MASTER BARBER, and underneath, "I Need Your Head In My Business." As I opened the door, he looked up from his work, and I detected in his glance only surprise—I had not told him I was coming—and pleasure. Stepping forward, he offered me his hand, and his grip was familiar and sturdy—warmth and affection in it, such as he had seldom shown me, but nothing patronizing: it was the glad warmth of an animal. Returning to his customer, he gestured me to a chair, the sweep of his arm embracing and offering his hospitality, making rich and desirable the confines of his shop. He asked many friendly questions . . .

I looked around. Every inch of space, beyond what held his equipment, was taken up with pictures, decorations, objects of one sort or another. I had no idea how he had made such a collection. There were rocks, minerals, semi-precious stones of all shapes, sizes, and colors, some of them shining. There were souvenirs and toys from every carnival and circus in the land. Airplane parts hung from the walls, a split half of a propeller was suspended on thin wires from the ceiling. Pictures, paintings, and textile fragments appeared everywhere, the subjects ranging from Mayan, Aztec, and Inca stone and art work, to movie stars, nude girls, and pornography. Relics from Alaska, and other Indian artifacts were stuck on shelves. The magazine table included the morning newspaper, and thirty-year-old copies of the *National Geographic* and the *Police Gazette*. There was a settled look, a look of age . . .

Hanging in front of the mirror, directly back of the chair, so that strands of black hair descended among the bottles of oil and tonic, was the shrunken Indian head that he had won in a poker game in Alaska. Carl stepped back to survey his customer, his own great cranium coming close to the shrunken one . . .

He began telling a story—a wild tale about barbering among primitive Eskimos in Alaska, the natives being confused between haircuts and scalping. The customers seemed to know that he was lying, and this added to it . . .

I listened to him talk, watched him cut several heads of hair. The warmth of the shop entered me, became quieting. In addition to being a storyteller, he had a skill at his trade; his hands moved deftly over the men's heads, weaving a phrenological spell.

The city of St. Louis, with the advent of the railroads after the Civil War, had turned its back upon the river and faced westward, had abandoned the old continental blood stream . . . Carl, setting up in this section, hugging the river, now drew warehousemen, truckers, straggling barge- and riverboat-men from blocks, perhaps miles around . . .

I became sleepy, began to drowse in my chair. Carl gave me the key to his room, suggested that I take a nap . . . I was almost asleep, as I stumbled out the door.

He lived in a furnished room, not far from the shop. It was small, poor, and bare, with the simplest furnishings—as barren of his personality as the shop was rich with it . . . too tired to look further, to dig beyond this front, I stretched across the bed and fell asleep.

When I awoke, it was midafternoon. Shaking myself, I sat on the edge of the bed, took a slower look around. On the floor, by the bed, were three books: a volume of Sappho, one of Homer, and the poems of Hart Crane . . .

Washing at the hand basin, I headed again for the shop. The rain had stopped, but cold wind blew off the river, pouring down the streets that led away from it.

A customer was just leaving and Carl was alone when I arrived. He suddenly decided to close, hustled me out, and locked the door, before anyone else showed up.

For several blocks we walked aimlessly, Carl—without coat or hat, his shirt open—sniffing the air like a dog. Then he stopped, clutched my elbow, and pointed . . . we turned and headed east, toward the river. A summer excursion boat was drawn up on the brick embankment, tilting at an angle. Together, just for the hell of it, we clambered aboard, laughing like kids, getting our feet soaked. I almost fell overboard when my foot slipped: Carl's hand flashed out, thrusting for my arm, and I got up safely.

Arms outstretched, balancing ourselves on the tilting planks, we made our way to the prow, and stood for some moments. The wind drove down on us from the north . . .

Melville:

> "Natives of all sorts, and foreigners; men of business and men of pleasure; parlour men and backwoodsmen; farm-hunters and fame-hunters; heiress hunters, gold-hunters, buffalo-hunters, bee-hunters, happiness-hunters, truth-hunters, and still keener hunters after all these hunters. Fine ladies in slippers, and moccasined squaws; Northern speculators and Eastern philosophers; English, Irish, German, Scotch, Danes; Santa Fe traders in striped blankets, and Broadway bucks in cravats of cloth of gold; fine-looking Kentucky boatmen, and Japanese-looking Mississippi cotton planters; Quakers in full drab, and United States soldiers in full regimentals; slaves, black, mulatto, quadroon; modish young Spanish Creoles, and old-fashioned French Jews; Mormons and Papists; Dives and Lazarus; jesters and mourners, teetotallers and convivialists, deacons and blacklegs; hard-shelled Baptists and clay-eaters; grinning negroes, and Sioux chiefs solemn as high-priests. In short, a piebald parliament, an Anacharsis Cloots congress of all kinds of that multiform pilgrim species, man.
>
> "As pine, beech, birch, ash, hackmatack, hemlock, spruce, basswood, maple, interweave their foliage in the natural wood, so these varieties of mortals blended their varieties of visage and garb. A Tartar-like picturesqueness; a sort of pagan abandonment and assurance. Here reigned the dashing and all-fusing spirit of the West, whose type is the Mississippi itself, which, uniting the streams of the most distant and opposite zones, pours

them along, helter-skelter, in one cosmopolitan and confident tide."

Carl faced north, his whitened knuckles gripping the rail. I turned away, headed toward the vacant cabin, the river flowing south. In a moment he followed me, put his arm on my shoulder, and I felt again an animal affection. Huddled in my overcoat, tilted against the angle of the deck, I stood by him . . .

All at once, his body drew in upon itself; he gathered his jacket to his throat, clutched it with his free hand . . . he was chilled and threadbare, and the scrubby look of poverty came over him . . .

Melville:

> *"In the forward part of the boat, not the least attractive object, for a time, was a grotesque negro cripple, in towcloth attire and an old coal-sifter of a tambourine in his hand, who, owing to something wrong about his legs, was, in effect, cut down to the stature of a Newfoundland dog; his knotted black fleece and good-natured, honest black face rubbing against the upper part of people's thighs as he made shift to shuffle about, making music, such as it was, and raising a smile even from the gravest. It was curious to see him, out of his very deformity, indigence, and houselessness, so cheerily endured, raising mirth in some of that crowd, whose own purses, hearths, hearts, all their possessions, sound limbs included, could not make gay.*
>
> *"'What is your name, old boy?' said a purple-faced drover, putting his large purple hand on the cripple's bushy wool, as if it were the curled forehead of a black steer.*
>
> *"'Der Black Guinea dey calls me, sar.'*
>
> *"'And who is your master, Guinea?'*
>
> *"'Oh, sar, I am der dog widout massa.'*
>
> *"'A free dog, eh? Well, on your account, I'm sorry for that, Guinea. Dogs without masters fare hard.'*
>
> *"'So dey do, sar; so dey do. But you see, sar, dese here legs? What ge'mman want to own dese here legs?'*
>
> *"'But where do you live?'*

"All 'long shore, sar; dough now I'se going to see brodder at der landing; but chiefly I libs in der city.'

"St. Louis, ah? Where do you sleep there of nights?'

"On der floor of der good baker's oven, sar.'

"In an oven? whose, pray? What baker, I should like to know, bakes such black bread in his oven, alongside of his nice white rolls, too. Who is that too charitable baker, pray?'

"Dar he be,' with a broad grin lifting his tambourine high over his head.

"The sun is the baker, eh?'

"Yes, sar, in der city dat good baker warms der stones for dis ole darkie when he sleeps out on der pabements o' nights.'

"But that must be in the summer only, old boy. How about winter, when the cold Cossacks come clattering and jingling? How about winter, old boy?'

"Den dis poor old darkie shakes werry bad, I tell you, sar. Oh, sar, oh! don't speak ob der winter,' he added, with a reminiscent shiver, shuffling off into the thickest of the crowd, like a half-frozen black sheep nudging itself a cosy berth in the heart of the white flock."

Moving to the down-tilted side where we had climbed aboard, Carl and I clambered ashore, soaking our feet again. At the top of the embankment we turned, shivering in the wind, and looked back at the boat . . .

. . . it seemed shrunken, a toy, helpless on its perch of bricks.

We headed back into the city, chattering, half-running with cold. Carl made straight for a neon sign, with the word BAR . . .

We had some drinks, and wandered on . . . I tried to talk with him, or get him to talk, but his eyes looked beyond me, his mind held to no thought . . . he took one drink at a bar, and was off again.

Then again he turned to me, all warmth and consideration, his hand on my shoulder, the gesture affectionate, and firm . . .

As we wandered, the buildings became poorer, dirtier, more popu-
lous. Strange figures huddled in hallways, clustered around the doors
of taverns—their lips thinned, thirsty, bitten back with poverty.

. . . at some time in the evening, we stood at the stage door of the
burlesque theatre, while Carl tried to talk his way in . . . there was a
glimpse of a near-naked girl . . .

Later, Carl ran out of money. I tried to loan him or give him some,
offered him my wallet, everything I had—but he protested fiercely,
the evening was to be his. The penurious, pinched look came over
him . . . he reached into his pocket, took out a couple of linty crack-
ers, and shared them with me . . .

> (and on the 4th voyage of Columbus the supply of
> biscuits became infested with worms . . . the men,
> refusing to remove these animals for fear of reduc-
> ing the volume of food, took to eating only at night
> so they wouldn't have to see them . . .

We passed another bar, and Carl brought me to a halt. He stood for
a moment . . . then cautioned me to wait outside, while he went in.

I watched him approach the first customer, standing at the rear end
of the bar. They shook hands, Carl slapped his back, put a foot on
the rail. The man gradually warmed, his body shifting, his coat
hanging looser . . . they had a drink together, and the customer
turned his back suspiciously to the rest of the room, drew some-
thing from his pocket, and he and Carl talked. After some
moments, Carl drew back, placed his hand familiarly on the other's
shoulder, his great head nodding assurances . . . and turned and
came out the door. He said nothing. . . but at the next bar, he paid
for drinks with a new $50 bill . . .

I have an image of the two of us—Carl stocky, broad-chested, jack-
et and shirt open to the rain, and I, slight, limping, hat and overcoat
hanging sloppily on my frame—the two of us ambling side by side,
drunk and speechless, a clown pair . . .

("Good friars and friends, behold me here /
A poor one-legged pioneer . . ."

The Melville line came to me as I pushed back the heavy door of a tenderloin tavern, the room cluttered with derelicts, sleeping, drinking, haranguing one another . . .

". . . a limping, gimlet-eyed, sour-faced person—it may be some discharged custom-house officer, who, suddenly stripped of convenient means of support, had concluded to be avenged on government and humanity by making himself miserable for life . . ."

". . . a lean old man, whose flesh seemed salted codfish, dry as combustibles; head, like one whittled by an idiot out of a knot; flat, bony mouth, nipped between buzzard nose and chin; expression, flitting between hunks and imbecile . . ."

". . . a singular character in a grimy old regimental coat, a countenance at once grim and wizened, interwoven paralysed legs, stiff as icicles, suspended between rude crutches, while the whole rigid body, like a ship's long barometer on gimbals, swung to and fro . . ."

Soaking, drinking in the words of THE CONFIDENCE-MAN, I leaned heavily across the bar, and turned to Carl. He seemed attentive, and I tried once more to get him to talk—asked him about the war, the POW camp, about Rico, Concha, and California . . . for a moment, he was serious and sad . . .

Then he pounded me on the back, waved his arm, and presented to me one of the characters, crippled and bearded, who had come to beg a drink . . .

Carl ordered for him, swerved himself to the old man's misery:—a relation of hollow vowels, toothless and full of beer . . .

"After three years, I grew sick of lying in a grated iron bed alongside of groaning thieves and mouldering burglars. They gave me five silver dollars, and these crutches, and I hobbled off. I had an only brother who went to Indiana, years ago. I begged

about, to make up a sum to go to him; got to Indiana at last, and they directed me to his grave. It was on a great plain, in a log-church yard with a stump fence, the old gray roots sticking all ways like moose-antlers. The bier, set over the grave, it being the last dug, was of green hickory; bark on, and green twigs sprouting from it. Some one had planted a bunch of violets on the mound, but it was a poor soil (always choose the poorest soil for graveyards), and they were all dried to tinder. I was going to sit and rest myself on the bier and think about my brother in heaven, but the bier broke down, the legs being only tacked. So, after driving some hogs out of the yard that were rooting there, I came away, and, not to make too long a story of it, here I am, drifting down stream . . ." (Melville)

Other derelicts left their tables, sidled toward us, clustering, jostling gently . . . Carl's arm swept out, gathered them in . . . every glass in the house was filled . . .

We passed the ruins of a cheap hotel, gutted by fire. Dark figures, cold and wet, stood about, staring at the stalagmites of charred wood . . . Carl spoke to one of them—he had been the night clerk, was still hovering over his job; he told us about the fire, about the man who drank rubbing alcohol, canned heat, and the like, and had managed to get his clothes soaked with the stuff, and then lit a cigarette—the bedding caught fire, the clerk had heard and seen him, screaming from his room, folded in blue flame . . .

Melville:

". . . to the silent horror of all, two threads of greenish fire, like a forked tongue, darted out between the lips; and in a moment the cadaverous face was crawled over by a swarm of worm-like flames.

". . . covered all over with spires and sparkles of flame, that faintly, crackled in the silence, the uncovered parts of the body burned before us, precisely like phosphorescent shark in a midnight sea.

> *"The eyes were open and fixed; the mouth was curled like a*
> *scroll, and every lean feature firm as in life; while the whole*
> *face, now wound in curls of soft blue flame, wore an aspect of*
> *grim defiance, and eternal death."*

Past midnight, Carl's manner became secretive, mysterious. For the
first time, he began to move as though he had a destination, and this
assurance made him the more devious, so that he acted

like Columbus, 4th voyage, treating the Indians with suspicion, misleading
even the Sovereigns as to his navigations and discoveries . . .

> ("The seamen no longer carried charts because the
> Admiral had taken them all . . ."

or like Melville's Benito Cereno, a man trapped . . .

We walked down alleys and across vacant lots, pausing with
grandiose watchfulness at the corners . . . more than once we dou-
bled back on ourselves . . . at the corner of a narrow street, among
warehouses, we stopped, smoked a cigarette, appeared casual . . .
then moved slowly down the street, turned into an alley, and
knocked at a lighted door. A man—short, bald-headed—opened
after a moment, recognized and admitted Carl, and stared hard at
me. I was passed, on Carl's word, and we moved through a long cor-
ridor, down some stairs, and, opening another door, entered a large,
low-ceilinged room, filled with men, mostly middle-aged and
beyond. Packing cases were set up at one side, serving as a bar, and
there was a rudimentary stage, a raised platform, with overhead
lighting, at the far end of the room. Nearby, a man beat notes out of
a decrepit piano. Tables and chairs were scattered about, facing the
stage. A few whores circulated among the men. We took a table,
and I waited, looked around, while Carl went to the bar for drinks.
The place had a familiar aspect, and I recognized it, from movies
and TV, as a duplicate of the old western music hall and saloon—bar
along the side, tables and chairs in the middle, stage across the end
of the room. The girls were in character.

Carl picked up a girl at the bar, brought her back with him, sat her between us. She was a gorgeous negress. The lights in the room flashed and went out, leaving only the stage lights. The men applauded, took their seats . . .

In a moment, a girl appeared on the stage. Tall, blonde, she wore a green evening dress, covered with tiny spangles, and her equipment included various accessories—gloves, scarves, fake fur, a jacket—to be handled, manipulated, shifted, and disposed of. She came to the front of the stage, so the light fell directly on her head and shoulders, creating shadows under her curves; she was still, hands held before her, her eyes, not calculating, not innocent, taking in the room.

The piano began to thump . . . the girl tapped her foot, her knee shaking the vertical lines of the gown . . . finger by finger, she removed one glove . . .

I sat back, the liquor, the closeness of the room, the people, the negress at my side, filling me. Carl and I lit cigars. There was satisfaction in the show, in the girl's presence on the stage, and I realized that in the flat gray of movies and television I had built up a hunger for just this: whatever the medium, just the flesh, here, in the room . . .

          (I recall, now, that, here in Indianapolis, the one burlesque theatre has been closed, to be converted into a revival hall . . .

          (as, in England, the Puritans closed the Elizabethan theatres, before getting to that other menace, the naked American Indian . . .

One by one the girl's accessories were removed and tossed aside. She stood in the strapless gown, at the very front of the stage, the light slanting on her from behind. There was, in her erect figure, an illusion of beauty, dignity, judgment, wisdom—of all desirable and satisfying values . . .

She turned, ambled upstage, and her hand went to the zipper in the small of her back . . .

> (and I thought that this was as intimate, as naughty as A Peep At Polynesian Life, Melville's Typee . . .

Turning again, she held the now unsupported gown with her fingers, cupping her breasts, practicing all manner of delay and ruse, before revealing herself.

Carl leaned in front of the negress to speak to me, and I tilted toward him, so that our heads met over her breasts . . . the liquor had gone to his voice, as well as to my head, and I couldn't make out all that he said, but his manner was professorial, instructive—something about the importance of revelation, as opposed to objective study—the loss, in a society with a scientific bias, of the art of discovery . . . the negress remained immobile, her eyes flashing, a smile rich on her face . . .

Little by little, the performer's gown came off, to the applause of the hard-breathing men . . . she stood, displayed herself, in a g-string . . . the applause grew harder,

and my body froze: a negro, full black, appeared on the stage, stripped to the waist—the girl went to him, stood before him, facing front, and in the white light, his large, magnificent hands moved over her . . .

The quality of breathing in the room, the girl's eyes, all changed . . . I couldn't look at the dark girl beside me . . .

> (Daggoo, in Moby-Dick: "Who's afraid of black's afraid of me! I'm quarried out of it!"

> (and Melville, elsewhere: ". . . as though a white man were anything more dignified than a white-washed negro."

I turned to Carl, just to see him rise, move to the back of the room, and the door . . . following him, I reached the door after he was already gone . . . I paused, glanced once more at the stage . . .

the girl was naked . . . the negro dropped to his knees before her, clutched her buttocks with his hands, and drew her toward him . . .

I found Carl on the sidewalk, his feet shifting, almost dancing, his eyes wild . . . as soon as I came up, he took off, and I struggled to keep up with him, following his back as fast as I could, down deserted streets and alleys . . . I ran as I had not run in years, perhaps never before, the light and heavy beat of my stride echoing from the buildings, the cold air burning in my lungs . . .

When I woke up, it was early morning, and I was sprawled across Carl's bed, hat and overcoat still on, my head hanging between bed and wall. I sat up, discovered Carl sitting on the floor, his head propped against the wall. He was surrounded by books and comic books, smoking a cigar, and reading

S U P E R M A N
in startling
3-D,

holding to his face the 3-dimensional glasses that come with the book—a bit of green cellophane before the left eye, and red before the right . . . turning the pages, laughing. Beside him, open at various places, were the volumes of Sappho, Homer, and Crane that I had seen before, a good many more comic books . . . and a copy of Melville's CLAREL.

Seeing me awake, he lit another cigar, handed it to me. I smoked, held my head in my hands, tried to reconstruct the evening. Carl finished SUPERMAN, picked up CLAREL, and

all at once, the tobacco went to my stomach . . . I made a rush to the hand basin, was violently ill . . .

*(Melville: "While for him who would fain revel
in tobacco, but cannot, it is a thing at which
philanthropists must weep, to see such an one,
again and again, madly returning to the cigar,
which, for his incompetent stomach, he cannot
enjoy, while still, after each shameful repulse, the
sweet dream of the impossible good goads him on
to his fierce misery once more—poor eunuch!"*

Staggering to the bed, I was galled to see Carl unmoved, reading.
Shifting himself, expanding his diaphragm, holding CLAREL before
him, he read aloud:

*"And he, the quaffer of the brine,
Puckered with that heart-wizening wine
Of bitterness, among them sate
Upon a camel's skull, late dragged
From forth the wave, the eye-pits slagged
With crusted salt."*

I made it to the basin just in time, hung over it a long time . . . there
was nothing in me. When I got back to the bed, Carl had changed:
not considerate, or even interested, he was watchful . . . then his eyes
went back to CLAREL, and he read:

*". . . Sequel may ensue,
Indeed, whose germs one now may view:
Myriads playing pygmy parts—
Debased into equality:
In glut of all material arts
A civic barbarism may be:
Man disennobled—brutalized
By popular science—"*

. . . he was declaiming, posturing outlandishly . . . and he threw
down the book, picked up SUPERMAN again, with the little red and
green glasses . . .

Squeezing my head in my hands, I closed my eyes. When I looked up, all color had vanished. Carl, the furniture, the room appeared in shades of gray. . . . I blinked several times, my eyelids serving as the shutter of a movie camera, then closed my eyes . . .

and behind the closed lids, I saw the room in color, but in disconnected, monocular images, one for each eye . . . in addition, there was a partition, a wall, reaching from the wall of the room to the vertical center of my face, separating the two images . . .

I opened my eyes again, and was at once dizzy: everything that I saw was inverted, upside down . . . rolling onto the bed, I buried my face in the pillow . . .

I slept through most of the day . . . when I got up again, it was late afternoon, and I was alone. Though weak and hungry, I was slept out . . . my body was quiet. I stood by the bed for some moments . . . emptiness and loneliness—the loneliness of public rooms, of personal things used and not loved—entered me. Books were put away, basin washed, ashtrays clean . . . Carl had erased himself from the room . . .

I found him at the shop—busy, loquacious, crisp—with no sign of fatigue. But his manner to me had changed . . . the warmth, the cordiality were gone, not deliberately, but in spite of himself, against his own will . . . I sat for some minutes, listening, chatting with him, trying to find what was there when I had first arrived, the morning before . . . but it was gone, the episode finished.

When he was between customers, I got up, prepared to leave. He followed me to the sidewalk, and we stood for some time at the corner, looking at the curb, at the street, at the gray darkening sky. It was already early evening, another night beginning—the streetlights and neon signs flickered on. Once more I tried to reach him, if only in a direct look from his eyes . . . he held my glance for an instant, and then changed—his posture, his manner, the very structure of his face—something kin to the look of poverty that I had seen before, but not quite the same . . . his shoulders collapsed inward, his eyes were downcast, his face troubled, his head moved restlessly . . .

I thought of the purpose of this visit, of my coming to St. Louis: that I was trying only to reach him, to open a channel . . . of how I had failed, how he had swept me into his own condition, and I had permitted it, allowed myself to become a part of all that he was caught in . . .

> *(Melville: "From being cast away with a brother, good God deliver me!"*

I thought of Melville, separated from Hawthorne . . . and of Columbus, at Valladolid, no longer able to reach the court . . .

I thought of China, the POW camp, of California and Joey: . . . I thought that what is more terrible, even, than all that Carl had done, was the original misery of his being, of his coming to be in a condition that made it possible . . .

> *Melville: "So true it is, and so terrible, too, that up to a certain point the thought or sight of misery enlists our best affection; but, in certain special cases, beyond that point it does not. They err who would assert that invariably this is owing to the inherent selfishness of the human heart. It rather proceeds from a certain hopelessness of remedying excessive and organic ill."*

I remembered the letter Carl had sent me, from the institution, announcing his complete cure . . .

"So far may even the best men err, in judging the conduct of one with the recesses of whose condition he is not acquainted" . . . Melville

I put a hand on his shoulder, took his hand into my other . . . he looked up, raised a smile, a little warmth . . . but it was not Carl . . .

The wind swept around the east corner . . . he looked cold . . . I gave him a squeeze, he slapped me on the shoulder, his chest expanding once more, and we parted . . .

Some days later, back in Indianapolis, I got a postcard from him.

"Dear Herman: The Gin got here!"

and I didn't understand the significance, until I read Melville's letters to Hawthorne—the passionate pouring-out, the reach of one man to another—written in the froth of finishing Moвy-Dиck:

> *"It is a rainy morning; so I am indoors, and all work suspended . . . Would the Gin were here!"*

SIX

"For Delly Ulver: with the deep and true regard and sympathy of Pierre Glendinning.

> *"Thy sad story—partly known before—hath now more fully come to me, from one who sincerely feels for thee, and who hath imparted her own sincerity to me. Thou desirest to quit this neighborhood, and be somewhere at peace, and find some secluded employ fitted to thy sex and age. With this, I now willingly charge myself, and insure it to thee, so far as my utmost ability can go. Therefore—if consolation be not wholly spurned by thy great grief, which too often happens, though it be but grief's*

great folly so to feel—therefore two true friends of thine do here
beseech thee to take some little heart to thee, and bethink thee,
that all thy life is not yet lived; that Time hath surest healing in
his continuous balm. Be patient yet a little while, till thy future
lot be disposed for thee, through our best help; and so, know me
and Isabel thy earnest friends and true-hearted lovers."

Melville, as Pierre . . . no longer chasing sperm oil monsters in the
Pacific, or writing the hard syllables of *Ahab, Flask, Stubb* and *Star-*
buck . . . but softened, turned inward, willingly charges himself to a
"ruined" servant girl: *Delly Ulver . . .*

PIERRE: *". . . this indeed almost unmans me . . ."*

The Pequod sunk and gone, Melville—1851 and '52—writes PIERRE
. . .

WOMAN SUFFRAGE AND POLITICS, Catt and Shuler: "No cause ever
made such rapid strides as that of Woman's Rights from 1850 to 1860."

The New York HERALD, September 7, 1853: "The assemblage of
rampant women which convened at the Tabernacle yesterday was an
interesting phase in the comic history of the Nineteenth Century . . .
a gathering of unsexed women, unsexed in mind, all of them publicly
propounding the doctrine that they should he allowed to step out of
their appropriate sphere to the neglect of those duties which both
human and divine law have assigned to them."

and earlier, Abigail Adams, March, 1776, to her husband, sitting with
the Continental Congress: ". . . and, by the way, in the new code of
laws which I suppose it will be necessary for you to make, I desire
you would remember the ladies and be more favorable to them than
your ancestors. Do not put such unlimited power into the hands of
husbands. Remember all men would be tyrants if they could. If par-
ticular care and attention are not paid to the ladies, we are deter-
mined to foment a rebellion . . ."

There is more, and earlier, in Melville: young Herman, age 21,
shipped on a whaler to the Pacific:
"Weary with the invariable earth, the restless sailor breaks from

every enfolding arm, and puts to sea in height of tempest that
blows off shore. But in long night-watches at the antipodes, how
heavily that ocean gloom lies in vast bales upon the deck; think-
ing that that very moment in his deserted hamlet-home the
household sun is high, and many a sun-eyed maiden meridian
as the sun."

... and there were the islands ...

> *"In mid Pacific, where life's thrill*
> *Is primal—Pagan ..."*

... Typee, Fayaway ...

> *"... the fair breeze of naked nature now blew in their faces."*

> *"'Tis Paradise. In such an hour*
> *Some pangs that rend might take release."*

Back in New England and New York, throughout the long years ...
"pale years of cloistral life" ... with Lizzie, the memory of Fayaway
remained, dug in ...

> PIERRE: *"For whoso once has known this sweet knowledge, and*
> *then fled it; in absence, to him the avenging dream will come."*

Dug in, avenging ... for Melville came to accept Fayaway as origi-
nal sin ...

> *(1850, checks and underscores in the Old Testa-*
> *ment: "... art thou come unto me to call my sin*
> *to remembrance ..."*

... to accept that he had "ruined" her ... and thus, locked in the old
Christian myth, in the burden of Adam, he must make it up to all
womankind:
as Pierre, to Delly ...

as Herman, to Lizzie.

> MARDI: *"And thinking the lady to his mind, being brave like himself . . . he meditated suicide—I would have said, wedlock— and the twain became one."*

> I AND MY CHIMNEY: *"By my wife's ingenious application of the principle that certain things belong of right to female juris- diction, I find myself, through my easy compliance, insensibly stripped by degrees of one masculine prerogative after another."*

> FRAGMENTS FROM A WRITING DESK *(written when he was 19): "What! to be thwarted by a woman! Peradventure baffled by a girl! Confusion! It was too bad! To be outgeneraled, rout- ed, defeated by a mere rib of the earth? It was not to be borne!"*

And there was BENITO CERENO, the Spaniard, captive of his blacks . . . sick of mind and body, loyally sustained (or so it seemed) by Babo, drifting at the mercy of the winds . . .

Melville as Cereno, captive not this time of the Typees, the friend- ly cannibals, but of his whites:

Lizzie, the Shaws, the right and just world (or so it seemed) of the 19th Century . . .

Lizzie as Babo, loyally sustaining Benito through misery . . .

> (and there was the other ship,
> the *Bachelor's Delight*, where all was
> trim and shipshape . . .

CLAREL:

> *"My kin—I blame them not at heart—*
> *Would have me act some routine part,*
> *Subserving family, and dreams*
> *Alien to me—illusive schemes.*

This world clean fails me . . ."

and

"Serve God by cleaving to thy wife,
Thy children. If come fatal strife—
Which I forebode—nay!' and she flung
Her arms about him there, and clung."

The rhyming couplets—Melville's aging force thrashing through eight hundred pages, two volumes, of CLAREL. No longer the powering prose of MOBY-DICK, mounting pilingly upon itself, but couplets: chains, darbies . . .

(the beloved irons that Columbus hugged to himself, swore to die with

(and did, the iron transmuted into his flesh, as arithritic gout . . .

Melville: ". . . so that the gallows presented the truly warning spectacle of a man hanged by his friends."

ISRAEL POTTER: *"The other officer and Israel interlocked. The battle was in the midst of the chaos of blowing canvas. Caught in a rent of the sail, the officer slipped and fell near the sharp edge of the iron hatchway. As he fell, he caught Israel by the most terrible part in which mortality can be grappled. Insane with pain, Israel dashed his adversary's skull against the sharp iron. The officer's hold relaxed, but himself stiffened. Israel made for the helmsman, who as yet knew not the issue of the late tussle. He caught him around the loins, bedding his fingers like grisly claws into his flesh, and hugging him to his heart. The man's ghost, caught like a broken cork in a gurgling bottle neck, gasped with the embrace. Loosening him suddenly, Israel hurled him from him against the bulwarks."*

Melville: still able to tire a Hawthorne:

Una, to her aunt: "Mr. Melville was here a day or two, and Mamma overtired herself during his visit, and was quite unwell for a day or two afterwards."

. . . and Lizzie:

reported by Sam Shaw: "Elizabeth's catarrh is somewhat relieved here but I am sorry to see how generally feeble she is, and prematurely old."

Melville: growing older—Lizzie outlived him by many years—no longer able to thrash . . .

From THE CAREER OF MOCHA DICK: *"From first to last 'Mocha Dick' had nineteen harpoons put into him. He stove fourteen boats and caused the death of over thirty men. He stove three whaling vessels so badly that they were nearly lost, and he attacked and sunk a French merchantman and an Australian trader. He was encountered in every ocean and on every known feeding ground. He was killed off the Brazilian banks in August, 1859, by a Swedish whaler, which gathered him in with scarcely any trouble, but it was always believed that poor old 'Mocha Dick' was dying of old age."*

There was Columbus, 4th voyage, forbidden by the Court to enter the principal island he had discovered . . .

"Moreover every man had it in his power to tell me that the new Governor would have the superintendence of the countries I might acquire."

. . . cruising elsewhere in the Caribbean, battling tempests and Indians, his ships rotting . . .

Ferdinand: "Being here at anchor ten leagues from Cuba, full of hunger and trouble, because they had nothing to eat but hard-tack and a little oil and vinegar, and exhausted by working three pumps day and night because the vessels were ready to sink from the multitude of worms that had bored into them . . ."

. . . putting ashore finally on Jamaica, where the two ships, the *Capitana* and *Santiago,* lashed together, beached, worm-eaten and rotten, ended their careers as houseboats . . .

. . . isolated among his islands—no tools for re-planking or building, his caulkers dead, his crew in mutiny, no ship likely to call as he had earlier reported no gold in Jamaica—Columbus survived for over a year on what food the Indians brought him, living on the arrested caravels . . .

> *There is the old Spanish proverb:* "La verdad no se casa con nadie" . . .

> *and Melville: "Truth will* not *be comforted."*

Shifting in my chair, I become aware again of the house, the attic, the rafters—poised in the quiet of the city, the dark, early-morning hours. I think of the early days in Indiana, the first settlements. I think of my great-grandfather, Hammond Mills, who built this house—and of his well worn philosophy: The Mind is to the Body as the Whole Man is to the Earth . . .

I remember fragments of medical school, the boys and men I studied and lived with . . . one became a gynecologist and surgeon, now has a lucrative, busy practice here in the city, scraping out the female troubles of Indiana . . . another has a commission in the Navy, does brilliant research in Space Medicine: the problems raised by sending human beings into outer space . . .

Shifting again, I am invaded with bitterness: I think of us as a nation of prurient neuters, bald-headed oglers, the men having laid down original tools and taken up others: become science fictioneers, space shippers, nuclear mystics, relinquishing the Body (Earth), seeking to escape it, save only to peer at it naughtily . . . become, with the aid of popular religion, the modern devout of the ether . . .

There is the population—not only of our own country but of the world—become anaplastic, growing, since World War ii, wildly, without roots or viable form . . .

the cells reverting to simplest, undifferentiated forms, breaking down so rapidly as to lose all trace of roots, of origin . . .

SEVEN

I lost track of Carl once again. Letters to both the shop and the room were returned by the post office.

When word came, after many weeks, it was not from Carl, but from doctors at the mental hospital, where he had again been committed. He had finally told them about me, had given them my address, and they wanted me to come: he was violent, and they thought I might help . . .

I boarded the train after midnight, as before. I was no longer interested in motion, in adventure . . . the journey was repetition, return over old ground . . . the fact of direction, of heading west, was not exciting: I was moving from one city to another, a simple act of travel, without meaning . . .

I thought of Carl, as my older brother—and I thought of Herman's older brother, Gansevoort, who failed in business, then in politics, and, heavily in debt, died, age 30, of "nervous derangement . . ."

> Herman, writing to Gansevoort—unaware that the latter had already died: "Remember that composure of mind is every thing."

> and later, writing of another: "This going mad of a friend or acquaintance comes straight home to every man who feels his soul in him,—which but few men do. For in all of us lodges the same fuel to light the same fire. And he who has never felt, momentarily, what madness is has but a mouthful of brains."

Tearing apart the paper cup from which I had finished my coffee, I scribbled a few lines on it:

In Memoriam: Gansevoort Melville

who fails in business
goes to politics;
who fails in politics
goes to heaven.

(who fails in all
goes to whale . . .

and I thought of the contemporary review of MOBY-DICK: *". . . so much trash belonging to the worst school of Bedlam literature . . ."*

Arrived in St. Louis, I went straight to the hospital, and the doctor in charge of Carl admitted me to his office.

I asked about Carl. He said that he was periodically violent, and for this reason was kept in restraint. He was at present in isolation, in a straight jacket. I stood up, paced nervously across the floor—exploiting in my own body the motion denied to Carl. I suggested that whatever else was the matter with him, whatever therapy they might be planning for him, it should be oriented in his having the simplest of personal freedom—that what he needed, first and foremost, was *space* . . .

The doctor looked at me candidly for a moment, and then begged me to follow him—we went out of the office, down a corridor, by elevator to another floor, around several corners, and into a room where masons and carpenters were at work. Motioning the workers aside, he showed me where Carl had terrorized a group of inmates: with nothing but his bare hands, he had ripped the paneling from a window frame, removed the window, and, unable to bend the iron bars, had dug with his finger ends into the stonework and masonry itself . . .

(MOBY-DICK: *"How can the prisoner reach outside except by thrusting through the wall?"*

I asked to see Carl, and the doctor readily assented. We passed through various other parts of the hospital, catching glimpses of patients, in private and public rooms, in varying states . . .

> Melville: *"I have been in mad-houses full of tragic mopers, and seen there the end of suspicion: the cynic, in the moody madness mustering in the corner; for years a barren fixture there; head lopped over, gnawing his own lip, vulture to himself; while, by fits and starts, from the corner opposite came the grimace of the idiot at him."*

We found Carl standing, spread-legged, defiant, in the middle of his barren room. The jacket made him appear armless. He began at once to speak, to declaim:

> "But this notion, that science can play farmer to the flesh, making there what living soil it pleases . . ."

> "Try to rid my mind of it as I may, yet still these chemical practitioners with their tinctures, and fumes, and braziers, and occult incantations, seem to me like Pharaoh's vain sorcerers, trying to beat down the will of heaven."

The words were familiar, though I wasn't sure of the source . . .

> "Please," I said, turning to the doctor, "take off the jacket . . ."

He hesitated a moment, and then complied.

Carl, standing rigid while the doctor untied the tapes, declaimed again.

> "Begone! You are all alike. The name of doctor, the dream of helper, condemns you. For years I have been but a gallipot for your experimentisers to rinse your experiments into, and now in this livid skin, partake of the nature of my contents.

Begone! I hate ye."

He held his arms to his body for some time after they were free. Slowly then, he unlimbered, heaving his shoulders . . .

The doctor warned that he would be outside if he were needed—and he left us alone.

Carl turned to me—and I recalled what it was he was quoting: THE CONFIDENCE-MAN . . .

"A sick philosopher," he continued ominously, "is incurable."

His body shifted, the defiance went out of it, and a warmth came in, clumsy and affectionate. Raising an arm, he clasped my shoulder, drew me toward him.

"Mike, boy," he said—this was the first indication that he recognized me—"Mike, boy, there's something I want to tell you . . ."

Bowing his head, he screwed his brow, punched it with thumb and forefinger. He looked up suddenly, declaimed again, vaguely, in fright rather than defiance:

"He tried to think—to recollect,
But the blur is on his brain."

I began to wonder when in his career he had read so much Melville—read him so well that he had memorized whole passages. Or perhaps he had never actually read him . . . maybe Melville, as history, had impressed himself into the fiber and cells of which Carl was made, had become part of his makeup . . .

He was sad now, unable to remember what he wanted to tell me, still clutching my shoulder.

"The Indians. . ." he began—this time he was not quoting—and he
breathed hard, letting the sentence hang for some moments . . .

"The Indians shrank the heads of their enemies. . ."—again he
breathed hard—". . . and we . . ."

"we shrink the hearts of our friends." He gripped my shoulder,
released it, and turned away . . .

Again, his mood changed, became matter-of-fact. He went to the
bed, lifted the mattress, took out some papers—scribblings, draw-
ings of one sort or another. We sat down together, and he passed
tbem to me, one at a time.

There was a flower picture, rich and luxuriant, the paper covered all
over with blossoms. Showing it to me, he waved his hand in free,
abstract motions, to suggest the manner of drawing it. There was a
title in the corner: "Herbage, not verbiage."

The next drawing was a vague impression, in good anatomy, of a
woman's womb, drawn as a transparent membrane: inside it, occu-
pying the entire space, was the head of an aged man, with a straight,
gray beard . . .

He shoved another paper into my lap, became suddenly angry. It
was a tortured, twisted figure, nailed to a cross.

> thrusting his finger at the face, shouting: "There's the first sono-
> fabitch! The first coward!" and then, sardonically: "the first bas-
> tard that couldn't control his imagination . . ."

He stood up, still angry, and stalked about the room, as I read
another paper:

ST. LOUIS MOTEL

1953

CARL AND BONNIE

Carl:

bonnie bonnie bonnie bonnie bonnie baw
buh buh buh

waga
waga

gwama   gwama
bay   bay   bay

bwana   bwana-bwana
bay bay bay bay bay,   buh

Wanna!
bwana.

great gorny
hag- worm,
wagon horn,
Oooooowwwwwwwwwww!

Bonnie:
Bog the corg
Carl:

Anny wen hog,
Ug.

waaaaaaaa!   waaaaaaaaaaaaaaaaaaaaaaaaaaaaaaaaa!

ᵂaaaaaaaaaaaaaaaaaaaaaa!

¡ɐɐɐɐɐɐɐɐɐɐɐɐɐɐɐɐɐɐɐɐɐɐɐɐɐɐɐɐɐɐɐɐɐɐɐʍ

Aw, the wa!
       Daw, the long wa!
              Wa!
hih!

Bonnie:
  shinny boy,
      long wog,
           flabble

Carl:
  l o n g   w o g !
  flat.
  agon worn,
    apple!   apple!   apple!   apple!

  schnad pool, bramble blan blag blzz

        waw

  W   a   a   a   a   a   a   a   w

Bonnie:
  flamble   flamble

I looked up, found him angry, posed.

          "Go mad I can not: I maintain
          The perilous outpost of the sane."

and he laughed, roared, at the quote from CLAREL—the book of chains.

          (Lizzie, when Herman was writing it: "If ever this
          dreadful *incubus* of a *book* (I call it so because it has
          undermined all our happiness) gets off Herman's
          shoulders I do hope he may be in better mental
          health—but at present I have reason to feel the
          gravest concern & anxiety about it—to put it in
          mild phrase . . ."

and Herman, in a footnote to a letter: "N. B. I ain't crazy."

The doctor came in, with an attendant. Carl, as one of the violent, was scheduled for hydrotherapy, which consisted of stripping the patients, herding them together at the end of a tiled room, and playing streams of water on them, at firehose pressure, in an effort to quiet them.

I protested that Carl was already quiet, that there was no need for it, but it made no difference—his name was on the list. He was cowed, his shoulders caving, as they led him away.

A news item from Honolulu—1854:

> *"Our readers will doubtless recollect the narrative published in the year 1851, respecting the whale ship 'Ann Alexander,' Capt. Dublois, being stove by a sperm whale in the Pacific ocean. Recently Capt. D. visited Honolulu . . . We learned from him many striking and remarkable circumstances respecting the attack . . . Without repeating the story we would state, that about five months subsequently, the same whale was taken by the 'Rebecca Sims,' Capt. Jernegan. Two harpoons were discovered in the whale, marked 'Ann Alexander.' The whale's head was found seriously injured, and contained pieces of the ship's timbers. He had lost his wildness and ferocity, being very much diseased . . ."*

Later, walking down the corridor, I heard the hollering and shrieking of the inmates as the hoses were turned on them—and I recognized, above the others, the vast, bellowing tones of Carl, urging out of his lungs, in defiance of the water streams, hollow vowels . . .

EIGHT

There was talk, in Carl's case, of performing a frontal lobotomy—cutting into the frontothalamic fibers (the *white* matter) of the frontal lobes of the brain . . . but, in correspondence with the doctors, I was able to discourage it . . .

Instead, he was given different forms of convulsion therapy—electroshock when either violent or calm, and metrazol, when in deep melancholy . . .

I thought of Moby-Dick, and Pierre . . . of a man sinking, pulling down and over him his family, his parents and ancestors—the mutations of all evolution—

struggling convulsively, even in drowning, to re-form himself, to grow or discover a new center . . .

as an epileptic, or in syncope: to fight out of the wrong center and into the right,

or to the left of it . . .

and I thought of the doctors, with electronics and drugs—one remove from his own, self-determined spasms of epilepsy—trying to force Carl

to create a new source and origin of motion . . .

NINE

Right after the First World War, when Carl and I were both small children, my father, encouraged by the Federal Farm Loan Act of 1916, added heavily to his holdings, paying exorbitant figures, assuming large mortgages, for adjacent farm land. We already had more than we could manage . . . but he wouldn't be stopped. In 1921, the bubble burst . . . our land dropped in value to less than half what we had paid for it, what we were committed to in mortgages. The prosperous Twenties, enjoyed by the rest of the nation, never existed for the farmer . . .

We were forced to sell—or, we thought at the time that we had sold. Father, in a state of despair and confusion, turned the affairs over to Mother, and she somehow managed, without telling the rest of us, to hang onto the house and enough of the land to be rented (the income to be applied against mortgages and debts) . . .

> (clinging to the land, as Columbus struggled, and failed, to hold the Indes . . .

. . . so that today, after the years of poverty, I and my family may enjoy once again the old house—a rural island, all but swallowed into the city . . .

We left Indianapolis, moved to Terre Haute—"high ground"—center of the Indiana coal mines,

birthplace of Theodore Dreiser, and Eugene V. Debs . . .

Down payment was put on a mean, one-story house, in a crowded part of the city. Failing to scrape a living out of the earth as a farmer, Father wanted to dig under the surface: he took a job in the mines . . .

Work was part-time at first . . . we skimped, saved, and mended. In
1922, just when he went on full shift and the job became steady, the
miners were called out on strike: Father was idle for nine bitter
months . . .

Theodore Dreiser: born, Terre Haute, 1871, twenty years before
Melville died, and a thousand miles deeper in the land . . . so that he
was full grown by the time Melville put down his pen . . .

The house on Ninth Street in Terre Haute, where Paul and Sarah
Dreiser lived, was infested with spirits and night-striders. On the
night of Theodore's birth, "Three maidens, brightly garbed, with
flowers in their hair, danced into Sarah's room and out again, to dis-
appear seemingly into the air; and when afterward the boy himself
proved perilously puny and sickly, inimical forces seemed to be in
command."

The family was poor . . . Theodore was sent home from school one
winter, because it was too cold to be without shoes. He was
ashamed to be seen carrying the laundry his mother took in, or
stealing coal, lump by lump, from between the railroad tracks.
When an old watchman died—a man he had known and who had
been kind to him—he went to stare at the remains, saw the two
coins on the eyelids, and reached for them . . .

and there was the father, Paul Dreiser: a transient, a failure, moving
from house to house, one jump ahead of the mortgage . . .

I recall my own father: he had become interested in Socialism,
talked about the life and work of Eugene Debs:

born, Terre Haute, 1855, when the ripples had scarcely ceased lap-
ping, or the water become smooth, over the sinking of the Pequod
. . . organized first industrial union (1893), led the Pullman strike
('94) . . . helped organize, 1900, the Socialist Party, polled nearly a
million votes for President (1920), campaigning from prison
against Harding, and, at the time of the coal strike—1922—was
still living . . .

I recall Father, during the strike, sitting at the kitchen table (in different kitchens, of different houses, each meaner than the one before), his face bland, naive, confident—no longer the man who had worked twelve, fourteen hours a day on the farm, who, with his own main strength, had held the house together during a tornado—replying, now, to most any question with a remark about Debs: he had faith in Gene, old Gene would help us, would take care of us . . . while Mother got a meal for a family of four out of a loaf of stale bread (sold, for a few pennies, at the back door of the bakery), and a jar of the precious, guarded, hoarded tomatoes—treasured above all other possessions—that she had put up years back, on the farm . . .

young Dreiser, taking refuge from his troubles, would get up early in the morning, walk into the country with his dog, to study the spider webs and morning glories, the wrens and swallows . . .

> (as, in the Gulf of Paria, Columbus observed the tiny oysters clinging to the mangrove roots: the oyster shells open, to catch from the leaves above, dewdrops that engender pearls . . .

The strike finally over, Father went back to work, his confidence in some measure restored. Mother had somehow managed to hold the family together . . .

and Dreiser, his mother dead, his father become impossible to live with, moved—1891, the year of Melville's death—to Chicago, to the slums: the smell of sour beer, sewer gas, and uric acid . . .

took to writing, produced a novel: SISTER CARRIE, written during the years 1899 and 1900, and standing therefore at the entrance, the beginning of the 20th Century . . .

Theodore Dreiser: gate-keeper, janitor to the century, presiding over the entrance upon and beginning of things,

> (and Debs, 1900, formed the Socialist Party . . .

Dreiser had his troubles getting the thing published: signed a con-
tract with a publisher—but the publisher's wife objected strenuous-
ly (Carrie was not moral), and they pulled a fast one: published,
according to contract (minimum edition)—and stored the books in
the basement . . .

PIERRE, dealing with incest, was produced without question—but
that was earlier, the pioneer days . . . by now—1900—Progress had
become Serious Business: adulterous CARRIE was stuffed in the
cellar . . .

and in both books we have the spectacle of a man sacrificing and
ruining himself . . . Pierre and Isabel, in the classic tragedy, end as
suicides, whereas, in Dreiser's work, Hurstwood vanishes a derelict,
and Carrie is left idle, floating into the new century:

> *"In your rocking-chair, by your window, shall you dream such*
> *happiness as you may never feel."*

As the failure of MOBY-DICK and PIERRE broke Melville's health,
so CARRIE's failure broke Dreiser's. Living in New York, bankrupt,
alone, he suffered hallucinations, his eyes itched and stung, his left
eye became weaker, lost its power of accommodation . . . sitting or
standing, he found himself compelled to turn around, to go in a cir-
cle, to bring himself into alignment with something . . . he nearly
jumped into the East River . . .

> (when he had first come to New York, first
> approached the ocean, he felt small and trivial
> . . .

> (the vast ocean, into which Hart Crane
> leaped . . .

> (where Melville had been so much at home . . .

> SISTER CARRIE: *"She also marvelled at the whistles of the hun-*
> *dreds of vessels in the harbor—the long, low cries of the Sound*

steamers and ferryboats when fog was on. The mere fact that
these things spoke from the sea made them wonderful. She looked
much at what she could see of the Hudson from her west win-
dows and of the great city building up rapidly on either hand.
It was much to ponder over . . ."

From Terre Haute, Father and Mother, Carl and I moved to Sulli-
van, where the job in the mines was steady, and the pay better . . .

(this being another of the towns where Dreis-
er had lived, as a child . . .

and my hand reaches across the desk for the clipping, yellowed with
age, from the 1925 newspaper: Mother saved and passed it on to me,
and I cannot bring myself to dispose of it:

FIFTY-ONE ARE

KILLED IN BIG

MINE EXPLOSION

Greatest Disaster in His-
tory of Indiana
Coal Fields.

ALL TRAPPED ARE

BELIEVED KILLED

More Than Hundred Men
in Mine at the Time
of Blast.

(BY THE ASSOCIATED PRESS)

SULLIVAN, Ind., Feb. 20—Fifty-one men are believed to have been killed
almost instantly today in an explosion of gas in the City Coal Company
mine on the outskirts of the city, that wrought the greatest mine disaster in
the history of the Indiana Coal Fields.

There were 121 miners in the mine at the time of the explosion which
occurred in the third and fourth entries North where most of the men killed
were at work.

(Melville, in the cave of Sybil: "What in God's name were such places made for, & why? Surely man is a strange animal. Diving into the bowels of the earth rather than building up towards the sky. How clear an indication that he sought darkness . . ."

The work of bringing out the dead proceeded slowly, the bodies being brought singly. Rescue workers were handicapped by gas fumes which flooded the mine immediately after the explosion.

Tremendous crowds thronged the scene soon after word of the disaster spread . . .

Wives and children of miners employed in the shaft crowded about, seeking information, and groups of waiting, sobbing women and children clustered about as the news was broken that 51 of the men were known to be dead.

I recall standing beside Mother—Carl on the other side, a hand of hers reaching to each of us—waiting, hour after hour, not moving . . . and when the body was brought up, the faces of the others turned toward us—curiosity locked in compassion—Mother waiting (Carl and I looking to her, even though it be disaster, wanting to be sure), waiting until the body were brought before her—and, as she recognized him, Father, her hand clutching, tightening . . .

Most authentic reports of the accident were that the explosion occurred when miners either cut into abandoned workings or a slight cave-in opened old entries in which gas had collected, the miners' lamps setting off the pocket of gas . . .

Men who had been in the mine said the explosion seemed to go in gusts, some being suffocated, others horribly burned, while others were but slightly burned. Many were hurled about rooms and entries . . .

Rope lines established by local authorities and miners failed to check the rush of hundreds who flocked to the mine.

(. . . rushing, eddying to the disaster . . .

there was the long period of waiting, and discovery—the knowledge, in the pit of my stomach, that something had happened, the excitement, the image of his face, as Carl and Mother and I saw it before us, his body—waiting for the realization, the understanding of it to burst upon me . . .

like a holiday: the normal, daily laws of living abrogated—waiting
to discover what it was, what it meant, that Father was dead . . .

. . . followed by disappointment, as there was no discovery, no burst-
ing upon me, but only dullness, a slow seepage of understanding . . .
and the poverty doubled in, feeding upon itself, as we lived now, a
family of three, on the compensation—$13.20 a week—allowed by
the law . . .

with the numbness: the absence of Father, who, even in failure, had
provided a dimension that was now gone . . .

Where Melville dove, Dreiser floated . . . a great mass of pity, cut
off . . .

Hurstwood, in SISTER CARRIE, as Dreiser's father, sitting alone,
apathetic in his rocker:

> *"Hurstwood saw her depart with some faint feelings of shame,*
> *which were the expression of a manhood rapidly becoming stul-*
> *tifed."*

and the drear, the cold, wint'ry drear of Hurstwood, struggling to
reclaim himself as a $2-a-day scab in the Brooklyn trolley strike . . .

Dreiser, who was sterile—terminating his sons before their concep-
tion, giving them, therefore, shorter lives, shorter agonies than
Melville's sons—nevertheless took the trouble, on a trip to Europe,
to hunt out his father's birthplace . . .

searching the sources, the roots, the blasted paternity . . . Theodore
Dreiser, Indiana-born, doorkeeper of the century . . .

> (in ancient Rome, the double barbican gate in
> the Forum—dedicated to Janus, supreme jan-
> itor—was closed during times of peace, open
> only in war . . .

BUD

ONE

AFTER MOBY-DICK, the sinking, Melville, with pseudonyms and anonyms, kept trying to die, as PIERRE . . .

> "*. . . death-milk for thee and me!*"

BENITO CERENO . . .

> "*seguid vuestro jefe*"

and BARTLEBY THE SCRIVENER . . .

> *opening lines, written when he was 34: "I am a rather elderly man."*

and like Columbus, in search of death, he turned to the Holy Land, Sodom, the Dead Sea . . .

> "*. . . foam on beach & pebbles like slaver of mad dog—smarting bitter of the water,—carried the bitter in my mouth all day— bitterness of life—thought of all bitter things—Bitter is it to be poor & Bitter, to be reviled, & Oh bitter are these waters of Death, thought I.—Old boughs tossed up by water—relics of pick-nick—nought to eat but bitumen & ashes with dessert of Sodom apples washed down with water of Dead Sea.— . . .*"

and Columbus, following the 3rd voyage, liberated from his chains by the Sovereigns,

(as Melville had been liberated, temporarily,
from the chains of poverty, by Judge Shaw,

turned inland

(as Melville turned inland, in PIERRE,

to another scheme: the liberation of Jerusalem . . .

retiring to the convent of Las Cuevas, he began work on the BOOK
OF PROPHECIES:

> "St. Augustine says that the end of this world is to come in the sev-
> enth millenary of years from its creation . . . there are only lacking
> 155 years to complete the 7000, in which year the world must end."

> "The greatest part of the prophecies and Sacred Writing is already
> finished."

thus foreclosing on the future of the hemisphere he had discovered,

. . . condoning and justifying all brutalities against the Indians, as
extreme haste must be made to convert the heathen . . .

Melville:

> *"With wrecks in a garret I'm stranded . . ."*

and

> *"Pleased, not appeased, by myriad wrecks in me."*

Columbus, on Jamaica:

> "Solitary in my trouble, sick, and in daily expectation of death . . ."

and back in Spain, 1504, still trying to get to the Court to present his
claims and grievances—too weak and ill to make the trip on foot or
on horseback—requests the loan of a funeral bier from the Cathe-
dral of Seville:

"This day, their Worships ordered that there should be loaned to
the Admiral Columbus the mortuary bier in which was carried the
body of the Lord Cardinal Don Diego Hurtado de Mendoza,
whom may God have in his keeping, in order that he may go to the
Court, and a guarantee was taken from Francisco Pinelo which
assured the return of the said bier to this church in safety."

. . . to be carried out of his disaster like Ishmael, on the floating
coffin . . .

TWO

But Melville, after trying through the long middle years to die, put
out a late, late bloom . . .

> *(scores & underscores, in a volume of Thomas
> Hood: ". . . the full extent of that poetical vigour
> which seemed to advance just in proportion as
> his physical health declined."*

. . . in his sixties and seventies, came to life:

> *"We the Lilies whose palor is passion . . ."*

> *". . . the winged blaze that sweeps my soul
> Like prairie fires . . ."*

> *"To flout pale years of cloistral life
> And flush me in this sensuous strife."*

> *"The innocent bare-foot! young, so young!"*

> *"The plain lone bramble thrills with Spring"*

"The patient root, the vernal sense
Surviving hard experience . . ."

In a volume, transparently dedicated to Lizzie.

". . . white nun, that seemly dress
Of purity pale passionless,
A May-snow is; for fleeting term,
Custodian of love's slumbering germ . . ."

"I came unto my roses late.
What then? these gray hairs but disguise,
Since down in heart youth never dies . . ."

"Time, Amigo, does but masque us—
Boys in gray wigs, young . . ."

and elsewhere:

"Could I remake me! or set free
This sexless bound in sex, then plunge
Deeper than Sappho, in a lunge
Piercing Pan's paramount mystery!
For, Nature, in no shallow surge
Against thee either sex may urge . . ."

Sappho, and Hart Crane . . .

surely, if Melville died before he was born, then, too, he was born before he died . . .

. . . and on the 4th voyage, aging and ill, forbidden by the Sovereigns to enter San Domingo, Columbus set sail for that very port. Ovando, the new governor, busy with a fleet of 28 vessels embarking for Spain, refused to admit the Admiral . . . on board the fleet were Francisco Bobadilla, who earlier had chained Columbus; Francisco Roldan, archrebel; and a rich cargo of West Indian gold . . .

Columbus warned them not to sail, that a storm was brewing . . .

perhaps he noted an oily swell from the southeast, abnormal tides, oppressive air, veiled cirrus clouds, gusty winds on the water's surface, brilliant sunset illuminating the sky, and large numbers of seal and dolphin on the surface . . .

        (as well as twinges in rheumatic joints . . .

But the others laughed, called him a diviner and a prophet,

    (Like Melville, in CLAREL, predicting for the New World:

> *("Not only men, the state lives fast—*
> *Fast breeds the pregnant eggs and shells,*
> *The slumberous combustibles*
> *Sure to explode . . ."*

Ovando's fleet set out boldly, under full sail: headed into the full blast of the storm . . .

Later, when all but 3 or 4 of the 28 ships had gone down, with all hands lost—his enemies accused the old discoverer of having raised the tempest himself, by magic art . . .

THREE

When I went to St. Louis a third time, Carl was out of the hospital. It was pleasant weather—brisk and sunny—and he met me at the station with a borrowed car—a '51 Plymouth station wagon.

There was vigor in his face, freshness in his actions. He had a crew haircut, and was sunburned. Standing at the train gate, his collar turned up, legs spread apart, hands thrust in his pockets, he looked boyish and strong.

(It wasn't until after I had left him, when I
was on my way back to Indianapolis, that I
realized he had said nothing about what he
was doing, where he was living, what his plans
were—so completely was he taken up with
the present moment—so thoroughly did he
capture my assurances . . .

We headed west on U.S. 40, out of the city. I recalled Carl's driving
from childhood—from the first time he massacred the cornfield on
a tractor. No less erratic now, he talked volubly, gestured with one
hand and the other, moved his feet restlessly over the pedals—
glanced only occasionally at the road, appropriating it as he wished.

He told me that U.S. 40 follows old animal and Indian trails, west-
ward migration trails. It was known for a time as the Boone's Lick
Trail, for the salt lick developed by Daniel Boone and his sons. Carl
told me—bouncing his broad rump, spreading his arms as he
talked—how Boone had moved out here because he wanted more
elbow room, Kentucky had become too crowded . . .

> (Melville: "You must have plenty of searoom to
> tell the Truth in . . ."

There was the stage driver in 1840, Carl mentioned, who, when the
road became too muddy and full of ruts, drove out on the prairie,
made a new road . . .

Reaching St. Charles, we turned off the highway, headed southwest
over back roads, along the Missouri River. We came into rich farm-
ing country, with fine old brick houses: long, sloping shingled roofs,
and generous porches. Carl mellowed as we rambled, became less
talkative, and warmer, his chest expanding with the rolling orchards
and fields of corn, timothy, alfalfa, and oats.

The midday sun warmed us, and we got out of the car, walked down
a deep creek valley to the river's edge. Carl had brought along some

cooked pork chops and a loaf of honest German bread . . . I had a bottle of redeye that I'd brought from home . . . we sat on the grass, near a patch of willows, and ate and drank, soaked in the sun that would be warm only through the broad noon hours . . .

We talked of Indiana, of Mother and Father, of the old days, and of ourselves. With Yankee and rebel blood in us—joining and hanging on in the prairie—we wanted to know the difference between north and south . . . we recalled that whenever Mother thought about something, she "allowed" it was so, whereas Father "kalklated" it . . . we thought of rivers and small streams—"brooks" in the North and "branches" in the South—and of the pioneer landing on the southern coast, following the main streams inland, or perhaps turning off on a branch while the northern pioneer found the rivers—the Merrimac, the Connecticut, the Hudson, the Delaware—coming out of the North and therefore heading in no useful direction: to be crossed, rather than followed . . .

. . . the rivers therefore becoming allies to the southerners, and, to the Yankees, obstacles, to be out-smarted and overwhelmed—as the North eventually outsmarted and overwhelmed the South. To the one, nature was objective, to be studied: the bird and flower books were written in the north, and Carl recalled the president of Indiana University, back in the last century, who must have been a Yankee: claiming that prayer could be used to arrest the laws of nature . . . the other, the southerner, was in and of nature, immersed in her . . . the likes of Daniel Boone . . .

Going barefoot, rolling up his trousers, Carl stepped into the chill, muddy water. The river, charged with fresh rains, was swift and treacherous . . . he held his hand out to me, and I stripped off shoes and socks, followed him in. Steadying each other, we walked out to our knees . . . we could see around a bend upstream, where the water was eating out the bank, undermining some poplars . . . now and then a stump or a full tree swept past us . . . leaning toward me, clutching my hand, shouting above the rush of the waters, Carl asked how I'd like to pole a keelboat, fully loaded, upstream to KayCee or St. Joe . . .

He became restless, turning his head one way and another . . . the sunlight sparkled on the water, and our legs were all but frozen, so that we were amputated at the knees, the joints set in ice . . .

Back on shore, we shivered, dried ourselves. The sun was past the meridian, the air was already cool. Carl offered me wine, and I drank. Upending the bottle, he finished it in one swallow . . . and, with all his strength, hurled it upstream. Standing together—his hand on my shoulder—we watched it, bobbing in the muddy, choppy waters, floating past us, downstream . . .

We climbed back to the car, and wandered for a while among back roads, circling, until we hit U.S. 40 again, and headed back to St. Louis. Carl was much quieter, his attention abstracted, his face almost morose. He seemed to look—and to drive—without seeing . . .

Reaching St. Charles, we stopped once more, by the river. Carl was stone-faced, immobile, facing upstream . . . when he began to speak, it was in mumbles—to himself, or to no one . . . I knew he was quoting, but I didn't at first know what . . .

> *"Rained the fore part of the day I determined to go as far as St. Charles a french Village 7 Leags. up the Missourie, and wait at that place untill Capt. Lewis could finish the business in which he was obliged to attend to at St. Louis and join me by Land from that place 24 miles*
>
> *"I Set out at 4 oClock* P.M. *in the presence of many of the neighboring inhabitants, and proceeded on under a jentle breese up the Missouri to the upper Point of the 1st Island 4 Miles and camped on the Island which is Situated Close on the right (or Starboard) Side, and opposit the mouth of a Small Creek called Cold water,*
>
> *a heavy rain this afternoon*
>
> *"at 9 oClock Set out and proceeded on 9 miles passed two Islands & incamped on the Starbd. Side at a Mr. Pipers Landing opposet an island, the Boat run on Logs three times to day, owing her being too heavyly loaded a Sturn,*

a fair after noon, I saw a number of Goslings to day on the
Shore, the water excessively rapid, & Banks falling in."

. . . his voice becoming clearer . . .

"pass a remarkable Coal Hill on the Larboard Side, Called by
the French Carbonere, this hill appear to Contain great quan-
tity of Coal from this hill the Village of St. Charles may be Seen
at 7 miles distance. we arrived at St. Charles at 12 oClock a
number Spectators french & Indians flocked to the bank to See
the party. This Village is about one mile in length, Situated on
the north Side of the Missourie at the foot of a hill from which
it takes its name Peetiete Coete *or the* Little hill *This Village*
Contns. about 100 houses, the most of them small and indeffer-
ent and about 450 inhabitants Chiefly French, those people
appear Pore, polite & harmonious."

. . . the opening, the very beginning, of the JOURNALS OF LEWIS
AND CLARK . . .

We got into the car, and drove to St. Louis.

Coming back to Indianapolis on the train, I reached to an inner
coat pocket for my ticket, and brought out a newspaper clipping.
Carl must have put it there, but I have no idea how or when, or by
what sleight of hand.

It was an obituary:

"Mills, Maria de la Concepcion—Resident of St. Louis, died in a
private hospital, after a brief illness. Survivors include the husband,
Carl Austin Mills, of this city, and a brother, Rico de Castro, with
the British Royal Air Force, stationed in China."

Holding the clipping before me—the conductor waiting for my
ticket—I was several moments in recalling that a common nick-
name for Maria de la Concepcion was Concha . . .

On the edge of the clipping, Carl had scribbled a pencil note:

"Cancer—in the gut—brutal—"

FOUR

There was the letter Melville received from an old shipmate:

> "... *first of all I will let you know who I am you probably have not forgotten all of the crew of the Old Frigate United States and more especially our visit to the city of Lima. my name is Oliver Russ, although I went by another name when at sea to conceal from my friends the unwise step I had taken and that name was Edward Norton I assumed my right name on coming home. Now what I wish to say is that I in the course of the next year after our return from sea I took to wife one of the fair daughters of the state of Maine and in two years from that day a son was born to us a substantial token of our mutual love and to manifest the high regard in which I have ever held yourself I named him Herman Melville Russ at that time I did not expect ever to hear of you again or that you would be numbered among the literary writers of the day. I say this to let you know that it was not the almost universal desire to name after great men that led me to do it, but a regard for those qualities which an acquaintance of eighteen month with you led me so much to admire.*"

... and on the lists of the 4th voyage, many names appeared—men from Palos and the Niebla—men who had shipped earlier with Columbus ...

they recalled, perhaps, the storm between Jamaica and Cuba, on the 2nd voyage, when the flagship was hove-to and all hands went below for a rest: the Admiral was the first on deck, and, noting that the weather was moderating, began to make sail himself, so as not to disturb his weary shipmates ...

> Melville: *"If ever, in days to come, you shall see ruin at hand, and, thinking you understand mankind, shall tremble for your*

friendships, and tremble for your pride; and, partly through love
for the one and fear for the other, shall resolve to be beforehand
with the world, and save it from a sin by prospectively taking
that sin to yourself, then will you do as one I now dream of once
did, and like him will you suffer; but how fortunate and how
grateful should you be, if like him, after all that had happened,
you could be a little happy again."

Columbus,

who had always been mysterious about his past, without mother or
father, a roving widower—takes a late interest in Genoa:

> From the Deed of Entail: "Item. I also enjoin Diego, or any one
> that may inherit the estate, to have and maintain in the city of
> Genoa one person of our lineage to reside there with his wife, and
> appoint him sufficient revenue to enable him to live decently, as a
> person closely connected with the family, of which he is to be the
> root and basis in that city; from which great good may accrue to
> him, inasmuch as I was born there, and came from thence."

> ". . . and Genoa is a noble city, and powerful by sea . . ."

> "I command the said Diego, or whoever may possess the said
> estate, to labor and strive for the honor, welfare and aggrandize-
> ment of the city of Genoa, and make use of all his power and
> means in defending and enhancing the good and credit of that
> republic."

Aging, lonely, the Admiral seeks his sources . . .

> writing to friends in Genoa: "Although my body is here, my heart
> is continually yonder."

> and to another, just before leaving on the 4th voyage: "The lone-
> liness in which you have left us cannot be described . . . I am ready
> to start in the name of the Holy Trinity as soon as the weather is
> good."

and another: "If the desire to hear from you troubles me as much in the places to which I am going, as it does here, I shall feel great anxiety."

On the 4th voyage, heading for Jamaica:

"... my ships were pierced with worm-holes, like a bee hive, and the crew entirely dispersed and downhearted."

"... all the people with pumps and kettles and other vessels were insufficient to bail out the water that entered by the worm-holes."

> *(Melville: "Bail out your individual boat, if you can, but the sea abides."*

Shore-bound, shipwrecked, on Jamaica ...

> *(Melville three times underscores, in the works of another: "He that is sure of the goodness of his ship and tackle puts out fearlessly from the shore ..."*

> *(and Melville, on his last sea voyage, age 68—a pleasure trip to Bermuda: "Rough passage home during blizzard Got around on hands and knees."*

Back in Spain, finished forever with the ocean-sea, Columbus writes his son Diego:

"Very dear son:

"Since I received your letter of November 15 I have heard nothing from you. I wish that you would write me more frequently. I would like to receive a letter from you each hour. Reason must tell you that I now have no other repose. Many couriers come each day, and the news is of such a nature and so abundant that in hearing it, all my hair stands on end, it is so contrary to what my soul desires.

"I told you in that letter that my departure was certain, but that the hope of my arrival there, according to experience, was very uncertain, because my sickness is so bad and the cold is so well suited to aggravate it, that I could not well avoid remaining in some inn on the road. The litter and everything were ready. The weather became so violent that it appeared impossible to every one to start when it was getting so bad . . .

". . . telling of my sickness and that it is now impossible for me to go and kiss their Royal feet and hands and that the Indies are being lost and are on fire in a thousand places, and that I have received nothing and am receiving nothing from the revenues derived from them, and that no one dares to accept or demand anything there for me, and I am living upon borrowed funds. I spent the money which I got there in bringing those people who went with me back to their homes, for it would be a great burden upon my conscience to have left them there and to have abandoned them.

"Take good care of your brother. He has a good disposition and is no longer a boy. Ten brothers would not be too many for you. I never found better friends to right or to left than my brothers. We must strive to obtain the government of the Indies . . .

"My illness permits me to write only at night, because in the daytime my hands are deprived of strength."

and another time:

"I wrote a very long letter to his Highness as soon as I arrived here, fully stating the evils which require a prompt and efficient remedy . . . I have received no reply . . ."

(Melville, in a letter, advertises CLAREL: *". . . a metrical affair . . . eminently adapted for unpopularity."*

and Columbus signs his letters to Diego, "Your father, who loves you as himself."

as Melville ended a letter to Stanwix: "Good bye, & God bless you, Your affectionate Father, H. Melville."

Melville,

age 69, begins work on BILLY BUDD, as an afterthought to his life . . .

creates "Starry" Vere, the educated, literary captain, aware (as Melville was) of history and tradition, knowing that their demands must and will be met . . . knowing, too, that the present act is a compound of many elements: out of the hazy near-past, the strong and clear distant-past, and the immediate moment . . .

Melville, as Captain Vere, creates himself a bachelor . . . the old dream!

and creates Billy, the Handsome Sailor—a foundling . . . the old Ishmael dream!

Vere and Billy, bachelor and bastard—the two elements of Melville, split . . .

and Vere it is (as the agent of tradition) who sends Billy to his death . . . Melville, as Vere, thereby accepting responsibility for his son Mackey's death; and perhaps, too, for the death of the Handsome Sailor in himself . . .

or perhaps Billy—pure and merry—was the sexual transposition of Fayaway: the dark savage girl become a pure white man,

> (Billy: ". . . *a lingering adolescent expression in the as yet smooth face, all but feminine in purity of natural complexion . . .*"

> (it being safer to love a man than a woman . . .

(as Dreiser transposed himself, saying, in effect, *it is not safe to be myself, I will be* SISTER CARRIE . . .

Melville, an old man, recalls Fayaway . . .

BILLY BUDD: *"In fervid hearts self-contained some brief experiences devour our human tissue as secret fire in a ship's hold . . ."*

and Julian Hawthorne reports an interview with Melville: ". . . he told me, during our talk, that he was convinced that there was some secret in my father's life which had never been revealed, and which accounted for the gloomy passages in his books."

Melville—ever the writer—placing things of self in someone else . . .

Mrs. Glendinning, in PIERRE: *"Oh, that the world were made of such malleable stuff, that we could recklessly do our fiercest heart's wish before it . . ."*

and my hand reaches for a newspaper clipping, the first in a series— date, 1953:

BOY, 6, IS KIDNAPPED
AT PRIVATE SCHOOL

**Son of Wealthy Kansas City
Family Taken by Woman Who
Gave False Story to Nuns**

KANSAS CITY, Mo., Sept. 28 (UP)—The 6-year-old son of a wealthy Kansas City business man was kidnapped from a Roman Catholic school here today by a woman who represented herself to be the boy's aunt.

The stocky, red-haired woman led Robert C. (Buddy) Williams Jr. from the French Institute of Notre Dame de Sion after falsely telling the nuns that his mother had had a heart attack. Hours later the police had been unable to find any trace of the boy or his abductor.

The child's father is the owner of the only Cadillac automobile agency in Kansas City, and has similar interests in Oklahoma City and Tulsa, Oklahoma. The family has a large, English-style home across the state line in Kansas.

The police said that there was no indication whether the kidnapper planned to seek a ransom.

The boy was in the primary grade of the school. He was a half-day pupil and was picked up each school day by the family chauffeur and taken home during the lunch hour. When the chauffeur arrived today the boy was gone.

FIVE

KIDNAPPED BOY FOUND DEAD
AFTER BIG RANSOM IS PAID

Two Jailed
In Missouri

KANSAS CITY, Mo., Oct. 8 (AP)—Little Buddy Williams' body was dug out of a shallow grave today, ending with sickening tragedy 10 days of waiting by his wealthy parents who paid a record $600,000 ransom for his return.

Arrested as his kidnappers were the woman who lived in the house in St. Joseph, Mo., where the body was found, and her ex-mental-patient boy friend Carl Austin Mills, 43, whose spending spree in St. Louis led police to part of the ransom money.

The slightly built, 6-year-old boy had been shot and killed the same day the woman, Mrs. Bonnie Brown Heady, 41, took him from his private school by ruse.

The city, the Indiana country around us, are dead quiet. Rising, I find my joints stiff, my body tired. I move around, amble to the end of the attic, loosening my limbs . . .

Carl, stealing a child, attempting by ransom to convert him to his own future, is a little like Melville—un-centered by the failure of MOBY-DICK—clutching Hawthorne: trying to push off on him the "Agatha" story, get him to do Melville's writing:

> ". . . *it has occurred to me that this thing lies very much in a vein, with which you are peculiarly familiar. To be plump, I think that in this matter you would make a better hand at it than I would.—Besides the thing seems naturally to gravitate toward you . . .*"

> ". . . *it seems to me that with your great power in these things, you can construct a story of remarkable interest out of this material . . . And if I thought I could do it as well as you, why, I should not let you have it.*"

and, perhaps, like Columbus, before or during the 3rd voyage, writing the Letter to the Nurse . . .

the center-line of communication with the Sovereigns broken: writing, therefore, to an underling, hoping by court gossip to reach the Royal ear . . .

no longer confident . . .

Through the little window in the gable end, I can see only darkness . . . staring through the glass, I think of the 1st voyage, return: Columbus on board the *Niña,* caught in a violent storm, writing "with caligraphic poise" on a single piece of parchment, trying to reduce to this space the content of his discovery . . . and sealing the parchment in a cask, throwing it overboard . . .

> there was the story that came out of Spain: "At noon of August 27 in the year 1852, an American three-masted brig named the *Chieftan,* of Boston, under command of Captain d'Auberville, found itself upon the coast of Morocco. As a storm was approaching, the Captain determined to increase his ballast, and while engaged in this occupation, the drag brought up what at first glance appeared to be a piece

of rock, but, finding it light in weight, the sailors examined it more closely, when they discovered it to be a coffer of cedar wood: opening this, there was disclosed a cocoa-nut, hollow, and containing a document written in gothic letters upon parchment. Not being able to decipher this, it was given to an American bookseller when the ship arrived at Gibraltar. The latter immediately upon glancing at the manuscript offered the American Captain one hundred dollars for the cocoa-nut and its contents, which offer the Captain declined. Thereupon the bookseller read to the astonished Captain the document, which was no other than the holograph relation of the discovery committed to the sea three hundred and fifty-nine years before." . . . but the fictional parchment disappeared . . .

and, likewise, "My Secrete Log Boke."—a "facsimile edition" of a version found by a fisherman off the coast of Wales—printed in English, the "universal maritime language"—and appropriately adorned with barnacles and seaweed.

but—in fact—there was Raymond Weaver—first of Melville scholars—who, in 1919, dug loose the tin bread box from the tight seaweed of Melville's heirs and descendants, and brought out the crabbed, incoherent manuscript of BILLY BUDD . . .

I think of Isabella, first permanent settlement in the Indies—swept by epidemic, poverty, and starvation, and rapidly depopulated . . .

"It was also said . . . that one day one man or two were walking amidst those buildings of Isabella when, in a street, there suddenly appeared two rows or choruses of men, who seemed to be noble and court people, well dressed, with swords girt and wrapped in traveling cloaks of the kind worn in Spain in those days, and when that person or those persons were wondering how such people so new and well dressed had landed there . . . on asking them whence they came, they answered silently by putting their hands to their hats to greet them and, when they took their hats off, their heads came off also and they remained headless, and then vanished: of which vision the man or men were left nearly dead and for many days pained and astonished."

and the Naval expedition, in the year 1891—the year of Melville's death:

"Commander G. A. Converse,
       "Commanding U. S. S. Enterprise.
   "Sir:–

"In obedience to your orders of the 13th inst. we respectfully submit the following report of the results of an exploration of the ruins of the city of Isabella.

"The party left the Enterprise, then anchored off Puerto Plata, Island of Santo Domingo, at 6:30 on the morning of the 14th of May and proceeded in the steamcutter thirty miles to the westward along the north shore of the island of Santo Domingo. We were accompanied by an old native pilot who was recommended by the U. S. Consul of Puerto Plata as familiar with the coast and such traditions as exist among the natives respecting the first settlement of Columbus. He has piloted vessels to and from the port of Isabella for many years.

"About eight miles inside the cape now known as Isabella there is a bay of considerable size; on its eastern shore a slight rocky projection of land formed by one of the numerous bluffs was chosen for the first permanent settlement of the Spaniards in the New World . . .

"No habitations are to be found within a mile and a half of the ruins . . .

"On landing we turned to the right and ascended a gentle slope to a little plain about two acres in area; this slightly projects into the bay and is bounded on the north and south by two dry water-courses forming natural ditches, or moats, and terminating abruptly on the western, or water side, in cliffs from twenty to thirty feet high formed by large boulders containing fossil coral and shells. Tradition points to this little plateau as the site of the ancient city and here we found scattered at intervals various small, ill-defined heaps of stones, remnants of walls built of small unhewn stones, evidently laid in mortar, pieces of old tiles and potsherds, some of the latter glazed, and fragments of broad, roughly made bricks. There were half a dozen or more blocks of dressed limestone that may have been part of the walls of buildings somewhat finished and permanent in character. The trees, matted roots and trailing vines overspread the ground . . .

"We overturned all the cut blocks of stone and examined them carefully in the hope of finding some marks or dates, but without success, and it is our belief that nothing of the kind exists.

"Should further exploration be made it would be of undoubted scientific interest to examine the fauna and flora of this region and there are evidences of interesting fossil remains. The caves in the cliffs of Cape Isabella and vicinity would probably yield interesting relics of the aborigines—the now extinct Caribs."

Melville—Customs Inspector #75—writes a letter to John Hoadley: "By the way I have a ship on my district from Girgenti—Where's that? Why, in Sicily—The ancient Agrigentum. Ships arrive from there in this port, bringing sulphur; but this is the first one I have happened to have officially to do with. I have not succeeded in seeing the captain yet—have only seen the mate—but hear that he has in possession some stones from those magnifcent Grecian ruins, and I am going to try to get a fragment, however small, if possible, which I will divide with you."

and Isabella today: a pasture by the sea, with only a few stones above the ground . . .

Turning, I amble back to the desk . . .

WOMAN WHO LURED BOY FROM SCHOOL
TELLS POLICE HE WASN'T FRIGHTENED

ST. LOUIS, Oct. 7 (AP)—The woman who lured Buddy Williams from his school in Kansas City on the start of a trip that was to lead to a shallow grave said today the 6-year-old boy wasn't frightened.

"He was such a sweet child," said Mrs. Bonnie Brown Heady. "He came so nice. He talked about getting a dog and ice cream."

(and there was Billy Budd: ". . . he showed in face that humane look of reposeful good nature . . ."

("The ear, small and shapely, the arch of the foot, the curve in mouth and nostril . . ."

(and he was called by his shipmates, Baby Budd . . .

PAIR PLEAD GUILTY
TO KIDNAP CHARGE

KANSAS CITY, Nov. 3 (AP)—Ex-mental patient Carl Austin Mills and his alcoholic companion, Mrs. Bonnie Brown Heady, pleaded guilty in federal court today to the kidnapping of 6-year-old Buddy Williams and were ordered to trial Nov. 16.

we thought that, because of his mental record, he would plead insanity, and all of us—Mother, Linda, and I—tried to persuade him to it; but Carl himself insisted against it, and such a plea was never made . . . instead, he took a rigorous psychiatric examination, and conned his way through it . . .

KIDNAP KILLERS WILL DIE
DEC. 18; 'TOO GOOD FOR
THEM,' WILLIAMS SAYS

Mrs. Hall,
Mills Stoically
Hear Sentence

KANSAS CITY, Nov. 19 (AP)—The kidnap slayers of Buddy Williams were sentenced to death today and will go to the gas chamber together for their ruthless crime.

I made several trips—to St. Louis, Kansas City, Jefferson City—but on all occasions Carl refused to see me, or acknowledge me . . .

PENITENTIARY GATES
CLOSE ON KIDNAPPERS

No Appeals Planned

JEFFERSON CITY, Nov. 20 (AP)—The Buddy Williams kidnap killers reached the Missouri Penitentiary tonight where they will die together in the gas chamber one week from Christmas.

Carl Austin Mills, 43, and Mrs. Bonnie Brown Heady, 41, were received at the grim gray-walled prison in gathering darkness at 5:35 P.M. They arrived in handcuffs and chains after an automobile trip from Kansas City . . .

On Thursday, the 20th of May, 1506, in the city of Valladolid, Christopher Columbus died . . .

(Melville:

("Like those new-world discoverers bold
Ending in stony convent cold,
Or dying hermits; as if they,

. . . .

Remorseful felt that ampler sway
Their lead had given for old career
Of human nature."

and Melville, in 1891, the year of his death, set aside BILLY BUDD, as finished—and picked it up again: added a chapter—afterthought to an afterthought—BILLY IN THE DARBIES:

". . . Sentry, are you there?
Just ease these darbies at the wrist,
And roll me over fair.
I am sleepy . . ."

There was the editor of the *Atlantic Monthly*, discussing a possible article on Melville:

"I can't help thinking that there must be some good material on the subject, though probably it would be better still if Melville would only let go of life. So much more frankness of speech can be used when a fellow is apparently out of hearing. What you say of his aversion to publicity makes me pause . . .
"On second thought therefore, I believe we had better wait for our shot at Melville, when his personality can be more freely handled."

. . . like Ovando, sending a ship to rescue Columbus on Jamaica: standing off shore, hovering, hoping him dead . . .

and Melville writes Daniel Orme:

> "But let us come to the close of a sketch necessarily imperfect. One fine Easter Day, following a spell of rheumatic weather, Orme was discovered alone and dead on a height overlooking the seaward sweep of the great haven to whose shore, in his retirement from sea, he had moored. It was an evened terrace, destined for use in war, but in peace neglected and offering a sanctuary for anybody. Mounted on it was an obsolete battery of rusty guns. Against one of these he was found leaning, his legs stretched out before him; his clay pipe broken in twain, the vacant bowl and no spillings from it, attesting that his pipe had been smoked out to the last of its contents. He faced the outlet to the ocean. The eyes were open, still continuing in death the vital glance fixed on the hazy waters and the dim-seen sails coming and going or at anchor near by. What had been his last thoughts! If aught of reality lurked in the rumours concerning him, had remorse, had penitence any place in those thoughts? Or was there just nothing of either? After all, were his moodiness and mutterings, his strange freaks, starts, eccentric shrugs and grimaces, were these but the grotesque additions like the wens and knobs and distortions of the trunk of an old chance apple-tree in an inclement upland, not only beaten by many storms, but also obstructed in its natural development by the chance of its having first sprouted among hard-packed rock? In short, that fatality, no more encrusting him, made him what he came to be? Even admitting that there was something dark that he chose to keep to himself, what then? Such reticence may sometimes be more for the sake of others than one's self. No, let us believe that the animal decay before mentioned still befriended him to the close, and that he fell asleep recalling through the haze of memory many a far-off scene of the wide world's beauty dreamily suggested by the hazy waters before him.
>
> "He lies buried among other sailors, for whom also strangers performed one last rite in a lonely plot overgrown with wild eglantine uncared for by man."

and on the 28th of September, 1891, Melville—unwilling to face another northern winter—died . . .

there was the dedication of BILLY BUDD: to an old shipmate, Jack Chase, "wherever that great heart may now be . . ."

and Melville's physician signed the certificate, ascribing death to "Cardiac dilitation . . ."

ENLARGEMENT OF THE HEART

I get up, stand by the desk, and turn off the light. A thin bit of gray comes through the attic window. There is a strange smell of gas, sulphurous, that I had smelled earlier, much earlier in the evening . . .

WILLIAMS KIDNAPPERS
DIE SIDE BY SIDE IN
MISSOURI GAS CHAMBER

Mrs. Heady,
Mills Chat
Before Death

From UP And AP Reports

JEFFERSON CITY, Mo., Friday, Dec. 18—Bonnie Heady and Carl Mills died side by side in a swirl of poison gas early today for kidnapping a little boy and killing him.

In the last hours before they were taken to the death house, the killers had kept a strange composure.

. . . deadly fumes with the faint scent of almonds.

the daylight is getting stronger . . .

treading softly, I go downstairs, both flights, and into the kitchen. I stand by the table, resting one hand on it, trying to listen to the silence. The refrigerator motor turns on, becomes a steady hum. I hear one of the children, Jenifer, stirring . . .

BIBLIOGRAPHY

Arey, Leslie Brainard. *Developmental Anatomy* (7th Edition, Revised).

[Associated Press Accounts]. Bobby Greenlease Kidnapping Story.

—— Sullivan County (Indiana) Mine Disaster

Berrill, N. J. "The Signs Columbus Followed," *Natural History* (October, 1950).

Bjorkman, Edwin. *The Search for Atlantis.*

Blakiston's New Gould Medical Dictionary.

Bondi, Herman.—*Cosmology.*

Carden, Robert W. *The City of Genoa.*

Catt, C. C., and Shuler, N. R. *Woman Suffrage and Politics.*

The Cyclopedia of Medicine, Surgery and Specialties (1949 edition).

de Madariaga, Salvador. *Christopher Columbus; being the life of the very magnificent lord Don Cristobal Colon*

De Voto, Bernard; editor. *The Journals of Lewis and Clark.*

Dreiser, Theodore. *Sister Carrie.*

Eggleston, Edward. *The Hoosier Schoolmaster.*

Elias, Robert H. *Theodore Dreiser: Apostle of Nature.*

Encyclopaedia Britannica (1946 edition).

Ford, P. L. editor. *Writings of Christopher Columbus, descriptive of the discovery and occupation of the new world.*

Goss, Charles Mayo, M.D., editor. *Gray's Anatomy of the Human Body* (26th Edition).

Homer, Samuel Butler, trans. *The Odyssey.*

Hubbard, L. Ron. *Dianetics: The Modern Science of Mental Health.*

——subsequent books, articles, etc., on dianetics and scientology.

Indiana Writers' Project. *Indiana: A Guide to the Hoosier State.*

Irving, Washington. *The Life and Voyages of Columbus.*

Jameson, J. F., editor. *Original Narratives of The Voyages of Columbus.*

Jones, William. *Credulities Past and Present.*

Jordan, Harvey Ernest and Kindred, James Ernest. *A Textbook of Embryology.*

Leyda, Jay. *The Melville Log.*

Martindale, Ramona. Unpublished manuscripts, letters, etc.

May, Alan G. "Mummies from Alaska," *Natural History,* March, 1951.

Melville, Herman. *The Apple-Tree Table, and Other Stories.*

——*Bartleby the Scrivener.*

———*Benito Cereno.*

——— *Billy Budd, Foretopman.*

——— *Clarel, a Poem and Pilgrimage in the Holy Land.*

——— *Selected Poems.*

——— *The Confidence-Man: his masquerade.*

——— *Daniel Orme.*

——— *The Encantadas, or Enchanted Isles.*

——— *Fragments From A Writing Desk.*

——— *The Happy Failure.*

——— *Hawthorne And His Mosses.*

——— *I And My Chimney.*

——— *Israel Potter, his fifty years of exile.*

——— *Journal of a Visit to London and the Continent, 1849-1850.*

——— *Journal Up The Straits, October 11, 1856.*

——— *Mardi; and a voyage thither.*

——— *Moby-Dick, or The Whale.*

——— *Omoo: a narrative of adventures in the South Seas.*

——— *Paradise of Bachelors.*

——— *Piazza Tales.*

——— *Pierre, or the ambiguities.*

——— *Redburn: his first voyage.*

——— *Tartarus of Maids.*

——— *The Two Temples.*

——— *Typee: a peep at Polynesian life.*

——— *White-Jacket; or The World in a man-of-war.*

Metcalf, Eleanor Melville. *Herman Melville, Cycle and Epicycle.*

Milne, E. A. *Kinematic Relativity.*

Writers' Program of the WPA in the State of Missouri. *Missouri: A Guide to the "Show Me" State.*

Morison, Samuel Eliot. *Admiral of the Ocean-Sea: a life of Christopher Columbus.*

Murray, Henry A. *Notes to Melville's Pierre.*

National Geographic Society (US). *The Book of Fishes.*

Olson, Charles. *Call Me Ishmael.*

Plato. *The Timaeus and Critias.*

Ragozin, Zenaide A. *A History of the World—Earliest Peoples.*

Roberts, John D. Personal letters.

Shipley, Joseph T. *Dictionary Of Word Origins.*

Spence, Lewis. *Atlantis in America.*

———— *History of Atlantis.*

Thacher, John Boyd. *Christopher Columbus, his life, his works, his remains* . . .

[United Press Accounts] Bobby Greenlease Kidnapping Story.

Vaillant, George C. *Indian Arts in North America.*

Vestal, Stanley. *The Missouri* (Rivers of America Series).

von Hagen, Victor W. "Shrunken Heads," *Natural History* (March, 1952).

Willy, A., Vander, L., and Fisher, O. *The Illustrated Encyclopedia of Sex.*

Yates, Raymond. *The Weather as a Hobby.*

PATAGONI

DARLINGTON, SOUTH CAROLINA

the modern south—pine barrens of lowcountry south carolina, where space appears to go on forever—is not at all unlike modern midwest:

where the land is flat, there is so much of everything to be seen: all that is green lies open, and the blue is cosmic, a true half-shell, full of yesterday's and tomorrow's and everybody else's thunderheads . . .

against this, darlington: labor day, the southern 500, stands and infield jammed, eighty thousand, like the sunday market at huancayo, the plaza filled with indians—americans gone mad with color and shape, shirts, hats, helmets, parasols—the biggest stock car race of them all

knifing around and through, the black oval: the track—the pitcrews all in white, cardoctors: black & white, asphalt & speed . . .

> black fords on
> black tires on
> black-ass
> fault

the cars in idiot pursuit of one another, round and round, all in line to catch the highbank turn, chomping butyl, gorging gas, puffing smoke—the chuff-chuff of Lawrence's whitman . . .

when the man ahead is too slow, you can't pass, you bump him, hinting, at better than 100 m.p.h. . . .

and the wrecks: a tire blows (track temperature: 130°) and the car hurtles the guard rail, rolls out of sight—spins and backs to a halt in midtrack, spews burning gas down the bank of the turn, the driver helpless, rest of the field coming at him, at better than 100 (when bobby myers got his, the one car hurtled straight in the air, smashed by another before it came down: the motor torn from the body, violent and then quiet)

> heavy limbed I
> rush to that space
>
> where I will crash
> and burn
> and scatter steel and gas
>
> and limbs will crush
> for want of air, butyl
> equilibrium
>
> and heavy footed men
> will pass

but it is carnival, and the white souls who came down the day before, drove their pickup trucks into the infield, built their raffish scaffolds, platforms, and tents, camped the night, drank their beer and fried their eggs, boiled all day in the sun of better than a hundred—are tired: quiet-like, they take down their rigs, start their motors, begin to file out, slow, tunneling under the track, before the race is over; this is carnival, a holiday, but next day is work day; they go out like sheep, like huancayo llamas, under the track, the motors silent against the unmuffled thunder above . . .

TIHUANACU

ONE

a.

the humboldt current moves northward, hugging the coast of chile and peru, the bottom waters, polar waters, upwelling

subantarctic into subtropical, juxtaposed—as climates slice each other, as jungle, mountain, and desert dispose themselves, on the adjacent land

bottom waters upwelling, turbid with plankton, a thick soup for herring, mackerel, and pilchard, these a pasturage for seal and porpoise, cormorant and penguin, petrel, kelp gull

plankton and crustacea, dead and dying, rain out of the churning, to feed the forests of rooted animals at the bottom, the bottom-living fish

the waters turning, cool, flow northward, swarm with whale and anchoveta,

> bonito, preying from beneath, the surface hissing as the anchoveta leaps

> ojo de uva

> rockpool fishes, schooling, planktonfeeding forms, freeswimming sharks

dogfish ratfish skate ray and silversides

the liza, stranded on the flats of paracas, corvina, at the flooding river mouths

borracho (a blenny) producing, when eaten, stupefaction, and

the cusk eel

and over these the birds! the thunderheads, the snakeshape clouds passing, passing, daylong clouds

cormorants diving, plunging, fishgorging at the surface

the gannets diving from a height, a barrage of boobies, the ocean a thick foam as they strike, fish, and rise

a booby squall, darkening the sky, spots a fish school—brought thick by upwelling waters to the surface—and the squall drops, vanishes, as one bird

there are camanay, alcatraz, piquero, and the guanay, kin to the blue-eyed shag, the rock shag, a circumpolar bird, panantarctic, swarming northward with the fishrich current

pelicans, gulls and guanayes, gorging, driving the silversides beyond the sideline, on the shore

at sunset, the crisscrossing lines of birds, filing to their islands, snowwhite islands black with birds, the air thick with mutterings, the hum of wings, grunts, and screepy calls

> the birds, the water fowl, circling and dropping
> snowfall upon snowfall, droppings of
> guano snow, circling on the islands

the newfallen guano white, the older, in the glacial depths, a gray, a brown, an oxide red—thick on the rainless islands, under the rain shadow, the rainless ceja de la costa

b.

into this pasturage plunged the indian

mounted his caballito, his bundle of reeds, and straddled, rising to cut through the breakers, and paddled—or lay on his breast, sculled, the waters washing over him

he swam with a cluster of calabashes, gourds

or mounted a float made of "skinnes of sea-wolves, blowne vp with winde," the seams carefully sewn, with an opening above water, and a small hose, "and from time to time they did blowe them like balles of winde"

or sailed on a raft of balsas—the pacific washing through—far out to sea, to fish

c.

the first indian, at the foot of the land, hunted the ground sloth and the native horse, took pilchards and olave fishes, cooked, there in tierra del fuego, on a wood that burned sweet, took the wild celery, cress, and parsnip, the young shoots of tussock, ate mussel, seal, por poise, cormorant—whale, crab, gull, and penguin.

later, when magellan came, there was "a Man of a prodigious Height, who was got upon a Hill, to see the Ships pass by," and there were others of 15 spans, and another that "was fo bygge, that the heade of one of owr men of a meane ftature, came but to his wafte"

"Such as measured their footesteppes in the sande, affirme with greate othes, that one theyr feete is almost as longe as twoo feete of owre men of the meane sorte," and

"The Capitayne named thefe people *Patagoni*"

d.

there were others, who sailed down the coast from the north on a
fleet of balsas, landing in peru at tumbez and puerto viejo, a race of
naked Giants: their knees reached to the natives' heads, their own
heads were mountains, hair to the shoulders, eyes the size of plates

plunging their hands into the living rock, they dug wells, spiral,
deep, and the water came up fresh

they ravaged the desert valleys for food, strode and rafted into the
ocean to take the tiburon and other large fish

they were without women, and used the native female, the gigantic
member killing her in the act, until, the number of females reduced,
they turned to one another, and plunged the big fish into the living
flesh

the Sin of Zodome

drugged, addicted, like the clayeaters of the jungle, a circle of giants
rocked on the brown sand, beneath the andes

e.

on the hot shores, the indian and his woman rolled, rollicked in the
sand, and his phallus—like the serpentphallus of chavín, flashing
flower petals—presented the seed to her lips

she kissed him, and the seed passed once more between them

in semen, sweat, and sea air, the indian and his woman performed,
mounted the positions

f.

"These two elements [land and water] have one spheare divided
between them, and entertaine and embrace one another in a

thousend sortes and maners. In some places the water encounters
the land furiously as an enemy, and in other places it invirons it after
a sweete and amiable manner. There are partes whereas the sea
enters far within the land, as coming to visite it; and in other partes
the land makes restitution, casting his capes, points, and tongues
farre into the sea, piercing into the bowelles thereof. In some partes
one element ends and another beginnes, yeelding by degrees one
vnto another. In some places, where they ioyne, it is exceeding
deepe . . ."

alluvial fans, terraces and deltas, narrow plains, and uplifted wave-
cut shelves . . . and in places, rocks, steep islands, the guano islands,
marine frontier of the andes

g.
maya type, or coclé, the chimu came out of the ocean and built
chan-chan

in the mountains above the city they turned the waters of the
moche, graded them the length of the valley, constructed cisterns
and stonelined channels, carried the water, by intricate distribution,
into the city itself

out of the gravel, the dry, nitrous sand, they built walls, mounds, ter-
races, marking the courses of the walls, in the building, with desert
reeds

from the moche waters gardens sprang up, the plain became lush,
greenery and flowers were tended in the public gardens and the
chimu's patios, the walls were carved and painted in designs, houses
were built with pitched roofs, terraced roofs of cane, totora—veran-
das, supported by the twisted algorroba timbers—patios, terraces,
all open, so that the gran chimu, in his house open and facing the
pacific, sat immersed in his element, counterpart of fish-in-ocean:
the chimu in the sea air

on pots and walls:

serpent, lizard, lobster, monkey
                              snakebird, turtle
                                        skate, crab, and plumed
snail
      birdman, sea bird, cactus—centipede soldier, magic bean sol-
dier, puma, pumabird, the hummingbird soldier

                              guano bird, crabsnake, hun-
dredfooted lobsterserpent

> the moon rules all elements, controls disturbances in the sea,
> makes thunder and lightning, brews the dew that causes
> crops to grow, is greater than the sun because he appears in
> the sky both day and night

offerings of maizemeal, white, were made to the sea

> pachacamac, built on an eminence on the bank of the rio
> lurin, turned its back, like chan-chan, to the rising sun, and
> faced the pacific, the beat of the breakers never out of hear-
> ing . . . the fishgod structure was filled with "Figures of divers
> sorts of Fish," and when an Indian died, the eyes were
> extracted from the skull, replaced by eyes of the cuttlefish

at chan-chan, the moche waters flowed in the gardens, the flowers
flourished

the sea "threw up vast quantities of Pilchards, with the Heads of
which they dunged their Lands," and the maize came up two crops
a year, "and they have great Plenty of it, and of Beans and Lupins,
with which, and the Fifth they take, they drive a Trade among the
People on the Mountains, and are always rich"

the chimu sat on his patio, beneath a totora veranda cooled by the
south breeze, his drinking waters potterycooled

TWO

a.

east of illimani, chimborazo, huascarán, the andean rivers burst the
mountains . . . at the puncu de manseriche, the marañon tumbles out

and a man among snow and thunder, plunging through drift banks,
over slabs of ice, comes up below on the sod, in a jungle sun

> snowwater drips off him, the honeybee swarms, kiss-flowers
> flash among heliconias, palm fronds, airfed orchids

> the bittern, the snowy heron are in the roundwaters, the fish-
> cow browses among riveredge herbs

seeds of wild fig dropped by birds in a crotch take root the young fig
shoots down forking reaching for soil forking new shoots like cut-
tlefish-tentacles push up hook and strangle

                          lianas run to the branch-
ends fall to the soil bounce to a new host or reach over riveredges
hook and grasp an indian his raft floating downstream from under
him

   the beanpod of the ingás grows an armlength

                                an indian child
rafts the waters on a lily leaf

                    rain falls in grape drops toadstools burst
brazil nuts crash from the trees snapping branches killing indian
beneath

       the dying palm collapses cracking like musketshot
termites grind timber to pulp

                    mucor covers the humus

b.

there were men with an eye in the center of the forehead, others
with dogs' heads, and mouths below their stomachs

juan alvarez maldonado found two pigmies and a man five yards in
height, with snout and fangs

"Bien adentro destas montañas había unas monas que parían mon-
struos que tenían las cabezas y miembros deshonestos como hom-
bres y las manos y pies como mona. Esos monstruos eran hijos de
los aborigenes" and others tell of indians with monkeytails, and the
woman who would not sell her pet black potbellied coata monkey
because he was her husband

c.

the centipede is a dog

the red grasshopper a hummingbird

the beetle is a flying mudturtle

the butterfly a bird

the snake of the bolivian yungas, or the amazon catfish, will eat an
indian

the spider a sparrow

the lizard walks upright, like a man

there are "battes as bygge as turtle dooues"—"exceadyuge great Tor-
toyſes"—"ſpiders of marueylous bygneſſe. And I haue ſeene ſumme
with the body and legges, bygger than a mannes hande extended
euery waye. And I ones ſawe one of ſuche bygne ſſe, that onely her
bodye was as bygge as a ſparrowe, and full of that laune whereof
they make their webbes. This was of a darke ruſſette coloure, with
ehes greater than the eies of a ſparow"

d.

bushmasters whine in their sleep, the anaconda wails, there is owl laughter, bullfrogs clang in the ironworks or bray as mules, the steamwhistle cicada is from a baldwin locomotive, macaws and parrots drown waterfalls

e.

the monkey's face reddens with passion, hummingbirds, crests erected, fight in midair

at the riveredge, the jaguar, at his leisure, eats the tail of the living alligator, or snarls, in the forest, over avocados

caterpillars go to bitters, bees and wasps are doped and drunk

pigbirds squat on a low branch motionless

the anaconda's breath is fetid, stupefying, and "In the frefh Water Rivers there are extraordinary large Alligators, and the Portuguefes fey their Tefticles fmell ftronger than Musk"

f.

the top of the jungle forest is an ocean surface, and, submarine, subarboreal, the indian slips along the bottom, a deepwater fish—or a blind foraging ant, creeping under fallen leaves and branches

he eats the marl, a milky clay—chicken gull stew—and puts his lips to a gash in the bark of the cow tree, sucks the milk

        (as the indian babe drew milk from his father's breast

a man blows a palmwood flute to welcome the ripening palm fruits, dons a herondown headdress, avoids bloodshed and the flesh of his patron fish, takes to wife a fat girl with a slender brow, and, to conjure, smokes an armlength cigar

a strip of yellow palm leaf, rolled and folded, with a pendant, a red
ornament, sheaths the penis, while the ceramic tanga, in the shape
of an arrowhead, a pointed tooth, is magic cover for the vulva

the liquor trough is filled with paiwarrie, the men running a race to
it, the winner plunging in, drinking, splashing, bathing in paiwar-
rie—like the pacific fisherman, immersed

g.

the earth is a great creature, the rivers the bloodvessels, the earth
turns one way and another, to warm itself at the sun . . . the first man
mated with a gentle doe, and deerlike, generation by generation, the
race of indians evolved . . . out of the phallus of the chief came the
first maize, from his head, gourds

the spirit of the bird is in his feathers, of the flower in its blossom—
a flower, at the fullest bloom, is dangerous, to be avoided
                                                        it is death
to sleep under the molle bush
                              the great serpent, mother of waters,
will draw an indian to his mouth with an inspiration of breath
                                                        a float-
ing log, fish or boa, or the rays of the sun, may invade a woman,
bring forth a child deformed . . . the rainbow—shadow of the great
waterserpent—will get her with demon
                                    there is the wild man of the
woods, a hairy little creature, strong and wiry, with feet on back-
wards, who loves to carry off indian women
                                        the freshwater dolphin
takes the shape and form, performs the office, of an absent husband
in a jungle full of ghosts, it is wise for a man to make many noises,
to establish his vitality
                        the falling stars are urine,
the dew saliva of the stars

h.
cut a piece from the stem of the ayahuasca, beat it in a mortar with
water—allow it to steep, and force through a sieve, to separate the
woody fiber—to the residue, add water, and drink:

demons in the stem of the plant, the old ones, are seen: jaguar, eagle,
anaconda, crocodile—the old ones who went west beyond the
mountains, feasted and drank beer, returned as

> fox   llama   puma   the giant blue morpho
> hummingbird   vulture
> uturuncu: the manjaguar
> nosebear   anaconda   dolphin
> otter   treetrunk   heron

i.
in the dance a man holds close to his body a phallus of bast and with
his hand spreads the seed through house and field

a girl wears the vaginal bone of the freshwaterporpoise, keeps a
bushhut for lovers, and

> the tortoises stumble over each other in the night, clawing
> the sand, digging nests for eggs, laying, crowding, covering
> and laying, breaking the eggs, digging and laying, shoving

> in the morning, when the indian moves among them, the
> mad tortoise still arches her hind leg, clawing, laying

j.

How to make Mosquito Soup.

RECIPE.—Descending the Missouri or Arkansas rivers in North
America, or the Corontyns or Uruguay in South America, run your
canoe ashore in a thick bottom, just at sundown, having filled your

tin kettle about half full of river water, which is very pure and wholesome. Before landing, however, throw a couple of spoonfuls of salt (or, what is better, if you have it, half a pound of salt pork) and one of black pepper into your kettle, and a dozen or so of the small prairie onion (cop-o-blos) . . .

All these things be sure to arrange before you land, as it might be difficult to arrange them on shore. Also, before being put on shore, if you be the cook, you should draw a pair of Indian buckskin leggings over your pantaloons, tying them very tight around the ankles. Leave your hat or cap behind, covering the head with a large silk handkerchief or shawl, passing under the chin, and covering the face as high as the bridge of the nose, and tie it firmly in the back of the neck: then, with a branch of willow boughs in your left hand to protect your eyes (keeping it constantly in motion), whilst your right hand is free to work with, a thick pair of buckskin gloves or mittens on your hands, and your pantaloon pockets turned inside out, your person is tolerably secure from all approach, and you may venture to step ashore but keeping your body and limbs constantly more or less in motion . . .

In these heavy wooded bottoms there is always a plenty of dried mulberry limbs and trees, which gather as quick as possible; they burn free, with a light flame and little or no smoke to frighten the mosquitos away. Set your kettle exactly in the middle of the fire, so that the flame will rise equally all around it, and some twelve or fourteen inches above its rim, which is abundantly high.

The rest of the party, having left you ashore, should then lose no time in paddling into the stream, each one with a bunch of willow-boughs whipping ashore all the insects that are attempting to follow the canoe, and leaving you, the cook, alone to 'walk the kettle,' as one alone concentrates the flying cloud better than several.

The cloud beginning to gather in promising quantities around you, you may commence walking at a regular pace, with short steps, around the fire and boiling kettle; and whilst keeping your eyes clear with the willow-boughs in your left hand, if you aim your blows right, a great many may be thus knocked into the kettle that perhaps are too wary to get their wings burned.

There is no limited time for this operation, nor any end to the arriving multitudes but you must be guided entirely by the apparent quantity, by lifting off the kettle occasionally, when the boiling ceases, and their carcasses rise in a large clotted mass on the surface, which with a large spoon you should throw off, as the *fat* is all extracted from them, and their bodies should give way to a fresh supply, in order to obtain the requisite richness of the soup.

If you observe occasionally a gallinipper or a mosquito hawk falling in, which is very apt to be the case, where they are so confusedly grouped together, all the better, for they are always gorged with a fresh supply of these insects; and if in the desperate struggle any part of your dress should have given way, and the mosquitos should have succeeded through the breach in getting a few ounces of your blood, no matter—never mind it; it will add to the richness of the soup.

The boiling operation being finished, and the canoe called ashore, the kettle should be handled as quickly as possible, and taken on board; all hands, as they are armed each with a bunch of willow-boughs, will be able to whip the following swarms ashore as the canoe enters the current, over which they never venture to fly more than a few rods.

Then, landing on some barren sand-bar which has no vegetation, and consequently is uninhabited by these torments, a comfortable night's rest may be enjoyed; and the soup, when it is sufficiently cooled, and the again collected mass of their light and emptied carcasses floating on the surface are again skimmed off with the spoon, and some hard biscuits crumbled in, your kettle of 'Mosquito Soup' is ready for use.

GEO. CATLIN, Rio Uruguay

k.

the rivers burst the mountains, pour and twine east—canoepaths in the varzeas—to the freshwater inland ocean:

the amazon

freshets at the foot of the andes, october rains in upland bolivia push into the madeira, tapajor, purus, spread over the flood plains, north into the juniperwaters of the negro—these subsiding, the spring rains in guiana, venezuela press down, drive into the now sluggish waters to the south:

an annual tide, the serpentriver—amarumayu—rolling and sway-ing, northward, southward, across the eastward flow

when the plains are in flower, fish swim over the land, the indian lives on mats hung from the crown of the palm, or retreats to his upland hut, where cricket, snake, and lizard creep into his thatch, the armadillo, the gran bestia sit by the door, the jaguar stands by, quiet, as the waters rise

padre fritz lived three months in a treetop, grasping fish, plantain, and fruit from the waters, fighting off crocodiles

the river undercuts the banks, and the land—a mat of roots and shifting silt—slips away . . . trees crash, the waves beat the opposite shore: back and forth, waves beating from riveredge to riveredge, hour after hour, land and trees crashing, terra cahida, the roar of artillery

bits of land tear loose and float: beds of water hyacinth, mats of brush, of soil, root, plant, and tree—rafts for anaconda, alligator, tapir—freshwater floating islands

at the mouth, beyond marajao, the amazonas, clayyellow, filled with timber, weed, and moss, turbid, an inland ocean folded northward by equatorial current, ocean river—the amazonas—freshwaters undercutting crumbling banks of salt atlantic—plunges, rolls, upwelling

THREE

a.

sodomite giant of tumbez, amazon marajao broke pride, converged,
and brought forth nudos, altiplano, cordilleras blanca and negra—
the mountains called antis

or an ancestorgod, incaic, shaped the ranges with boulders shot
from his huaraca—as huanacaure, brother to manco ccapac, later
split the hills with a throw

on chimborazo, icecliffs, fed by the jungle trades, project from the
peak, westward—tons of ice break away, fall, touch nothing, crash at
the glacier's head, the ice shattering, fragments clambering over one
another, grinding, rolling, clouds of ice spraying beyond

cinderash from cotopaxi fills the air, blinds alvarado's soldiers—the
sky is misted, snow falls

vicuñas idle in the snowbanks, viscachas in the rocks—the llama
munches ichu, and moves over the puna

above, the condor's wings are motionless, doorhinged

below the snowline grow the tola, the queñua, the saffron quishuar

the nazca indian comes up from the coast, welcomes the soft
wools—alpaca, vicuña—for his loom

for campaigns and conquests, the inca makes maps in relief, little
models of the mountains

b.

near titicaca it is better than a hundred in the sun, near frost in the
shade—on illimani, below zero at dawn, above seventy at noon

the indian in ecuador, in a day, brings ice from glacier, chirimoya
from jungle, to where apple, peach, pear grow

the fig tree in mala gives fruit on the sierra side in one season, the
coastal side in the other

at tequendama the rio de bogotá falls in one leap from cold country
to palms

the hummingbird of patagonia flies in the snow

c.
snow and thunder drive across the altiplano, the snowy egret rises,
circles

on a glaring, cloudless day the gale drives stones across the ground,
cuts hand and face, dries the dead without putrefaction

"Without doubt this is a kinde of cold so piercing that it quencheth
the vitall heate, cutting off his influence"

the man on the high peak, the sun blazing on him, looks down on
snowclouds, on lightning cracking over banks of snow

d.
fireshowers of fallingstars pour on cayamba, in the clear air of copi-
apo a planet is seen at noon

at sunrise the mistsea rolls, rises, breaks against grass, snow, rock-
escarpment, and the sun fires an arm through

a man stands, his head between sun and mistbillows, and the anthe-
lion, the rainbownimbus, shines: the shadow of his head in the mist
haloed in circlets, coronets

setting, the sun drops below cloudwaves, shooting in retreat
through gaps, the world upsidedown, sunlit from below

e.

the heart gives a bruit, a sawlike sound—the red marrow is abundant, active—the little indians' cheeks are plumcolored, blue in the red, cyanotic

the problem being, at high altitude, ventilation

> the indian draws in breath and blows on the quena . . . at night he draws his knees to his chin, to sleep, the thighs conserving vital heat

"the quality of the ayre cutteth off man's life"

in some, a depression, a lack of will

in others, *surumpe:* the sun breaks through snowclouds, with wind and dry air pierces the eyes—the indian sits by the roadside, shrieking, eyes in flames, lids bleeding, swollen, stuck fast—snowblind

or *soroche:* the head swims, throbs, the veins turgid—breath comes short, the heart a drumbeat—hands and feet chilled, lips and eyelids swollen, bleeding

jose de acosta "was surprised with such pangs of straining and casting as I thought to cast vp my soul too: for having cast vp meate, fleugme, and choller, both yellow and greene, in the end I cast vp blood, with the straining of my stomacke"

the will oppressed, the urge to drown, or fornicate

> Rx: *surumpe:* fresh bloody flesh of vicuña, laid on the eyes

> *soroche:* unguent of tallow, garlic, and wild marjoram on the forehead . . . infusion of coca . . . copulation

FOUR

a.

in the eastandean foothills, fossil lacustrine limpets are found, and in the upland, above timberline, pliocene marine deposits—testaceous remains . . . at the summit of the andean arch, subtropical fossil floras

walled in to the east, the continent enclosed vast mediterraneans: the amazon sea, mojos lake, the sea of the pampas

rain fell over the old mountains, preandean, and over the low altiplano . . . the clouds refilled from titicaca, and the deserts of gran peru flushed green

but the continent thrust to the west, against basement complex rocks, precambrian—a resistant mass—and the young andes uparched—epeirogenic—overlying, truncating the old mountain roots

b.

a man is anxious, restless, a pressure on the breast—the frame shudders, limbs tremble

seabirds fly inland to the cordillera, dogs disappear, vicuñas descend from the mountains, mingle in the streets with indians

the sound is lowpitch, between hearing and feeling, as, remote thunder, a groan and rattle, the crepitation of burning wood—the earth a thinshell cavern, thumping

a man's footing is oscillatory, fluid: the desert curls, sand-columns rising, whirling, the mountain peaks wave like reeds

the river at arequipa turned black and sulphurous

near chillan the

earth bubbled and burst, hot, fetid waters swelled out

                                        not far from
arica a number of skeletons, legs flexed on the pelvis, were heaved
from the ground steam issued from pasagua bay, itself a crater

                                                              the
ocean bubbled, smoke and bursts of flame erupting

                                        at callao the pa-
cific withdrew from the shore, paused, and, foam-capped, smooth
as milk, rolled inland

lava welled out of cotopaxi, shoved blocks of ice and snow before it,
caused floods in latacunga (indians thought the crater yielded sea-
water and fish

ashclouds rose, the sun turned green, the sky verdigris, copper,
bloodred, brass

at riobamba, below sangai, the land reshaped, mountains sprouted,
rivers shifted, disappeared
                        cache vanished
                                    near cuzco rivers sprang
in dry gullies
                a ridge thrust across the rio seco
                                        the shellmarked coast
lifted, uparching from the ocean, and held

old stream beds and valleys—babes to the andean canyons—are
crossed, buried beneath vulcanism, intrusive granite

the cordillera blanca, uparching, cuts the trades, jungle rains
become ice sheets, and coastal gran peru, green, dries to a desert

toxodons, camelidae vanish in the puna beds

        hot sun follows the snow, the hills groan, rocks split, flakes of
        stone and soil fall down the slopes

the limestones are pitted, the porphyries sculptured—skull-
shape granites onionpeel, quartzite erodes

young andes reshape rock wastes, reform the stream flows

and the indian intrudes

FIVE

a.
at the crux, the area of titicaca:

                              opposite the golfo del peru, a
structural reentrant in the westward thrust of the continent

crustally unstable, subject to shallow and deepfocus vulcanism, with
thrust faults and overturned folds on the long axis of the lake

                                                          titicaca:

caught viselike between the cordilleras

        (kjopa-kjahuana is produced by blockfaulting, soto island
        may be a horst

dust is washed from the uru, as he sails in his balsa through water-
spoutcolumns, rising from titicaca
                        hailstones—chij-chi—whiten the ground,
the june snows cover koati
                        winds flash in sudden gusts through the straits
of tiquina and yampupata
                        bluewinged teal, black diver, white-and-black
gull feed in the waters, snipe skim the beach, white crane stalk the
lake-edge shallows

the wind throws a thicketful of parrots into the air, herons
issue from the yellow waterreed

near the lake, a stunted olive, wild
strawberry and cabbage grow

the andes thrust up, passed an arm around pacific waters,
cupping them from the ocean—when bottoms in the shal-
lows are stirred, seashells foam to the surface: early titicaca,
an inland ocean, fed by glaciermelt and rains from the yun-
gas, grew and spread

the world was dark, and the sun, flameshape, burst
from wildcat rock

at tihuanacu, on the south shore, titicacatihuanacu man, lacustrine,
andeanocean man, intruded

b.
at the center, willka, the sun: rising over snowy cordillera, warming
the high plain, the sunvicuña, sunllama, early american camel,
sunanimal: wariwillka

world, the center of the universe, tihuanacu, the center of the
world—at tihuanacu, taypicala: taipiri, center, and ccala, worked
stone: a block of andesite, worked by man—wariwillkastone, the
sunstone:

faced full front, he stands on a socle, at the summit of the
hollow cavern, earth

(the earth is a stepped pedestal, terraced: ocean to
desert to mountain to high plain to mountain to jun-
gle—earth salient, reentrant—acute and obtuse

and within, the inner earth, the moonhouse: the puma,
enclosed—with longnecked condor, and wariwillka,
upreaching—in the cavern, earth

at the extreme of the sign—the ends of the earth—
wariwillkas, the eyes winged (impregnating), head
crowned, condorfeathered

and above, at the summit of the socle, the springequinox,
wariwillka, septembersun

the head is crowned, the supreme crown: star signs
and sunanimal heads (the necks jointed, moving—
condorfeathered puma at the brow, faced full front

around the full face, as a fillet, signs of earthsteps, with skies
superimposed

the face human, a full nose, sight in full flight from the
phalliceyes, winged, sunanimalcrowned

from the jaw, five stars (flight of the voice), and on the chest,
full center, a birdtailed puma (the body in motion) over the
sun, with condors bordering, upreaching

across shoulders, condors and sunsigns, and at the belt,
sunanimals, with pumaheads, trophies, suspended

warwillkas, earth and sky on the arms—from the elbow, a
trophy head faced full front: the sunthief, killed at the solstice

in the hands, scepters, top and bottom condor
crowned, the female and the crested condormayku

this—the sunfigure—springsun at the year's beginning—the indian
worked in andesite

and beneath, spreading at its feet, carved a frieze, a meander,
with the year's other parts, the months solstice to solstice

the world—tihuanacu—guarded from suntheft—june
and december—the northern and southern ends of
the earth—by a mighty, crested condor mayku

c.

the blocks quarried in the north, floated on rafts of totora reed, across titicaca

the carving: conflation of llama, puma, fish, cougar, condor

                                                            earth,
sun, moon, sky

                    of the stepsign, stepsign with volute

                                                    chachapuma,
pachamama

the sunfigure, rafted and carved—mounted, by andean man, on the platform of kalasasaya

at akapana, the fortress: stone angles salient and reentrant, for defense—as at kalasasaya, salient and reentrant stone repelled ignorance, conserved knowledge: the southern cross, solstice and equinox, distribution of the seasons

        in the center of the earth, a puma, nibbling the moon—from full to crescent

    and letting it grow again

            and a giant wariwillka—sunanimal—stamping, shaking

SIALIA

a.
d'Etroit,
as sieur de la mothe cadillac
saw it:

the narrows would
control the lakes . . .

b.
Preliminary Remarks:

> *RULE.*—Before attempting to read a lesson, the learner should make himself fully acquainted with the subject, as treated of in that lesson, and endeavor to make his own, the feelings and sentiments of the writer.

Articulation:

> *RULE I.*—Avoid the omission or improper sound of unaccented vowels, whether they form a syllable or part of a syllable . . .

> *RULE II.*—Guard particularly against the omission, or the feeble sound of the terminating consonant.

> *RULE III.*—Avoid uniting into one word, syllables which belong to different words.

Tones:

> *RULE I.*—The reader or speaker should choose that pitch, on which he can feel himself most at ease, and above and below which he may have the most room for variation.

> *RULE II.*—The tones of the voice should always correspond with the nature of the subject.

Inflections:

> *RULE I.*—The falling inflection is generally proper, wherever the sense is complete . . .

> *RULE II.*—Language which demands strong emphasis, generally requires the falling inflection.

> *RULE III.*—Questions, which *cannot* be answered by *yes* or *no*, together with their answers, generally require the falling inflection . . .

> *RULE IV.*—Where a pause is rendered proper by the meaning, and the sense is incomplete, the rising inflection is generally required . . .

> *RULE V.*—Questions which may be answered by *yes* or *no*, generally require the rising, and their answers the *falling* inflection . . .

> *RULE VI.*—The different members of a sentence expressing comparison, or contrast, or negation and affirmation, or where the parts are united by or used disjunctively, require different inflections: generally the *rising* inflection in the *first* member, and the *falling* inflection in the *second* member. This order is, however, sometimes inverted.

McGuffey's
Newly Revised
Eclectic Fourth Reader

c.

east of the appalachian barrier the pioneer brought out jebediah morse's geography, and studied: the fertility of michigan, the fruit and wild grapes, the freshwater lakes

he headed west, over corduroy and gumbo, beneath treetops shaken by the wind as an ocean surface, agitated

the man moved into the forest with an axe, to fight it, drive it back

as the distance grew—from albany, new york, philadelphia—words turned to whispers, whispers to silence—he read an old newspaper, and, wordless, held with cool ardor to his axe: immersed and virgin in the timber

out of dearbornville he felled logs for a house, and men came to help raise them—black ash were cut and peeled, the bark laid on for a roof

a green black oak was felled, the man sawed off bolts, rived out shakes with a froe, laid them up with clay, for a chimney

at night he got a backlog in—rolling it on sticks, moving chairs and table aside, crowding it in place, over the clay hearth—against it he set michigan andirons: bolts of green wood—and laid the foresticks on

late, as the coals glowed, a boy could stand on the hearth, look through the flue at michigan constellations

a clearing was made, trees ringed or felled

the axe driven into rooty dirt, corn seed dropped in the cleft, the axe driven close to close the cleft

pontiacers—flies the size of young hummingbirds—swarmed in the brush, and the blue racer outraced the pioneer the first crop—wheat or corn—fought in the clearing with stumps, trunks, shoots, weeds, and vines

one william ford—who had known tenantry in ireland—cleared ninety acres, with patches of timber, called it Springwells Township Farm

july 30 1863, his wife mary gave birth to a first son: the boy henry

d.
it was like jefferson: to play roughly at the fiddle, and to lighten—or enlighten!—the burden

out of springwells—or skylighted monticello—the rustic, giving play to gyrations, to wheels

> (young jefferson pushed through the snows with his bride to reach the little cottage off the main house

> and years later, stood on the monticello porch watching progress at the university, through a telescope

jefferson: backeast, east of appalachia, but hugging the mountains, pushing—the modern mind spilling over, to all louisiana

and later, northward, to michigan

"Mr. Ford still believes it is early morning in America . . ."

father took the little boy by the hand to show him a song sparrow nest: by the big oak, twenty rods east of home and birthplace, and the boy heard the bird sing

he took walks alone in the ten eyck estate, or in the virgin tracts east of the rouge

in winter, skated down roulo creek to the rouge, down the rouge to
the detroit, and up to woodward avenue

in summer, bathed in the rouge, south of michigan avenue: dared to
swim far out, to pick water lilies

or, saturdays, hitched the team, with father and brother, hauled hay,
grain and wood, apples, potatoes, to the haymarket

      (which is now a greensward, a stadium

        (for lions and tigers

f.
they asked the grown man, years later, the lawyer at the chicago tri-
bune libel trial, mr. ford, he said, what was the united states origi-
nally? and henry unclasped a jackknife, honed it on the leather of
his shoe, took his own good time and replied, without looking up,

land, I guess

g
they asked him, elsewhere, what he would do if he were to take
charge of american farms
     tear down all the fences, he said.
     but what about animals overrunning your crops?
     there wouldn't be any animals, he replied. there is no reason
why any farmer should have horses. tractors are better and cost
much less. better milk can be and has been made out of vegetable
products than any cow can give. the cattle that we need for food and
sheep that we need for wool should be raised on great ranges in the
west . . .

he built a chemurgical workship, hired greenhorns with no notions,
poured cabbages, carrots, onions, melons into the caldrons . . . word

came that before long we should grow most of an automobile, per-
haps grow a complete car of wheat

stacks of cornstalks and sunflowers went into the hoppers

h.
january 12 1904—ford, with clara and edsel, and spider huff, drove
northeast to anchor bay, lake st. clair

scraped snow from the ice, spread cinders

turned loose the model b, an overpriced lemon (the particular car
being barney oldfield's 999), ford at the wheel and spider blowing in
the tank to keep the gas feeding, made the measured mile—the car
leaping, skidding over ice, fissures, cinders—in 39 seconds plus

i.
"Everything is in flux, and was meant to be. Life flows."

there was this thing he had about water: the love of old water pow-
ered mills, the fixing of factories and assembly plants by rivers, for
power, the placing of freight on ships rather than RRs

he hated history: "The water that is up the river, and the water now
going over the wheel, are of more importance to youngsters than
water that already has gone out to sea."

books "mussed up his mind" and "Reading can become a dope habit
. . . Booksickness is a modern ailment."

threw out paperwork, recordkeeping, statistics—the *statics* (as ole
diz calls 'em)

had no fixed corporate structure, no titles (the men in his research
labs had desks but no chairs)—preferred, instead, a *fluid* structure,
executives with no defined responsibilities, competing, warring with
one another, the organization kinetic, life and factory an assembly
line, moving, an amazon, mainflow and effluents

"Life . . . is not a location but a journey"

"Life is a going concern"

"The most beautiful things in the world are those from which all excess weight has been eliminated"

j.
june 1 1909—start of a crosscountry race, new york to puget sound:

> (the checking stations: new york—poughkeepsie—albany—
> syracuse—rochester—buffalo—erie—cleveland—toledo—
> south bend—chicago—bloomington—st. louis—centralia—
> kansas city—manhattan—ellsworth—oakley—denver—
> cheyenne—rock river—wamsutter—granger—pocotello
> bliss—boise—walla walla—pendleton—seattle
>
> the pathfinder car couldn't make it, quit in idaho—another,
> starting in seattle, found snow, snoqualmie pass, seventeen feet

new york city, president taft pushed a gold key, the mayor fired a gold revolver, five cars started: an acme, a shawmut, an itala, and two fords

at cleveland, the summer rains: the toledo run made in "mud in bunches . . . gummy, clayey, clinging mud"

st. louis west, rain and hail, hensegg metaldenting hailstones, cloudbursts, beside which a michigan downpour was but the "falling of the dew"

gumbo and quagmire, mud to the axles, swollen streams, with quicksands, to be forded, driver and mechanic tearing down old pigpens, running on the planks

wagonroads, mule trails, or no trail at all, misguided guides in the desert east of topeka, ford #2 slid off a bank into a stream—the two men removed the damaged axle, carried it 3 miles to a blacksmith, got repairs, carried 3 miles back, installed, and resumed

crossed the river platte on the ties of a RR bridge

west of cheyenne, driver and mechanics held tight, so not to be thrown, as the fords climbed

snoqualmie pass: #1 smashed a rock, and the crew rebuilt the motor at the continental divide

                #2 skimmed over the frozen surface of snow, sank as the sun warmed, was dug out by a section gang

                                 and came on to puget, the winner!

      carrying, in its front tires, original air from new york city

k.
Processes On The Crank Box:

> Apply drop-forging half ring to rear end, drill three pin holes, put in pins.
> Rivet pins both ends.
> Seat and drill front vertical wall for four rivets.
> Burr up rivet ends to retain rivets.
> Head front-wall rivets, by hand.
> On anvil with hand-hammer and 'staking' tool, stake front wall to fill.
> On surface plate, gauge and with hand-hammer bring job to overall length.
> Apply globe seat for front-axle globe-end radius fork.
> Drill for two rivets, to fix globe-bracket position.
> In press, rivet ends of globe-bracket.
> First braze; rear-end reinforce, made in four-fire, hand-revolved brazing-furnace.

Braze globe-seat bracket. Vertical flames both upward and
    downward.
On emory wheel, polish arm-seats.
Face end of rear annular collar flush with crank-box shell
    end.
Back to big press line, and in final die straighten up the job,
    far as completed.

> *I asked my mother for fifty cents*
> *To see the elephant jump the fence.*
> *He jumped so high*
> *He reached the sky*
> *And never came back till the Fourth of July.*

Re-rivet front-wall rivets, stretched by preceding operation.
Bring walls to length with press surface-jig.
Grind flat over walls at ends.
Pierce two holes for drain-cock flange; also, same operation,
    seat and close in the drain-cock seat ready for tapping.
Rivet splash-plate.
On driller, half-globe ream front axle radius-ball seat.

> *Mary had a little lamb*
> *Its fleece was black as tar.*
> *And everywhere that Mary went*
> *They thought it was a b-a-a-r.*

Drill thirty-one holes, Bausch Machine Company's driller.
Burr thirty-one drilled holes.
Punch three rivet holes in each armseat.
Drill fourteen transmission cover holes.
Burr fourteen drilled holes.
Punch three holes in front and bottom.
Ream front wall for starting-crank sleeve seat.
Punch overflow screw-seat-bush holes.
Fix front-end malleable-iron casting trunnion in place with
    two rivets.

Drill six more trunnion rivet holes.

Hand-rivet six rivets in trunnion.

Close in the two overflow-plug bushes, to be tapped to take the overflow screws. These screws are at different levels, to show maximum and minimum oil plash-pool depths in crank-box fly-wheel-housing depression.

Press-rivet six rivets in end trunnion shell.

Turn crank-box shell projections down over trunnion shell, with hand-hammer.

Braze trunnion shell to crank-box shell, in four-hole, hand-revolved brazing furnace.

On a large cast-iron jig, with legs and clamp and spotting pins, gauge and straighten the trunnion.

Drill trunnion hole.

With angle plate on face-plate and lathe and back rest fixture, turn trunnion.

I eat my peas with honey,
I've done it all my life.
It makes the peas taste funny,
But it keeps them on my knife.

With crank-box clamped to lathe-saddle spotting fixture, bore and face rear-end brazed-in drop-forging annular collar.

Drill and tap screw holes in rear-end collar.

Place the two pressed-steel hangers by which crank box is held to chassis frame, drill for and insert three pins, and rivet pin ends, to hold hangers to crank-box shell.

Braze crank-box hangers to crank-box shell, four fires in a bank, with swinging flames on top, stationary flames below.

By hand, with big file end, scrape and clean inside of crank-box shell.

By hand, finish-tap rear-collar screw holes.

Place transmission covers, with gaskets applied to covers; place horse-shoe reinforces inside of crank-box, and put in fourteen transmission cover screws, through covers, through gaskets, through crank-box shell, and turn screws down hard; screws threaded into the two horseshoe reinforces.

Oats, peas, beans, and barley grows,
Oats, peas, beans and barley grows,
How, you nor I nor nobody knows,
Oats, peas, beans, and barley grows.

In large fixture, with gauge and hand-hammer, bring the crankbox hangers to place.

Lay crank-box, flat side down, on large surface plate, and with hand-hammer make the crank-box top flange lie down on the surface plate, all the way around.

Entry, kentry, cutry, corn,
Apple seed and apple thorn.
Wire, brier, limber lock,
Three geese in a flock.
One flew east, one flew west,
One flew over the cuckoo's nest.
O-U-T spells out goes she.

In a large fixture, with clamps, with hand-hammer, bring the hanger holes to slide on fixture pins.

Tap globe-seat cap holes for cap retention.

Tap drain screw seat.

Tap the two overflow screw seats.

Fill overflow screw seats with temporary brass screws, screwdriver cuts, to close holes for gasoline leak tests.

Tap two holes in rear-end annular collar, and two holes in front vertical wall.

Heat front side of front wall, and clean wall and box wall seat with muriatic acid, to clean the surfaces for soft-soldering.

With tinning fluid and hand soldering-copper, soft solder front wall in place to the crank-box shell inside.

With hand copper, fill joint with soft-solder and also fill top
joint between box wall and the front wall, if joint is
open on top side.
With hand-file end clean off surplus solder.

> *Hacker, packer, soda cracker,*
> *Hacker, packer too.*
> *Hacker, packer, soda cracker,*
> *Out goes you.*

Place drain screw and turn it down hard.
Press the hand starting-crank bushing into place in center of
trunnion.
Place crank-box, open side up, in gasoline vat and see if any
gasoline leaks into the box at any point.

> *Onery, uery, ickory Ann,*
> *Filisy, folasy, Nicholas John*
> *Queever, quaver, English neighbor,*
> *Stinkem, stankem, B-bo-buck.*

Final. Dip in air-drying japan vat, to japan outside of crank-
box.

> *Quaker, Quaker, how is thee?*
> *Very well, I thank thee.*
> *How's thy neighbor next to thee?*
> *I don't know, but I'll go see.*

l.

among maples, where the ann arbor trail crosses the rouge, stood
nankin, the old grist mill restored, producing dies and engravings
for fords—the neighboring farmers gained winter employment in
the mill, sent their children to the red brick schoolhouse

The rural production center, ideal community:

jefferson at monticello, ripley at brook farm, ford at nankin
                                                          oneida,
new harmony, joseph smith and elbert hubbard
                                        hedgerow theatre, black
mountain college; community in the arts
                              mack avenue, highland park:
for the deserving worker, the $5 day
                        blithedale: the plant on the river
rouge

m.

on a picnic with edison, ford ran, jumped, yelled, and hollered,
chopped logs, climbed trees
                he and edison once held a kicking contest, new york
hotel: it was edison who won, bringing down the chandelier
                                                    again, ford
disappeared on board a train, returned later covered with soot: he
had climbed the coalcar, hobnobbed with the engineer, ran the
locomotive

often he hopped in and out of his office by way of the windows

n.

the oscar ii, the peace ship—her hull glistening in the low winter
sun—slipped into the hudson currents

                    I saw a little fordship
                    go chugging out to sea . . .

in the atlantic, ford, taking his brisk michigan morning walk, was drenched by a wave—he caught cold and retired to his cabin

(the newsmen made up their own stories, from the ship's bar)

once he snuck out, went below, was for a moment happy, inspecting machine shop and engine room

the ship docked in norway, ford was sick and grim—the winter sun set early

dean marquis—working for the family to persuade ford to give it up—put him in a gloomy room, heavily curtained, with northern exposure—and locked the door

it was christiana!

ford passed hours alone, working—alone—for peace

o.
the sense of touch, the real thing

>   (when bill durant, forming general motors, tried to buy
>   out ford, ole hank said, all right, but gold on the table!

>   (a money he could touch

he disliked blue prints, worked from models

"I wouldn't give five cents for all the art in the world" and once spent time hanging around artist's studios trying to find out what it was, the intangible

"History is more or less bunk" but there were wayside inn and greenfield village, a *real* history

touch sense, the genius of touch:

they decide to contract for a part of the car, say a distributor head—the samples come in, maybe 30 of them, the engineers spend days studying, take them apart, work them over, figure out which is the best

all 30 are spread on a table and ford comes in, squints at them, picks one up here and there—after a couple of minutes says, that one

and so it is

> and some wag brought him an alien washer, asked where it belonged on a model t—he grasped it and threw it out the window, knew by the touch that it didn't

william carlos williams: ideas only in things . . . *the animism of the indian!*

the hand at work, in touch—the mind liberated, made meditative

or ford's fellowmiddlewesterners, dreiser and anderson, groaning to make their art real, to put the self on the page—man and art indistinguishable

the man and the thing made—ford & ford—one

p.
when asked the secret of his life, he replied that he was leonardo da vinci, reincarnate

"What we call death doesn't end all for us, by any means"

"When the automobile was new, and one of them came down the road, a chicken would run straight for home—and usually get killed. But today when a car comes along, a chicken will run for the nearest side of the road. That chicken has been hit in the ass in a previous life."

His own first car was only part of an accumulated experience,
inherited at birth

> (the transmission was planetary)

and three worlds from now the ford would be a better car than ever

> for the nation, a car—a carnation!
> not an inca, but re-inca—in car!
>
> *r e i n c a r n a t i o n !*

q.
little harry bennett came out of the navy, to run the show at the rouge

hired cons, thugs, pluguglies—on the side raised beef, chows, horses,
played the sax, thought *moby-dick* the greatest book ever written

when he rode with ford, he was armed—the chauffeur had a gat
under each arm, and there were magnum revolvers in a holster built
into the car

in his office he shot target practice with goldplated revolver

harry bennett was director of personnel

> march 7 '32—an icy day—a crowd—fordjobless, commies,
> hangerson—gathered in detroit, and marched to the rouge . . .
> at the city line—baby creek park—the dearborn cops pumped
> tear gas shells: the mob got mad, hurled rocks, fought through,
> unarmed, to miller road, the overpass at gate 3:
>
> bennett's thugs, inside the gate, turned firehose and firearm on
> the hunger marchers, wounding, killing: the battle of the rouge
>
>> and later, ford men tore up the soybean acres, planted
>> them in cement for bombers, at willow run

r.

milk is poisonous, and salt is good for the hair

"I've got no use for a motor that has more spark plugs than a cow has teats"

s.

at fair lane, virgin oaks, willows, elms stood among the second growth

handmade bricks from coon ten eyck's tavern were built into the fireplace

the bobolinks came back to dearborn every year on april 2 . . . there were five hundred bird houses at fair lane, the largest, the martin house, held seventy-six apartments—the wren boxes hung from strips of spring steel, to discourage sparrows—pheasants and quail were hatched, incubated, and through the winter wire baskets of food hung from the trees, and the bird baths were electrically heated

corn was grown, left standing for the squirrels, and little stacks of rails and hay were built to house the rabbits

> (but the english birds imported—hammer, chaffinch, twit, bullfinch, thrush, linnet, lark—scattered and vanished in the michigan plain, and the doves at greenfield fell prey to michigan hawks

> (the rabbits flourished, overran fair lane, destroyed the orchards, he had his men tear down their homes, shoot them as pests

>> (as, the workers: five-dollar-day to hunger march

> (and the heated bird baths failed to break the cycle of migration

ford took a daily walk, chinning himself on lowhanging limbs, and ending at a trot, or a sprint through the cornstalks

entering the door at fairlane, he stood in the hall and whistled for clara . . . they sat on the sunporch and watched birds, binoculars and audubon in hand . . . at night she read aloud to him from *bambi* and *the yearling*, and they listened to lum and abner

or he skated alone on the frozen rouge, by moonlight

at the engineering lab in dearborn he maintained musicians: dulcimer, cymbalo, violin, and sousaphone . . . the craneway was removed, the machines pushed back: henry and the motormen folkdanced

he named his yacht *sialia*—indian for bluebird—but on board he was restless: as they locked through a canal, he vaulted a rail, and footed the distance

"The stars are so bright in Florida, we saw many that cannot be seen here in Dearborn"

sailing the caribbean, he would spot a lonely beach: a launch would set him ashore, with clara, and the *sialia* would stand offshore, while the couple rested, or hunted seashells in the sand

t.
"The Rouge is so big that it is no fun any more"

after the old french landrich of detroit came the younger lumberrich, and after them the still younger motorrich—and with all of these ford mixed not at all

he called on grandpa mellie dunham for a fiddletune, and skipped—alone, solemn—through the steps of a waltz or ambled in the late evening to the stephen foster cottage, green-field village, and—hunched at the organ—picked with one finger at *the old folks at home*

> (the manager of fordlandia, the rubber plantation on the amazon, came from detroit, and at christmas time he had in his jungle home a christmas tree!

at dearborn, april 7 1947—five days after the arrival of the bobolinks—a rain and windstorm raged, the power failed—the lit-tle suwanee, fed over a wheel by waters of the detroit river, overfl-owed in greenfield village, and the sidewheeler foundered . . . up the rouge at fair lane—by the light of oil lamps—ford's own motor came to a halt

> in a cardboard box in his private experimental lab, they found a test tube, tightly sealed and neatly labeled:

"Edison's last breath."

SALT, GARLIC, & COITION

ONE

a.

" . . . knobby joints and a somewhat zigzag stalk, hairy leaf sheathes and stiffish leaves, purplish color in all or several parts of the plant, coarse root system, ears of pyramidal shape (markedly tapering and having a heavy butt), soft, brittle cobs and long glumes, irregularly rowed seeds, and crest tassels."

> " . . . as bygge as a mannes arme in the brawne: The graynes whereof are sette in a marvelous order, and are in fourme somewhat lyke a pease. While they be soure and unripe, they are white: but when they are ripe they be very black. When they are broken, they be whyter than snoww. This kynde of grayne, they call *Maizium.*"

out of the montaña, west of the clogged rainforest, but climbing out of it, a typical amazonian plant, with "pendulous leaves, colored foliage, long aerial roots, a cauliflorous inflorescence, small flowers with conspicuous coloring, and a tendency toward the separation of the sexes in the flowers."

maize moved under the hand of the indian, and the podded hawks-bill seeds became naked

marched north, the culturehero!—maize and indian, exfoliating, spreading

crossed the isthmus and in mexico became tripsicoid: " . . . slender, canelike growth, elastic and little subject to breaking or lodging, often of bright green color; cylindrical ears; dense woody cobs and short glumes; seeds in straight rows; widely branching tassels; and free tillering."

flooded north and east: navajo and cherokee

the indian putting the plant to use in every growth stage: leaf, blossom, immature and fullgrown fruit—his garden in the field

b.
on the rainless coast of peru the indian grew maize with fishheads and dew, fattened the ground with guano

in the mountains he straightened the rio urubamba—a snake thrashing between valleyedges—contained it within walls, filled soil over loose rock, replaced full stretches of earth, reshaped, regraded the valley

stepped the slopes with terraces, filled with jungle earth, directed glacial water

and, with potatoes, drove glaciers up the ridges

on the steep slopes, he held with one hand and worked the ground with the other—staked the squashes, so they would not roll off

handplowed in crisscross, to hold the steepfalling rains

built cities on hills and hummocks, to save the fat bottoms for cultivation

TWO

a.

the inca drove a wedge between the men drugged—coast indians addicted to the hills and hummocks, the fat bottoms, the buttocks of their own: the sodomites

cut off the moche waters to chan-chan, brought the gran chimu to his knees

took virgins to himself, burned and buried alive those who drove the fish into unproductive flesh, and

with lusty indians, built an empire to the borders of the condor's range, panandean

b.

in peru, when the palta ripens, the men and girls fast, abstain from salt, garlic & coition, for five days . . . they gather in the fruitgardens, nude, and hold a footrace: as each man reaches a girl, he plants and ripens her, on the spot

(intercourse must always occur outdoors, in the cultivated fields— the indoor child will be blind or lazy

between the dying and new moons, the indian goes to his wife, and for nine months, as each month turns new, he goes to her again, engendering the child by degrees, man and moon enlarging it, bringing it full

c.

andean man played the mansize syrinx, drum, tambor and cowhorn—deerbone fife, deerskull whistle, quena, conchshell and bullhorn—a tibia flute (from an enemy), a fivehole flute, a fifteen-foot bamboo horn—and at huantar, set flutes in rockclefts in the mountain, for the updrafts to make music he spoke quechua: quehuasca, twisted straw—the language agglutinate, polysynthetic, the meanings twisted together—woven to the root, the actionword—or joined, as at machu picchu, stone by stone: meanings so precise that, though without mortar, not a knifeblade may pass between them

his wife twisted vicuña with viscacha and bat wool, spun it clockwise—she gained a carmine dye from the cochineal, used urine as a mordant, and wove three hundred threads to the inch

d.

in the valley of yucay—from pissac to ollantaytampu—the inca might listen to chiuiuiuñichi—air whistling among the leaves of trees—or the songbirds, the doves and pigeons, the tuya, ccenti, checollo, the golden-breasted quitu

he might be misqui-tullu—a sweetbone, lazy fellow—and bathe in mingled hot and cold spring waters, in freestone baths

he wore a mantle of batfur from tumbez, or a garment composed of thousands of the tiny goldgreen feather from the hummingbird's breast

he would dine in the morning, and spend the day drinking (the inca huana ccapac could outdrink his captains, three to one) . . . in the evening, a light supper

his gardens gave chirimoya, palta and lucma, the white maize of yucay, wild cherries from andahuaylas

the cherry tomato grew wild in urubamba

e.

LLANTO

HUK URPICATAM UYWAKARKANI

Jauja (Perou)

BAILE DE LOS DANZANTES

Vallée du Chanchamayo (Perou)

KASWA

PASTORALE

f.

the inca tupac amaru—his sunvirgins—and a few effeminate males
were the last to live at machu picchu—a refuge past pizarro

in the air, the blackheaded grosbeak, a sparrow and finch, the gray
dove, the brown robin

bear and deer on the ground—bushmaster and coral

water came from springs on the mountainside, carried by stone into
and through the city: pool, drain, stone, fountain, to pool

                    (but in the dry season it must be hauled from
                    the urubamba two thousand feet below, or
                    from springs miles away

D'ÉTROIT

when I go out to gloucester to see charles olson everything works
out fine the east wind the april fog rolling in off the harbor 28 fort
square cozy charles just out of bed rolling out over dinner a rich
meal and he drives me back to the station I make the 8:12 with time
to spare due north station 9:19 35 minutes to the airport and anoth
er half hour to flight time the stations click off on schedule until we
back out of the salem station a mile or so and sit for half an hour just
the margin I needed to make my connection we get rolling again
and take our time when I get to north station I rush to the phone
call the airline find the plane is delayed 20 minutes and I just might
make it I roar to a taxi and bribe the driver heavy to make time
through sumner tunnel and out to east boston at the reservation
desk I find the flight is now delayed indefinitely they have no planes
everything coming in late account of the weather I can't possibly
make my connection at idlewild new york for the flight to detroit
I'm about to give up go back to boston get a hotel or take the sleep-
er when they announce an earlier flight also delayed just now leav-
ing for new york I beat my way back to the desk make them hold
the flight while I buy a ticket rush out the gate cross the pavement
through driving april rain board the plane surrender ticket to stew-
ardess door slams motors rev we cruise to runway gun the sons of
bitches and we're aloft

comes now above the cloud layer over the intercom the electronic
voice of the stewardess welcome aboard eastern flight number such-
and-such your hostess miss so-and-so this flight for la guardia field
new york and I think oh great oh great for la guardia and my flight
is out of idlewild across long island with an hour and fifteen min-
utes to contemplate this we settle in still raining at la guardia I rush

to the reservation desk present my problem plane leaving idlewild
for detroit in half an hour I can't get there and he says yes you can't
get there and I look at him and he looks at me and then he goes to
an inner office calls a number to idlewild comes back out beaming
you're in like a bird northwestern flight number such-and-such
idlewild to detroit also delayed by weather yes by taxi four bucks I
can make it

pleasant ride groundborne la guardia to idlewild discuss with driver
problems of manhattan hack stuck late at night on the island only
thing to do is work the airports hope for a fare back to the city and
here I've crossed him up but at least a fare maybe now he'll be lucky

wild it is but not idle and my flight is further delayed nothing to do
for a couple of hours but find the men's room closed for cleaning sit
and contemplate the crowds the dirt the noise and think this I could
do at one third the cost in any united states bus station like every-
one else I've been took and study spanish from the bilingual eastern
and national plane announcements for san juan puerto rico es la
ultima llamada

3:10 A.M. airborne for detroit, rain, fog, heavy wind, the plane, cargo
with a few passengers, rocked. I manage to sleep a little

around 5:30, circle into detroit metropolitan airport and land still
raining and blowing hard emerge under the flat steel dawn and
cross to the huge modern terminal building miraculously vacant
claim my baggage and catch a greyhound to the city

       detroit
       a city   no city
           but
             only the suburbs of its
             (as e. e. would say)
             unself

get a hotel change get breakfast get by phone the routine on the
ford plant rubberneck tour catch an interurban for dearborn walk to
the ford rotunda make the tour

the ingot afire,
blasted from the hearth,
hot in the
tincovered squaremiles:
                    the rouge

the ingot: lithic, thick
—tihuanacu, chavín, san
agustín—this it is—mesabi:
decanted on a flat car
to cool beaten, slapped, chopped, rolled
on the line, rolled
thin   thin   thin

cool & thin
a toy
for a drug store,
a salesroom

back up to dearborn for beer and lunch another bus and another
walk to the edison museum

> henry's agglomeration of all americana, with the crazy
> machines, the old cars, the impact of including the recent
> past (the link), the big machines, steam plants, etc: the
> flywheel, 4' wide, 24' diameter, and the avery traction engine,
> 1916, with the bulldog on the front and the words, "teeth talk"

and greenfield village all sentiment all indulgence and here I begin
to give a little

the rain has quit but it is still blowing hard and a few tiny flakes of
snow bite like bugs on my face and the little girl who is to be our
guide says in her funny middle western way there WILL be such and
such and you WILL see so and so and you WILL walk three miles I
make it through henry's birthplace perfectly restored and learn
much from this boxing in of little middle western spaces before

frank lloyd wright and into edison's buildings from menlo park with the carloads of original jersey clay dumped around them the first floor is all right *it's all so very historical* but on the second in the laboratory where I can look out the windows across the brick wall and over the highway to the ford experimental grounds I begin to lose track of the nineteenth-century spiel and watch the thunderbirds racing around the experimental track testing testing and here I crap out

the little girl is upset but I tell her I haven't time, I make my way back through the biting weather to the entrance, back on foot to dearborn

> (at the rouge, the overpass on miller road, the blood of them—of harry bennett, and those others, the ones who died, the hungry white indians who had marched out from the city—the blood of them still (so it seems) on the pavement)

and the first drink and think of the second and more and dinner and maybe the gayety burlesque a less official survival in detroit of an older age and a long long night in the madison lenox hotel

7 A.M. two days later a sunday off from willow run the day still gray a delta sixty-seater headed south but a midspring sunday only three or four on board and the stewardess miss so-and-so confused by the mob of us gets the mudtasting coffees mixed the squared fields below still unsprung a gray green and cutting the corner of lake erie over the western islands the freshwater below a graybrown in the smoldering trying-to-emerge early sun that is still only yellow clouds and later to the east tumbling in the low the graylow clouds the land thumping into hills—the hills that barriered jefferson so, to the west, and ford, to the east . . . and west, the flat

SONATAS IN CAJAMARCA

ONE

to the indian, the castilians were

"banished men, with haire on their faces, yea, such as were bred of ye scum of the Sea, without any other Origen or Linage, because the Sea had brought them thither: demaunding also why they wente like Vagabondes wandring the World: it should appeare said they, that you are ydle persons, and have not wherein to imploy your selves, because you abide in no place, to labour and till the ground."

TWO

in manaos, in the rubber boom cobbles from lisbon paved the streets, houses were built of italian tile and marble, with furnishings from france, linen from london, venetian tapestries, mirrors from brussels

grand pianos rotted in the damp, the ladies sent linens to lisbon, to be laundered

tracks of the madeira-mamoré RR were laid on formosan ties, by men from malta, jamaica, wales, barbados, china, martinique, turkey, persia

(coripuna indians hovered in the jungle

a limeñan hidalgo traveled to iquitos, across the andes and in his own country, by way of panama, transshipping at darien, thence to liverpool, transshipping, again, to belem—and up the amazon

THREE

"I have tightened my flute
with the nerves of a bull
so that its voice would be clear . . ."

in the jungle colonel fawcett read and reread a wormriddled *martin chuzzlewit*—teddy roosevelt sat on a log, with headnet and gauntlets, and read "Madame Desbordes Valmore's lines on the little girl and her pillow, as dear little verses about a child as ever were written . . ."

in peru, a relay of 40 indians brought a piano over the trail to cajamarca, and the owner played sonatas

other indians carried pianos, coast to cuzco, and in bolivia, an exceptional mule became a pianera: able, singlebacked, to carry a piano over the andes

midnineteenth century, the literati in cuzco favored fenimore cooper

the salives indians play well now on the violin-cello

FOUR

a certain limeñan merchant got stuck with a consignment of eye-glasses, so he went to his amigo, a corregidor in the provinces, and an order was issued, that no indian in this corregidor's district should appear at divine services without spectacles . . . the consignment moved rapidly

the rubberworkers in the jungle traded rubber for tradeguns: the barrels were made of wire, wound, heated, dipped in solder, and painted—when fired, the cap snapped, the powder fizzed at length, and the charge left the muzzle snorting like a wild pig—after 40 or 50 shots, or if too big a charge were used, the barrel unwound in the indian's face, and he would go to work again, for rubber, and another tradegun

       (the indians in peru at one time were forbidden to cut their hair, that they might more easily be dragged by it

       (santa rose indians tied a condor to a bull, exploded firecrackers from the bull's horns

       (in jauja, they went wild, killed white dogs and white chickens, scraped whitewash from the walls

FIVE

into the humboldt current the indian smuggles dynamite, spreading it—the american net—to take fish

       (in rare years, coastal currents and climate are disturbed, rain falls, the seabirds go loco, fly inland, feed with cattle and swine

when the guano islands were raided, coolies were shipped in by the hundreds from macao, slavedriven to dig guano, to pour the harvest down a chute into a ship's hold, where more coolies—lost in the yellow smoke of it, as in a lardfire—balanced the cargo

parts of coolie corpses, vanishing, embalmed in fresh guano, protrude now, make perches

SIX

at tihuanacu, building block and carved stone went into home and church, were blocked and crushed, by the trainload for fill, bridge and culvert, on the RR

the tracks were laid on tihuanacu stone, over ties from oregon

> (in detroit, workers make abstract art from junk, old tailpipes, crankboxes

SEVEN

the dogs at tihuanacu dug up the newburied indian infants, and in chile, the tavernowners bid at auction for the body of an infant: the buyer dressed and painted it, propped open the eyes, set it among candles, and fired off rockets, to announce the wake . . . for three days and nights, business was good

EIGHT

MANUAL OF INSTRUCTIONS

to catch a condor:

> hide under a freshly killed animal skin (with meat still adhering) until a condor alights, for the carrion
>
> grasp him by the legs

to prevent excessive rain:

> expose a skull
> put a cigarette in its mouth

NINE

a wedding—andeanindian—is an orgy, a

vaginafiesta!

PENSACOLA, NORTH CAROLINA

thars this lil ole dirt road, you know, like they had, this lil ole cabin settin up above the road, this ole feller asettin on the porch, and this moll t comes chuggin round the bend, feller drivin it along, an that ole feller up on the porch, he rises up, his eyeballs just abuggin an he says,

"maw, git the shawtgun—ah doan know whut hit is, but doan let hit git away"

maw gits don the shawtgun and comes ott, she takes keerful aim and fars

them shawtgun pellets splays all over thatair moll t and that feller adrivin he jumps and jes lights ott across the pasture, the moll t keeps rot on amoseyin don the road

"did ya git hit, maw?"—the ole feller can't see too good

"no paw" she says, lowerin the gun—the moll t amoseyin on don the road—"but ah made it let loos-a that man"

DIARIO Y CARTAS

Aloha Bar
Miami International Airport
5 P.M.   5/18/59
(budweiser)

wall, so mebbe ya got my wire by now, made the western onion man
garntee delivery at 6 PM (the witching hour)—

things not too hectic, wms. in a temperate frame, eastern flight very
smooth

well, have ya stopped bawlin? I don't understand wimmin—ya beat
'em, cuss 'em, maltreat 'em and when ya leave, they bawl—

couple hours from now I climb me into a tin can and go like the
very wind—

next communique from parts further south

love & stuff

Paul

aw, quit bawlin, I'm comin back

Lunes 18 de Mayo

como una niebla gruesa
el hispanoamericano

cuelga
entre nos y el indio

the caribbean is the oak bluffs of south america, a sink trap

flying over the caribbean at night, over a flaky layer of clouds—muy
hermoso

heat lightning over Colombia, like it spread the length, the unob-
structed alleys of the cordillera, panama to patagonia

funny difference: the U.S. is breadth, S.A. *length*

2:30 A.M.—
over the pacific

runnin 2 hours late which suits me fine, I'll get to see more o' them
handy andes, got a good window seat, east side

panama hot slimy full of furriners slingin' us hammerican tourists
the slick eye, glad to be away & above it all—my panamanian plane
pal was real palsy, though, I could dig his spanish better than his
english, so help me

with the aid of god, seconal & bellows club, I've had one thick hour
of sleep, figure that's enough

P.

guayaquil another dirty little place feller took my letter with a dirty
look & a rattle of spanish wouldn't even let me buy a stamp & don't
believe I sealed it, you got, no?

she-Injun in felt hat and poncho tried to sell me a shawl but I figure
I wait

well, I've seen it all a few moments ago: dawn over the andes:
might's well turn around at lima & come home

extra stop at Talara, first footing in Peru: a freshness, even though a desert: cool wind, brown sand sterile, but maritime, a pleasure after the thick sticky sick spanish heat of Panama & Guayaquil

and now breakfast, huevos revueltos, revoltin' eggs, that is, and coffee with Pream, the invention of some diabolo norteamericano

---

I have just enjoyed my first southern hemisphere defecation, albeit airborne. I am at home.

Love,

el caballero

Martes 19 de Mayo

Flying just offshore, from Talara to Lima: the garua, the cloudfog obscures ocean & shore completely, the guano islands and the first hills of the mainland emerging from the puffy snowcotton blanket—beyond, to the east, the cordillera negra and the cordillera blanca, glistening

landing at Lima, dipping, as though blindly, into this puffy stuff, real eerie feeling—on the land, all gray, foggy, grunting to rain, and dismal

weird barren brown treeless grassless mountain coastline, and inland, south of Lima—here and there a narrow streambed that hasn't dried up, with strips of farm pursuing it to the sea, pinching it all the way

Lake Titicaca: on a clear sunny winter day the most magnificent body of water, the bluest bluest deepest bluest lapis lazuli indigo cerulean bluest azul, makes the rich blue sky pale, it is just unimaginable, the lake & sky, the brown mountains, here is the whole story of the basic colors of so much of Indian design, the brown & blue— if the race didn't originate on these shores, it shoulda knowed better (on copacabana, there was, antiguamente, an idol of carved lapis lazuli, highly polished)

La Paz a fantastic city, at first it seems sorta brown and unattractive, scattered in its little saucer, but you get into it, walk the streets, nose the shops, etc., and it is fascinating, everywhere the subterranean Indian—cold shadows, warm sun, all buildings wide open, no heat—the american consul complains of the altitude, it makes him dream too much—mixed effect of climate and steep streets: to exhilarate & slow, at the same time—mad location & distribution of city, sunk in the midst of the barren hills & upland, you turn down a street and all of a sudden there's that damn brown barrenness again, or maybe a vast snowy peak, as though you could reach & touch

Col. Medina: very possibly the greatest single archeological collection in the world, packed into one room—the immense amount of fine, detailed, minute work—in sculpture & pottery, the facial types of all races; hence, the prime race—Sun god as leader with worshipers, of which there may have been, at least in plan, many more—presence of swastika in tihuanacu design

many wari-wilka (cameloid) types—also, most fabulous along these lines, the twin dinosaurs, goddammit, joined together (see dragon as folk memory of dinosaur)—many phalli, stylized & representational

superb mochica love vase, man & woman caught at it

gold work as fine as the colombian

2 types of trepanning: cutting & rasping—the complete set of surgical tools, of minute gradation, for trepanning—also, the female mummy showing a caesarean

Medina: que hombre—"Una coleccion magnifica, indescriptable, hecho por un caballero verdadero del viejo mundo"—this I write in his guestbook, as we drink a liqueur

> 20 de mayo
> hotel sucre palace
> 7 ayem

if I tried to give you details of all the superb & unimaginable impressions I received yesterday, I couldn't—so I won't.

suffice it to say that Lake Titicaca, from the plane, on a brilliant winter day, is just beyond belief—this is THE place in THE world

had excellent conversation with plane pal, Lima to La Paz, a suave frenchman now living in Lima, he gave me much lowdown so that I landed sort of with my feet on the ground

here at sucre palace (the local gentry, I find out, call it sucker's palace) instead of austria, sort of worked out that way

now, La Paz: it is just another one of those things I can't begin to explain, but you might as well start packing—this is, beyond all doubt, THE CITY—incredible

now, Col. Medina, whom I visited yesterday: one of the strangest, most intense, remarkable men, almost dead from sheer physical and mental deterioration and exhaustion, poor as dirt, but with the fire of his possession, his madness—Tihuanacu—burning in him, holding him together—he had a bad cold, he showed me around for a while, went back to his chair, coughed, wheezed, drowsed, opened an eye, saw me looking at something new, he just HAD to come charging out of the chair, a little weary bull, to explain . . . if you can imagine a c---- with a glowing coal, the last spark of the conquistadors driving him, forcing him—que hombre!

his collection is dynamite, incredible—am going back again before I leave—

everything thus far is incredible—which is why I believe it

> throw out your bum ear and
> start packing

> Señor Boliviano

Miercoles 20 de Mayo

T-day: made my arrangements with the taxi man, and we're off—
the climb out of the city, etc., and across la puna—harvest time, the
injuns digging out the spuds, spreading them to freeze, then turn-
ing in the hogs to root what they missed—much barley—as before,
this insane geography, them early joes didn't *choose* the blue-brown
color scheme, they were *driven* to it—here every fragment of the
landscape constantly impels, you're like under a pressure, but dis-
tant, again that funny combination of exhilaration and relaxation—
about the barley, the injuns use the grain for themselves, feed the
rest to the stock, see Carl Sauer (also mebbe Anderson), field &
garden one, important to get this in—on to tihuanacu, the ruins
themselves at first glance not impressive, but just wait, buster—am
impressed again, as at Medina's, with the delicacy of the work, the
pieces are not as large, as grandiose as expected—it is this: the
intense refinement of a style, over a period of centuries, *clustered* at
one place—incredible, the delicacy of the work in this astounding
geography—thank god & pachamama for their only begotten son:
Sarjento Chura, indio casi puro, devoted student of Posnansky &
Medina, another little man, like the colonel, with a hot coal burn-
ing in him, he is a guide in more ways than he knows (love his term
for the bolivian archeologists: muchachos)—the straightness of
those goddamned lines, these were a people who knew something
and were organizing it—it is no virtue, size: what began at tihua-
nacu exploded at the river rouge, the temple kalassaya, be it 1/2 a
futbol field, gives the feeling of delicacy, especially conceived as an
instrument (calendarial) (but for that matter you could lose the
rouge plant in la puna—and let's do it)—later, a lovely time, drink-
ing beer and smoking my norteamericano cigars with Sarjento
Chura and the taxi guy (in his own way, a good joe, asks many
pathetic questions about the states) (he bought his chevrolet via
New Orleans, they told him it would do very well in La Paz, it was
used to the mountains of Louisiana)—the beautiful church of
tihuanacu, almost enough to drive a man to god, a huge thing, long,
with galvanized tin roof, wooden cross beams, adobe walls, and
sculpture and building blocks pilfered from las ruinas—inside, the
blue dome (that damn sky again!), the dull old spanish colonial

paintings, the gaudy remnants of the fiesta pasada—outside, again, in the sun, in the broad abandoned plaza (the village dead with poverty), chatting with the padre, the taxi driver, Sarjento Chura (truly we are a gentle troup), the padre pointing out to me the wild, early tiahuanaco sculptured heads, built, for no particular reason, into the high eaves of the church

near the entrance, the figures of the virgin and the piles of rock, catholic and indian, side by side

back to La Paz and Sr. A—— P——, manufacturer, young, rich, and aggressive, wants nothing more than to live in the states, where he has traveled extensively, t'hell with 'im

the great thing about tiahuanaco and its stone art, it is expuesto to the weather (like the coastal fisherman, to the water)—hence, unlike protected art, it survives

4:30 P.M.—sucre palace

well when you go out to tihuanaco—the origin of early man in america—what do you expect to find?—two california coeds, doin' the ruins—they talked a slick spanish and took pitchers and gave me a lot of tips about cuzco, how to avoid the tourist traps, etc.—so, the contemporary, together with the most ainshunt

it was quite a day—incredible, the survival of that delicately carved stonework, thru the centuries—location magnificent, sense of the original presence of the lake, the geologic changes, etc.—extra kick, though, was the man: Sarjento Chura, almost pure Indian, local guide, uneducated, poor as dirt, but knows the place in and out, has dug for Posnansky, Medina, Bennett, etc., calls the present Bolivian archeologists "children"—remarkable little man—why do I keep running into people who remind me of C—— but with that extra inner hot coal glowing—convinced it has something to do with tihuanacu itself

so much to say, so little time, etc,—are you packed yet?

leaving here day after tomorra, you'll be glad to know, boat trip on the lake and RR to Cuzco, if I think of it I might send a cable

half-hour interruption, went down to the lobby to meet Sr. P——, he's a nuisance, american-type business man, scared to death of R——, I think, I now have to have 2 lunches with him and a tour of the city

a moment to remember: chatting outside the church at Tiahuanaco (dig up Posnansky in the studio, there's a beautiful photo of it) with the unshaven almost poor-as-an-Indian padre, a lovely man, who came out to open the church for me, also Sarjento Chura, and the driver who brought me out (who now seems, after P——, a real good joe)—chatting, in the open spanish-style plaza, almost abandoned, under the goddamdest bluey blue sky

later, drinking beer with Chura, he pours a little on the ground first, for pachamama

ah, there is so much!

el indio puro

my first antinorteamericano demonstration: a waiter passes behind my back and says to his friend "yanqui!" and they both go giggling into the kitchen

favor de aguadar la llegada which means please keep all these god-dam letters, I'm putting some things in here which don't get into my notes and visee versee

don't forget your woolies, it gets chile at night

May 21, 11.30 A.M.

I'm moving kinda slow today, but I'm moving, it's a joke how it happened: that lousy american vice-consul told me to try the hotel copacabana for food, so I go try it, the food is good, and I order a little white wine to go with, turns out I've bought a whole goddam bottle, by now everyone's staring at me, the waiters giggling, hell, I ain't gonna give in, nothing to do but drink it and walk out like a gentleman which absolutely I do (with chilean wine, the best made anywhere, this is possible) a southern gentleman no less, I pay with a $20 bill U.S. which creates an international crisis and I've got more goddarn bolivianos in change, etc., etc.

at six this morning I thought I was dead, but I started blowing on my own little hot coal, and now I'm glowing

all of which proves: we pay the least for things that matter most to us—the most for trash

just found out that I haven't been putting a complete address on my letters to you, they may all be wandering around brazil, some joke, huh?

Jueves 21 de Mayo

Wonderful personal tour of Tiahuanaco Museum by painter guy—sense of evolution of style, through the periods, in ceramic arrangements—collection not as rich, though, as Medina's—best piece: carved quena, made from condor bone—Posnansky's room, fireplace, etc., fine old half-delapidated building—machine-gun chitchat with two painters on the place tihuanacu might occupy in a modern artist's development—feel sorry for them, afraid they don't have an angle on it, they are impelled by it—the straight guys (medina, chura) are cooking on a better (older) fire

p——s not bad, had midday dinner at their home, martinis, wine, beer, etc., p—— and wife and brother, little boy with Roy Rogers pistol little girl with hula hoop—sort of funny to see the split level ranch-type set grafted onto old Spanish colonialism (Luther Burbank should live so)

sinister cholo slums, bullet holes of last revolution (month ago), Indian markets, wideopen thieves' market, etc.—bargaining for goods

Bolivian landscape, outside city, like Arizona or Utah

Openair park—tihuanacu pieces—sort of dismal, it and I keeping the wrong company—imagine, for god's sake, the great monolito Wendell Bennett in situ, against that Tihuanacoid sky

Moisés Chire Barrientos *(Artist Pintor)* telefono 2239. Mueso Nacional tihuanacu—La Paz—Bolivia.—

just bought a couple of this guy's paintings, not too bad, he and I are cooking on the same gas, we've both got tiahuanaco in our guts—he has great respect for the work of the present bolivian archeologists

remarks about a pre-tihuanaco civilization, very undeveloped, recently excavated, underneath everything else

Sr. p——'s remark, about the ancient tree trunk, 4 ft. thick, recently excavated, further justification for the lush vegetation theory, antiguamente

send Will Wests to Medina, P——, Barrientos—also, It Is to Barrientos

now, why in hell are the present tihuanacu excavations being sponsored by some *japanese* group?

May 22—ayem

leaving today, just sent you a cable, did ya get it, huh? look forward to mail in kuzzgo

el boliviano

May 22

pleasant shopping tour in the Indian market this morning, stopped in at big dilapidated old San Francisco cathedral, date on it says 1549, guess I'll go see mother quinn about a conversion shoeshine in front of cathedral, beggars, Indians, organ music, jeeps, trucks, colectivos—Indians don't believe in autos, walk in middle of the street, must be constantly tooted out of the way, La Paz a city peppered with toots—from a radio in the remote corners of an Indian grotto, Elvis Presley—

lunch today with P—— then board the train for Guaqui night boat to Puno, train tomorrow for Cuzco—unless I jump ship somewhere, to stay with that goddam lake—

on board ferrocarril La Paz Guaqui: RR travel in bolivia is like minsky's: interminable intermissions while characters come on board and try to sell you trash

Sabado 23 de Mayo

Sitting in RR car just off the boat at Puno, gray, snow falling heavily, like that insane bolivian blue was centuries away—boy who carried my bags, barefoot, freezing to death, sits and stares at me, wonders what it is to sit and write notes

well, this is a strange world—drinks dinner more drinks last night with 2 serious bohemian french university students bumming around south america, plus young american slob, ICA, one of those government men down here teaching the bolivians how to be good yankees (muchos weeskee con soda on his expense account)—plus his associate, henrique, bolivian gentleman, real nice, keeping in spite of all hell his dignity (even when he insists we call him hank), all this on top of the world, Lake Titicaca—the only place in the world where you can be seasick and mountainsick at the same time—fine little steamer, we talk international politics, titahuanaco, etc., the world is a strange place

watching the loading of freight, in the titicaca dusk—some kind of mineral in bags—the indians chattering, flying in and out of the hold, their ponchos flapping like batwings—the ICA man commenting, over my shoulder, on their inefficiency under way, Peru gray and grimy after bolivia, the Indian poverty without relief, sinister, Pukara a filthy little hole (can't help thinking that the puna-bolivia-titicaca area did something to those around it (tihuanacu) that it still does, despite all hell—but all hell makes upland Peru grimy)

ferrocarril friends: Carmen (muy guapa, muy viva, we have fun) and her sisters (3 peruvian gals on a vacation), and good ole Frank and his gang (Clearwater, Fla.), he has good Spanish, roughed it in Peru 25 years ago as a mining engineer, has come back now with wife and friends to relive it all, they sit in perfect isolation, squirt insecticide from time to time, he calls the trip a "course in home apprecia- tion"—we have one end of the car while the La Paz (professional) futbol team—*The Strongest*—has the other

Carmen and her sisters buy me delicious little potato cakes, give me apples, etc.

nice scene with another lovely impoverished padre, on his way to some un-padred little town para hacer un matrimonio, again exchange of cakes and fruits, very festive

snow again at 14,000' pass, but cleared up—getting better now, vil- cañota valley, descending toward Cuzco, the farming makes the land interesting, the barley fields as though wave-washed all the way up the mountainsides, and the river itself, well, enough water will make anything clean, no?

arrival in cuzco in pitch dark, seems the municipal power system is overloaded, every time a thundercloud appears they pull the main switch— the station a madhouse, muchos muchachos trying to grab my bags, I tag after my three gals and we share a taxi—I pay bill, they put on wild scene, involving Cuzco police con flashlight, seems I was being overcharged 10¢, very funny

Hotel Cuzco elegant, spacious, clearly the peruvians are more efficient than the bolivians—the incredible vulgarity of the murals in the dining room—damn good steak

Domingo 24 de Mayo

Waked up by the bells of Cuzco, and they ain't pretty, more like the puerto rican beer can serenade in new york—after this, a brass band

Carmen Blossiers, Cortes 166 No. 204 (Department or Floor), Lima, Peru—Will West

Much of Cuzco is gentle, attractive, delightful—unlike brutal, unsettled La Paz—which, I guess, is why I prefer La Paz—amazing how the character of what the spaniards found, at each place, dictated what they created there—which persists today—as, Tiahuanaco→La Paz and Cuzco→Cuzco (in each case, through 3 periods: Indian, Colonial, & now)

Why I don't take photographs: those rocks must be aching from throwing themselves at all that goddam film

Out to Pisac, the market, ruinas, etc., this morning—Pisac sordid, dirty, the market a travesty, with that unenlightened grime I come to associate with Peru—the farm valleys, though, are magnificent, jesus, these incas, in handling agriculture & water (the two being the same) are magnificent

the baño del inca is lovely, you get a sort of shrine feeling in the stonework—ceremonial approach to water *first:* then, its distribution for irrigation, agriculture, use—note the hard rock over which water emerges, showing no erosion (perhaps hardening with the years, like the puerta del sol

Sacsahuaman: very norteamericano, like, how big a rock can we carve and move? a kind of brute sluggishness at the heart of this—

a thought: the "bigness" we put in our works is not so much the size of the land around us—this serves mainly to confirm—as it is the distance from roots, from sources—the dimension of john henry, paul bunyan, the rouge plant, etc., is not that of the space and resource they conquered, but of the atlantic ocean: the distance the mythmakers traveled, to reach

. . . again and again, at tihuanaco, in the andean vastness, I was impressed that these sculptures are not gross but concentrated, complex, delicate—resourceful . . . look, however, at the massiveness of sacsahuaman and easter island

Just back from the futbol, que partido! *The Strongest* (La Paz) 2, "Lucre" (Cuzco) 0, and I'm glad—a beautiful game at this level of skill, the speed, flow, delicacy of manipulation, teamwork make it almost like ice hockey—note the reverse kick, both feet up, and you land on your can—

south america is the last outpost of insanity, it's our only chance

May 24

my latest international bum is a Danish architect out of Toronto, bumming central & south america, we're going to Machu Picchu together Tuesday, he thinks me funny for traveling like a gentleman, staying in hotels, etc., apparently south america is full of jack kerouacs, their only pride is their poverty, their ability to get things for 1/20th what it costs the tourists (me), but it's all so aimless, a desperate sort of exhaustion underlying it

5:30 P.M.—just back from the stadium (where else?) where I watched the futbol (what else?) very exciting, a good tonic for ruins

Lunes 25 de Mayo

Archeological museum closed for repairs, goddamit, even Clearwater Florida with his bribes and letters of introduction can't get us in—

Mercado Central: greens & bloodmeat & hot smells, all wrapped in dirt, I must be a goddam gennulman, I don't love this dirt for its own sake

Hectic pace of life in these S.A. cities, it ain't much pretty

South Americans are animals, live, think, eat, compete like animals—death is implicit in one misstep, security no existe—culture the product of leisure?—but there is no leisure, so the indian gets dirtier and the spain-blooded struggles to stay afloat, maybe rise enough to get to the states—the cholo sits in the middle and churns (revolts)

there is only one straight line in all south america, one gesture of clarity and distinction: tihuanacu

bolivian beer is good, peruvian beer tastes like rhinegold—but Inca cigarillos are all right

completely norteamericano evening with bunch of young slobs from miami and san diego, feel like now I've got my second (Indian) wind, god dam, let's get out of cuzzgo—

(the horrible bizzness of the shunting aside of the wellmeaning peruvian gentlemen, the one who worked to get the coca for the detroit bitch, and the other who went out of his way to get the information on the larco herrera museum for me, their hearth, hotel, etc., pre-empted) (at least more theirs than ours)

it's a question of energy: at anywhere near the exhaustion level, south america is impossible—there must be enthusiasm—south america being the chaos of ourselves, this is important

May 25

3 of us together in hotel at Machu Picchu, Pete the Dane, Don the New Yorker (met him on train out this morning), and me—I must say it's pretty god damn impressive, nothing I've seen in pictures has given me a sense of it, the purity of color (this is where those photographers, damn 'em, tell lies, LIES!) and those goddam stalagmite mountains all around—they have done a remarkable job of leaving it pure and clean

Martes 26 de Mayo

PETER STUDSGATH, SØBORGHUSPARK 9, SOBORG, DENMARK—compañero de machu picchu

Lima: El Patio Restaurant (near Plaza de Armas)
Norte Pacifico Bus (near Bolivar Hotel)
Granada restaurant
Chiappi—avenida pierola (cheap, italian, good)
El Vencedor—125 Jiron Cuzco
(above information provided, in advance, by Don Leinbach)

Miercoles 27 de Mayo

Machu Picchu—from huayna picchu, the peak, how much impressive—the tall peaks all around, the guard points up & down river, the needle sharp mountains—the vastness of the thing, spreading over its crown, its saddle, at the crucial point—climbing huayna picchu—Don, Pete, & I—straddling the ridge, 2000' straight down on either side—at the right moment, after sunset, the condor flight—the beautiful greenness of these mountains, almost tropical, but rising to snow peaks—the rockwork: the city emerging from the living rock, many great boulders, uncarved or partially carved—one carved up to the top, where it is left in the shape of mountains—machu picchu spring water now used in the hotel, the best I've had in South America—beautiful train ride with Don Leinbach, Machu Picchu to Cuzco, on the platform all the way (against rules but brakeman didn't bother us)—view of Ollantay-tambo, terraces, etc., massive—delicious tangerines, bananas, oranges (lunch for 2, 6¢)

machu picchu sunrise: the first pink touch on the snow caps—you wouldn't believe it, pal

the high points thus far: tihuanacu & the puna, and machu picchu & the mountains—(also, medina)

back in Cuzco: playing bumper pool with Arturo and Rojer, peruvian caballeros—they let me win—nothing will take the place of manners, suh

Machu Picchu: wild strawberries, and many flowers—the hotel manager's kids playing futbol in the open court

May 27

Just back in Cuzco—more later

May 27

yes, machu picchu, machu picchu, god dam, you have to see it to believe it—

beautiful ride back to cuzco on the filthy indian train, on the platform all the way—sunshine, magnificent scenery

these travel friendships you make are delightful, and fortunately they come to an end, on to the next

Jueves 28 de Mayo

the indians liked to pick a spectacular spot and then get just behind it—para ocultar—this true, certainly, of machu picchu, probably chavín & san agustín

yesterday, the filthy indian train from Machu Picchu—today, Aviacion Fawcett, DC-4 to Lima—life here, like the mountains, is tilted, faulted, and stratified—I slice it like fruit cake—nowhere as in S.A. is individual character impressed against its background, framed, clarified—personality emerges with a sharpness as terrifying as the geography

On plane, Cuzco to Lima: lady across the way, clutching her oxygen tube and her beads, together—getting it both ways

Passing 21,000' mountains, close by—oh, it's vurry drum attic—

May 28

just arrived hotel maury, very nice, cheaper than advertised—flight down quick, easy, right past 21,000' snow peaks—going Machu Picchu-to-Cuzco-to-Lima is strange, the reverse of Miami-to-

Tiahuanaco, like I was shot out of a cannon (Zacchini) into the present, Lima big, modern, commercial, it's just impossible to imagine the contrasts in this continent, nothing comparable—all South America shut down today for Corpus Christi, I may not be able to mail this until tomorrow

May 28—II P.M.

well, this time it's a funny little student from San Marcos University, picked me up on the street when I was looking for the airline office, learning english (they all are), loves norteamericanos (they all do), took me to the movies (Frank Sinatra, Dean Martin, what else?), drinks, dinner, drinks, I had to fight to pay the dinner check, etc., is gonna take me to the museum, pachacamac, everything, all weekend, I feel somehow I'm taking advantage, to him I'm the biggest thing that's hit since Nixon

Lima is Lima. if they spoke a little more english, it would be Miami.

have just found out I go monday by camioneta (pickup truck, oh boy) to Huarás, will cable

what's the popular soft drink here? of course: Inka Kola

your letters, plus anniversary card, all waiting for me here, muy buenas, maybe, who knows, someday you'll get some of mine—

picked up 2 chiggers in machu picchu, no place like home

May 29

Roger—my buddy—laid up this morning with "dolor de cabeza" (hangover), so I do errands, get information, etc.—on way back to hotel, get involved in street demonstration, revolutionary sympathizers, shopkeepers hustling to slam doors, pull iron bars over windows, demonstrators in tight formation, cavalry charges, throws tear gas, they—and I—disperse, muy rapido, just a quiet latin american morning—

II P.M.

out to Pachacamac, 20 miles south, hill & ruins on the coast, magnificent location, whole pacific ocean at your feet—the weather never clears in Lima in the winter, but today it was sunny and bright, nobody understood but me—

Roger expert & generous guide, but he begins to be a nuisance, he gets tanked every night & maudlin, I must be the whole magnificent U.S.A. to him—he of course had never seen Pachacamac, didn't know it was there, tried hard to understand why I cared—tragic spanish eyes, brooding, in a kid so happy he can say "ruck 'n' rull"— a spanish gentleman, about to be fractured

well, on soon elsewhere

happy anniversary!

Viernes 29 de Mayo

as far as Limeñans are concerned, the Rio Rimac runs the wrong way, from the mountains they take nothing, turn their backsides to them, and their faces to the movie screen

but in Lima, you can smoke an Inca, light it with a Llama, while you drink an Inca Kola—

nice feeling in hotel maury—even though remodeled—of being one of many extranjeros viajando en el perú—they have the fine old espejos de luna, comedor and lobby—

street demonstration, revolutionary sympathizers, cavalry, tear gas, etc. —what the hell am I doing here, anyway?

institute of contemporary art, exhibition of one Ricardo Grau, slick coastal modernism, a faint touch of the indian in his colors, but it all looks like fingernail polish

best south american meal yet, Granada Restaurant, Don Leinbach's recommendation, sopa criolla, liza con ensalada, cerveza alemán—

Lima is a cleaner city, fewer beggars, but one feels the grind, the animal scarce veneered—

Pachacamac: again, as always, it is location: indentation in the coast, with the desert correspondingly in the mountains, imposing hill, guano island offshore, magnificent command, almost "possession" of that dark goddam ocean extension, spread of the city, much of Frank Lloyd Wright in the terraces, walls, etc.—as with Machu Picchu, it is the distant view that makes it

here, even in bright sunshine, the colors are pastel: mountains, desert, ocean, sky

birds: gallinazo, ugly buzzard-type, and lechuza, nocturnal, que træ mal suerte

words, described in the shrubbery: "soy puta." Roger carefully destroys, saying "I'm doing this for the peruvians, not the norteamericanos, everyone knows the norteamericanos can't read spanish."

Roger, orphan boy, adds his scribbling to the others on the adobe bricks: "Mi abuelo vivió aquí." He didn't, really.

Road south out of Lima is *exactly* like Detroit-to-Dearborn: an unsettled people squatting on a desert

a thought: early man was a hunter, living in nomadic hordes, following game—the great event of culture, of civilization, was a process of *rooting,* of acquiring *place:* a fishing group (Humboldt Current?), stationary on land by virtue of the fishrich ocean, spreading, experimenting into agriculture (*rooting*)—this led to astronomy, study of the seasons, in the modern sense, *knowledge*—hence, an aristocracy (knowledgeable group) and *centers of knowledge:* Tihuanacu, Chavín, San Agustín, Pachacamac—*to know, one must root*—now, thanks to the Incas (Roman) (spread of knowledge) (welfare state) (colonizing, uprooting local cultures)—and Ford— we are once more nomadic—

Pachacamac: it is that magnificent sense of the *right* location: this is not a gesture, but a matter thought with precision

me, a yankee, eating a chinese dinner in lima, peru, while the band plays the blue danube—what I mean, native culture

all south americans can say "sawnawvabeech" and "boolsheet," and some of them can say "cawksookare"

May 30—9 P.M.

well, Roger had to turn out to be what he is, which god made him, and I ain't—which all, I suppose, goes with Lima—again, the spanish gentleman came to his aid, there was a scene, but a clean scene—by the way, did you ever turn down a fairy in spanish?

incidentally, you don't have to worry about the gold standard, I seem to have no economy at all—who knows, this is the end of everything, maybe?

tomorrow at 3/30 A.M. they call me (this is the strangest goddam continent) and at 4 I go by "colectivo" (taxi that you share with 4 other people and costs practically nothing) all the way to Huaras—later in the week, Chimbote, Trujillo, etc.—looks like I'll make the goddam trip in about 4 weeks, frightening, isn't it?

Sabado 30 de Mayo

To the museum today, magnificent collection, fine spanish patio type building (but I miss that tumble down old building in La Paz)—best stuff the chavín, as in tiahuanaco, strength & delicacy, combined: feline conflations—snakes with fangs, felines condorclawed—

phalloliths, elliptic, glyphed

estela raimondi a great piece: the indian continuous, the generations joined, mouth to crown, mask to mask, in the headdress—the phallic tongue a river, passing name and race

superb textiles, paracas, over & over repetition of blue-brown motifs, sense of red purified out of red-brown earth—collections of other colors more common in US, they are not typical, representing rather the collector's taste

monolitos from Casma, suggesting both tiahuanaco & chavin—

Roger M——   —   Will West   —   and so much for that

Domingo 31 de Mayo

Wild colectivo ride, Lima to Huarás, ugly cholo driver, violent indianspanish peruvian scenery, interminable goddam moonscape, desert, rocks, straw & adobe huts, dry as dust, nothing, nothing, nothing—delicious 28¢ beefsteak breakfast—filthy, almost haunted little town where we stopped for the control, radio blaring ruck 'n' rull—climbing then, gradual return of green, as we get to where the rains can reach

and now the Hotel Monterrey, a day of rest, swiss & precious in this weird continent: clean room, good food, swimming pool, mineral baths, genteel american missionaries to talk to, etc., all unreal

every place I visit produces an indigenous personality type by way of companion, even those who travel seem to present themselves to me in the place that naturally, incisively frames them—it is this, the place-sense, the background at all times pushing, projecting, that gives to human personality here an at times well nigh insane clarity, precision

Monday, June 1

this little hotel is incredible—am sitting now on the terrace overlooking a border of flowers, swimming pool, weeping willow, eucalyptus, mountains, etc., air fresh & clear, sun warm, cute little peruvian chick sitting next to me—later today, a trip to Huaras for the museum, and maybe a swim—tomorrow, Chavín, in the hotel station wagon (chick's poppa in offing, don't worry)

tea yesterday with 4 american missionaries, they know somebody named Innes who has a chicken farm on Starne's Cove Road,

Asheville, NC—one of them lost a brother to the headhunters a while back, I'm in favor of this sort of thing

another author-type here, swiss, he sits out on the terrace with his typewriter—competition

just back from a walk down the road—fun saying "buenas tardes" to all the indians, watching the reaction—they had to go empty and clean the swimming pool today, so no swim—instead, I went down and sat by the river—

Lunes 1 de Junio

Huarás beautiful, the loveliest I've seen in South America—everything that Cuzco claims to be and isn't—as Cuzco fronts for Machu Picchu, so Huarás for Chavín—a connection here?

the autos here in the little streets (calles estrechísimas) are quaint, not ruthless—there is a survival of spanish leisureliness

beautiful faces, the most beautiful women in south america, these people haven't been slashed by the harshness—even a puta, glorious

not antinorteamericano, the first time I haven't felt a hardness—curious, polite

poverty here, but gentle, no starvation, the land too rich—in La Paz & Cuzco, one feels the grindstone daily casts out hulls—

lovely waiter, Hotel Monterrey, heard me last night talking, in english, about tiahuanaco & chavín, wants to make sure I get to the museo here in Huarás—I reached *him,* if not the missionaries

just realized, Roger M——'s whine for "service" was the same whine used by the beggars—

indian funeral, everyone talking, laughing, the casket a light burden—must have been a cholo, they're glad he's dead

the south american fruitcake: the indian at the bottom, doing the work, turning out the food, etc.; then the cholo—he drives taxis and buses, waits on table, tends store, anything uncreative and, if possible, destructive; next, the spanish colonial, who used to be boss but who has now been superseded by the yankee, descending from the north via panagra, radioactive fallout, the real topdog

sign on the front of a camión: si dios quiere, volveré

another: amarte es mi delirio

Martes 2 de Junio

damn, this waiter's making a big thing about my getting to the museum, "ojalá" he says "ojalá"—it's like his ancestry is at stake, everything depends on my getting the right impression—hope I don't disappoint him—

just back from museo, will say what I can, which is mostly the magnificent vistas, the primitive monolitos in rows in the patio, against the flowers, the spanish wall, and in the background the magnificent cordillera blanca, huascarán, etc.—after a while, the little monolitos seem to be people, so many intelligent monkeys, watching

ride to chavín worth the price, even if there were nothing there to see—climbing to snowline, tunnel through the cordillera blanca, descending other side, interminable switchbacks, descent to one of those marvelous, warm, rich valleys east of the andes, giving toward the selva

chavín at first sight a shambles, thanks to the ministerio de whatever it is, but swinging around to the river, the ball court or whatever, you get an idea, magnificent block of condors, 7 running toward the jefe, almost in the style of tihuanacu, but distinto—this business of influence very touchy, the similarity intense but at the same time the individuality intense: if they did take from the boys to the south—as it appears—they sure god made it their own

you find the guy with the key and start crawling around the under-
ground vaults, fine pieces, original of monolito tello, smaller tiahua-
nacoid pieces—crawl on your belly through a 2 x 2 hole and come to
a room with camarones carved on the ceiling, and there it is:
camerones are found only in the rivermouths on the pacific coast:
this valley gives east, to the selva, but chavín gave west, to the
coast—*over* those two goddam mountain ranges—them dam
shrimp, hiding on the ceiling, this is the height of the occult, the
mysterious

manager of Hotel Monterrey drove me over, I got to know him
pretty well, almost spoiled the whole hotel for me—we killed a dog
and a chicken on the way, would have killed indians if they hadn't
jumped fast ("indians aren't people, they're animals" he sez)—I can
take this stuff from cholos, they have blood reasons, but not from a
goddam swiss—of course he hates it here, can't wait to get out to
europe or the states

Miercoles 3 de Junio

The western hemisphere is a man: patagonia—pie grande—the
foot: tihuanacu—between the legs, the two cordilleras—the gener-
ative: más al norte—brazil, etc.—the cuerpo: and U.S.A., the head,
the sense of it all . . . it is with this geographic man that, as hombre
americano, I am possessed

       a man dropped,
       airwelled
       to the patagoni

       (bigfoot at the bottom)

       to rise through gran chaco
       amazonas
       coclé

       to spread:
           toltec, texan
                pueblo north american

scary roads, hard driving, magnificent scenery, Huarás to Chimbote—crossing the cordillera negra, at the very top, an indian boy pissing, no hiding, a celebration, for us—boy, piss, bus, all the world, the top of the world—

the feeling, the touch of the condor stone, chavín—

> when you incise the rock
> cut it sharp
> cut it deep
>> then turn loose
>> the alluvium

sanitary rule, south america: always wash your hands before picking your nose

nice young chino-peruano on the colectivo, he carries huge picture of Clark Gable, we talk across the sleeping drunks, he assures me that my spanish pronunciation is lousy, I'm assured

there is much fine modern stonework on peruvian roads, adaptation of ancient methods, use of living rock, etc.—one beautiful example, fullness and refinement, on road Huarás to Casma

Hotel Trujillo

8 :30 P.M.—June 3

just arrived, your 5 letters and cable waiting for me, feel like I'm on my way home

tell anne I've met some wonderful priests here, if she wants to marry one it's okay with me, and tell adrienne I've been drinking beer here with honey's father

today, another day of scary roads, hard driving, magnificent scenery colectivo ride, chimbote to trujillo, with drunk indian asleep on my shoulder—very restful

about colombian bandits, will go to bogotá, inquire at u.s. consulate, also lalley's friends, be guided accordingly—everything else has been so great, would shoot myself if I missed san agustín—don't worry, this cookie can take care of himself

Jueves 4 de Junio

Trujillo—a slimy charleston-type coastal city—eye doughnut lock day cussed a pea rue—

big excitement of the day: cops on bicycle chasing a thief—they cotch

herrera musem, like everything else in peru, gone to lima—local museum I cannot find, don't care enough to ask, the hell with it, I drink beer instead

chino-peruano friend again, claims to be peruvian FBI-man, trailing smugglers, etc., who knows, maybe so

funny shoulder-rubbing in government hotels, norteamericanos, they come to work, they come to play—slacks, sport shirts, zipper jackets, etc.—and local peruvian uppercrust, rotary club or whatnot, dressed to the hilt, shirts crackling with starch—the yankee sprawls, the peruvian gentleman, unable to be himself in his own hotel, retreats finally into icy reserve

lima-trujillo-charleston-oak bluffs: all ports of llegada and salida are sink traps, serve to deceive as to the nature of what they serve

only us northers can afford to be candid—formalities are the solace—and revenge—of the underprivileged

I keep going back to the first experience: plummeting out of the modern sky into medina's sanctum of pre-geologic origins: the day that had everything, from dawn over the andes, garua in Lima, that goddam lake, to liqueurs with precious, hot, little coronel federico diez de medina—everything I've done since has in a way been a confirmation of that first day

chan-chan a ghost city, the filthy gallinazos perching & crapping (white craps on the land waves) on the crumbling walls (climbing on which I contribute to the delapidation)—as at chavín, but worse, a sense of delapidated disregard

the taxidriver's two phrases in english: all reet, and les go—serve for all purposes

a weirdness, a ghostliness to this whole coast, the rain that over-hangs and never materializes

chan-chan: the original vastness, houses and open courts, can only imagine what a garden steady water would make this—the city spreading almost to the seaside, the faintly damp seabreeze, roar of the surf

the little fragments that bring it back, the signo escalanodo, the bird figure, what it must have been: the imposition of a unified idea of order on a ruthless geography

Trujillo—June 5
THE GIRL WHO TALKED WITH GOD

sitting in the plaza last evening, listening to the band concert, watching the teenagers walking around, one of whom, a she, gets up nerve to come up and ask me, you're not from here, are you? and I say, no, and she says, from where? and I say, the united states, and she says, a-h-h-h-h-h, flutters, well nigh faints, can say no more

Chiclayo—3 P.M.

the goddam tourist hotel that shows on the esso map isn't built yet, so I'm staying at a funny little place called hotel europa, real good food—discovered a delicious dark beer called maltina, they say it's very nootrishus chiclayo I like—maybe it's just that the sun shines, but there's a nice shaded plaza, the breezes blow, and the town doesn't have that filthy old-spanish pretentiousness of lima and trujillo

two letters from you before I left trujillo—including dad's—how's the alfalfa, with all that-there rain?

just found out I have to take a bus at 5 ayem tomorrow, oh, boy

no, I ain't goin' down the amazon, it would be an expensive bit of sightseeing—for no particular purpose—have been convinced by many that my iquitos-leticia connection is too risky in this uncertain world—so, another few days & dollars saved

there's an esso distributor in trujillo named F. A. Harman, yup, that's the way he spells it

Viernes 5 de Junio

hora peruana: the time things actually happen, not when they say they will

funny sounds in SA: church bells, revolution or plumbing?

chiclayo: usual crop of highbreasted beauties, swinging their hips through the erected male glances in full flight

in a restaurant: an ancient asthmatic, scarfed, hobbling-each breath followed by a period and a long pause: like a fish flopping, dying, in the bottom of the boat—comes in, and orders, for survival, a coca cola

oh how these characters love noise, just noise: church bells, unmufflered motors, radios, P.A. systems, dice cups (beat 'em on the table for luck) and most of all, oh, most of all, the goddam human tongue

glimpse into a doctor's office: picture on the wall showing the various vital organs—very convincing glance at a printshop: bearded christ-like character working at a press in a 2 x 4 cuartito, pictures of christ on the wall—chiclayo jargon?

damn I like this chiclayo, mebbe I was just in the mood for it, but this is a hot little town

Sabado 6 de Junio

negro-peruano, heaving me an insult at 5 ayem: italiano!—then he turned around and clipped me for 10 soles, fake excess baggage charge

bus day, Chiclayo-Piura-Talara—excellent breakfast at La Choza, openair bamboo-style roadside restaurant, genuine tropical feeling

the game's getting bigger: today we killed a cow—look on the driver's face, sad & gritty, as he drove on

spot on this page is sacred: beer spilled at the Bar of the Royal Hotel, Talara, Peru, a seaside tropical joint to be remembered—rambling old hotel—two frame structures joined together—at the edge of the harbor, view of tugboats and little lateen-sail rigs, makes me feel woppish, like, say, Ezra's first trip over

Talara a "modern" town, full of US-type houses for the petroleo workers—who somehow manage to live in them like peruanos—the Royal Hotel on the edge of all this, a real antediluvian (anteamerican) (but not antiamerican) JERNT—architects could labor for years and not get with the style of these two ramshackle shacks, rammed together—the right way to leave peru, almost redeems this whole dull coast—

few words with peruvian west-pointer, seems like, god bless 'im, he was born in texas—

mad scene in Royal Hotel Bar—peruvian army officer, talking much of US-Peruvian friendship, admires my expensive (cuzco) dark glasses, gracefully pockets same—I say nothing, but later complain to first lieutenant, peruvian police, who asks tactfully (drunkenly) for them, is denied drunkenly (tactfully) (glasses bulging in pocket) that they exist—result: another bit of U.S. foreign aid, much beer, no glasses, no love lost —hail & farewell, peru!

police lieutenant admits to me that he doesn't like Talara, it isn't Peru, too many norteamericanos—more and more it becomes apparent that we (U.S.) lie, horizontally, with no vertical penetration, on top of peru—an added complication to the catholic-on top-of-indian structure

Talara

bus ride today, chiclayo to talara, you see this coast once and you've seen it all

bus buddies: a slick little red-headed peruvian floozie and a sharp little italiano, lives now in venezuela, traveling salesman type— their's obviously an arrangement, but I didn't seem to interfere with their plans, so we lunched together—they spoke clear spanish for me, mumbly spanish among themselves

in haste, must get to panagra and P.O.

mañana, bogotá

¡caramba!

Domingo 7 de Junio

Walk down to the pacific this morning, first time—water mild— join romantic-maritime-looking boys to watch docking of "esso norfolk," tanker—scene eugene o'neilish

Flying again, panagra, avianca, etc.—rubbing shoulders, lunching, drinking, etc., with assorted fools, tourists, and business men, from guess where? the US—best part of flight: departure from talara, view of town, ocean, hotel, etc.

arrival bogotá after dark, looks bigger, sharper than lima—hotel granada full of futbol players, no room, so I pick up my mail and follow hack to funny little pension-type hotel crillon—¿quien sabe, muy bueno, no? anyway, a solid dinner—tomorrow, to find out about buses & bandits, etc.

Lunes 8 de Junio

Bogotá less spanish, snappier than Lima, more New York than Miami, the layers deeper buried—you feel the proximity of the Great White Father, to the north—the occasional beat Indian on the street more a stranger—first city I am not stared at—

really, the only place the U.S. is attractive is in the U.S., abroad we are something awful to behold—

well, the word is that the bandits ain't banditting south of neiva, so mañana put on my old duds hide my watch my wealth and head for san agustín

US embassy bogotá most US-looking goddam place you ever did saw—all plush and chrome, clean as no blowed whistle ever was—but they done treated me right, ah kent complane

Monday A.M.—Bogotá

good talk with consul, he say little or no risk, so I go—RR or air thru danger zone, no difficulty from Neiva south—maybe you get cable from me?

it looks now like I home about a week from today, no?

Martes 9 de Junio

Avianca Bogotá to Neiva, bus Neiva to Pitalito, no further than this I can go today, wait until noon tomorrow and San Agustín only 21 miles away

Colombia much different from Peru and Bolivia, settled, green, etc., the geography less drastic—paved roads, barbed wire (in Peru, an eight-year-old girl fences cattle)—travel generally more settled, less scary, despite tales of bandeleros

country read, corn & banana patches, hogs, burros, brahma bulls, lovely tile- or thatch-roofed adobe houses, split-bamboo fences— all of a sudden-like, a farmhouse made of aluminum

Pitalito: the inevitable beercan church bells

but the central plaza is lovely, well-tended, and the church itself a nice building

no electricity tonight, so the girls bring candles—bet they had 'em saved for church

Tuesday P.M.—Hotel Monaco
Pitalito, Colombia

Well I aims one way or another to be back in Bogotá by Saturday afternoon, on time to get Avianca's $75 excursion flight to Miami, spend the night there, and fly into Asheville Sunday, no? maybe you got my cable this morning

funny scene in this hotel when I landed, they had one room where the bed wasn't made up, other where the water wouldn't work— great crisis until I solved: move bedding into room where water works—so here I am

Miercoles 10 de Junio

The lovely Hotel Monaco, they knock on my door at 7:15 A.M., bring me orange juice and coffee (room & board & all this, $1.80 a day)

beautiful breakfast, caldo, eggs in individual little pan, bread, plus a big cup of hot chocolate

guy tells me, don't try to hotel in san agustín, rough, so I go out in the rain with muchacho, find taxi, we make deal, sesenta pesos, for this afternoon, bueno, do it all and return pitalito

nice in the morning, lean on the railing on the hotel balcony, watch
the town come alive

vegetable market, rainy, muddy, everything fresh & green, bueno

in colombia they know the U.S. must be listening, they've mufflered
their motors

magnificent midday dinner—reminded of filthyrich US-er warning
me, cali airport, "don't go anywhere in colombia you can't fly"—
flying, amigo, is for the birds

en route san agustín: rich rainrich land, like w.n.c. but without the
harsh winter—hard to imagine poverty here, must take extremes of
collective mismanagement to achieve it

great idea, pursuing a river to its source—nacimiento—as did them
indios the magdalena—the land gets exciting, the cut of the river,
the knees of land pushing into it, the waterfalls, and above this, a
sweeping arable upland: the place to build

San Agustín: primitivo: the force, at its best

the rock, emerged, conceived first as phallus, and from the head of
phallus, emerging, sculpturewise, the head of man

man himself, todo, as phallus—symbol, staff of authority, headdress,
the head itself a dress to the body, as to the phallus

the great work is the work of great heads

emphasis on the mouth, things emerging, extension of tongue—
raimondi stela, chavín, and posnansky, flight of the voice—

tongue, speech, phallus, as continuity of the race

the tongue, the race, the phallus, the flute—speech, seed, music

semi-tropics, wild-colored birds, a thing flashing red and yellow, etc.

lavapatas (like the baño del inca) the rocks carved, serpents, etc., serpentine canals, the water directed so that it flows over the carved figure, the god, perpetually washed, cleaned

as in the little outdoor museum in huarás, the feeling that the figures, the clusters of figures, are alive, watching: this the power they gain from being outdoors, as was, as is

the absolute isolation, absolute concentration of these central sites, sitios, all of 'em—essential, this sense of *place* for anything above random rambling—pound's "rose in the steel dust," a focus, a locus

magnificent arrangement of park, wonderful sense you get—from things being left where discovered, almost scarce excavated—of being in on it all, like, this is how it was, the dirt, the land, the place, the thing

> is
> of itself,
> and grows,
> in place . . . (in situ

San Ag a demonstration of how it can be done

nice scene with park director, Sr. Guerrero, when I brought out magazine article with pictures of himself and family—called all the family (beautiful wife) they gathered around, he ordered muchacho to serve me as guide, show me everything—like I said before, nice places attract nice people: the warm-eyed muchacho, who had to talk to me about his father: mi papá está en Venezuela, he sez—they all are, son

Hotel Monaco: at first I thought this place was run by a bunch of teenage girls, but I finally met the manager, speaks good english, seems he went to high school in a place called detroit, michigan after the breakthrough on the english gambit, I now have many friends in the joint—after supper, I give english lessons to all the kids—

Jueves 11 de Junio

lluvia lluvia lluvia pare regresar—hoy, pitalito a neiva, por bus—

later, it clears up, the sun comes out, the mountains get kinda pretty

big deal this morning with Sr. Edmundo Aljach Zajar, manager of the Hotel Monaco—he speaks english, spanish, french, and arabic, has lived colombia, us, & beirut, I'm to bail him outa pitalito, get him a job in the u.s., oy vay—but a nice little guy, I'll try, I'll try

now the hotel tayrona, neiva, poco más moderno, no?

big fat china-colombiana, camarera, the way she floats into the room—her eyes out of chichen itza

Viernes 12 de Junio

oy, what a night—the beauties of open spanish hotel architecture, todo expuesto a todo, what the radioactive hispanoamericano does to this

hoy, neiva a bogotá, por avion

at the airport, neiva: business men are the same everywhere

bogotá: horrible semi-destroyed reproductions of san agustín figures, sinking in the mud between the billboards, highway from the airport to town

tickets, money, cambio, etc., u.s. embassy again to convince the fools that colombia is safe (earn their salaries for them), then a couple lousy french movies, to kill time

Sra. M—— , and her two boys who went to asheville school, well if this ain't home, it's just about

I like the hotel granada, it once was and it ain't and it's trying to still be, I like the lady because she makes no concessions to my ignorance of spanish, tough

wild night, last of the trip, with compañia colombiana petroleo, or somesuch, pretty decent guy, native—like everybody else, in a peck of trouble —really the best of the "contemporaries" I've met, appropriate for last night—solid perception, without rancor, of the idiocy of U.S. position in south america

Sabado 13 de Junio

in bed 5 A.M. muchos weeskee con agua, up at 9 fresh as the proverbial, ham 'n' egg breakfast, ready to roll

cambios, cambios, cambios, cheques de viajeros, pesos, dólares, etc.—god bless exprinter cook wagons-lits first national city bank of new york, etc.

national museum bogotá a waste of time, nice building inferior collection, really the only thing in colombia is san agustín

tonight, my lovely, I bed me down in miami

mad business of the lost bag in the taxi, desperate trip in 1948 Ford (35 m.p.h. top speed) 12 miles back to bogotá, chasing, no luck, back to aeropuerto (35 m.p.h.) rush thru despecho, aduana, etc., bag given up for lost—at last minute, two taxi guys rush in, bag in arms, first guy had gone back to bogotá, found it in back seat, come back out to find me: saludos, abrazos, handshakes, dólares, pesos, etc., avianca anuncia la salida de vuelo seis seis seis a vecinos de miami, abordo, abordo

slick chick on plane, bogotá to baranquilla—baranquilla no hay, sez I, vamos a miami baranquilla to miami, homely indiana type, abe lincoln without a beard

spraying the plane with insecticide just before arrival, u.s. public health service regulation, get us all good & sterile

miami, customs, taxi, motel, etc.—rum & coke with eastern air lines student pilot, he lends oido simpatico to my much unloading

I keep thinking of the lovely guy in bogotá, petroleo, looking in his wallet after another big bar bill, *cada vez menos,* he says, the tenderness, the delicacy, the galloping sadness of the man, like the indian woman, a heap of rags and filth, squatting in the patio, cuzco correos, digging with a pin at the cut, the open running sore on the sole of her foot

> bulking in her stealth
> aloof in public
> huddling, huddling
> flocked in
> hush

> flesh a filth
> mountain skirts and bowlerhat
> downthrust
> black black eyes

like the lavapatas at san agustín and the baño del inca in cuzco, the water running out, pouring over the delicate surfaces, deep cut—

Domingo 14 de Junio

lousy coffee, miami restaurant, I know I'm in the states

eastern airlines, miami to atlanta, standby for flight to asheville, abordo at the last minute—

a volver

POSTLUDE

between the writing and publication of this book, two characteristically south american events have occurred:

el strongest—the futbol team—has been wiped out in a plane crash

and the superbly beautiful town of huarás has been devastated by an earthquake

> in memorium: huarás
> &
> *el strongest*

BIBLIOGRAPHY

Many chapters in *Patagoni* are obvious conflations of other men's work—I am grateful to the many who went before me, who reported what they saw and did. This list is by no means complete, nor is it a recommended bibliography—but for one reason or another (often the disciplines of my own book) their material didn't appear in the finished work, and have not been listed.

SOUTH AMERICA

Acosta, Father José de. *Natural and Moral History of the Indians.* London, 1879.

Acuña, Father Christoval de. *A New Discovery of the Great River of the Amazons.* Trans. C. R. Markham, London.

Agassiz, Professor, and Mrs. Louis. *A Journey in Brazil.* Boston, Mass., 1868.

Alexander, Hartley Burr. *The Mythology of All Races: Latin American.* Boston, 1920.

Arber, Edward, ed. *The first three English books on America.* Birmingham, Al., 1885.

Arguedas, José María, and Ruth Stephan. *The Singing Mountaineers.* Austin, Tex., 1957.

Ashmead, P. H. *The Madeira-Mamore Railway.* Washington, D.C., 1911.

Bandelier, A. F. "The Aboriginal Ruins at Sillustani, Peru," *American Anthropologist*, vol. 7, No. 1, 1905.

_____. *The Islands of Titicaca and Koati.* New York, N.Y., 1910.

Barcroft, Binger, Bock, Doggart, Forbes, Harrop, Meakins and Redfield. "Observations upon the effect of high altitude . . ." *Philosophical Transactions of the Royal Society of London*, Series B, vol. 211, London, 1922.

Bates, Henry Walter. *The naturalist on the River Amazons.* London, 1863.

Beals, Carleton. *Fire on the Andes.* Philadelphia & London, 1934.

Bingham, Hiram. *Across South America.* Boston, Mass., 1911.

_____. "Further Explorations in the Land of the Incas," *National Geographic Magazine*, Washington, D.C., 1916.

_____. *Inca Land.* Boston, Mass., 1922.

_____. *Machu Picchu, a Citadel of the Incas.* New Haven, Conn., 1930.

_____. *Lost City of the Incas.* New York, N.Y., 1948.

Bird, J., and Bellinger, L. *Paracas Fabrics and Nazca Needlework.* Washington, D.C., 1954.

Bollaert, W. *Antiquarian, Ethnological and Other Researches in New Granada, Ecuador, Peru and Chile.* London, 1860.

Bouger, M. *An Abridged Relation of a Voyage to Peru,* in *Pinkerton's Voyages and Travels,* vol. 14. London, 1813.

Bowman, Isaiah. *The Andes of Southern Peru.* New York, N.Y., 1916.

Brown, John. *Two Against the Amazon.* New York, N.Y., 1953.

Brown, Rose, and Bob. *Amazing Amazon.* New York, N.Y., 1942.

Bushnell, G. H. S. *Peru.* New York, N.Y., 1957.

Catlin, George. *Rambles Among the Indians of the Rocky Mountains and the Andes.* London, 187-?.

Church, George E. *Aborigines of South America.* London, 1912.

Cieza de León, Pedro de. *The First Part of the Chronicle of Peru.* London, 1864.

Cole, George R. Fitz-Roy. *The Peruvians at Home.* London, 1884.

Cook, O. F. "Staircase Farms of the Ancients," *National Geographic Magazine,* Washington, D.C., 1916.

Craig, Neville. *Recollections of an Ill-Fated Expedition.* Philadelphia, Pa., 1907.

Darwin, Charles. *Journal of Researches in the Natural History and Geology of the Countries visited during the Voyage of* H.M.S. Beagle *round the World.* New York, N.Y., 1890.

Edwards, William Henry. *A Voyage up the River Amazon.* New York, N.Y., 1847.

Eiby, G. A. *About Earthquakes.* New York, N.Y., 1957.

Fawcett, P. H. *Lost Trails, Lost Cities.* New York, N.Y., 1953.

Frezier, Amedee Francois. *A Voyage to the South-Sea and along the Coast of Chili and Peru in the Years 1712, 1713 and 1714.* London, 1717.

Garcilaso de la Vega, El Inca. *The Royal Commentaries of Peru.* London, 1688.

Gregory, Herbert E. *A Geographical Sketch of Titicaca, the Island of the Sun.* New York, N.Y., 1913.

Hagen, Victor W. von, editor. *The Green World of the Naturalists.* New York, N.Y., 1948.

Harcourt, Raoul d', and Marie d'. *La Musique des Incas et ses survivances.* Paris, 1925.

Herndon, W. L., and Gibbon, L. *Exploration of the Valley of the Amazon.* Washington, D.C., 1854.

Herrera y Tordesillas, Antonio de. *The general history of the vast continent and islands of America . . .* trans. by John Stevens. London, 1725-26.

Heyerdahl, Thor. *American Indians in the Pacific.* Chicago, Ill., 1953.

Holstein, Otto. "Chan-Chan: Capitol of the Great Chimu," *Geographical Review,* vol. 17, New York, N.Y., 1927.

Humboldt, Alexander von. *Researches concerning the Institutions and Monuments of the Ancient Inhabitants of America.* Trans. Helen Maria Williams. London, 1814. 2 vols.

_____. *Personal Narrative of Travels to the Equinoctial Regions of the New Continent.* London, 1849.

Hutchinson, T. J. *Two Years in Peru with Exploration of its Antiquities.* 2vols. London, 1873.

Karsten, R. *The Civilization of the South American Indians, with Special Reference to Magic and Religion.* London, 1926.

Keleman, Pal. *Medieval American Art.* 2 vols. New York, N.Y., 1943.

Keller-Leuzinger, Franz. *The Amazon and Madeira Rivers.* London, 1874.

Kelsey, Vera. *Seven Keys to Brazil.* New York, N.Y., 1941.

Kravigny, Frank W. *The Jungle Route.* New York, N.Y., 1940.

La Condamine, Charles-Marie de. *Abridged Narrative of Travels Through the Interior of South America,* in *Pinkerton's Voyages and Travels,* Vol. 14. London, 1813.

Lehman, Walter, and Doering, Heinrich. *The Art of Old Peru.* New York, N.Y., 1924.

Mangelsdorf, P. C., and Reeves, R. G. *The Origin of Indian Corn and its Relatives.* Texas Agricultural Experiment Station, Bulletin 574, College Station, May, 1939.

Markham, C. R. *Cuzco & Lima.* London, 1856.

_____. *Contributions toward a Grammar and Dictionary of Quichua, the Language of the Incas of Peru.* London, 1864.

_____. *The Incas of Peru.* London, 1910.

Mathews, Edward D. *Up the Amazon and Madeira Rivers.* London, 1879.

Means, P. A. *A Study of Ancient Andean Social Institutions.* New Haven, Conn., 1925.

_____. *Ancient civilizations of the Andes.* New York, N.Y., 1931.

_____. *Fall of the Inca Empire and the Spanish Rule in Peru: 1530-1780.* New York, N.Y., 1932.

Millar, George. *A Crossbowman's Story of the First Exploration of the Amazon.* New York, N.Y., 1955.

Montesinos, Fernando. *Memorias Antiguas Historiales del Peru.* ed, and trans. P. A. Means. London, 1920.

Mortimer, W. G. *Coca, the Divine Plant of the Incas.* New York, N.Y., 1901.

Mozans, H. J. *Along the Andes and Down the Amazon.* New York, N.Y., 1911.

Murphy, Robert Cushman. "Fisheries Resources in Peru," *Scientific Monthly,* vol. 16, 1923.

_____. *Bird Islands of Peru.* New York, N.Y., 1925.

_____. *Oceanic Birds of South America.* 2 vols. New York, N.Y., 1936.

Newell, N. D. *Geology of the Lake Titicaca Region, Peru and Bolivia.* Geological Society of America, Memoir 36, New York, N.Y., 1949.

Ogilvie, Alan G. *Geography of the Central Andes.* New York, N.Y., 1922.

Orton, James. *The Andes and The Amazon.* New York, N.Y., 1876.

Picart, B. *Ceremonies of the Idolatrous Nations.* London, 1734.

Pizzaro, Pedro. *Relation of the Discovery and Conquest of the Kingdoms of Peru.* New York, N.Y., 1921.

Posnansky, A. *Tihuanacu. The Cradle of American Man.* 2 vols. New York, N.Y., 1945.

_____. *Tihuanacu. The Cradle of American Man.* 2 vols. La Paz, 1957.

Price, Willard. *The Amazing Amazon.* New York, N.Y., 1952.

Prodgers, C. H. *Adventures in Bolivia.* New York, N.Y., 1922.

Rivero, M. E., and von Tschudi, J. J. *Peruvian Antiquities.* New York, N.Y., 1853.

Roosevelt, Theodore. *Through the Brazilian Wilderness.* New York, N.Y., 1914.

Sauer, Carl. "American Agricultural Origins: A Consideration of Nature and Culture," in *Essays in Anthropology.* Berkeley, Cal., 1936.

Saville, M. H. *Antiquities of Manabi.* 2 vols. New York, N.Y., 1907-10.

Southey, Robert. *History of Brazil.* 3 vols. London, 1810-19.

Spruce, Richard. *Notes of a Botanist on the Amazon and Andes* (ea. A. R. Wallace). London, 1908. 2 vols.

Squier, E. G. *Peru: Incidents of Travel & Exploration in the Land of the Incas.* New York, N.Y., 1877.

Stevenson, W. B. *A Historical and Descriptive Narrative of Twenty Years' Residence in South America.* 3 vols. London, 1825.

Steward, Julian H. ed. *Handbook of South American Indians.* 6 vols. Washington, D.C., 1946.

Sutcliffe, Thomas. *Sixteen Years in Chile & Peru.* London, 1841.

Temple, Edmund. *Travels in Various Parts of Peru.* London, 1830.

Tschudi, J. J. von. *Travels in Peru.* New York, N.Y., 1854.

Uhle, Max. *Pachacamac.* Philadelphia, Pa., 1903.

Up De Graff, F. W. *Head Hunters of the Amazon.* New York, N.Y., 1923.

Verrill, A. H. *The American Indian, North, South and Central America.* New York, N.Y., 1927.

_____. *Old civilizations of the New World.* New York, N.Y., 1929.

Villavicencio, Victor L. *La Vida sexual del Indigena peruano.* Lima, 1942.

Wallace, A. R. *Narrative of Travels on the Amazon and Rio Negro.* London, 1889.

Whymper, Edward. *Travels Amongst the Great Andes of the Equator.* London, 1892.

Zarate, Agustín. *The Discoverie and Conquest of the Prouvinces of Peru . . . Written in foure bookes, by Augustine Sarate.* (Translated out of the Spanish tongue, by F. Nicholas). London, 1581.

HENRY FORD

Anonymous. "Mr. Ford Doesn't Care," *Fortune Magazine,* December, 1933.

Arnold, Horace L., and Faurote, Fay L. *Ford Methods and Ford Shops.* 1915.

Bennett, Harry. *We Never Called Him Henry.* New York, N.Y., 1951.

Benson, Allan L. *The New Henry Ford.* New York & London, 1923.

Bowie, Beverley M. "The Past is Present in Greenfield Village," *National Geographic Magazine,* July, 1958.

Burlingame, Roger. *Henry Ford, A Great Life in Brief.* New York, N.Y., 1955.

Ford, Henry, and Crowther, Samuel. *My Life and Work.* Garden City, N.J., 1924.

Garrett, Garet. *The Wild Wheel.* New York, N.Y., 1952.

Lochner, Louis P. *Henry Ford: America's Don Quixote.* New York, N.Y., 1925.

Marquis, Samuel S. *Henry Ford: an Interpretation.* Boston, Mass., 1923.

McCarthy, Joe. "The Ford Family," *Holiday Magazine,* June–September, 1957.

McGuffey, William H. *Eclectic Fourth Reader.* New York, N.Y., 1849.

Merz, Charles. *And Then Came Ford.* New York, N.Y., 1929.

Nevins, Allan, and Hill, Frank Ernest. *Ford: the Times, the Man and the Company.* New York, N.Y., 1954.

_____. *Ford: Expansion and Challenge: 1915-1933.* New York, N.Y., 1957.

Nowlin, William. *The Bark Covered House.* Chicago, Ill., 1937.

Petersham, Maud, and Miska. *The Rooster Crows: A Book of American Rhymes and Jingles.* New York, N.Y., 1953.

Pierson, George W. ed.. *Tocqueville and Beaumont in America.* New York, N.Y., 1938.

Pound, Arthur. *Detroit, Dynamic City.* New York, N.Y., 1940.

Richards, William C. *The Last Billionaire.* New York, N.Y., 1948.

Ruddiman, Margaret. "Memories of My Brother Henry Ford," *Michigan History,* Lansing, Mich., September. 1953.

Simonds, William A. *Henry Ford: His Life, His Work, His Genius.* New York, N.Y., 1943.

_____. *Henry Ford and Greenfield Village.* New York, N.Y., 1938.

Sinclair, Upton. *The Flivver King.* Pasadena, Cal., 1937.

Stern, Philip Van Doren. *Tin Lizzie.* New York, N.Y., 1955.

Sward, Keith. *The Legend of Henry Ford.* New York, N.Y., 1948.

Wilson, Edmund. "The Despot of Dearborn," *Scribner's Magazine,* July 1931.

THE
MIDDLE PASSAGE

A TRIPTYCH OF COMMODITIES

LUDD

1811

11 March. Protest meeting in Nottingham market place and breaking of about sixty frames at Arnold.

16-23 March. Outrages in many villages in the north-west. More than 100 frames broken, including Sutton in-Ashfield, Kirby, Woodborough, Lambley, Bulwell, and Ilkeston in Derbyshire.

29 March. Framebreaking at Mansfield.

13 April. Reward of 100 guineas offered after destruction of six frames at Bulwell.

14 July. Destruction of frames at Sutton- in-Ashfield (Kirby-in-Ashfield according to one account).

4 November. Six frames broken at Bulwell.

10 November. Attack on house of person named Hollingworth at Bulwell, involving death of a Luddite, John Westley of Arnold, who was shot as he entered the house. Ten to twelve frames broken at Kimberley, allegedly for the employment of colts.

12 November. Eight or nine frames broken at Basford.

One Reverend William Lee, born at Woodborough—or in Calverton—of kin to the Champion Lee of Ditchley—was destitute of patrimony—or owner of a small freehold estate at Woodborough—was in 1589 twenty-three years of age, a student—or graduate—or Master of Arts—at Cambridge and curate at Calverton,

> a man of pale, hard, cold aspect,
> but with an inner fire,
> and a well-knit frame . . .

Was deeply smitten with the charms of a young townswoman, and paid court to her in an honorable way,

but she seemed always more intent on knitting stockings, and instructing pupils in that art, than upon the caresses and assiduities of her suitor

—or he married the young lady in secret, and was expelled from the University when the alliance came to light, was forced to live on the earnings that his wife gained from knitting stockings.

In either case: from necessity—or from pique at her preoccupation at the expense of his suit—he determined to mar her hand work, and to invent a frame or machine for knitting stockings.

> Seeing a woman knit,
> and having an excellent head,
> Lee curiously observes the working needles in knitting,
> and studies fondly the dextrous movements;
> becomes himself an adept
> and in his mind frames a model,
> a scheme of *artificial fingers,*
> for knitting many loops at once.

> Wm. Lee buys planes, files, and pincers,
> excellent close grained woods from Midlands forests—
> he is in fact constructing the stocking loom!

> knitting many loops at once,
> with artificial fingers!

With his brother James, Lee performed and exercised the loom before Queen Elizabeth.

"My Lord," said the Queen, "I have too much love for my poor people who obtain their bread by the employment of knitting, to give money to forward an invention, that will tend to their ruin by depriving them of employment, and thus make them beggars."

Wm. Lee, of well-knit frame, took the invention to France—but failed with it there, and died in poverty. His brother James brought it back across the water, and the industry, established first in London and later shifted to the Midlands and to Yorkshire, began.

> *18 November. Some fifty-four to seventy frames broken at Sutton-in-Ashfield.*
> *18 November. One wide frame broken at Old Radford. Many threatening letters received. Rick-burning at Mansfield, Sneinton, and Hucknall Torkard; victims supposed to be those active against the frame breakers.*
> *23 November. One frame broken in Nottingham, one at Ilkeston.*
> *23/24 November. Thirty to thirty-four frames broken at Basford in various workshops. One broken at Chilwell during the same night.*
> *25 November. Eleven frames broken at Basford during the afternoon, several broken in Nottingham itself. Reports of breakings at Eastwood, Heanor, and Cossall.*
> *27 November. Frame broken at Carlton. Daytime attack on frames being transported under escort at Redhill.*
> *28 November. Four frames broken at Basford, and three to five at Bobber's Mill.*

". . . are we to conclude that machinery is in itself an evil? You are all aware that cropping by hand as you now practice it is by no means easy work; nay, we all know that it is very painful for learners to handle the shears until the wrist has become hoofed. Now look at one of these machines. Observe how smoothly and how beautifully

it works! How perfectly it does for the workman the most arduous
part of his task."

The Art and Mystery of Frame-Work Knitting

a curious and complicated piece of machinery possessing six times
the speed of the original mode, and capable of an endless variety of
substantial and fancy productions

an engine to knit by machinery, in-
creasing speed twenty-fold!

a small machine at which the workman
sat—as it might be at a piano or a typewriter—working it both with
hands and feet. In hand knitting the needle deals with one stitch
after another all down the row: in the stocking frame each stitch
had a needle to itself, and all the needles worked simultaneously!

direct and absolute knitwork
in the stitches thereof,
nothing different therein
from the common way of knitting
(not much more anciently for public use
practiced in this nation than this)
but only in the number of needles,
at an instant working in this
more than in the other by an hundred to one;
set in an engine or frame
composed of above 2000 pieces
of smith's, joiner's, and turner's work;
after so artificial and exact a manner,
that by the judgement of all beholders,
it far exceeds in the ingenuity, curiosity, and subtilty
of the invention and contexture,
all other frames or instruments of manufacture
in use
in any known part of the world!

throwing the thread from a bobbin over the hooks or 'needles' by hand drawing the slur by one of the treddles to force down the jacks and their sinkers and so to form loops between every other pair of needles sinking the lead sinkers down on the thread to divide the loops between all the needles locking up jacks at the same time by the thumbs and so equalizing all the loops by these cleverly combined movements bringing the loops thus formed to the needle heads throwing up the frame assisted by the strong central spring leaving the loops at the needle heads and the work at the stem to be pressed over in forming the new course or series of loops then putting down the spring bar or presser by the foot on the middle treddle and putting forward the web already made upon the needle beards which are now pressed into the grooves of the needles then letting the press-er rise and at the same time bringing the web over the needle heads bringing down the frame to the bottom standard to catch the work with the nebs of the sinkers which are for that purpose made in the shape of a long arch taking back the web by the nebs of the sinkers holding the frame firmly down and finally letting the frame rise to the catch of the copens holding the thumbs firmly to the thumb plate and then quit the thumbs for another course the slur is moved for one course to the right and for the next back to the left

5 December. One frame broken in Nottingham, several at Basford.

6 December. Seven frames broken at Holbrook, eighteen at Pentrich.

7 December. Six frames broken at Bulwell, four at Arnold, ten at Pentrich.

11 December. Several frames broken at Ripley, one at Burton Joyce.

12 December. Stacks fired at Basford and one frame destroyed at Benton. Attacks also reported in Hucknall Torkard, Ilkeston, Makeney, Heage, Holbrook, Crich, Swanwick, Riddings in Der-byshire.

14 December. Three frames broken in Notting-ham.

15 December. Several frames broken in Notting-
ham, including lace-frames.
16 December. Rick-burning at Basford.
21-28 December. Robberies in Derbyshire by 'Ned
Ludd's men' and frame-breakings in Notting-
ham, Basford, and Arnold.

The stockingers employed apprentices—pauper children—a prac-
tice known as colting—and worked them from five in the morning
until ten at night, for 4 shillings 6 pence a week.

Often the frames were not worked on the employer's premises, but
were scattered about in workmen's cottages, in the various centers of
trade and neighboring villages. They belonged sometimes to the
workman himself, sometimes to his employer, sometimes to specu-
lators.

> and the workers were forced to make pieces
> cut up
> into gloves, socks, sandals—
> cut, shaped with
> scissors,
> without proper loop selvedges,
>
> underfashioned & unsound,
> deficient in threads,
> dyed with logwood instead of madder,
>
> cut goods,
> stretched to required shape,
> to become worthless
> with a washing

1812
15 January. Leeds meeting of cloth workers, some
with blackened faces and stated to be armed with
hammers and clubs. James Shaw apprehended

and committed. Information given on oath to Leeds magistrates of conspiracy to destroy machinery in certain mills. No attacks made following meeting.

19 January. Leeds. Oatlands Mill, near Woodhouse Carr, the property of Messrs Oates, Wood, & Smithson, was discovered on fire. Contained gig-mills. Believed to be act of incendiarism as no one had worked there that day, Sunday, and combustible materials were discovered in several places.

22 February. Huddersfield. Attack on dressing-shop of Joseph Hirst of Marsh; shearing frames destroyed. Similar attack on workshop of James Balderson of Crosland Moor. Luddites organised in two parties, the attackers and the watchmen.

26 February. Huddersfield. Attack on dressing-shop of William Hinchcliffe of Leymoor. All machinery destroyed. Committee of manufacturers and merchants formed in Huddersfield with large discretionary powers.

5 March. Huddersfield. Four houses entered near Slaithwaite and frames and shears destroyed.

11 March. Huddersfield. Houses of John Garner of Honley, Clement Dyson of Dungeon, and Mr Roberts of Crosland, attacked and obnoxious machinery destroyed.

Ned, or Edward,
Lud, Ludd, or Ludlam,

a lad from Leicestershire —Anstey, or Loughborough—

of weak intellect and irritable temper,
a common object of ridicule,
a reckless character,
averse to confinement or work,

was ordered by his father
—or his employer—
to *square his needles,*
i.e., to place them in a perfectly straight line
in the front of his machine,

and he took up his hammer

and beat them into heaps

> *15 March. Huddersfield. Workshop of Francis Vickerman of Taylor Hill attacked, twenty to thirty pairs of shears broken, woollen cloth destroyed, and private property in house destroyed.*
> *23/4 March. Rawdon. Attack on shearingmill of William Thompson & Bros. Thirty to forty pairs of shears destroyed in twenty-minute attack. Thirty-six windows broken and three pieces of fine woollen cloth damaged.*
> *25 March. Leeds. Dickenson, Carr, & Co's workshop attacked and eighteen pieces of dressed cloth destroyed.*
> *1 April. Special General Sessions of the Peace to institute Watch and Ward.*

"I, *A.B.* of my own voluntary will, do declair and swear that I never will reveal to any person or persons, under the canopy of Heaven, the names of any of the persons composing the secret committee, either by word, deed, sign, or by address, marks, or complexion or any other thing that may lead to the discovery of the same, under the penalty of being put out of the world, by the first brother whom I may meet; and of having my name and character blotted out of existence. And I do further swear, that I will use my utmost endeavors to punish with death, any traitor or traitors, who may rise up against us, though he should fly to the verge of existence. So help me God, and bless me to keep this oath inviolable."

. . . the which, by swearing, the frame-work knitters were twisted in
. . .

    . . . generally of the stubborn, resolute Yorkshire race:
    ignorant, violent, determined,
    holding close together,
    a well-knit group

three hundred frames broken, thrown into the streets, a house burnt
down
    numerous acts of lawless outrage
                   military training, and the
seizure of arms
          clubs & sticks, swords, guns and pistols, with sledge
and axe to wreck the frames
              meeting secretly upon commons and
moors, with sentinels posted, in case of discovery, the alarm to be
given by firing a gun, or by rocket and blue-lights
                     the men in dis-
guise, answering to numbers and not names
                   throughout the exten-
sive and populous tracts of the Lancashire and Cheshire cotton
manufacture, and the clothing part of the West Riding
                   the Luddites
small in numbers, but with popular support, and the frames scat-
tered across the countryside, impossible of protection
                  the villages pa-
trolled by troops, but to no avail
             the machine-wreckers divided in-
to groups, in parties from six to fifty, frame-breaking in villages
miles apart
         (by an Act of Parliament, 1812, frame-breaking became
a capital offence)
             at Basford, a house entered and frames broken
within ten yards of a magistrate and a party of Dragoons
                   ". . . down with
all kings but King Ludd."

"On Friday afternoon, about four o'clock,
a large body of rioters
suddenly attacked the weaving factory,
belonging to Messrs. Wroe and Duncroft,
at West Houghton,
about thirteen miles from this town;
of which, being unprotected,
they soon got possession.
They instantly set it on fire,
and the whole of the building
with its valuable machinery, cambrics, &c.
were entirely destroyed.

The reason assigned for this horrid act
is,
as at Middleton,
'weaving by steam.'

The rioters appear to level their vengeance
against all species of improvement in machinery.

Mistaken men!
—what would this country have been
without such improvements?

No one of the incendiaries are taken . . ."

". . . that, about the hour of One in the Morning of the 27th. of February Instant himself and family were alarmed by a Gun being fired through his window, when he saw a large number of people about his house—that soon afterwards the Door of his Shop was broken open and he heard a number of People rush in, and a great Noise of Hammers striking the frames and Shears there . . . That as soon as they were gone, this Examinant went out to see what they had done and found Five Dressing or Shearing frames and about Thirty pairs of Shears broke to pieces."

_____

"The stragglers are called together by a low whistle, and Mellor's deep voice is heard as he puts them in order. They form in a long lane, down which the various leaders walk, calling over their rolls, not by names but by numbers. This being done, they are next formed into companies. The men with guns are called to march first, and Mellor assumes the command of this detachment. Next follows the pistol company, headed by Thorpe. A hatchet company comes after, and the rear is brought up by the men wielding huge hammers, and by those who carry only bludgeons or are without weapons of any kind. They are rapidly put through a short drill and then formed into marching order, John Hirst, of Liversedge, and Samuel Hartley, of Rawfolds, who was or had been in Cartwright's employ, being told off as guides. It is now approaching midnight and they have some three miles to walk."

. . . marshalling, then, at the obelisk, or Dumb Steeple, before the attack.

> at the mill in Rawfolds,
> the watchdog roused,
> barked . . . howled
>
> the sentries were surprised and silenced.
> but Cartwright and his men awoke,
> gathered their muskets,
> rang the milltop bell
>
> Mellor's men swung their axes,
> but the mill door,
> heavily studded with nails,
> blunted and fended the blades
>
> Luddite hammers fell on,
> failed to smash through

the alarm bell boomed above the mill,
Cartwright's men fired
. . . flashes of musketry . . .
the defenders shielded well within

the Luddites fell back . . .

> *1812*
> *11 April. Spen Valley. Attack on Rawfolds Mill of*
> *William Cartwright by a crowd of around 150*
> *men gathered from various parts of woollen dis-*
> *trict. Mill was stoutly, if not strongly, defended.*
> *Luddites met first serious armed resistance and*
> *suffered first defeat. Some damage was done to the*
> *exterior of the mill, but no machinery was broken.*
> *Two of the assailants were killed and others*
> *wounded. With this abortive attack, Yorkshire*
> *machine-breaking was virtually at an end . . .*

> *1813*
> *January. York Assizes. Three men convicted and*
> *executed for the murder of William Horsfall, five*
> *for the Rawfolds job, and nine more for stealing*
> *arms or money.*
> *March. Bulk of forces withdrawn.*

EFIK

"The Land-breeze . . . is . . . fmall, fultry, and ftinking, efpecially
when from Rivers whofe Banks are peftered with rotten *Mangroves,*
ftagnating Waters, &c."

"The heats are here intolerable in the day-
time, even in December, and efpecially at noon; for it is then gener-
ally a dead calm at fee, and no manner of air can come to it from the
land, by reafon it is fo clofe fhelter'd behind by the thick woods
ftanding about it. The heat is fo ftifling, that neither man nor beafts
can endure it, or fcarce breathe, efpecially near the ftrand, at low
water; for there the reflection from the fand almoft fcorches the
face, and burns the very foles of the fhoes in walking on it . . ."

rotting mud rivers,
sheets of filthy waters,
drop their heaviest harvest
before the bars

the lighter silts carried
—patchy, frothy—to
sea

(rotting water walled in swamps)

"While your eyes are drinking in the characteristics of Bonny
scenery you notice a peculiar smell . . . the breath of the malarial
mud, laden with fever . . ."

(putrifying ooze)

the soft, steamy air, the mist, creeps out of side creeks, among man-
grove roots, laying itself upon the river, stretching and rolling

crawling out of bushes, crouching toward sand and surf, reaching,
withdrawing, curling, a white wall, over dead waters

"...Muſque-
toes and Sand Flies, who diverted us ſo prettily that we could not
get any Sleep . . ."

"On landing, they would be taken to the trader's sheds, where they
would be fed, rubbed down with palm oil and made up for sale."

the trade: blackfish oil

"You are to be very careful and circumſpect in your Choice of
Slaves, that you on no account purchaſe any but ſuch as ſhall be
merchantable, free from Sickneſſ, Diſtempers, Ruptures, and loſſ of
Limbs . . ."

"But our greatest care of all is to buy none that are
pox'd, lest they should infect the rest aboard . . . therefore our sur-
geon is forc'd to examine the privates of both men and women with
the nicest scrutiny . . ."

"When theſe Slaves come to *Fida,* they are
put in Priſon all together, and when we treat concerning buying
them, they are all brought out together in a large Plain; where, by
our Chirurgeons, whoſe Province it is, they are thoroughly exam-
ined, even to the ſmallest Member, and that naked too both Men
and Women, without the leaſt Diſtinction or Modeſty."

"He handled
the naked blacks from head to foot, squeezing their joints and mus-
cles, twisting their arms and legs, examining teeth, eyes, and chest,
and pinching breasts and groins without mercy."

"Thofe which are approved as good are fet on one fide; and the lame or faulty are fet by as *Invalides*, which are here called *Mackrons*. Thefe are fuch as are above five and thirty Years old, or are maimed in the Arms, Legs, Hands or Feet, have loft a Tooth, are gray-haired, or have Films over their Eyes; as well as all thofe which are affected with any Venereal Diftemper, or with feveral other Difeafes."

"The *Invalides* and the Maimed being thrown out, as I have told you, the remainder are numbred, and it is entred who delivered them. In the mean while a burning Iron, with the Arms or Name of the Companies, lyes in the Fire; with which ours are marked on the Breaft."

"I doubt not but this Trade feems very barbarous to you, but fince it is followed by meer neceffity it muft go on; but we yet take all poffible care that they are not burned too hard, efpecially the Women, who are more tender than the Men."

"*Saturday 3rd November*. Fair weather, fresh land and sea breese. The carpenter finishes his work on the longboat. In the morning had a visit from some Portuguese of Pirates bay, brought a woman slave, who I refused being long breasted, but dismissed them in very good humour with their reception, and they promised to bring me 2 young slaves in a little time."

"Yellow Will brought me a woman slave, but being long-breasted and ill made, refused her, and made him take her on shoar again."

"The *Women* are not nigh fo well fhaped as the Men: Childing, and their Breafts always pendulous, ftretches them to fo unfeemly a Length and Bignefs, that fome, like the *Ægyptians*, I believe, could fuckle over their Shoulders."

. . . driven by black Krumen, with whips of the hide of the hip-
popotamus, into the water's edge,
scrubbed with sand grains,
loaded
into native canoes and ridden through the surf, Krumen paddles
controlling waters and slaves,
transshipped to large slave boats (care
being taken that all do not leap at once) and carried to the off-shore
ship,

> the slaver,
> slaving up

"On being brought on board . . . they show signs of extreme distress
and despair, from a feeling of their situation . . . the slaves on board
his ship being often heard in the night making a howling melan-
choly noise, expressing of extreme anguish, he repeatedly ordered
the woman who had been his interpreter to inquire into the cause.
She discovered it to be owing to their having dreamed they were in
their own country again, and finding themselves when awake, in the
hold of a slave-ship."

> ". . . I could not help being fenfibly affected
> . . . at observing with what apparent eagernefs
> a black woman feized fome dirt
> from off an African yam,
> and put it in her mouth;
> feeming to rejoice at the opportunity
> of poffeffing
> fome of her native earth."

"When the land breeze died away, it fell entirely calm, and the sea
continued an unruffled mirror for three days, during which the
highlands remained in sight, like a faint cloud in the east.

The glaring sky and the reflecting ocean acted and reacted on each other until the air glowed like a furnace. During night a dense fog enveloped the vessel with its clammy folds."

> "crawling up the ship side,
> wrapping us in
> dankly smelling moisture,
>
> green mildew"

and meals were cooked on board over fires of green mangrove—the smoke of which "for want of a current of air to carry it off, collects itfelf in large quantities, and infefts every part of the fhip, rendering a veffel during its ftay here very unhealthy. The fmoke alfo, by its acrimonious quality, often produces inflammations of the eyes, which terminates fometimes in the lofs of fight."

"I began to notice a strange, fetid smell pervading the vessel, and a low, heavy fog on deck, almost like steam, and then the horrid truth became apparent. Our rotting negroes under hatches had generated the plague and it was the death-mist that I saw rising."

> departed the coast at night, after dark,
> the slaves secure below,
> to prevent murmuring

"We had about 12 negroes did wilfully drown themselves ... for 'tis their belief that when they die they return home to their own country and friends again."

". . . the captain and officers, when at dinner, heard the alarm of a slave's being overboard, and found it true, for they perceived him making every exertion to drown himself. He put his head under water, but lifted his hands up; and thus went down, as if *exulting that he had got away.*"

> "he dived under water, and rising again at a

distance from the ship, made signs which words cannot describe, expressive of his happiness in escaping. He then went down, and was seen no more."

"... when to our great amazement above an hundred men slaves jumped overboard"

"... they had no sooner reached the ship's side, than first one, then another, then a third, sprang up on the gunwale, and darted into the sea"

"... continued dancing about among the waves, yelling with all their might, what seemed to me a song of triumph, in the burden of which they were joined by some of their companions on deck. Our ship speedily left the ignorant creatures behind; their voices came fainter and fainter upon the wind; the black head, first of one, then of another, disappeared"

"... and many of the moft mutinous, leapt over board, and drown'd themfelves in the ocean with much refolution, fhewing no manner of concern for life"

"... forty of the moft obftinate of them, men and women, leap'd into the fee together, where turning on their backs, they called to the French to obferve them, and holding their mouths quite open, fwallow'd down the fee-water, without moving arms or legs, till they were drown'd, to fhow their intrepidity and little concern for death"

"one of the blacks
whom they were forcing into the hold
suddenly knocked down a sailor
and attempted to leap overboard.

He was caught by the leg
by another of the crew,
and the sailor hamstrung him with a cutlass.

I ran to the main chains and looked over;
for they had dropped the black into the sea
when they saw that he was useless.

He continued to swim,
even after he had sunk under water,
for I saw the red track extending shoreward;
but by and by, it stopped,
... widened ...
... faded"

"The slave ships were peculiarly constructed, with a view to prevent the negroes from ending their misery by plunging into the sea; nevertheless, the utmost vigilence was not able to frustrate such manumission, and a score have been known to muster up all their strength, burst from their chains, and leap overboard, exulting, with apparent joy, as they sank in the waves, or fell prey to the procession of sharks that followed in the wake of the Guineamen."

"... but before the poor creatures had got a few yards from the ship the sharks had torn them in pieces, and not a fragment of them to be seen except the water tinged with their blood"

                                                    "... we have likewife feen divers of them eaten by the fharks, of which a prodigious member are about the fhips in this place, and I have been told will follow her hence to Barbados, for the dead negroes that are thrown over board in the paffage"

                    " ... out of the whole we lost 33 of as good men slaves as we had on board, who would not endeavor to save themselves, but resolved to die and sunk directly down. Many more of them were taken up almost drowned, some of them died since, but not to the owner's loss, they being sold before any discovery was made of the injury the salt water had done them"

----

boarded naked,
or given an arse-clout ...

"... it is pitiful to fee how they croud thofe poor wretches, fix hundred and fifty or feven hundred in a fhip, the men ftanding in the hold ty'd to ftakes, the women between the decks, and thofe that are with child in the great cabbin, and the children in the fteeridge ...""

or stowed on platforms, each lying on his right side, "which is considered preferable for the action of the heart"

or seated within one another's legs, pressed together, backbone to breastbone

or stacked in tiers, spoon fashion, knees flexed, eyes forward, head to windward

or packed against the ship's
curved planks,
so that when removed,
"many can never resume
the upright posture"

"Monday, May 15.—When the squalls, breaking heavily on the vessel cause her to heel over, and the negroes to tumble against one another in the hold, the shrieks of the sufferers, through the gloom of the night, rising above the noise of the winds and waves . . ."

"He has seen the slaves drawing their breath with all those anxious and laborious efforts for life, *which are observed in expiring animals, subjected by experiment to foul air.*"

"Being thrust back,
and striving the more to get out,
the after-hatch was forced down on them.
Over the other hatchway,
in the fore part of the vessel,
a wooden grating was fastened.
To this,
the sole inlet for the air,
the suffocating heat of the hold,
and perhaps panic from the strangeness of their situation,
made them press;

and thus a great part of the space
was rendered useless.
They crowded to the grating,
and clinging to it for air,
completely barred its entrance . . .
The cries, the heat, 'the smoke of their torment'—
which ascended,
can be compared to nothing earthly.

. . . some were found strangled,
their hands still grasping each other's throats,
and tongues protruding from their mouths.
The bowels of one were crushed out."

Scraped the rooms,
then smoked the ship with tar,
tobacco and brimstone
. . . afterwards washed with vinegar.

"We were very nice in keeping the places where the slaves lay clean
and neat, appointing some of the ship's crew to do that office con-
stantly and several of the slaves themselves to be assistants to them
and thrice a week we perfumed betwixt decks with a quantity of
good vinegar in pails, and red-hot iron bullets in them, to expel the
bad air, after the place had been well washed and scrubbed with
brooms; after which the deck was cleaned with cold vinegar . . ."

but often the shit tubs could not be reached by the shackled blacks,
and

"in this situation,
unable to proceed
and prevented from going to the tubs,
they desist from the attempt;
and as the necessities of nature
are not to be resisted,
        they ease themselves as they lie"

"The place allotted for the sick negroes is under the half deck, where they lie on the bare planks. By this means those who are emaciated frequently have their skin and even their flesh entirely rubbed off, by the action of the ship, from the prominent parts of the shoulders, elbows and hips so as to render the bones quite bare. And some of them, by constantly lying in the blood and mucous that had flowed from those afflicted with the flux and which is generally so violent as to prevent their being kept clean, have their flesh much sooner rubbed off than those who have only to contend with the mere friction of the ship."

"Some of the most diseased were obliged to keep on deck with a sail spread for them to lie on. This, in a little time, became nearly covered with blood and mucous, which involuntarily issued from them, and therefore the sailors, who had the disagreeable task of cleaning the sail, grew angry with the slaves, and used to beat them inhumanly . . ."

> ". . . after all our pains and care
> to give them their messes
> in due order and season,
> keeping their lodgings as clean and sweet as possible,
> and enduring so much slavery and stench
> so long
> among a parcel of creatures
> nastier than swine . . ."

"The slaves in consequence grew fearful of committing this involuntary action, and when they perceived they had done it would immediately creep to the tubs, and there sit straining with such violence, as to produce a prolapsis ani, which could not be cured."

". . . the shrunk and wrinkled skin hanging in loose folds over the regions of the bowels . . . the horrid appearance of blood on the lips . . ."

> (stuffed their mouths with oakum,
> (to prevent the African screaming

(and in Barbados,
(stuffed oakum up assholes,
(to plug the flux

"In one of these voyages . . . the slaves had the small pox. In this case
he has seen the platform one continued scab; eight or ten of them
were hauled up dead in the morning, and the flesh and skin peeled
off their wrists when taken hold of."

"There they lay in one mass of scab and corruption, frequently
sticking to each other and to the deck till they were separated to be
thrown overboard."

        the crew, ". . . arming their hands with tarred
mittens, flung the foetid masses of putrefaction into the sea!"

                           "The
distemper which my men as well as the blacks mostly died of, was
the white flux . . ."

   . . . pox,
small pox,
flux,
white flux . . .

   . . . gravel
 and stoppage of urine . . .

" violent cholicks . . ."

". . . inflammation
and swelling
of the eyes and eyelids,
with a difcharge of
fetid rheum."

"*Thursday, April 20th.*—A negro died this morning from having gorged himself on dry meal and crude beans. When thrown overboard, it being a dead calm, the body floated for upwards of half an hour, the face above water, close to the vessel, and sometimes striking against the side . . ."

"*Tuesday, April 25th.*—The poor wretch who has wonderfully lingered twelve days, since the contusions received on the first night, terminated his miseries today, and, when thrown overboard, sunk as lead."

"The great physical suffering of all seems to be raging, unquenchable thirst. They eagerly catch the drippings from the sails after a shower; apply their lips to the wet masts; and crawl to the coops to share the supply placed there for the fowls."

". . . for tho' we ſeparate the men and women aboard by partitions and bulk-heads, to prevent quarrels and wranglings among them, yet do what we can they will come together, and that diſtemper which they call the yaws, is very common here, and diſcovers itſelf by almost the ſame ſymptoms as the *Lues Venerea* or clap does with us . . ."

"*Thursday 13th June* . . . This morning buried a woman slave (No. 47). Know not what to say she died of for she has not been properly alive since she first came on board."

". . . when they arrive near the markets
for which they are destined,
care is taken to polish them for sale
by an application of the lunar caustic
to such as are afflicted with the yaws."

———————

"*Wednesday, May 31.*—It is remarkable that no death has occurred to-day . . ."

———————

"I do not think the forms of these Fullah girls, with their complex-
ions of freshest bronze, are exceeded in symmetry by the women of
any other country. There was a slender delicacy of limb, waist, neck,
hand, foot, and bosom, which seemed to be the type that moulded
every one of them. I saw none of the hanging breast; the flat,
expanded nostrils; the swollen lips, and fillet-like foreheads . . ."

> "Towards the evening
> they diverted themselves on the deck,
> as they thought fit . . .
> which pleafed them highly,
> and often made us paftime;
> efpecially the female fex,
> who being a-part from the males,
> on the quarter-deck,
> and many of them young fprightly maidens,
> full of jollity and good humour,
> afforded us abundance of recreation;
>   as did feveral little fine boys . . ."

"In the afternoon while we were off the deck, William Cooney se-
duced a woman slave down into the room and lay with her brutelike
. . ."

"Once off the coast the ship became half bedlam and half brothel.
Ruiz, our captain, and his two mates set an example of reckless
wickedness. They stripped themselves and danced with black
wenches while our crazy mulatto cook played the fiddle. There was
little attempt at discipline and rum and lewdness reigned supreme
. . . The shrieks and groans of the stifling wretches below echoed our
orgies above."

———————

"Only one birth occurred on the passage. A woman was delivered of
twins—one dead, and the other living but a few hours after birth."

"No gold-finders can endure fo much noifome flavery as they do who carry negroes . . ."

————

Friday, May 12—I have today witnessed a spectacle
such as I had frequently heard to have occurred
in slave-vessels,
but barely know how to describe.

In a tub,
placed on the slave-deck,
for necessary purposes,
a boy was found, who had fallen backward,
and, too weak to extricate himself,
was smothered in it.

He appeared quite dead . . .

ORCA

PART ONE

March,
the testes of the bull sperm awaken,
fatten and ripen,
until in May
they will swell to sixty pounds or more

and the female ovaries are roused,
becoming turgid and inflamed,
the follicles quickening

swimming by her side, frolicking, running submerged and skim-
ming on the surface, the bull strokes the cow gently with the length
of his body, with fins and flukes . . . pats and slaps with his pectorals,
rubs against her, shoots ahead and rides on his back, flippers held
out stiffly . . . returns

and the cow allows him to swim across her
inflamed belly, to nuzzle, to clap jaws, slam heads together

(gently,
unlike the donkey
or the polecat)

the gray whale's penis is curved like a cane,
and they lie together,
male and female, belly to belly,
cow embracing bull with her flip-
pers, to hold him in position for possession,

noise and figures blotted,
perhaps, in waves, rain, storm,
                              and a third whale, a male, may lie
across them, to ease the mating, the meeting of the organs,
                                                  the three
whales churning the waters to a foam, as the bull struggles for pene-
tration

over and over again attempting,
                              and a spot of froth—sperm that
missed the mark—rises to the surface

male and female, struggling to co-ordinate the rising and falling,
inhaling and spouting, thrusting and receiving

until, chest to chest, the pair rise together

    —the male penetrates—

and they fall with a crash . . .

                              (among dolphins,
                              (the cow celebrates
                              (by giving forth
                              (a string of piping sounds,

                              (little bubbles
                              (escaping
                              (from the blowhole

                    ——————

a land mammal, slipped back into the rivers:

on the rosy, inch-long embryo, a pair of fleshy pimples—vestigial
hind legs, grows and disappears
                              a floating hip bone, no longer use-
ful (save to hold the muscles that urge the penis)

                                            a vestigial femur

                                               hu-

merus, radius and ulna, the five digital bones, within the flipper

                                            fading

toothbuds, in a baleen finback

                        in the 9-month fetus, grayish-white,
half grown, the digits flatten in the flippers, ears and olfactories
recede, the skull telescopes, with interdigitation of bones—mam-
maries and genitals become internal, the clitoris receding to a long
groove:

    riverine,
    and then pelagic,
    streamlined,
    all surfaces smoothed

---

the mother blue whale bends her trunk and tail, whips them back

                                              her

vagina flares pink

                   the fetus shifts within, pounding her flanks

    with bicornuate uterus
    —the musculature in an inner circular
    and outer longitudinal
    layer—
    the peristaltic uterine contractions
    —with gravitation—
    turn the fetus,
    in the rich embryonic fluid,
    from head to tail presentation,

    and the fetal flukes drive to the outlet.

    Mother contracts,
    and the tail appears . . .
    . . . retreats . . .
    reappears;

she convulses,
the infant slides partway—
but the flippers catch,
and hold,
          and the mother rests,
                    the infant half-born.

With final thrust,
in a flood of pink

the infant slips out
the umbilicus—drawn taut—snaps

and the mother blue whale—placenta expelled—turns to her child,
nudges him to the surface.

Cold water, dry, cool air, nudge and urge the infant lungs

––––––––––

The mother nudges the infant with her flipper, guides him to the
soft spot on her belly
          and he works his mouth to the nipple, presses
hard . . .
          the long gland, golden brown, extrudes and distends, and a
flow squirts to the back of the infant throat:
                    pink and creamy white,
thickly fat, with a fishy smell
          better than two gallons, flowing

––––––––––

mother and infant,
rising, dipping near the surface,
in the Pacific swell . . .

          and the infant smiles,
          a smile ingrown,
          remaining on his face life long

––––––––––

Weaning, two years alive, the calf leaps free of the mother, skims the surface, is, for a moment, air borne;

or swims beneath the surface, softly accommodating to the waves, his double flukes in a nearly rotary action, sculling the waters, without turbulence;

or dipping a few fathoms down, turns, and sculling violently, leaps, angularly, hesitating, and crashes back, the waters pyramiding around him

The young calf joins a school, swimming, sporting, with the others,

diving, breaching, the school, in a body, in one instant, supramarine;

the school discovers a ship, follows it, forms a circle around it, only their heads visible above the surface, the eyes staring, winking;

and, suddenly inverting, each whale, standing for an instant upon its head, descends, elevates only the flukes—so many black butterflies skimming the surface—

commences lob-tailing—flukes waving back and forth, beating slowly, and then more powerfully, against the waters, shooting up clouds of foam

As though at a signal, the school dives, disappears.

———————

dives, perhaps, three thousand feet, to hunt the giant squid

octopod, decapod, cuttlefish,

swimming at the bottom with open mouth, the prey enticed by white gums and purple tongue,

battling the squid, the tentacles and suction cups that reach for eyes and blowhole,

the whale tearing at the soft body with his teeth, struggling upward,

to reach the surface, perhaps, at night, squid fragments dribbling from his lips, glittering, phosphorescent . . .

. . . or swallowing the squid—or a ten-foot shark—whole.

---

        the urine is clear and pale,
        the feces a brick-red patch,
        or a yellow, diffusing cloud

        the stomach rumbles,
        the whale has the colic,
        lumps of ambergris emerge
        (the fruit of peptic ulcers)

        the whale belches:
        horrendum emittit ructum!

---

his eyes are weak,

                        myopic, astigmatic,

                                        without power of accommo-
dation,
            filmy,
                    lubricated with greasy tears

he has no sense of smell

he breathes a noisy wheeze, a fog, with a scent of musk

---

bones are light and spongy, with air spaces

. . . and when the whale dives, the pulse rate drops dramatically, oxy-
gen for the dive being stored not only in the lungs but in blood-
stream and muscles

the blood carried
to the vascular networks
by the intervertebral
and intercostal arteries,

by the costocervical and
supreme intercostal,
                    dividing,
in a serpentine course, into
innumerable branches
imperceptibly interwoven and
anastomosed,

                    a veritable
retia mirabilia!

breaching and sounding, blood pressure and heartbeat alter
                                        (between
snout and tail, the water pressure may vary three atmospheres)

the breathing violent,
lungs contracting,
expanding,

entire

_____

by cavitation—a string of vacuum bubbles—the whale trills, whis-
tles, squeaks, ticks, and clucks—

and hears snapping and crackling of shrimps and crabs,
                                        puffing and
grunting, grating and booming of fishes,
                              whining dolphins,
                                        sea birds
screeching overhead

the water moving,
            wind humming:
                        "creaks and cries, barks, groans,
and whoops"
            the sound waves landing on his length, his flanks a
sounding board

      and makes his way
      ocean to ocean,
      bottom to shore
      to food
      to whale

      by radar,

      sonar,

      sofar

PART TWO

      Scammon discovered the lagoon in the Baja,
      Scammon Lagoon,
      where the California gray
      foregathered for foreplay
      and mating.

      Scammon waited.

the harpooned whale lob-tailed, thrashing,
                        breached, leapt clear,
crashed back,
            snowing foam on the whaleboat;
                        writhed, sounded and

somersaulted, breaching behind,

                    "he went clean rampageous loony"

lashed the waters into a pink foam,

                  crashed the whale-boat into the

ship's side,

       or breached at night, the sky blue-black, the water

falling from his flanks in green columns, the foam phosphoric,

                        and

wrapping himself in whale lines, splintering the boat, rolled over
and over and over

"Then the bow actually touched the animal. The Lieutenant leaned forward and thrust in his lance quite near the eye, about a yard from the spot where the harpoon was fixed. After the thrust he began to shake the weapon, twisting it with a rotating movement, as if he meant to enlarge the wound. Red blood appeared on the brown body . . ."

"He thrust in the second lance, farther back this time, and stirred it in the wound. The blood came gushing as if from a tap."

"They also launce the whales near their privy-parts, if they can come at it; for if they are run in there, it doth pain them very much; nay, even when they are almost dead, if you run in your launce thereabout it causes the whole body to tremble."

. . . the whale enters his flurry, turning on his side, swimming in a circle, slowly, at first, then faster, and faster,

                    head above water, jaws

clashing;

       there is a hissing sound, then a fountain of steam, first

pink, then red,

         floods of blood spurting from the blowhole:

                        enters his

flowering, blows his blood . . .

            "Some whales blow blood to the very

last," says Scammon, "and these dash the men in the long-boats most filthily, and dye the sloops red ..."

"... the very sea is tinged red ..."

There is a low groan, growing to an echoing bellow—the lungs' last heavings through bloodclogged tubes

the bloodfountain dies to a few drops, a gurgle ...

"Those whales that are mortally wounded heat themselves, that they reek while they are alive, and the birds sit on them, and eat on them ..."

"... long and white maggots grow in their flesh,
they are flat,
like unto worms that breed in men's bellies,
and they smell worse
than ever I smelt anything in my life.
The longer the whale lies dead in the water,
the higher he doth swim above it;
some swim a foot high above the water,
others to their middle,
and then they do burst easily,
and give a very great report.
They begin immediately to stink,
and this encreases hourly,
and their flesh boils and ferments
like unto beer or ale,
and holes break in their bellies,
and their guts come out."

———

"My dear Wife and Mother,
Saturday of the 7 I got a whale that made 80 bbls after great del of trouble. He was one of the knowing kind. I strok him to my boat. The whale went off a little way and then came for the boat. He stov the boat ver bad so he seam to be contented with that and lade clost to me as the other to boats was off about 4 miles from me in chase

of other whales. Finly the Mate came to me. I told him never mind
me but get the whale if he cold. He went and struck him and the
whale stove his boat wost than mine, and heart 3 of the men. He
nock the Mate as hie as our house. Well I began to think that fish
was not for me. Her war to stoven boats and 12 men swimming in
the sea and the Ship and other boat long way off."

> ... rogue whale,
> biting whale, fighting
> whale ...

> ... Payta Tom, New
> Zealand Tom, Timor
> Jack ...

". . . I observed a very large spermaceti whale, as well as I could
judge about eighty-five feet in length; he broke water about twenty
rods off our weather bow, and was lying quietly, with his head in a
direction for the ship. He spouted two or three times, and then dis-
appeared. In less than two or three seconds he came up again, about
the length of the ship off, and made directly for us, at the rate of
about three knots. The ship was then going with about the same
velocity. His appearance and attitude gave us at first no alarm; but
while I stood watching his movements, and observing him but a
ship's length off, coming down for us with a great celerity, I invol-
untarily ordered the boy at the helm to put it hard up; intending to
sheer off and avoid him. The words were scarcely out of my mouth,
before he came down upon us with full speed, and struck the ship
with his head, just forward of the fore-chains; he gave us such an
appalling and tremendous jar, as nearly threw us all on our faces.
The ship brought up as suddenly and violently as if she had struck
a rock, and trembled for a few seconds like a leaf. We looked at each
other with perfect amazement, deprived almost of the power of
speech. Many minutes passed before we were able to realize the
dreadful accident; during which time he passed under the ship,
grazing her keel as he went along, came up alongside of her to lee-
ward, and lay on top of the water (apparently stunned with the vio-

lence of the blow) for the space of a minute; he then suddenly start-
ed off, in a direction to leeward. After a few moments reflection,
and recovering, in some measure, from the sudden consternation
that had seized us, I of course concluded that he had stove a hole in
the ship, and that it would be necessary to set the pumps going.
Accordingly they were rigged, but had not been in operation more
than one minute before I perceived the head of the ship to be grad-
ually settling down in the water; I then ordered the signal to be set
for the other boats, which, scarcely had I despatched, before I again
discovered the whale, apparently in convulsions, on the top of the
water, about one hundred rods to leeward. He was enveloped in the
foam of the sea, that his continual and violent thrashing about in
the water had created around him, and I could distinctly see him
smite his jaws together, as if distracted with rage and fury. He
remained a short time in this situation, and then started off with
great velocity, across the bows of the ship, to windward. By this time
the ship had settled down a considerable distance in the water, and
I gave her up for lost. I, however, ordered the pumps to be kept con-
stantly going, and endeavored to collect my thoughts for the occa-
sion. I turned to the boats, two of which we then had with the ship,
with an intention of clearing them away, and getting all things ready
to embark in them, if there should be no other resource left; and
while my attention was thus engaged for a moment, I was aroused
with the cry of a man at the hatchway, "Here he is—he is making
for us again." I turned around, and saw him about one hundred rods
directly ahead of us, coming down apparently with twice his ordi-
nary speed, and to me at that moment, it appeared with ten-fold
fury and vengeance in his aspect. The surf flew in all directions
about him, and his course towards us was marked by a white foam
of a rod in width, which he made with the continual violent thrash-
ing of his tail; his head was about half out of water, and in that way
he came upon, and again struck the ship. I was in hopes when I
descried him making for us, that by a dextrous movement of putting
the ship away immediately, I should be able to cross the line of his
approach, before he could get up to us, and thus avoid what I knew,
if he should strike us again, would prove our inevitable destruction.
I bawled out to the helmsman, "Hard up!" but she had not fallen off

more than a point, before we took the second shock. I should judge the speed of the ship to have been at this time about three knots, and that of the whale about six. He struck her to windward, directly under the cathead, and completely stove in her bows. He passed under the ship again, went off to leeward, and we saw no more of him."

"I began to reflect upon the accident, and endeavoured to realize by what unaccountable destiny or design (which I could not at first determine) this sudden and most deadly attack had been made upon us: by an animal, too, never before suspected of premeditated violence, and proverbial for its insensibility and inoffensiveness. Every fact seemed to warrant me in concluding that it was anything but chance which directed his operations; he made two several attacks upon the ship, at a short interval between them, both of which, according to their direction, were calculated to do us the most injury, by being made ahead, and thereby combining the speed of the two objects for the shock; to effect which, the exact manoeuvres which he made were necessary. His aspect was most horrible, and such as indicated resentment and fury. He came directly from the shoal which we had just before entered, and in which we had struck three of his companions, as if fired with revenge for their sufferings."

Did a whale grasp a loose sailor? . . . sound with him? . . . breaching, spit him out?

Is the spermaceti gorge too narrow to admit a man? . . . but a 10' shark? . . . a 35' squid?

Was a man swallowed, and recovered, later, dead? . . . the chest crushed? . . . the skin eaten, by gastrin and pepsin?

Was another swallowed, and lived, 24 hours, in a whale's stomach? . . . and when released, on the deck of *Star of the East,* was he revived with a bucket of sea water? . . . was he then a raving lunatic, two weeks, before recovering his senses?

And another, did he remember a great darkness? . . . slipping along a smooth passage? . . . his hands touching a slimy substance that seemed to shrink from his touch? . . . could he breathe? . . . and was the heat terrible—not scorching or stifling, but seeming to draw out his vitality through opened pores? . . . and were face, neck, and hands changed to parchment—bleached by cetacean juices?

The killer whale, *orca*, with truly falcate flukes, and an enormous dorsal fin—so slender that the tip turns over like the ear of a dog—

—the killer, though barrel-shaped and bulky, is capable of bursts of immense speed. Knife-edged, recurved, interlocking teeth line his jaws, and he swims in ranks five abreast, heads and tails turned downward, backs elevated all in one instant, with great sabre-formed fins

a shoal of killers, spouting as one, renders the ocean a plain of waving geysers.

Orca eats anything: seal, porpoise, penguin, salmon, a finback or humpback whale,

and will, in packs, attack the great blue:

the school dividing, some attack the flukes, biting in,
                                                    and the great

blue, fighting, hurls killers aloft,
                                descending flukes and *orcas* resounding on the seasurface,
while others of the school swim to the head, nipping the muzzle,

but all, all killers, working from the sea side, driving the quarry to the shallows.

When the tail is nailed to the seasurface, more killers plunge for the head, the eyes, the lips, while others leap over the blowhole, to smother,

      while one, lashing flukes, thrusts his snout between the lips, pushing against the horny strips, reaching for the tongue.

the great blue writhes, lunges clear of the foam, the clinging killers borne aloft,

and the one *orca* reaches the tender great blue tongue, bites in, begins to eat;

      the great jaw relaxes, goes slack, the tongue lolls out,
                        while
others churn for the eyes, the belly, the teats,
                 working always in an
arc, pushing the blue to the shallows, to the surf, to the beach

one killer sinks his teeth in the genitals,

and the great blue whale, insane with pain, brain flooded with fouled blood—thrashes, lunges inland—free, now, of *orca*—rolls in the breakers, comes to stillness in the backwash, the ripple, near the dry sand

              ——————

with an arm-length razor-knife the man stabs the sperm whale's head—the tough, spongy cells, the whitehorse—and lets the spermaceti flow

     clean and clear,
     clear as water,
     barrel after barrel,
     bubbling

         a film forms on the surface, and the stuff slows to a trickle, cools to ropy strings, icicles, frozen waxy waterfalls

     spermaceti, sperm

              ——————

the blubber-room men are bathed in oil,

       slipping with the ship's roll,
       rolling in blubber . . .

. . . on the butchering deck, piled high with meat, bones, steaming
intestines, the men work . . . in the clatter of the bone saws, steam
of the boilers, stench of guts . . . cables and winches, meat hooks,
whale oil, and bone dust

       and spread their legs,
       the wasted meat lumps,
       bone hunks,
       thickets of gut,
       sliding away

and after—a warm bath, a balanced meal, a show in the on-board
movie theatre,

and every year, in the long antarctic summer, some will lose their
reason.

---

out comes the fatty tongue, two tons, soft as a cushion
                            seven strong
men, or perhaps a steam winch, drag the half-ton head across the
oily deck
      and the blood pours, and pours, and pours
                      the intestine, re-
laxed, measures twelve hundred feet
                   the balls weigh a hundred
pounds, each
       and the prick is a thin, hard rope—like a bull's, a ram's,
a goat's, or a stag's—ten feet long and a foot thick

or, from inside the cunt, out come the ovaries, sixty-five pounds,
each
      and within, there may be an ovum—visible to a man's naked eye

---

the beached great blue,
alone and helpless,
heaves,
struggling to breathe

but the water-molded muscles,
the soft, spongy bones,
will not lift the
unsupported carcass,
for ventilation,

and the whale begins
to suffocate,

heaving in convulsions,
bellowing.

the scientist,
alerted to the prize,
stands aside,
appalled,
as the writhing dwindles,
the bellows soften to a wail—

until the man can stand it no longer,

puts a bullet through the great blue brain,

gets him out of his suffering,

and then goes about his work

BIBLIOGRAPHY

LUDD

Anonymous. *The Beggar's Complaint*. Sheffield, England, 1812.

Felkin, William. *History of the Machine Wrought Hosiery and Lace Manufactures*. London, 1863.

Hammond, J. L. & Hammond, B. *The Skilled Labourer*. London, 1919.

Peel, Frank. *The Risings of the Luddites*. Heckmondwike, England, 1895.

Pellew, G. *Life and Correspondence of H. Addington, 1st Viscount Sidmouth*. London, 1847.

Raynes, F. *An appeal to the public, containing an account of Services rendered during the Disturbances in the North of England in the year 1812*. London, 1817.

Rude, G. F. E. *The Crowd in History*. New York, 1964.

Thomas, Malcolm I. *The Luddites*. Newton Abbot, Devon, England, 1970.

Thornbury, Walter. *Old Stories Re-told*. London, 1870.

Ziegler, Philip. *Addington*. London, 1965.

EFIK

Atkins, John. *A Voyage to Guinea, Brazil and the West Indies*. London, 1737.

Blake, William O. *The history of slavery and the slave trade*. Columbus, Ohio, 1861.

Bosman, Willem. *A New and Accurate Description of the Coast of Guinea*. New York, 1966.

Brawley, B. G. *A short history of the American negro*. New York, 1927.

Churchill, John. *A collection of Voyages and Travels*, vols. 5 & 6. London, 1732.

Davidson, Basil. *Black mother*. London, 1961.

Dow, George F. *Slave Ships and Slaving*. Salem, Mass., 1927.

Drake, Richard. *Revelations of a Slave Smuggler*, ed. Henry B. West. New York, 1860.

Falconbridge, Alexander. *An Account of the Slave Trade on the Coast of Africa*. London, 1788.

Hawkins, Joseph. *A history of a voyage to the coast of Africa*. Philadelphia, 1797.

Hill, Pascoe G. *Fifty Days on Board a Slave Vessel*. New York, 1844.

Kingsley, M. H. *Travels in West Africa*. New York, 1897.

Manning, Edward. *Six Months on a Slaver*. New York, 1879.

Mannix, Daniel P. *Black cargoes.* New York, 1962.

Moore, Francis. *Travels in Africa.* London, 1738.

Newton, John. *The Journal of a Slave Trader.* London, 1962.

Pope-Hennessy, John. *Sins of the Fathers.* New York, 1968.

Richardson, William. *A Mariner of England.* London, 1908.

Williams, Gomer. *History of the Liverpool Privateers . . .* London, 1897.

ORCA

Andrews, Roy C. "Observations on the habits . . ." *Bulletin,* American Museum of Natural History, v. 26. 1909.

———. *Whale-hunting with a gun and camera.* New York, 1916.

Bennett, Frederick D. *Narrative of a Whale Voyage . . .* London, 1840.

Blond, Georges. *The Great Story of Whales.* New York, 1955.

———. *The Great Whale Game.* London, 1954.

Bullen, Frank T. *The Cruise of the Cachelot . . .* London, 1898.

Chase, Owen. *Narrative of the most Extraordinary and Distressing Shipwreck . . .* New York, 1963.

Cheever, H. T. *The whale and his captors.* New York, 1850.

Cousteau, Jacques-Yves. *The Whale.* New York, 1972.

Eschrift, D. F. *The Northern Species of Orca.* The Ray Society Publications, v. 40.

Kellogg, Remington. "The History of Whales," *Quarterly Review of Biology,* vol. 3, 1928.

McCombe, E. *Whales and whalers.* Sydney, Australia, 1940.

Riedman, Sarah R. and Gustafson, Elton T. *Home is the Sea: Whales.* New York, 1966.

Sanderson, Ivan T. *Follow the whale.* Boston, 1956.

Sawtell, Clement C. *The Ship Ann Alexander of New Bedford, 1805-1851.* Mystic, Conn., 1962.

Scammon, Charles M. *The Marine Mammals of the Northwestern Coast of North America.* San Francisco, 1874.

Scheffer, Victor B. *The Year of the Whale.* New York, 1969.

Slijper, E. J. *Some Remarks on Gestation and Birth in Cetacea and other Aquatic Mammals.* Oslo, 1956.

———. *Whales.* New York, 1962.

Wilson, Ambrose J. "The Sign of the Prophet Jonah and its Modern Confirmation," *Princeton Theological Review,* vol. 25, 1927.

APALACHE

"... the reverberation often exceeds through silence the sound that sets it off; the reaction occasionally outdoes by way of repose the event that stimulated it; and the past not uncommonly takes a while to happen ..."

—Ken Kesey

BASH BISH

ONE

it happens that the land is smelt before it is seen

The fragrance drifts seaward / we smelled the land a hundred leagues, and farther *when they burned the cedars* / before we come in sight of it thirty leagues, we smell a sweet savour / we had now fair sunshine weather, and so pleasant a sweet air as did much refresh us, and there came a smell off the shore like the smell of a garden / the air smelt as sweet and strong / richly scented with *the fragrance of the pines* / the wind brought to us the finest effluvia / the odorous fmell and beawtie / small wooddes very well smellinge / the sweet fragrance *of spruce* / adorned and clothed with *palms, laurels, cypresses* . . . which, for a long distance, exhale the sweetest odors / a marvelous sweet smell

WE HAD SMELLING OF THE SHORE

(noddy tern, moonfish, grunt)

> chub, jack, garr
> pike, cat, carp

(the progress of the ships impeded?)

maids and wives
sheldrake, brant

---

wee difcouered and clearely perceyued a fayre Coaft, ftreschyng of a
great length

(prima vista!

     high craggy Cliffy Rocks
     whitish, low
     stony Iles
     and higher up covered with firs
     a twinkling mountaine
     high and fayre trees

we fayled and vewed the coaft all along with unfpeakable pleafure

(terra optima! et temporata!

---

it is not possible to describe how this bay swarms with fish, both
large and small

     (wild duck, oyster, squirrel)
     (tunny, porpoise, whale)

a flocke of stocke-doues in so great number

birds diversely feathered

---

we viewed the land about vs, being . . . very sandie and low towards
the waters side, but so full of grapes, as the very beating and surge
of the sea ouerflowed them, of which we found such plentie, as well
there as in all places else, both on the sand and on the green soile on
the hils, as in the plaines, as well on euery little shrubbe, as also
climing towardes the tops of high Cedars

as the very beating and surge of the sea ouerflowed them

Sept. 9th. In the afternoon we remarked that in fome places the colour of the fea (which has been hitherto of a deep blue) was changed into a paler hue: fome of thefe fpots were narrow ftripes of twelve or fourteen fathoms breadth, of a pale green colour, which is fuppofed to be caufed by the fand, or, as fome fay, by the weeds under water

       the bottome of the bay then appearing as a greene meadow

      at night, we heard the rut of the shoare

the woody islands at the sea
         the sea shore covered with myrtle,
peach-trees, orange trees and vines in the wild woods
                     not
choaked up with undershrubs
         the soiles there upon the sea
coaste, and all along the tracte of the greate broad mightie
ryvers, all alonge many hundreth miles into the inland,
are infinitely full fraughte with swete wooddes
               compassed
about . . . with oaks, pines, juniper, sassafras
            wooded to the
brink of the sea

wild Vines runne naturally / the ground doth naturally bring foorth vines / the wild vines cover all the hills along the rivers / I have seen whole pieces of land where vine stood by vine / and diverse grape vines which though growing without Culture in the very throng of weedes and bushes were yett filled with bunches of grapes to admiracon / Vines in many parts on the Sea Shore, bearing multitude of Grapes, where one would wonder they should get Nourishment / in suche abundance, as where soever a man treads they are ready to embrace his foote / Those Grapes, I say, lying over bushes and brambles / to behold the goodly vines burthening every neighbor bush, and clymbing the toppes of highest trees, and those full of

clusters of the grapes in their kind, however dreeped and shadowed
soever from the sun / Grapes so prodigiously large / Vines, in big-
ness of a man's thigh / having the trunke three and foure foote high
and as bigge as ones fist in the lower part, the Grapes faire and great
/ of such greatnes, yet wild / grapes exceedinge good and sweett of
to Sorts both red butt the on of them ys a marvellous deepe red /
swollen grapes / grape neere as great as a Cherry . . . they bee fatte,
and the iuse thicke / black Bunch-Grapes which yield a Crimson
juice . . . well knit in the Clusters

And beyond this we saw the open Countrey rising in height aboue
the sandy shoare with many faire fields and plaines full of mighty
great woods
               a beautiful hill, rising gently from the sea, its sides
bathed by two springs
                    the bordering land is a most rich neighbor
trending all along on both sides, in an equal plaine, neither moun-
tainous nor rocky, but verged with a greene bordure of grasse
                                                        And
sayling forwards, we found certaine small Riuers and armes of the
Sea, that fall downe by certaine creekes, washing the shoare on both
sides as the coast lyeth
               An outstretched country . . . rising
somewhat above the sandy shore
                         all the low land . . . is conjectured to
have been naturally gayned out of the sea
                                   virged with a green bor-
der of grasse . . . so making tender unto the
eye of the surveyor her fertility and pleasure

I have nowhere seen so many ducks together . . . and when they flew
up there was a rushing and vibration of the air like a great storm
coming through the trees, and even like the rumbling of distant
thunder, while the sky . . . was filled with them like a cloud
                                                  Birds fill
also the woods so that men can scarcely go through them for the
whistling, the noise and the chattering

Pigeons fly wild and in the
Woods great Flocks of Parrakeetos

In march the eeles come forth
out of places where they lie bedded all winter, into the fresh
streames

it is a thing unſpeakable to conſider the thinges that bee ſeene there
... in this incomparable lande

as the very beating and surge of the sea ouerflowed them

The land towards the Mouth of the Rivers is generally of a low
moist and fat Mould such as the heavier sort of Grain delight in
The Mould in some Places is black fat and thick laid The vesture of
the earth in most places doth manifestly proue the nature of the
soile to be lusty and very rich exceeding fat and fertill a good Soyl
covered with black Mold The crust of the earth a spit's depth excel-
lent black earth a fast fat earth fat and lustie strong and lustie of its
own nature

(In many places are lowe Thicks
(low land that is stiff and rich
we stood a while like men ravished at the beautie and delicacie of
this sweet soile

All the spring-time the earth sendeth
forth naturally

Going forward we found rich ground but having curious rising hills
and brave meadows

at the top of a hill we saw lying south west a
curious prospect of hills like waves raised by a gentle breese of wind
one upon another

the countrey was marvellously sweet, with both
marish and medow ground

every day we did more and more discov-
er the pleasant fruitfulness

many ample rich and pregnant valleys

the

farther we went, the more pleasing it was to every man, alluring us
still with expectation of better

for the continent is of an huge and

unknowen greatnesse

several springs and fallings / pure springs of most excellent water
pleasantly distilling from their rockie foundations / fresh water,
which streameth doune / the Water is clear, fresh and fit for Brew-
ing / and such intersections and doublings of wood and Water /
with such Fresh-waters running through the woods as I was almost
rauished at the first sight / This river, running along the valley to
seek the sea, comes to this hill where it runs over a large blue rock,
which is broken in two, obliquely with the river / As you come near
the falls, you can hear the roaring which makes everything tremble
/ there is constantly spray ascending like smoke, which scatters itself
like rain. In this spray, when the sun shines, the figure of a rainbow
is constantly to be seen trembling and shaking, and even appearing
to move the rock

Great haboundaunce of woddes ther be
the grafs man-high unmowed tall Timber
Trees unlopped and the wodd she beareth
is not shrubbish . . . but goodly oake,
birch, tall firre and spruse mulberrie,
applecrab Cedar and Cypress Vines, Saxe-
fras Oakes, and Wal-nut trees, and Chest-
nut trees, Ewe trees, and trees of sweet
wood blue plums and finest oaks some small
young birch, bordering low upon the river
an infinity of Candleberry Myrtle Willough,
Alder and Holly with other trees, which
issues out sweet Gummes our way em-
barrassed by trees an absolute Forrest

The excellencie of this part of the River, for his good breadth, depth, and fertile bordering ground, did so ravish us / a brave pleasant River as can be desired / blessed with . . . fishful rivers

The ground in the flat land near the rivers is covered with strawberries, which grow here so plentifully in the fields, that one can lie down and eat them

the aboundance of grasse that groweth everie where . . . But it groweth verie wildly with a great stalke and a broad and ranker blade

Here growes in the Woods abundance of wortleberries or Whorts

strawberryes and mulberyes new shaken of the tree the fields Covered with Strawberries and wild Onions

the ground all flowing over with faire flowers

The sight of the faire medowes is a pleasure not able to be expressed with tonge

(the crye and brayeng of wild beastes herde

in the night tyme

(Elks are very plenty

(and buffalo east of appalatcy

and what else we know not yet, because our daies are young

TWO

accokeek acquack

up the susquehanna and juniata, across the mountains at kithanne

sasquesahanock, patowomek, chesepiook

choccoloco,

chockolog
>fakahatchee, loxahatchee
>>meddybemps, saukatunkarunk

out of the valley of menaun-gehilla to the mouth of little kanawha

chaubuqueduck, messatsoosec . . . twada-alahala . . . machaquama-
gansett . . . the kenogamishish . . . connoharriegoharrie . . . near
egunk hill, the upper part of moosup's: peagwompsh

a branch to the forks of youghiogheny

chinklamoose askiminikonson kaskaskank *across the north and east
forks of quemehoning* aggamogin rippogenus quinnehtokqut *across
the nipnet and between the breastshaped hills* sisquisie taghkanick
wyalusing wyomissing *at quabaug six trails converged* mobjack coin-
jock *the big bone blue lick trail* skunkscut nipsic chipchug scantic *from
the head of clinch to the fork of tug* nisquitianxet gungywamps scitico
woxodawa *the licking route* sankety unkety nausset *the north prong of
nickajack* scusset

*the black fox trail began at the cherokee towns along the hiwassee,
passed rattlesnake springs, crossed the hiwassee and followed down-
stream along the north side, crossed the tennessee at hiwassee island,
and continued west to the mounds in sequatchie valley*

>sopchoppy chequepee quaddic
>capawack cotuit quidnic
>sebec naugus obscob
>moxie nissitisset wisconk

>stissing catsjajock

hackinkasacky hobocan nayack picipsi sinsink

>chenango cheningo
>(cheningo chenango)

from the lower towns of the cherokee to babahatchie

ochriskeny lackawack   *from cisca, by the*
ruttawoo ocitoc   *black fox spring, to*
navisink goynish   *the great lick*

catawissa shantituck   *by way of tioga, lycoming*
santuit tatnuck   *creek, to tuscarora valley*

tellico jellico   *through auchquick, the*
chopmist popsic   *kusk kusks, to hockhockon*

shagwango congamuck   *over stony hills, across*
snipsic boxet   *sholola creek at the falls*

sneeksuck yawgobby   *on the border of the hard*
sunquams passquesit   *land, and up to the great rocks*

minisink appoquinimink   *portage at pemaquid,*
succabonk pagganck   *thence up the damariscotta*
machepaconaponsuck   *to sheepscot waters*

```
        moose                    scook
            sneech                                    sag
      sip
                          scug
tug               tist
                                              slank
      puss cuss
```

---

*left the river beyond the openings, to a spring that issued from a
ravine—up the mohawk, across schoharie & canajoharie, thence onei-
da country, across oriskany, oneida, canasawga & chittenango, thence
to the deep spring on the onondaga boundary, and onondaga villages on
the river—across owasco outlet, into land of the cayugas, and the lake
—to the seneca river, the territory of the senecas: canandaigua, and the
genesee—across tonawanda, to the tuscaroras, and niagara*

euchee nacoochee elloree sewee
wateree sugaree santee tybee
congaree sautee yemassee wimbee

otsego owego otsquaga otsdawa
otseningo oghwaga otego otstungo

passadumkeag mattawamkeag kassanunganumkeag
nahumkeag maskeag amoskeag kenduskeag

*from pontegwa, the river falls, past watanic and ko–iss, to namaskik for
the fishing—thence to penikook, past lake winnisquam, lake opeechee
and aquadoctan, to chenayok: the mouro–mak–winnebis–aki trail*

naumkeag okfuskee ochenana   meduxnekeag withlacoochee
oswegatchie   penobskeag hatchechubbee owasco *on the east bank
of the susquehanna, the paxtang path*   transquaking rockawalking
*by the great pond from high land aslant to the lower part of the great
plain*   pissepunk podpis
    owego to susquehanna: the lake-to-lake middle trail   sunsicke
arrowsic   *from the long calm to the falls of potapsco* bigbee lublub
tashmoo tombigbee *across the mauromak, following the ocean sand,
reaching the penobscot, and upstream*   nipscop tickfaw moodus
trails on both sides of the genesee   bash bish shickshock   *across
fishing creek to shickshinny* anacostia anticosti *between the alarka and
the tuckasegee, with a stone cairn on the ridge*   quassaconkanuck
to allaquapy's gap yawgunsk

great salted standing water
where the sun shines out
at the bushy place
at the place of mud
first or oldest planted ground
the dancing place
at the pine spring
a long straight river
a meadow

bull thistle
tidewater covered with froth
the place where clams are found
the sprucy stream
at the sweating place
at the sweet land
the place of fear
the place where deer are shy

beginning at conestoga, the trail crossed the susquehanna at connejoho-
la, crossed the headwaters of conewago creek, crossed catoctin creek, the
monockissey and the potomac, and extended on to opequon

zinnodowanha

THREE

the earth an ocean. the earth ocean.

and here and there,

an island.

---

eruption (the magma plastic,

erosion (the gravitic creep of scree,

uplift
and
deposition

islands and rims of mountains emerging offisland, embayed water-
bodies silting and filling, new land joining old land, the land isosta-
tic, land cores filling to rims, single and double arcs, new rims
erupting

the islands grew,
the islands
became c o n t i n e n t a l

———————

appalachia:

manufacture of rock:

the compression of sediments washed from
old mountains to the east, the moisture squeezed out, mud pressed
to shale

tropical forests hardened to coal

and the making of mountains:

the wedge of sediments pressed and up-
lifted
crumpled squeezed wrinkled
raised and eroded
overturned
and overthrust over the planes of fracture
anticline
arches, syncline troughs
folded, faulted
lowangle dips, pitching
folds, warped, pitching at random
inlying coves
the overthrust slab
worn through, to become a window to the ancient complex rock
beneath

appalachia:

resistant relic of metamorphism, the
roots and stumps, the truncated base of
diastrophic tilts and folds

the forelands, the sediments, the clastic wedges

flanked by monadnocks in the piedmont, by swarms of ultrabasic rock in the crystalline oldland of new england

and marching to burial, beneath its own sediments in the deep marine embayment to the south . . . to the north, drowned, at percé, gaspé

---

appalachia, uplifted to a peneplain, incised by drainage superposed:

the watersheds divided asymmetrically, the streams rejuvenated, the patterns dendritic, trellised, rectangular, parallel

the rivers washing out the softer sediments, cutting through ridges at the water gaps

strong streams working headward, beheading the weaker, pirating the waters

> (strike tributaries gained strength, effected captures

> (the shenandoah crept up the great valley, beheaded virginia rivers, leaving a trail of wind gaps

> (the tugaloo captured the chattooga at tallulah

the appalachian river, the ancestral tennessee, flowed to the south-west, through the great valley and into the gulf

and save only for swamps and bogs, cliffs or river bluffs, windfalls, burns, serpentine barrens and balds—all appalachia forested

going east → oldland, coastal plain, fluctuant shoreline, continental shelf the shoreline:

> the atlantic plain, moderately elided, a faint escarp-
> ment at the barrier islands

shelf & plain,

> low country & shallow sea,
> > interchangeable, interchanging

and northward ↑ the plain submerging, reaching zero at the deep
and ancient hudson, emerging northward only as islands, as

the inner and outer cuestas:
> long island, the vineyard, sable island
> cape charles, cape may, nantucket

> > (the new england coastal plain submerged,
> > transected still with old rivers

the low country a gently tilting coastal plain,
> and florida a low anticline, a limestone upwarp
> > (ground water rising to fill lake swarms
> > > (and two miles deep, appalachian
> > > depositional distribution

> florida,

> > the grand banks,

sable island: the crest of the inner cuesta, isolate from the oldland,
an emergence . . .

the continent downtilted northeastward

> > uplifted southwestward

on the fulcrum of the narrows

———————

in ancient mature soils (melanized and lateritic), the mixed mesaphy-
tic forest of midappalachia:

>   *beech, tulip, basswood in the arboreal layer, the superior layer,*
>   *sugar maple, sweet buckeye, chestnut, oak and hemlock*

>>   *dogwood, magnolia in the understory, sourwood,*
>>   *striped maple,*

redbud, ironwood
hophornbeam, holly

>>   *mull plants rooting in the porous and fri-*
>>   *able soil*

>>   *(along the streams: willow, sycamore,*
>>   *sweet gum and river birch*

the cumberlands: a large fault block with upturned edges

the oldest, most complex association: towering columnar trees, widely
spaced, growing in crumb mull humus / the southern highland hemlock
of undoubted antiquity / on sandy soils of the dip slopes, pine / umbrel-
la magnolia a conspicuous ravine tree / white oak dominant on lime-
stone / pitch pine on the massive rock outcrops / hemlock in the rocky
talus / shellbark and pignut hickory

>>   *gnarly hardwood stands, subalpine*
>>   *orchards, balds with grass and sedge*

heath shrubs, spruce flats,
hemlock bottoms, oak barrens,
on the black shale slopes

>>   *the vernal and estival*

>>   *flora of the cove*
>>   *hardwoods*

a luxuriant herbaceous layer.

as a species dies in the transitional forest, another is released

> *old endemics, relics of an earlier*
> *community*

———————

the coast was drowned, the streams dismembered

> elliptical drumlins, nw by se, weymouth great
> hill, the harbor . . . and beyond the narrows, a
> river channel mountaindeep . . . to the north,
> hard rock, and south, the drumlins crushed,
> sand, tombolos

the northflowing rivers ponding, filling with ice, reversing direction

> ice overtaking a mountain, the stoss side rounded and pol-
> ished, the lee slope made rugged by plucking

> > (on the lee side, steps, a cliff, a
> > chasm, talus and erratics

> > (surfaces polished and striat-
> > ed by the rockshod ice

cirques & scarps

> frontal, terminal and ground moraines,
> outwash veneers, outwash plains,
> glacial & fluvioglacial remains

eskers & drumlins

> on the passadumkeag sheet, morainic areas, kames

and in boston harbor, the drumlins swarm.

as the ice retreated, the land lifted, the ephemeral lakes became
rivers, leaving terraces and varves at annual horizons

> in the outwash plains,
> sanded wind shaped the stones:
> ventifacts

*angiosperms, rafted south on the melting bergs, came to rest, to form a
disjunct community*

———

woods hole and the narrows: morainal deposits transected
                                        old rivers
blocked by till and drift, new lakes, swamps and falls
                                        new rivers:
creases, furrows in the outwash plain
                        the land uplifted, a terrace
added, okefenokee sound captured behind trail ridge, swamped
                                                        the
hudson scoured, the ocean flowing to lake albany, or, perhaps a
marine strait, to the st. lawrence
                        the adirondacks draining radially

———

*at the highest elevations: firforest,
with oxalis, liverwort,
shieldfern and moss*

> *forbs and dwarf shrubs*

the hobblebush and yew

> *(in the seven mountains,
> a boreal relic*

the forest migrating to and fro, with advance and retreat of the ice

midappalachia: the tension zone, northern and southern species inter-
penetrating—inliers, outliers

semivirgin (primary but not virgin

>   *xeric cliff margin communities,*
>   *gnarly oaks and crevice shrubs*

north appalachia: a deciduous-coniferous mosaic

>   *lichened sandstone blocks.*
>   *scrub pine on the shaly slopes*

>   *virgin stands and coppice sprouts*

>   *pond pines in*
>   *the shrub bogs*

>   *a salt spray climax*
>   *at sandy hook:*
>   *red maple and holly*

>   *red and sweet bay,*
>   *following old white cedar*

with the final retreat of ice, the seed fell and grew in ground rock, rock
flour

(young soils, podzols, partake of the character of the substratum)

>   wave action, the land frontally attacked, distributed
>   north to long point, south to nausset, monomoy

>   rockaway, sandy hook, and
>   south, the long bars mask the
>   drowned line, the lagoons and

estuaries silting, the sea en-
croaching

the boston drumlins swarm, cliffed by waves

the plain terraced with faint scarps, old shorelines, shore
to piedmont

the land planed by waves, veneered with sediment

broken into necks and islands, fresh swamp, salt marsh,
fresh and salt estuary

attacked and erroded, washed and deposited

in spits:

compound, parasitic, barbed, and baby

THE FEARE IN YE BUTTOCKS

ONE

Many have trauayled to fearch
the coaft of the lande of Labrador,

> afwell to th intente to knowe
> howe farre or whyther it reachethe,

> > as alfo whether there bee any paffage by fea through
> > the fame into the fea of Sur and the Ilandes

... which are vnder the Equinoctiall line:

> > thinkynge that the waye thyther fhulde greatly
> > bee fhortened by this vyage ...

This yeere one Sebastian Gaboto,
a Genoa's sonne, borne in Bristow,
professing himself to be experte in
knowledge of the circuite of the
worlde and Ilandes of the same,
as by his charts and other reasonable
demonstrations he shewed, caused
the King to man and victual a shippe
at Bristow, to search for an Ilande ...

> > Sebastion Cabot was the fyrft that brought any
> > knowledge of this lande. For being in Englande in the

dayes of Kyng Henry the feuenth, he furnyſſhed twoo
ſhippes at his owne charges or (as ſum ſey) at the kyn-
ges, whome he perſuaded that a paſſage might bee
founde to Cathay by the north ſees, and that ſpices
myght be brought from thenſe ſoner by that way . . .

(Voyages, Navigations and Discoveries . . . to . . .
the backeside of Gronland . . .)

He sailed in the spring with three hundred companions, set his
course to the west until he sighted land in forty-five degrees of
north latitude, and went on by that land to sixty degrees, where the
days are eighteen hours long and the nights are very clear and
bright.

. . . even in the moneth of July
he found monstrous heapes of ice
swimming on the sea,

and in maner continuall day light,

yet saw he the land in that tract free from ice,
which had been molten by the heat of the sunne.

The soile is barren in some places,
and yeeldeth litle fruit,
but it is full of white beares . . .

In the yeare a thouſande and fiue hundreth, Gaſpar Cortefreales,
made a vyage thyther with two carauelles: but founde not the
ſtreyght or paſſage he ſought . . .

In their iourney they were so farre Northwards, that they sawe
mightie Islands of yce in the sommer season, on which were haukes
and other foules to rest themselves being wearie of flying over farre
from the maine.

The 21. day we had sight of a great drift of yce, seeming a firme lande, and we cast Westward to be cleare of it.

This day at 4. of the cloke in the morning, being faire and cleere, we had sight of a head land . . . and when we came thither, wee could not get to the lande for yce: for the yce stretched along the coast, so that we could not come to the land . . .

. . . this night we wer trobbled with much drift ise . . .

. . . the ise being some tymes very thick and some tymes more skattringe.

. . . mountayns of ise fleting and driving with the wyndes and tydes and streams . . .

. . all this 24 howers we were so pestred with ise . . .

From satordaye at noone tyll mydnyght we gyded our shipp to the westward amongst the ise with our ores, hoaping to get through, butt we were sodaynly compassed about with many great ilands of ise, and continewed sore distressed with a sore storme of winde at southeast, being fogie and thick wether, that we were so crushed betwixt myghty great Ilands that we were in danger every minet to be crushed in peeces with force of the heaving and setting of the sayd ise with the great sea that the wynd made . . .

we found our Greene Sea againe,
which by proofe we found to be
freest from Ice,
and our Azure Blue Sea
to be
our Icie sea . . .

The seuenteenth, at night, we heard the rut of the shoare, as we thought; but it prooued to be the rutt against a banke of Ice that lay on the shoare. It made a hollow and hideous noyse . . .

. . . that great Island of yce fell one part from another, making a noyse as if a great cliffe had fallen into the Sea.

> . . . we tasted cold stormes, in so much that it seemed we had
> changed summer with winter . . .

> . . . being the sixe and twentieth of July, there fell so much
> snow, with such bitter cold aire, that we could not scarce see
> one another for the same, nor open our eyes to handle our
> ropes and sayles . . .

> . . . such an horrible snow, that it lay a foot thick upon the
> hatches . . .

> . . . every man perswading himselfe that the winter there
> must needes be extreme, where they found so unseasonable a
> Sommer.

> > . . . such a high and hollow sea . . .

> > . . . thicke fog, cold and slabbie weather . . .

> > . . . very thick and foggie weather . . .

> > . . . a high-growne Sea . . .

> > . . . a stinking fogge . . .

> Our sole hope was in seeing, at times, great numbers
> of birds . . .

And on the 21st of the said month of May we set forth from the
harbour with a west wind, and sailed north, one quarter north-east
of cape Bonavista as far as the isle of Birds, which island was com-
pletely surrounded and encompassed by a cordon of loose ice . . .

> In spite of this belt our two long boats were sent off to the
> island to procure some of the birds, whose numbers are so

great as to be incredible, unless one has seen them . . .
            In the air and round about are an hundred times as
many more as on the island itself . . .

            And these birds are so fat that it is marvelous . . .

Isle des Ouaiseaulx . . .

    auks, murres, puffins,
    gannets, guillemots

    . . . certain great white foules with redde billes and redde legs
    . . .

They affirm that the sea is full of fish . . .

This morning, one of our companie looking over board saw
a Mermaid, and calling up some of the companie to see her,
one more came up, and by that time shee was come close to
the ships side, looking earnestly on the men: a little after, a
Sea came and overturned her: from the Navill upward, her
backe and breasts were like a womans, (as they say that saw
her) her body as big as one of us; her skin very white; and
long haire hanging downe behind, of colour blacke: in her
going downe they saw her tayle, which was like the tayle of a
Porposse, and speckled like a Macrell.

Heading north-west we ranged these coasts, first on one side and
then on the other, to see if this was a bay or a strait . . .

And as we wished to examine this opening, to see if there was any
good anchorage and a harbour, we lowered the sails for the night.

    a dangerous gulf
    between land new found,

and unknown land
. . . east-north-east and south
with a little westing
and the passage is a narrow one.

> We found also birch and willow
> growing like shrubbes
> low to the ground.

. . . thirty-eight fathoms
and weedy bottom.

Here runnes a quicke tyde into the Straight . . .

> . . . this place seemeth to have
> a marvellous great indraft,
> and draweth unto it . . .
> things which doe fleete in the Sea . . .

Indeavoring to goe forward,
wee were fast inclosed amongst it
and so droue to and againe with it . . .

> . . . the sea falling down
> into the gulfe
> with a mighty overfal,
> and roring,
> and with divers circular motions
> like whirle pooles . . .

. . . this day we entred the streight.

> . . . and we found we were shot farre into the Inlet,
> being almost a Bay, and environed with very high
> Mountaynes, with low land lying between them . . .

> . . . in the mouth of the Straights,

our passage was very narrow,
and difficult
but being once gotten in,

we had a faire open place . . .

. . . you may anchor in ten-fathom water
over against a little nook . . .

(. . . and found there duck eggs
in great quantity . . .)

We named the sayd gulfe Saint Laurence his bay.

. . . in the very mouth
of the great river
that runneth up to Canada . . .

. . . *and the Indians predicted that if Cartier attempted to ascend*
the great river, he would be destroyed by snows, tempests and
floating ice . . .

Our wild men told vs that there was the beginning of Saguenay, and
that it was land inhabited . . . The sayd men did moreouer certifie
vnto vs, that there was the bay and beginning of the great riuer of
Hochelaga and ready way to Canada, which riuer the further it
went the narrower it came, euen vnto Canada, and that then there
was fresh water, which went so farre vpwards, that they had neuer
heard of any man who had gone to the head of it, and that there is
no other passage but with small boates . . .

The whole country on both sides of this river . . . is as fine a
land and as level as ever one beheld. There are some moun-
tains visible at a considerable distance from the river, and
into it several tributaries flow down from these. This land is
everywhere covered and overrunn with timber of several

sorts and also with quantities of vines . . .
There are numerous gooseberry bushes, strawberry vines,
Provins roses, as well as parsley and other useful, strong-
smelling herbs.

. . . with trees unto the brink of the river.

Our Captaine then caused our boates to be set in order, that with
the next tide he might goe vp higher into the riuer, to find some safe
harborough for our ships: and we passed vp the riuer against the
streame about tenne leagues . . . where is a little riuer and hauen,
where by reason of the flood there is about three fadome water. This
place seemed to vs very fit and commodious to harbour our ships
therein, and so we did very safely . . .

The first winter, snow rose past the sides of the ships, anchored in
the river . . . and at Port Royal, Champlain's cider and wine
froze in the casks . . .

And as we came out of the river, we saw one of the headmen of the
Stradacona Indians coming to meet us, accompanied by several
men, women and children; and he began to make an harangue,
expressing joy and contentment after the manner of the country,
while the squaws danced and sang uninterruptedly, being in the
water up to their knees . . . And when we were a league or so away,
we still heard them singing, dancing and rejoicing over our visit.

. . . and there the River of Canada beginneth to be
fresh and the salt water endeth.

. . . we were led by a number of the men and women to the aforesaid
mountain which we called Mount Royal . . . When we reached the
summit, we could see for more than thirty leagues around. To the
north is a range of mountains, running east and west, and a similar
range to the south; between which is a most goodly district, fertile,
flat, and level; through the middle of it, beyond the spot where we

had left our boats, we saw the river flow, and a most furious water-
fall, impossible for us to pass, and as far as eye could reach we saw
the river extend to the south-west, great and broad and wide, pass-
ing close to three beautiful round hills which we saw . . . and we
were told and shown by signs . . . that there were three such water-
falls in the river like the one where our boats were . . .

> Then they made signs that after passing these falls one could
> sail up the river for more than three moons . . .

. . . and that beyond Saguenay the said river entereth into two or 3
great lakes . . .

That there is a fall about a league in breadth, where a wondrous
great rush of water plunges into this lake . . .

. . . and that there is a Sea of fresh water found, and . . . there was
never man heard of that found out the end thereof . . .

> *Mer Douce,*
> *the sweetwater sea . . .*

TWO

In order to practice patience in good earnest and to endure hard-
ships beyond the limit of human strength it is only necessary to
make journeys with the savages, and long ones especially, such as we
did; because, besides the danger of death on the way, one must make
up one's mind to endure and suffer more than could be imagined,
from hunger, from the stench that these dirty disagreeable fellows
emit almost constantly in their canoes, from walking with great
labour in water and bogs and in some places over rocks, and through
dark thick woods, from rain on one's back and all the evils that the
season and weather can inflict, and from being bitten by a countless
swarm of mosquitos and midges . . .

Add to these difficulties that one must sleep on the bare earth, or on a hard rock, for lack of a space ten or twelve feet square on which to place a wretched hut; that one must endure continually the stench of tired-out savages; and must walk in water, in mud, in the obscurity and entanglement of the forest . . .

Be with whom you like, you must expect to be, at least, three or four weeks on the way, to have as companions persons you have never seen before; to be cramped in a bark canoe in an uncomfortable position, not being free to turn yourself to one side or the other; in danger fifty times a day of being upset or of being dashed upon the rocks. During the day, the Sun burns you; during the night, you run the risk of being a prey to Mosquitos. You sometimes ascend five or six rapids in a day; and, in the evening, the only refreshment is a little corn crushed between two stones and cooked in fine clear water; the only bed is the earth, sometimes only the rough, uneven rocks, and usually no roof but the stars; and all this in perpetual silence.

> It is a strange thing when victualls are wanting,
> worke whole nights & dayes,
> Lye downe on the bare ground,
>   & not allwayes that hap,
> the breech in the water,
>   the feare in yᵉ buttocks . . .

. . . harden thy soul, resist hunger; thou wilt be sometimes two, sometimes three or four days without food; do not let thyself be cast down, take courage . . .

> There is no safety in crossing the rivers of this country by fording unless one knows them well, because there are a great many quicksands, in which one sinks so far that it is impossible to get out.

It was snowing hard; but, with necessity urging us on, the bad weather could not stop us.

We ftayed 14 dayes in this place moft miserable, like to a
churchyard; ffor there did fall fuch a quantity of fnow and
froft, and wth fuch a thick mift, that all the fnow ftoocke to
thofe trees that are there fo ruffe, being deal trees, pruffe
cedars, and thorns, that caused ye darkneffe uppon y^t earth
that it is to be believed that the fun was eclipfd . . .

In some places, where the current is not less strong than in these
rapids, although easier at first, the Savages get into the water, and
haul and guide by hand their canoes with extreme difficulty and
danger; for they sometimes get in up to the neck and are compelled
to let go their hold, saving themselves as best they can from the
rapidity of the water, which snatched from them and bears off their
canoe.

> We left the Iroquoits in his fort
> and the feare in our breeches,
> for w^thout apprehenfion
>   we rowed from friday to tuefday
> w^thout intermiffion.

> We had fcarce to eat
> a bitt of fault meat.

> It was a pitty to fee our feete & leggs in blood
> by drawing our boats through the fwift ftreames,
> where the rocks have fuch fharp points
> that there is nothing but death
> could make men doe what we did.

———

If you go to visit them in their cabins . . . you will find there a minia-
ture picture of Hell,—seeing nothing, ordinarily, but fire and
smoke, and on every side naked bodies, black and half roasted, min-
gled pell mell with the dogs, which are held as dear as the children
of the house, and share the beds, plates, and food of their masters.
Everything is in a cloud of dust, and, if you go within, you will not

reach the end of the cabin, before you are completely befouled with soot, filth, and dirt.

Instead of being a great master and great Theologian as in France, you must reckon on being here a humble Scholar, and then, good God! with what masters!—women, little children and all the Savages,—and exposed to their laughter. The Huron language will be your saint Thomas and your Aristotle; and clever man as you are, and speaking glibly among learned and capable persons, you must make up your mind to be for a long time mute among the Barbarians. You will have accomplished much, if, at the end of a considerable time, you begin to stammer a little.

> . . . to tell the truth, the life of missionaries in this country is the most dissipating life that can be imagined. Scarcely anything is thought of but bodily necessities, and the constant example of the savages, who think only of satisfying their flesh, brings the mind into an almost inevitable enervation . . .

As to the matter of food,
it is such as to cause all the books to be burned
that cooks have ever made . . .

> The ordinary diet is Indian corn . . .
> the seasoning with meat or fish,
> when you have any.

Now when they were in the open country and the hour for encamping arrived, they would seek some fitting spot on the bank of a river for a camp, or in another place where dry wood could easily be found to make a fire; then one of them set himself to look for it and collect it, another to put up the lodge and find a stick on which to hang the kettle at the fire, another look for two flat stones for crushing the Indian corn over a skin spread out on the ground, and afterwards to put it into the kettle and boil it . . . there was always dirt and refuse, partly because they used fresh stones every day, and very dirty ones, to crush the corn. Besides, the bowls could hardly have a pleasant smell, for when they were under the necessity of making water in their canoe they usually used the bowl for the purpose . . .

> . . . a Beaver in the morning,
> and in the evening of the next day
> a Porcupine as big
> as a sucking Pig.

> . . . we were forc'd to feafon our *indian* Corn . . . with little Frogs that the Natives gather'd in the Meadows . . .

> . . . we lived on wild garlick, which we were obliged to grub up from under the snow.

> . . . the entrails of deer, full of blood and half-putrefied excrement, boiled fungus, decayed oysters, frogs eaten whole, head and feet, unskinned, uncleaned . . .

Then they offered us some of their sagamité to eat, as they often have some remains of it in the pot; but for my part I very rarely took it, both because it usually smelt too strong of stinking fish and also because the dogs frequently put their nose into it and children their leavings.

> . . . the women savages eating the lice from their own bodies
> . . .

> . . . mingling some yallowifh meale in the broath of that infected ftinking meate . . .

> . . . they feeded me wth their hodpot, forcing me to fwallow it in a maner . . .

> . . . unfavoury and clammie by reafon of the fcume that was upon the meat . . .
> . . . their filthy meate that I could not digeft, but muft fuffer all patiently.

. . . the stink worse even than sewers . . .

. . . I ate old Moose skins, tougher than those of the Eel; I went through the woods biting the ends of the branches, and gnawing the more tender bark.

As we went backe uppon our ftepps for to gett any thing to fill our bellyes, we were glad to gett the boans and carcaffes of the beasts that we killed.

. . . in the next place, the fkins that were referved to make us fhoofe, cloath, and ftokins, yea, moft of the fkins of our cottages, the caftors fkins, where the children befhit them above a hundred times. We burned the hair on the coals; the reft goes downe throats . . .

Every one cryes out for hunger; the women become baren, and drie like wood. You men muft eate the cord, being you have no more ftrength to make ufe of the bow. Children, you muft die. french, you called yourfelves Gods of the earth, that you fhould be feared, for your intereft; notwithstanding you shall taft of the bitterneffe, and too happy if you efcape. Where is the time paft? Where is the plentyneffe that yee had in all places and countreys?

We were out of provisions, and found only some dried meat . . . which we took to appease our hunger;

but soon after perceiving it to be human flesh, we left the rest to our Indians.

(It was very good and delicate)

The letter is badly written, and quite soiled, because . . . he who writes it has only one whole finger on his right hand; and it is difficult to avoid staining the paper with the blood which flows from his wounds, not yet healed . . . He writes it from the country of the Hiroquois . . .

. . . gathering all their rage, they fell upon me, and with their fists, thongs and clubs beat me till I fell senseless. Two of them then dragged me back to where I had been before, and scarcely had I begun to breathe, when some others, attacking me, tore out, by biting, almost all my nails, and crunched my two fore-fingers with their teeth . . .

> They made a great fire
> and tooke my comrade's heart out,
> and choped off his head . . .

. . . there came a little boy to gnaw wth his teeth the end of my fingers.

They burned a frenchwoman; they pulled out her breafts and tooke a child out of her belly . . .

. . . for they had cut off both his thumbs, and through the stump of the left one they . . . drove a pointed stake up to his very elbow.

> (If he cannot fing
> they make him quack like a henne)

. . . the first thing they did to him afterward was that one of them cut with a knife around his scalp, which he stripped off in order to carry away the hair, and, according to their custom, to preserve it as very precious.

After such treatment one would hardly believe that there could remain any sensation of life in a body so worn out with tortures. But lo! he suddenly rises, and . . . takes in his hands, which were all in shreds, a firebrand, that he might not die as a captive, and that he might defend the brief liberty he had recovered a little while before death. The rage and the cries of his enemies redouble at this sight;

they rush towards him with pieces of red-hot iron in their hands. His courage gives him strength; he puts himself on the defensive; he hurls his firebrands upon those who come nearest him; he throws down the ladders, to cut off their way, and avails himself of the fire and flame, the severity of which he has just experienced, to repel their attack vigorously. The blood that streamed down from his head over his entire body would have rent with pity a heart which had any remnant of humanity; but the fury of our barbarians found therein its satisfaction. Some throw upon him coals and burning cinders; others underneath the scaffold find open places for their firebrands. He sees on all sides almost as many butchers as spectators; when he escapes one fire, he encounters another, and takes not one step without falling into the evil that he flees.

While defending himself thus for a long time, a false step causes him to fall backward to the ground. At the same time, his enemies pounce upon him, burn him anew, then throw him upon the fire. This invincible spirit, rising again from the midst of the flames,—all covered with cinders that were imbued in his blood, two flaming firebrands in his hands,—turns towards the mass of his enemies, to inspire them with fear once more before he dies. Not one is so hardy as to touch him; he makes a way for himself, and walks towards the Village as if to set it on fire.

He advances about a hundred paces, when some one throws a club which fells him to the ground; before he can rise again, they are upon him; they cut off his feet and hands, and, having seized the rest of this mangled body, they turn it round and round over nine different fires, which he almost entirely extinguished with his blood. Finally they thrust him under an overturned tree-trunk, all on fire, so that, at the same time, there may be no part of his body, which is not cruelly burned . . . having neither feet nor hands, he rolled over in the flames, and, having fallen outside of them, he moved more than ten paces, upon his elbows and knees, in the direction of his enemies, who fled before him, dreading the approach of a man to whom nothing remained but courage . . .

(They cut off yor ſtones and the women play wth them as wth balles)

(I was covered with loathsome vermin, and could neither get rid of them nor defend myself from them. In my wounds, worms were produced; out of one finger alone, more than four fell in one day)

———————

After this they fearched me and tooke what I had, then ftripped me naked, and tyed a rope about my middle . . . they removed me, laughing and howling like as many wolves, I knowing not the reason, if not for my fkin, that was foe whit in respect of theirs . . .

> . . . they combd my head, and wth a filthy greafe greafed my head, and dafhed all over my face wth redd paintings.

> . . . the young men tooke delight in combing my head, greaff ing and powdering out a kinde of redd powder, then tying my haire wth a read ftring of leather like to a coard, wch caufed my haire to grow longer in a fhort time.

> They took a fancy to teach mee to fing; and as I had already a beginning of their hooping, it was an eafy thing for me to learne . . .

> In this place they cutt off my hair in the front and upon the crowne of the head, and turning up the locks of ye haire they dab'd mee wth fome thicke greafe. So done, they brought me a looking glaffe. I viewing myfelfe all in a pickle, fmir'd wth redde and black, covered wth fuch a cappe, and locks tyed up wth a peece of leather and ftunked horribly, I could not but fall in love wth myfelfe . . .

I more and more getting familiarity wth them, that I had the liberty to goe from cottage, having one or two by mee. They untyed mee, and tooke delight to make me fpeake words of their language, and weare earneft that I fhould pronounce as they . . . There was nothing elfe but feafting and finging during our abode.

The old woman wifhed that I would make myfelfe more familiar wth her 2 daughters, wch weare tolerable among fuch people. They weare accuftomed to greafe and combe my haire in ye morning. I went wth them into the wildernefs . . .

All the way the people made much of me, till we came to the village, and efpcially my 2 fifters, that in all they fhewed their refpects, giveing me meate every time we refted ourfelves, or painting my face or greafing my haire or combing my head. Att night they took the paines to pull off my ftokins, & when I fupped they made me lay downe by them . . .

The women are tender and delicat . . .

The weather lovely,
the wind fayre,
and nature fatisfied.

. . . we wanted not bear's greafe to annoint ourfelves, to runne the better. We beated downe the woods dayly for to difcover novellties. We killed feverall other beafts, as Oriniacks, ftaggs, wild cows, Carriboucks, fallow does and bucks, Catts of Mountains, child of the Devill; in a word, we lead a good life.

Wee had allways great preparations, and were invited 9 or tenne times a day. Our bellyes had not tyme to emptie themfelves, becaufe we feed fo much . . .

. . . there weare playes, mirths, and bataills for fport, goeing and coming wth cryes; each plaid his part. In the publick place the women danced wth melody. The yong men that indeavoured to gett a pryfe, indeavoured to clime up a great poft, very fmooth, and greafed wth oyle of beare & oriniack greafe . . . The feaft was made to eate all up. To honour the feaft many men and women did burft.

I lived 5 weeks
without thinking
from whence I came.

The boats ready, we embarque ourselves . . .
It was a pleafur to fee that imbarquing,
ffor all the yong women went in ftark naked,
their hairs hanging down . . .

They fing a loud and fweetly.

They ftood in their boats,
and remained in that pofture halfe a day,
to encourage us to come and lodge wth them againe.

Therefore they are not alltogether afhamed
to fhew us all,
        to intice us,
and inamimate the men to defend themfelves valiantly
and come and
            injoy them.

Friends, I muft confeffe I loved thofe poore people entirely well . . .

THREE

. . . there is a river that goeth Southwest,
from whence there is a whole moneth's sayling
to goe to a certaine land,
where there is neither yce nor snow seene . . .

───────────

The great river St. Lawrence takes its rise in several great lakes,
among which five are of extraordinary size . . . They are all of fresh
water, very good to drink, abounding in fish, and surrounded by fer-
tile lands . . .

At last, with all our misery, we discovered Lake Ontario on
the second day of August, which comes in sight like a great
sea, with no land visible but what you coast along.

Betwixt the Lake Ontario and Erié, there is a vaſt and prodi-
gious Cadence of Water which falls down after a ſurprizing
and aſtonishing manner, inſomuch that the Univerſe does
not afford its Parallel.

The Waters which fall from this vaſt height, do foam and
boil after the most hideous manner imaginable, making an
outrageous Noise, more terrible than that of Thunder . . .

The rebounding of theſe Waters is ſo great, that a ſort of
Cloud ariſes from the Foam of it, which are ſeen hanging
over this abyſs even at Noon day, when the Sun is at its
heighth.

That after passing this fall no land is seen on either side, but
only a sea so great that they have not seen the end of it, nor
heard tell of any who had done so . . .

. . . we came to an Anchor at the Mouth of the Streight,
which runs from the Lake *Huron* into that of *Erie.* The 11th,
we went farther into the Streight, and paſs'd between two
ſmall Iſlands, which make one of the fineſt Proſpects in the
World . . . The Navigation is eaſie on both ſides, the Coaſt
being low and even. It runs directly from North to South.

It was a sight to arouse pity, to see poor Frenchmen in a Canoe,
amid rain and snow, borne hither and thither by whirlwinds on
those great Lakes, which often show waves as high as those of the
Sea. The men frequently found their hands and feet frozen upon
their return, while occasionally they were overtaken by so thick a
fall of powdery snow, driven against them by a violent wind, that
the one steering the Canoe would not see his companion in the
bow.

At length . . . we entered the largest lake in all America called
the fresh water Sea of the Hurons . . .

This lake is not deep and is subject to terrific winds from

which there is no shelter . . .

(white fish
& moose meat)

the Sweetwater Sea . . .

I embarked with M. Joliet, who had been chosen to conduct this enterprise, on the 13th May, 1673, with five other Frenchmen, in two bark canoes. We laid in some Indian corn and smoked beef for our voyage.

> . . . two Miamis whom they had given us as guides, embarked with us, in the sight of a great crowd, who could wonder enough to see seven Frenchmen alone in two canoes, dare to undertake so strange and so hazardous an expedition.

We first took care, however, to draw from the Indians all the information we could, concerning the countries through which we designed to travel . . . they were much surprised, and said all they could to dissuade me from it. They told me I would meet Indians who spare no strangers, and whom they kill without provocation or mercy . . . That the Great River was exceedingly dangerous, and full of frightful monsters who devoured men and canoes together, and that the heat was so great that it would positively cause our death. I thanked them for their kind advice, but told them I would not follow it . . .

> . . . the way is so cut up by marshes and little lakes, that it is easy to go astray, especially as the river leading to it is so covered with wild oats, that you can hardly discover any channel.

As our guides had been frequently at this portage, they knew the way, and helped us to carry our canoes overland into the other river, distant about two miles and a half; from whence they returned home, leaving us in an unknown country . . . We now left the waters which extend to Quebec, about five or six hundred leagues, to take those which lead us hereafter into strange lands.

> The river on which we embarked is called Meskousing; it is very broad, with a sandy bottom, forming many shallows, which render navigation very difficult. It is full of vine clad islets.

After forty leagues on this same route, we reached the mouth of the river, and . . . safely entered the Missisipi on the 17th of June, with a joy that I can not express.

> We met from time to time monstrous fish, which struck so violently against our canoes, that at first we took them to be large trees, which threatened to upset us.

As we were descending the river we saw high rocks with hideous monsters painted on them, and upon which the bravest Indians dare not look. They are as large as a calf, with head and horns like a goat; their eyes red; beard like a tiger's; and a face like a man's. Their tails are so long that they pass over their heads and between their fore legs, under their belly, and ending like a fish's tail. They are painted red, green, and black.

Several years ago, M. de la Salle had reached the conclusion, based upon the information he had derived from many Savages of various nations, that settlements might be established to the southwest of the great lakes of New France; and moreover, that a way might be found to the sea by following a great river named by some Savages Ohio and by others Mississipi.

> On the following day, the 19th of September, he pushed forward with fourteen persons in four canoes laden with a forge, with all the tools of house and ship carpenters, cabinet-makers, and sawyers, and with arms and merchandise.

In the middle of the passage, there suddenly sprang up out of the deepest calm a dangerous storm, which made him fear for his vessel, inasmuch as it raged during four days with a fury equal to that of the severest ocean storms.

> On the 25th he continued his course along the coast all day and a part of the night, being favored by the moon; but the wind rising, he landed with his whole party. They found themselves upon a naked rock, where they bore rain and snow for two days, wrapped in their blankets and hovering near a little fire of driftwood.

On the 1st of October they pushed on, and having made ten leagues, fasting, arrived near another Pottawattamie village. The high, steep coast was exposed to the northeast wind which was then blowing and increasing at such a rate as to cause enormous waves to break against the shore. The only course that M. de la Salle could take, in order to effect a landing safely, was to throw himself, in company with his three men, into the water, and to carry the canoe, laden as it was, to shore, in spite of the breakers which sometimes rolled over their heads.

> M. de la Salle departed on foot to join M. De Tonty, who had preceded him with his followers and all his equipage 40 leagues into the Miamis country, where the ice of the River Chekagou . . . had arrested his progress, and where when the ice became stronger, they used sledges to drag the baggage, the canoes, and a wounded Frenchman, through the whole length of this river, and on the Illinois . . .

M. La Salle having arrived safely at the Miamies . . . began with his ordinary activity and vast mind, to make all preparations for his departure. He selected twenty-three Frenchmen, and eighteen Mohegans and Abnakis, all inured to war. The latter insisted on taking along ten of their women to cook for them, as their custom is, while they were fishing or hunting. These women had three children, so that the whole party consisted of but fifty-four persons . . .

In thefe Parts the Frofts continue all Night even at this time of Year; fo that our Legs were all over Blood, being cut by the Ice, which we broke by degrees in our Paffage as we waded o'er the Lakes and River. We never eat but once in four and twenty Hours, and then nothing but a few Scraps of Meat dry'd in Smoak . . .

I was fo weak that I often laid me down, refolving rather to die than follow thefe Savages any farther, who travell'd at a rate fo extraordinary, as far furpaffes the Strength of any European. However, to haften us, they fometimes fet fire to the dry Grafs in the Meadows through which we pafs'd; fo that our Choice was march or burn.

> . . . we arrived at the end of January at the great River Mississippi.

> . . . as soon as we were on the Micissipi we no longer perceived that it was the winter season, and the further we descended the river the greater we found the heat.

. . . a fine, large river flowing from the north. It divides into several channels at the spot where the River of the Illinois falls into it, forming very beautiful islands. It winds several times, but seems always to keep its course to the south as far the Acanscas.

> This open country, we were told, continues . . . westward and southward . . . so far that its limit is unknown, especially towards the south, where treeless meadows are found more than one hundred leagues in length, and where the Indians who have been there say very good fruits and extremely fine Indian corn are grown.

. . . we descended the Mississippi. The first day we went six leagues, encamping on the right bank near the mouth of a river which falls into the Mississippi, makeing it very turbid and muddy. It is named the river of the Missouris.

The country is good, somewhat high, abounding in great trees . . . It was in the month of March that this took place; a sweet breath was in the air; the peach trees were in bloom.

We saw . . . peaches already formed on the trees, although it was only the beginning of March.

> . . . the most beautiful country in the world, prairies, open woods of mulberry trees, vines, and fruits that we are not acquainted with.

The peach-trees are quite like those of France, and very good; they are so loaded with fruit that the Indians have to prop up with forks those they cultivate in their clearings. There are whole forests of very fine mulberries, of which we ate the fruit from the month of May; many plum-trees and other fruit-trees; some known and others unknown in Europe; vines, pomegranates, and chestnut are common. They raise three or four crops of corn a year . . . Winter is little known except by the rains.

> Thus the little fleet advanced toward the south, finding the country ever fairer and more temporate.

At the door of the cabin in which we were to be received, was an old man awaiting us in a very remarkable posture; which is their usual ceremony in receiving strangers. This man was standing, perfectly naked, with his hands stretched out and raised toward the sun, as if he wished to screen himself from its rays, which nevertheless passed through his fingers to his face. When we came near to him, he paid us this compliment: 'How beautiful is the sun, O Frenchman, when thou comest to visit us! All our town awaits thee, and thou shalt enter all our cabins in peace.'

> These Indians do not resemble those at the north, who are all sad and severe in their temper; these are far better made, honest, liberal, and gay.

The fourth day we departed. The Arkansas escorted us to the

water's edge, passing their hands over our bodies. This is their caress, signifying that we should take courage.

> In the fields one scares up quail, in the wood one sees
> parrots . . .

> We begin to see here those reeds
> which
> shoot up to a height of fifteen feet.

On the 19th of December he
observed the comet
for the first time . . .
Several times . . . he also observed
parhelia,—among the rest, one
which showed eight suns . . .

At last, after a navigation of about forty leagues, we arrived, on the sixth of April, at a point where the river divides into three channels. The sieur de la Salle divided his party the next day into three bands, to go and explore them. He took the western, the sieur Dautray the southern, the sieur Tonty, whom I accompanied, the middle one. These three channels are beautiful and deep. The water is brackish; after advancing two leagues it became salt, and advancing on, we discovered the open sea . . .

> . . . the mouth of the river,
> which ran far out into the sea . . .

. . . the warm, enclosed Gulf,
with all the creatures swimming in it . . .

SOUTH→

1625, or before,
 William Blaxton, or Blackstone,
  settled alone on the tri-mount,
   and along the south shore of Charles River

750 acres,
 more or less, at Shawamet . . .

". . . betook him
. . . to till the land,
 retaining no symbol of his former profession
  but a Canonicall Coate."

raised English roses
 and yellow sweetings,
  and when

the colony of Puritans under Winthrop
 landed at Mishawamet,
  suffering from sickness and impure water,

Blackstone crossed the river,
 and invited them to join him at Shawamet,
  where his land abounded in sweet springs . . .

"December 27. The Governor and Assistants met at Boston, and took into consideration a treatise, which Mr. Williams (then of Salem) had sent them, and which he had formerly written to the

Governor and Council of Plymouth, wherein, among other things, he disputed their right to the lands they possessed here, and concluded that, claiming by the King's grant, they could have no title, nor otherwise, except they compounded with the natives."

> " . . . where the king of *England* had granted a royal *charter* under the *governour and company* of this colony; which patent was indeed the very *life* of the colony; this hot-headed man publickly and furiously preached against the *patent* . . . on an insignificent presence of *wrong* thereby done unto the *Indians* . . ."

"1634, No. 27. The Court was informed, that Mr. Williams, of Salem, had broken his promise to us, in teaching publicly against the King's patent, and our great sin in claiming right thereby to this country, &c. and for usual terming the churches of England antichristian. We granted summons to him for his appearance at the next Court."

"1635, Mo. 5, 8. At the General Court, Mr. Williams, of Salem, was summoned and did appear. It was laid to his charge, that being under question before the magistracy and churches for divers dangerous opinions . . . The said opinions were adjudged by all, magistrates and ministers, (who were desired to be present) to be erroneous and very dangerous and that the calling of him to office, at that time, was judged a great contempt of authority. So, in fine, time was given to him and the church of Salem to consider of these till the next General Court, and then either to give satisfaction to the Court, or else to expect the sentence . . ."

> " . . . the Church, affected with the *fierceness* of his *talking* in publick and the *starchtness* of his *living* in private, so far forget themselves, as to renew their invitation unto him to become their *pastor* . . ."

> "In the year 1654,
> a certain *Windmill* in the Low Countries,

whirling round with extroardinary violence,
by reason of a violent storm then blowing;
the stone at length by its *rapid motion*
became so intensely hot,
as to fire the mill,
from whence the flames,
being dispersed by the high winds,
did set a whole town on *fire.*

But I can tell my reader,
that about twenty years before this,
there was a whole country in America
like to be set on fire
by the *rapid motion* of a *windmill,*
in the head of one particular man.

Know then,
that about the year 1630,
arrived here one Mr. Roger Williams . . ."

" . . . the giddy courses . . .
whereto he would *abandon* himself . . ."

". . . this incendiary . . ."

"At this General Court, Mr. Williams, the teacher of Salem, was again converted, and all the ministers in the Bay being desired to be present, he was charged . . . He justified . . . and maintained all his opinions . . . So, the next morning, the Court sentenced him to depart out of our jurisdiction . . ."

"Sept. 3, 1635.—Whereas Mr. Roger Williams, one of the elders of the church at Salem, hath broached & dyvulged dyvers newe and dangerous opinions, against the aucthority of magistrates, as also writ lres of defamacon, both of the magistrates & churches here, & that before any conviccon & yet mainetaineth the same without retraccon, it is therefore ordered that the same Mr. Williams shall dpte out of this jurisdiccon within six weeks nexte ensueing, wch if hee neglect to pforme, it shalbe lawfull for the gounr & two of the magistrates to send him to some place out of this jurisdiccon, not to returne any more without licence of the court."

"The increase of concourse of people to him on the Lord's day in private, to the neglect and deserting of public ordinances and to the spreading of the leaven of his corrupt imaginations, provoked the magistrates rather than breed a winter's spiritual plague in the country to put upon him a winter's journey out of the country."

"11 mo. January. The Governor and Assistants met at Boston to consider about Mr. Williams, for that they were credibly informed, that, notwithstanding the injunction laid upon him (upon the liberty granted him to stay till the spring,) not to go about to draw others to his opinions, he did use to entertain company in his house, and to preach to them, even of such points as he had been censured for; and it was agreed to send him into England by a ship then ready to depart. The reason was, because he had drawn about twenty persons to his opinion, and they were intended to erect a plantation about the Narraganset Bay, from whence the infection would easily spread into these churches, (the people being many of them much taken with the apprehension of his godliness.) Whereupon a warrent was sent to him to come presently to Boston to be shipped, &c. He returned answer (and divers of Salem came with it,) that he could not come without hazard to his life, &c. Whereupon a pinnace was sent with commission to Capt. Underhill, &c. to apprehend him, and carry him aboard the ship, (which then rode at Nantasket;) but, when they came at his house, they found he had been gone three days before; but whither they could not learn."

" . . . driven from my
howse & land & wife & children
(in the midst of N. Engl: winter . . ."

" . . . unmercifulIy driven from my chamber
to a winter's flight . . .
For one fourteen weeks I
. . . knew not what bread or bed did mean."

" . . . the miserie of a
Winters Banishment."

But the Puritans—annoyed
by that Canonicall Coate—
tried to dislodge him from his land,
using the king's grant for excuse.

Blackstone replied:

"The king asserteth sovereignty
over this New England because
John and Sebastian Cabot sailed along the coast,
without even landing at any place;

and if the quality of sovereignty can subsist
upon the substratum of mere inspection,
surely the quality of property can subsist
upon that of actual occupancy,

which is the foundation of my claim."

So the Puritans were forced to buy him out,

and Blackstone noted, further,

"I came from England
because I did not like the lord-bishops,
but I cannot join with you,
because I would not be under the lord-brethren."

1635, with his cattle,
   shoots from his apple trees,
     slips from his rose bushes,
       his library of 86 volumes,

Blackstone entered the wilderness
   headed south,
     or, as some say, for the "Far West."

With sundial and pocket compass, Williams departed Salem, no doubt following the Boston road as far as Saugus, then turning west, and again, due south, into the Narragansett country . . . the ground was covered with snow . . .

    " . . . I steered my Course from Salem
    (though in Winter snow wch I feele yet)
    unto these parts . . ."

"Aboute the year 1634 Mr. Roger Williams was banished from boston, hee differing from them in sum religus pints was forsed to fley in the winter seson by reason thereof hee was forsed to great hardships so that If the Indians which were the natives of the land had not hope him hee might have suffered deth but they was very kind to him and hope him a long in his Jurne . . ."

        ("These ravens fed me in the wilderness."

" . . . tel hee came to a place sence caled mantons neck where hee had much kines sheued him from the Indians . . ."

      . . . near a spring, where
      "the water boils from the ground
      rapid and clear . . ."

      "a great spring of sweet water"

"I first pitcht & begun to build & plant at Secunk . . . : But I recd a
Letter from my ancient friend Mr Winslow, then Govr of Ply-
mouth, professing his owne & others Love & respect to me, Yet
lovingly advising me (since I was falled into the Edge of their
Bounds, & they were loth to displease the Bay) to remove but to the
other side of the Water, & then he said I had the Country free
before me . . ."

. . . down the Seekonk, around Fox Point, up the Great Salt River
and the Moshassuck, to an unfailing spring of sweet water . . .

> ("The savages will not willingly drink
> but at a spring head . . .")

> Westward, salt marshes, islands overgrown with coarse grass,
> sand hills with scrubby pines . . .

> At the river's edge, beaches and clam flats— "This is a sweet
> kind of fhelfifh . . ."

> Eastward, a steep hill, rising in back of the spring, then slop-
> ing gently to the Seekonk—thickly covered with oak and
> cedar . . .

It was named Providence— "from the freedom and vacancy of the
place . . ."

" . . . and when I came, I was welcome to Ousamequin, and to the
old prince Canonicus, who was most shy of all English, to his last
breath."

" . . . and I desire posterity to see the gracious hand of the Most
High, (in whose hands is all hearts) that when the hearts of my
country-men and friends and brethren failed me, his infinite wis-
dom and merits stirred up the barbarous heart of Canonicus to love
me as his own son . . ."

"Be it knowne unto all men by these prsentes, That I Roger Williams of the Towne of providence in the Narragansett Bay in New England, having in the yeare one Thousand Six hundred thirty Foure, And in the yeare one Thousand six hundred Thirty Five, had severall Treatyes with Counicusse, and Miantenome, the Two cheife Sachims of the Narragansett; And in the End, purchased of them the Landes and Meddowes upon the Two Fresh Rivers called Moshosick And wanasquattuckett . . ."

("I desired not to be troubled with English Company . . ."

"By God's merciful assistance, I was the procurer of the purchase, not by monies nor payment, the natives being so shy and jealous, that monies could not do it, but by that language, acquaintance and favor with the natives . . . which it pleased God to give me . . ."

". . . Counanicus . . . was not I say to be stirred with money to sell his Lands to let in foreigners. Tis' true he recd presents and gratuities many of me, but it was not Thousand not Ten Thousands of money could have bought of him an English Entrance into the Bay. Thousands could not have bought of him Providence . . ."

"It was not price nor money that could have purchased Rhode-Island. Rhode-Island was obtained by love . . ."

From the three hills of Shawamet,
Blackstone journeyed to a three-terraced hill
on the river upstream
from Narragansett tidewater . . .

He built a house on the first terrace,
a few rods from the water's edge,

Dug a well on the second,

And at the top built a shelter
   which he used as a study.

His home became known as
   Study Hall, on
      Study Hill . . .

North and north-east of the house,
   he turned a garden,
      and planted his orchard to the
         south . . .

"God was pleased to give me a painful, patient spirit, to lodge with them in their filthy, smoky holes, even while I lived at Plymouth and Salem, to gain their tongue."

"I Prefent you with a Key; I have not heard of the like, yet framed, fince it pleafed God to bring that mighty *Continent* of *America* to light . . .

This *Key*, refpects the *Native Language* of it, and happily may unlocke fome *Rarities* concerning the *Natives* themfelves, not yet difcovered.

I drew the *Materialls* in a rude lumpe at Sea, as a private *helpe* to my owne memory, that I might not by my prefent abfence *lightly lofe* what I had fo *dearely* bought in fome few years *hardfhip*, and *charges* among the *Barbarians* . . .

A little *Key* may open a *Box*, where lies a *bunch* of *Keyes*.

With this I have entred into the fecrets of thofe *Countries* . . . for want of this, I know what groffe *mif-takes* my felfe and others run into."

         "But for their later *Defcent,*
         and whence they came into thofe pars,
         it feemes as harde to finde,
         as to finde the *Well-head* of some frefh *Streame,*
         which running many miles out of the *Countrey*

to the falt *Ocean,*
hath met with many mixing *Streames*
by the way.
They fey themfelves,
that they have *fprung* and *growne* up
in that very place,
like the very *trees* of the *Wilderneffe.*"

("... they are so exquifitely skilled in all the body and
bowels of the Countrey ...")

"... I humbly pray your consideration, whether it be not only pos-
sible, but very easy, to live and die in peace with all the natives of
this country."

"... that the whole land, English and natives, might sleep in peace
securely."

"... for the eftablifhing of peace through all the bowels of the coun-
try ..."

"Yet I have found leffe noyfe, more peace
In wilde *America* ..."

———

Blackstone broke a bull to bit and bridle,
    rode from Study Hall on Study Hill, from time to time,
        to Providence or Boston,

distributing fruits
    from his orchard
        to children on the way ...

                "... perhaps,
                the richest and most delicious
                apple
                of the whole kind ..."

1659, aged about 60,
*   he rode his bull to Boston,*
*   to court a bride . . .*

"I desire not to sleepe in security & dreame of a nest which no hand can reach. I cannot but expect changes . . ."

> (" . . . there is so much sound and noise of purchase and purchasers . . .")

". . . Having bought Truth deare, we must not sell it cheape . . ."

"If riches, if children, if friends, if cattle, if whatsoever increase, let us watch that the heart fly not loose upon them."

> ("P.S. My love to all my Indian friends.")

In his old age,
*   Blackstone rode his bull,*
*   where previously he had walked.*

" . . . it is famous that the *Sowweſt (Sowaniu)* is the great Subject of their discourſe. From thence their *Traditions.* There they ſey (at the *South-weſt*) is the Court of their *great God Cautanouwit*: At the *South-weſt* are their *Forefathers* foules: to the *South-weſt* they goe themselves when they dye; From the *South-weſt* came their Corne, and Beanes out of their Great God *Cautantowwits* field: and indeed the further *Northward* and *Weſtward* from us their Corne will not grow, but to the *Southward* better and better."

May 26, 1675,

> "Sir, about a fortnight ſince your old acquaintance, Mr. Blackſtone, departed this life in the fourſcore year of his age; four days before his death he had a great pain . . . afterward

he ſaid he was well, had no pains, and ſhould live, but he
grew fainter, and yielded up his breath without a groan."

He was buried two rods west
  of his cottage . . .
    left books

valued at 15£, personal effects
  of 40£ value; also,
    sixty acres of land

and two shares in meadows
  in Providence.
    The west plain, the south neck,

and land about the house and orchard,
  amounting to two hundred acres,
    and the meadow called Blackstone's meadow . . .

1683,

"The Lord hath arreſted by death our ancient and approved
friend, Mr. Roger Williams . . ."

"Sowwanakitauwaw — *They go to the South ward.*"

TELEMAQUE

1809, a ship's steward, Negro, was arrested for smuggling inflammatory pamphlets into the port of Charleston, South Carolina, from New York City, on board the ship MINERVA ...

> *Meanwhile*
> *the goddess with gray eyes had*
> *other business:*
> *disguised as Telémakhos, she*
> *roamed the town*
> *taking each likely man aside and*
> *telling him:*
> *"Meet us at nightfall ..."*

1781:
Capt. Joseph Vesey—commanding a slaver sailing between St. Thomas (Virgin Islands) and San Domingo—took on board a cargo of 390 Negroes, including among them a boy of 14, *of great beauty, alertness and intelligence.* Vesey and the officers made a pet of the boy, taking him into the cabin, fitting him out in new clothes, and giving him the name Telemaque.

Arrived at San Domingo, Vesey had no further use for Telemaque, and sold him with the rest of the slaves ...

(8/1/61)

MONROE GETS FIRE JITTERS AFTER SIXTH

By Don Gray
Observer Staff Writer
MONROE - Six fires in five nights, believed to be the work of arsonists, have Monroe citizens jittery.

The sixth blaze erupted Monday night and destroyed a small packing plant ...

Police are holding three Negroes for questioning. But they haven't released their names.

On his next voyage, however, he was
forced to take back the boy, as the
planter who had purchased him
claimed, with support from the
king's physician, that he was subject
to epileptic fits.

Capt. Vesey accepted Telemaque,
made him his personal servant . . .
Telemaque served Vesey for 20
years, in good health . . .

1783—Capt. Vesey settled ashore in
the port of Charleston, engaging in
the gentler trade of shoreside slave
merchant . . . :

Negroes,
On Wednesday the first of October, at
Mrs. Dewees, No. 43, Queen-street,
Will be exposed for sale, 104 Prime
Slaves, just imported in the schooner
Eagle, *Captain David Miller. The*
sale will continue every fair day (Sun-
days excepted) until all be Sold.
  The conditions will be made as con-
venient as possible to the purchasers.
J. Vesey & Co.
No. 27-1/4 Bay.

Telemaque was not sold: servant to
Vesey, he became Telmak, and then
Denmark . . . Denmark Vesey.

1800—now perhaps 33 years old—
Denmark drew a prize of $1500 in
the East Bay Street lottery . . . for
$600 he purchased his liberty . . .

. . . hired out as carpenter, was well
thought of in the white community
. . .

... built or bought a house at 20 Bull
...

... took seven wives, all slaves (with whom he consorted with their owners' permissions ...)

Long before anyone else, the prince Telémakhos
now caught sight of Athena—for he, too,
was sitting there, unhappy among the suitors,
a boy, daydreaming. What if his great father
came from the unknown world and drove these men
like dead leaves through the place, recovering
honor and lordship in his own domains?

According to white report, Denmark Vesey was distinguished for great strength and activity . . . among his own color he was looked up to with awe and respect . . .

You need not bear this insolence of theirs,
you are a child no longer.

———

Ned and Rolla Bennet, Jack Purcell . . . Peter Poyas, Gullah Jack and Monday Gell . . . later, Frank Ferguson and Lot Forrester, from the country: all were slaves of the highest calibre, above white suspicion, enjoying the unlimited confidence of their owners . . . Ned and Rolla were confidential servants, Peter was a slave of great value and a first

(8/6/61)

CITY OFFERS $1,100 FOR ITS FIREBUG

By Don Gray
Observer Staff Writer
MONROE - The Monroe Police Department is now offering $1,100 in reward money in an effort to track down arsonists believed responsible for seven fires here in less than two weeks ...

Total damage caused by the fires has now reached an estimated $218,000. Local police are working overtime to break the case and ease the fears of business men throughout the city.

(8/21/61)

NEW YORKER SAYS 3 MEN ATTACKED HIM

MONROE - (AP) - Richard Griswold, 35-year-old white man from Brookyln, N.Y., who came here to observe what he called racial tensions, claims that three white men

rate ship carpenter, and Monday an expert harness maker, much indulged by his owner, enjoying all the substantial comforts of a free man . . .

I know Peter, he belongs to Mr. James Poyas; in May last, Peter and myself met in Legare street, at the corner of Lambol . . . he said, by George! we can't live so. I replied, how will we do? He said, we can do very well, if you can find any one to assist us—will you join? I asked him, how do you mean? He said, why! to break the yoke. I replied, I don't know. He asked me, suppose you were to hear, that the whites were going to kill you, would you defend yourself? I replied, I'd try to escape. He asked, have you lately seen Denmark Vesey, and has he spoken to you particularly? I said no. Well then, said he, that's all now; but call at the shop to-morrow after knocking off work, and I will tell you more!

As many as thirty at a time, the men crowded into Vesey's quarters at 20 Bull Street . . .

. . . he asked me if . . . I remembered the fable of Hercules and the Waggoner whose waggon was stalled, and he began to pray, and Hercules said, you fool put your shoulders to the wheel, whip up the horses, and your waggon will be pulled out . . .

Denmark Vesey's temper (according to the whites) was impetuous and domineering, ungovernable and savage . . . to his wives and children (they said) he displayed a haughty and capricious cruelty.

choked him and threw him to the ground Saturday while he was taking pictures . . .

Griswold, who is staying with Robert Williams, Negro leader here, said he was roughed up while taking pictures of 10 Negroes and white persons . . .

Dear friend, you are tall and well
    set up, I see;
be brave—you, too—and men in
    times to come
will speak of you respectfully.

———————

Four years, the plans were held in the heads of Denmark and a close few . . . until Christmas, 1821, when he began to speak out:

Even whilst walking through the streets in company with another, he was not idle; for if his companion bowed to a white person, he would rebuke him, and observe . . . that he would never cringe to the whites, nor ought any one who had the feelings of a man. When answered, we are slaves, he would . . . reply, "You deserve to remain slaves . . ."

In Cow Alley, at the African Church—around the corner from the Planter's Hotel—at prayer meetings and Sunday service, Vesey and the others recruited . . .

I met him the next day, according to appointment, when he said to me, we intend to see, if we can't do something for ourselves, we can't live so. I asked him, where he would get men? He said, we'll find them fast enough, we have got enough, we expect men from country and town. But how, said I, will you manage it. Why, we will give them notice, said he, and they will march down and camp round the city.

(8/25/61)

MONROE PICKETS' SIGNS POINT TO 'INJUSTICES'

By Don Gray
Observer Staff Writer

MONROE - A group of white and Negro pickets marched the sidewalks of the courthouse square here for the fourth straight day Thursday. They carried placards bearing anti-segregation slogans such as "Jim Crow Must Go," "We Want Justice" and "The Fourteenth Amendment Means Nothing Here" . . .

Monroe police chief A. A. Mauney identified some of the white pickets as members of a delegation visiting controversial Negro leader Robert F. Williams.

To the North of Charleston many miles towards Santee, and into St. John's Parish . . . to the south to James' and John's Islands . . . to the West beyond Bacon's Bridge over Ashley River . . .

. . . trying all round the country, from Georgetown and Santee, round about to Combahee . . .

Gullah Jack, in Goose-Creek and Dorchester, spoke to 6600 persons, who agreed to join.

Charles asked a negro woman on the furm, if the old daddy was home, and she called him—this old daddy is an African, marked on both sides of his face—Charles took him in the stable, and also myself, and told him about the country negroes coming . . .

Peter Poyas, who wrote a good hand, drew up the lists, his own containing 600 names, and all the lists together, over 9000 . . .

> *(. . . but take care
> and don't mention it
> to those waiting men
> who receive presents
> of old coats, &c.
> from their masters, or
> they'll betray us . . .)*

According to Monday Gell, Denmark was satisfied with his own condition, being free; but, as all his children were slaves, he wished to see what could be done for them.

Slowly he shook his head from side to
side,
containing murderous thoughts.

But what, said I, will they do for arms.
He answered, they will find arms
enough, they all bring down their hoes,
axes, &c. I said, that won't do to fight
with here. He said, stop! let us get can-
didates from town with arms, and we
will then take the guardhouse and
arsenal in town, the arsenal on the
neck and the upper guardhouse, and
supply the country people with arms.
How, said I, will you approach those
arsenals, &c. for they are guarded? Yes,
said he, I know that, but what are these
guards, one man here, and one man
there, we let a man pass before us. Well,
said I, but how will the black people
from the country, and those from the
islands, know when you are to begin, or
how will you get the town people
together. Why, said he, we will have
prayer meetings at night, and there
notify them when to start, and when
the clock strikes twelve, all must move.

When the men met at 20 Bull, the
hat was passed, for collections to
purchase arms. A blacksmith was
engaged to make pike heads and
bayonets with sockets, to be fixed at
the ends of long poles, the poles well
selected, neatly trimmed and
smoothed off. Peter Poyas had a
sword, Charles Drayton a gun and
sword, John Horry a sword, and
Adam Yates a knife . . . Monday
Gell had a sword, and Bacchus
Hammett gave Peirault a sword and

(8/28/61)

OFFICER SHOT DURING MONROE RACIAL CLASH

By Don Gray, John York
and Davis Merritt
Observer Staff Writers
MONROE - A week of picketing in
front of the Union County Court-
house by a group of white and
Negro anti-segregationists flared
into racial violence Sunday. A white
policeman was wounded by a pistol
bullet and at least 32 persons were
arrested.

Sporadic and scattered fights
broke out among white spectators
and the pickets . . .

Mayor Fred Wilson called an
emergency meeting of the City
Council . . .

Officers said a white couple was
reportedly held "hostage" at the
home of Negro leader Robert Wil-
liams for a short period in the
evening.

They said Williams threatened to
hold the couple, identified as M. &
Mrs. G. Bruce Stegal of nearby
Marshville, until all members of the
picketing group were released, but
Williams released them unharmed a
short time later . . .

Several shots were reported fired
in the area of the courthouse in the
late afternoon, and police confiscat-
ed a variety of weapons from whites
and Negroes.

Police Chief A. A. Mauney said
barricades had been erected by mid-
evening on the street which runs in
front of the home of Robert
Williams, local Negro leader in-

carried another and a pistol to Vesey, together with a keg of powder, stolen from the owner . . . Arms were stolen from the Revenue Cutter, and musket balls were hidden under water at one of the docks . . .

I met him one day with a scythe in his cart, which he told me he was carrying to a blacksmith's to have made into a sword.

. . . on Queen Street, opposite the Planter's Hotel, arms could be stolen . . .

Bacchus Hammett brought a keg of Powder to my shop, and said he would procure five hundred muskets from his master's store . . .

Black draymen and carters of the city, as well as many slaves, had horses under their control; also, butcher boys and slaves at the livery stables controlled horses, and slaves whose owners belonged to the cavalry corps could steal them . . . at the appointed hour, stable doors would be opened, the horses saddled, and the insurgents mounted . . .

Blacks from the country and island Blacks would commandeer canoes, and the many-oared plantation boats, used to carry vegetables to the city, capable of handling upwards of a hundred men . . .

Pompey Haig told me that there were some Frenchmen, blacks, very skillful in making swords and spears, such as they used in Africa . .

volved in the picketing action.

The barricades were to stop cars filled with white adults and teenagers from riding up and down in front of Williams' house. Patrol cars were circulating in the area.

(8/29/61)

NEGRO LEADER

JURY INDICTS WILLIAMS ON KIDNAPPING CHARGE

FBI ISSUES
WARRANT
FOR ARREST

WILLIAMS MISSING:
REPORTEDLY FLEES

Related Stories on Page 2A
See Editorial on 2B

MONROE- (AP) - A kidnap indictment was returned Monday against Robert Williams, 36, controversial Monroe Negro who long has advocated violence by his race.

Williams could not be located and the FBI issued a warrant for his arrest on charges of unlawful flight to avoid prosecution.

The warrant was issued shortly before midnight Monday by U.S. Commissioner Robert L. Scott in Charlotte.

The Union County Grand Jury returned a true bill after hearing testimony by a white couple held hostage by Negroes Sunday night.

On King Street, beyond the city limits, in a common wooden store, unguarded, were deposited the arms of the Neck Company of Militia: between two and three hundred muskets and bayonets, and a few swords . . . in Mr. Duquercron's store on King Street, also beyond the city limits, there were five hundred muskets and bayonets, deposited for sale . . . Vesey had made a purchase of dark lanthorns, to guide the insurgents . . . Mr. Schirer's store of arms on Queen Street, and the stores of Gun Smiths, were noted . . . at the Arsenal on Meeting Street, opposite St. Michael's Church, where the greatest proportion of the arms of the State were lodged, the doors were weak and wooden . . .

Peter Poyas was to lead a party to assemble on South Bay, to be joined by a force from James Island, to march and seize the Arsenal . . .

But, I replied, when you are coming up the sentinel will give the alarm—he said he would advance a little distance ahead, and if he could only get a grip at his throat he was a gone man, for his sword was very sharp; he had sharpened it . . .

A barber and hair dresser—a white man—was employed to make wigs and false whiskers of the hair of white men . . . with these, and faces painted white, the insurgents could advance undetected—and Peter Poyas could reach the arsenal, the sentinel, without suspicion . . .

A few Negroes sat on the grand jury.

The couple said they were abducted by about 200 armed Negroes, tied up and later released.

About 30 officers raided Williams' house, where the Negro leader has kept a large store of arms. Williams was believed to have fled.

No arms were found during the raid.

In New York Sylvester Leaks, co-chairman of the Crusade for Freedom, said that Williams, an associate, fled from Monroe late Sunday night because he feared arrest. The Crusade for Freedom planned a rally in support of Williams in New York.

Also raided was the rented so-called "Freedom House" near Williams' home. Pickets from outside the state have been staying there.

Monroe police asked the FBI to issue a nationwide alert for the goateed Williams.

The reported kidnaping climaxed a weekend of racial violence in this city of 10,000, where Negro and white pickets, one from as far away as England, have marched with placards for days.

A policeman was wounded Sunday by a Negro the policeman said he was trying to disarm. Sporadic fighting over the weekend resulted in 47 arrests. Extra highway patrolmen were ordered in to help keep order and the city appealed to the federal government for help.

Williams is an avowed admirer of Fidel Castro. Police patroled the area of his home, where Williams

The Arsenal secured, a party would be detached, to prevent whites from assembling at their alarm posts . . . a second body, consisting of Neck and country Negroes, was to assemble on the Neck and seize the Arsenal there . . . a third to assemble at Bennett's Mills, to murder the Governor and Intendant, march through the City and take station at Cannon's Bridge, to prevent the inhabitants of Cannonsborough from entering the city . . . a fourth to rendezvous at Gadsden's Wharf, march and attack the Upper Guardhouse . . . a fifth to assemble at Bulkley's Farm, two and a half miles from the City, secure the pikes secreted there, seize the powder magazine, and march into the City . . . a sixth would assemble at Vesey's and, under his command, march to the Arsenal . . .

. . . and a number of unattached insurgents would ride through the City, killing on sight . . .

Gullah Jack—or Couter Jack, as sometimes called—was from birth a sorcerer and necromancer, this being in Angola a matter of inheritance . . .

Although he had been fifteen or twenty years in this country, yet he appeared to be untouched by the influences of civilized life.

At a meeting at Bulkley's Farm, Jack and others roasted a fowl, and ate it half raw, as evidence of brotherhood . . .

has boasted of maintaining a large arsenal. Reporters have seen a large number of firearms there.

The 36-year-old, muscular Williams has said he was stockpiling weapons in "an armament race with the white people of Monroe."

An uneasy quiet returned to this county seat 24 miles east of Charlotte. The pickets did not march, and extra law officers patrolled the city. Mayor Fred Wilson called the city council into emergency session to consider ways of preventing further outbreaks.

In Raleigh, Gov. Terry Sanford said that the Monroe situation "is under control, and is going to be kept under control."

Sanford declined with thanks an offer from Alabama Gov. John Patterson to send Alabama troops here if needed.

Sanford had declared earlier Monday that "We are not going to allow outside agitators to promote violence in our state. We're going to put an end to it immediately."

Sanford said that the local officers, patrolmen and FBI agents "were on the job."

"It is well known," Sanford said, "that North Carolina has no trouble from people who seek their goals from legitimate means. It is also known that this state will not tolerate violence from anybody for any purpose."

Sanford asserted that "the band of agitators who have descended on Monroe came at the request of an outspoken advocate of violence, a self-styled Castro who has attempt-

Jack Pritchard called on me, he is some-
times called Gullah Jack, sometimes
Couter Jack, he gave me some dry
food, consisting of parched corn
and ground nuts, and said, eat
that, and nothing else, on the
morning when it breaks out, and
when you join us as we pass, put
into your mouth this crab claw,
and you can't be wounded, and,
said he, I give the same to the rest
of my troops—if you drop the large
crab claw out of your mouth, then
put in the small one.

. . . the country born promised to join
him, because he was a doctor . . .

He said, his charms
would not protect him
from the treachery of his
own colour . . .

—————

. . . to set the town on fire in several
places, at the Governor's Mills, and
near the Docks, and for every servant
in the yards to be ready with axes and
knives and clubs, to kill every man, as
he came out when the bells began to
ring.

. . . an indiscriminate slaughter of
whites, and also Blacks who had not
joined them, or did not immediately
do so . . .

Well, said he, if you don't join you'll be
killed.

Asked if white women and children
would be killed, Denmark answered,

ed to grow a beard, who wears a
beret, and who carries a loaded car-
bine. It is significant that he has
been denounced by the respected
leadership of both races."

Although the governor did not
identify Williams by name, the ref-
erence was obvious.

Atty. Gen Robert F. Kennedy
described the situation in Monroe
as under control.

Kennedy said he had received a
full report on the disturbance. "On
the basis of facts reported to me, I
would hope and expect that persons
responsible for the violence, includ-
ing the holding of a man and his
wife as hostages, will be prosecuted
to the full extent of the law,"
Kennedy said.

"The local authorities in Monroe
and the officials of the state of
North Carolina moved vigorously
and effectively under difficult cir-
cumstances to control the distur-
bance. The situation is under con-
trol and no action by the federal
government is contemplated."

The governor ordered 50 highway
patrolmen and two State Bureau of
Investigation agents here to assist
the overworked Monroe Police
Department in restoring order.

The FBI, asked by the Justice De-
partment to learn the facts, also dis-
patched agents to watch the situa-
tion.

The middle-aged couple who
were held hostage, Mr. and Mrs. G.
Bruce Stegall of nearby Marshville,
testified before the grand jury that
Superior Court Judge Allen H.
Gwyn ordered to look into the
interracial situation.

What was the use of killing the louse and leaving the nit?

And another time,

> *. . . it was for our safety not to spare one skin alive.*

The City would be fired,

> *. . . because nothing could be done without fire . . .*

. . . a quantity of *slow match* was secreted at Gibb's & Harper's Wharf . . .

Telémakhos left the hall, hefting
> *his lance,*
with two swift flickering
> *hounds for company*

July 14, 1822, at midnight—the second Sunday in the month—was the date appointed by Vesey . . . at this time of year, many of the Whites would be gone, summering at Sullivan's Island, up-country, or in the North . . . on Sundays, country Negroes could come into town, without exciting suspicion . . . and Charleston would be dark, the last quarter of the moon occurring on the 11th and the new moon not due until the 18th . . .

Saturday afternoon, May 25th, Wil-
(*. . . but take care*
liam Paul, slave, tried to enlist a new
> *don't mention it*
recruit, one Peter,
> *to those waiting men*

The Stegalls said they took a shortcut on their way home, and a band of about 200 Negroes, many of them armed, stopped them on the street where Williams lives.

"We were scared," said Mrs. Stegall, who said they had nothing to do with the racial disturbances and had passed through Williams' neighborhood by chance. "They took us into Williams' house and tied us up. They had guns on us. The house was filled with Negroes and others were outside in the yard around the house."

(8/31/61)

POLICE DIG
UP ARSENAL
IN MONROE

Related Stories on Page 7A
MONROE- (AP) - Police raided the home of the president of the Monroe Non-Violent Action Committee tonight and confiscated a small arsenal of weapons, including one of Russian make.

Richard Crowder, 19-year-old Negro head of the group, had been picked up earlier for investigation in the kidnaping of a white couple during the aftermath of an interracial disturbance Sunday.

Crowder was charged with kidnaping and was held without bond.

Officers said they found 11 weapons, most of them rifles, in the attic of Crowder's home. They said the weapons were among those collected recently by Robert F. Wil-

personal servant to Col. Prioleau . . .
who receive presents
Peter was astonished, said that he
of old coats, &c.
was grateful to his master for his
from their masters,
kindness, and withdrew . . . the con-
or they'll betray us
versation was reported to the auth-
. . . *)*
orities . . . William Paul was arrest-
ed, grilled, and remanded to the
black hole of the work house . . .
May 30, after much persuasion, he
broke down, admitted there was a
plot, and pointed to Peter Poyas and
Mingo Harth as leaders . . .

Peter and Mingo were picked up,
but remained cool and composed,
treated the charges with great levity
. . . they were released for want of
evidence . . .

Black and white were now on guard
. . . Vesey advanced the date of
attack to Sunday June 16 . . . messen-
gers tried to reach the country
Negroes, but travel was difficult . . .

June 8, William Paul—still in the
black hole—talked again, but the
plot was not revealed . . .

June 14, George Wilson, half-breed
blacksmith and slave to Major John
Wilson, revealed enlarged informa-
tion to the Major, including the date
of attack: June 16, two days hence . . .

Militia was called out, arms pre-
pared, the arsenals heavily guarded:
by Sunday night, Charleston was an

liams, 36-year-old militant Negro
leader, who is being sought on a kid-
nap warrant. Williams, with his wife
and children, fled the city Sunday
night in the wake of the distur-
bances.

State Bureau of Investigation
Agent John Vanderford said one of
the weapons was a large caliber rifle
of Russian make and bore the ham-
mer and sickle emblem on its side.

(9/1/61)

WILLIAMS
REPORTEDLY
SEEN IN N.C.

CLINTON, N.C. - (AP) - A man an-
swering the description of Robert F.
Williams, militant Negro leader
wanted for kidnaping in Monroe,
was the object of a search in eastern
North Carolina Thursday night.

Highway patrolmen were told the
man stopped his black, 1958 car for
mechanical repairs at a garage on
U.S. 701 just north of here.

The patrol station at Eliza-
Raleigh said the car proceeded
north on U.S. 701 before repairs
could be made. The station did not
know the nature of the mechanical
trouble.

This description of the driver was
broadcast to patrolmen in the area:
Negro, 5 - 11, 210 pounds, wearing a
goatee and having a heavy build.

The patrol station said the car
bore National Association for the
Advancement of Colored People
stickers on its front bumper and
windshield.

armed camp, and white civilians filled the streets, full of curiosity . . . a few country Negroes made their way to the City, but Vesey sent word to them to return:

there would be no insurrection . . .

June 17, arrests were made: Peter and Mungo Poyas, and Ned, Rolla, Batteau, and Mathias Bennet. A special court was formed, convening June 19, and arrests continued . . .

June 20, suspicion fell for the first time on Denmark Vesey . . .

. . . he had disappeared . . .

Search began, and on the night of the 22nd,

during a perfect tempest

the city guard entered the house of one of his wives, and dragged him out . . . one more day and it was expected he would have boarded ship, and escaped—perhaps to a Negro Caribbean island . . .

The defendants, on trial, failed to gratify the court with displays of fear . . . Rolla showed *great presence and composure of mind,* and Ned *was stern and immovable* . . . Peter's behavior *indicated the reverse* of fear . . . Denmark folded his arms, listened attentively, and fixed his eyes on the floor . . .

Denmark Vesey—The Court, on mature consideration, have pronounced

There was a 20-minute lag between the time the car left the station and the time a patrolman arrived. This would have given the driver sufficient time to reach the Newton Grove traffic circle, about 17 miles north, and cut off in almost any direction.

(9/30/61)

WILLIAMS REPORTED IN CUBA

MONROE - (AP) - "That's fine," Mayor Fred Wilson said . . .

you Guilty—You have enjoyed the advantage of able Counsel, and were also heard in your own defence, in which you endeavoured, with great art and plausibility, to impress a belief of your innocence. After the most patient deliberation, however, the Court were not only satisfied of your guilt, but that you were the author, and original instigator of this diabolical plot. Your professed design was to trample on all laws, human and divine; to riot in blood, outrage, rapine . . . and conflagration, and to introduce anarchy and confusion . . . Your life has become, therefore, a just and necessary sacrifice, at the shrine of indignant Justice . . .

. . . a few tears fell from Denmark's eyes . . .

At the trial of Peter Poyas, he was asked if it was possible he could wish to see his master and family murdered—who had treated him so kindly! . . .

. . . Peter smiled . . .

To fellow prisoners, Peter said,

Do not open your lips! Die silent, as you shall see me do.

July 2nd, the gallows were set up on Blake's lands, outside the City . . . Peter Poyas, Ned, Rolla, and Batteau Bennet, and Denmark Vesey were hanged . . .

(July 4th, at six A.M., troops gath-
ered at Broad and Meeting,
marched east on Broad to East Bay,
and south on East Bay to the Bat-
tery: the 46th anniversary of the
establishment of Liberty . . . at St.
Phillip's Church, Washington's
Farewell Address was read, and at
St. Michael's, the Declaration of
Independence . . .)

Executions continued: July 26, a
long gallows was set up on The
Lines and 26 were hanged . . .

         Total arrests 131
         Convicted. 67
         Hanged 35
         Banished 32

. . . later, Peter Prioleau and George
Wilson—informers—were emanci-
pated, exempted from taxes, and
given a grant of $50 a year, for life
. . .

(10/1/61)

NEGRO ASKS, GETS ASYLUM FROM CUBA

HAVANA - (AP) - Robert F. Wil-
liams has escaped to Cuba.

The 36-year-old militant integra-
tionist leader, wanted for kidnaping
a white couple during racial violence
in Monroe, N.C., has long been an
admirer of the Cuban government.

A Havana radio report, moni-
tored Saturday in Key West, Fla.,
said that Williams asked and
received political asylum.

The FBI and the Royal Canadian
Mounted Police were seeking Wil-
liams . . .

OKEFENOKEE

Mose Thrift, early Okefenokee pioneer, white, had two sons,
Hard and George . . .

. . . they
set up a saw mill south of Waycross, hauled cypress out of the swamp,

and cut it

Hard

Thrift

logged

the

trembling

earth

SHICK SHOCK

Where the sun sleeps, our fathers came thence.

. . . the Earth opened in the West, where its mouth is.

*In Siberia, the Angara culture: sedentary, fishing through the ice on
Lake Baikal, the Amoor and Shilka Rivers . . .*

Everybody from over there across the water stayed in
the large villages of the first land.

*. . . until the snow shoe was developed, and Siberian Indian and Eski-
mo separated, race and language diversifying, as they pursued game
across the tundra . . .*

The water froze over where they stayed: snow came,
the wind blew, and it was cold.

*Later, the climate changed, as the glaciers began to melt, the game
retreated northward . . .*

Long ago they didn't know there was land here.
He said long ago they began to starve.
In the old world nothing would grow.
For many years they were starving.

So they gathered together.
They held a council.
Because they were starving they decided to go and
    look for another land.

They made up their minds.
They thought elsewhere there was land.
They will try to eat.

... eastward, onto the Siberian coastal plain, the Chukchi peninsula ...

There where the land slopes north and at the time
when the wind was blowing and the weather was get-
ting cold . . .

... to Bering Strait:

There at the edge of all the water where the land ends
. . .

... and across:

. . . the Northerners were of one mind and the East-
erners were of one mind: it would be good to live on
the other side of the frozen water.

*... ice corridors opening in the Sangamon Interglacial, or during and
following the Wisconsin ...*

As they were walking suddenly they knew they were
      walking on ice.
For many days they walked on ice.

One group didn't want to go.
One group went to the east.
They went where the sun rises.
They went in search of food.

*... man and animal, sub-Arctic plant and forest of conifer, following
the retreating glaciers ...*

. . . so that the water ran and ran, spreading in hollows

and making hollows, penetrating here and penetrating there.

. . . northeastward, to the mouth of the Mackenzie . . .

As the water rippled on, long extended areas became dry even where there were hollows and in caves . . .

. . . or due south, into the valley of the Yukon . . .

Ten thousand men went upstream, went right on upstream during a single day, upstream to the eastern lands . . . every man kept going along.

. . . the ice melting, the upper Yukon opening to the Liard and the Peace, and thence to the Fraser . . .

men and women, following the inter-montane valleys, to the area of the Columbia: rich in fish, roots, and game . .

Those who were strong and those who had power came away, separating from those who remained living there.

The strongest, the gentlest, and the most religious did this: they were the hunters.

To the north, east, south, and west the hunters traveled.

The Rockies—"the backbone of the earth"—a staging area . . . in the foothills to the east, an axis of colonization . . .

Early in the morning several of the runners went away
　　to the east.
They continued a long time in the direction of the
　　east.

Eastward further, the great plains, the open prairie, without tree or shelter, formed a barrier (so that a family, dipersing from the valley of the Columbia, might reach Patagonia before Florida . . .

But there were passages through the plains: north of the Saskatchewan to Lake Winnipeg, by the chain of lakes to the St. Lawrence . . . by the Yellowstone and Missouri to the Mississippi . . .

> Once again they were in a settlement by the Yellow River, where berries were abundant among the rocks and stones.

. . . by the Platte to the Missouri, or by the Arkansas, and thence to the Mississippi . . .

> Now when daylight came, he spoke three times: 'Let those going east be many.'

Buffalo paths—"threads of soil" . . .

> By the good hills and along the plains, buffalo were beginning to graze.

Along the streams, game, water, fuel and shelter . . . pioneer plants of the mid-latitudes springing from the earth-debris that mantled the melting ice blocks . . .

> When the seventh runner arrived he saw a big woods
>   with abundant food.
> There was so much food to eat here they decided to go
>   back for the others.
> Here they will also live.
> They went back to find where they had come across.
> They were not able to find it.
> The ice had melted.

In the lower Missouri valley, the first taste of mid-latitude woodlands: walnut, hickory, and pecan, on the uplands . . . stands of oak, with sweet acorns . . . grape, black cherry, persimmon, and pawpaw . . .

. . . a vast country, a good land, where cold winds never blow . . .

. . . Virginia deer, opossom, turkey, quail, and woodcock . . . migrant waterfowl, spring and fall, in the Mississippi flyway . . . chert, suitable for tools, in the Ozark hills . . . salt licks in the shale beds . . . caves and rock shelters in the creek and river bluffs . . .

A long time ago several young men made up their minds to find the place where the Sun lives and see what the Sun is like. They got ready their bows and arrows . . . and started out toward the east. At first they met tribes they knew, then they came to tribes they had only heard about, and at last to others of which they had never heard.

The Coweta, on top of a high mountain at the backbone of the earth, could see both the setting and the rising of the sun. They debated whether to go toward the sunset or the sunrise, but finally turned eastward, toward the sunrise. They traveled slowly, stopping where the hunting was good, and going on again, until they came at last to a river, wide and muddy, so wide that they stayed on its banks longer than anywhere else . . .

They came to a thick, muddy, slimy river, camped there, rested there, and stayed over night there. The next day, they continued their journey and came, in one day, to a red, bloody river. They lived by this river, and ate of its fishes for two years; but there were low springs there; and it did not please them to remain.

They also saw a trail which led into the River; and as they could not see the trail on the opposite bank, they believed that the people had gone into the River, and would not again come forth.

They separated at Fish River . . .

Northward, the Great Lakes: Algonquins and others, invading from the Mackenzie River, Great Bear and Great Slave Lakes, Lakes Athabaska and Winnipeg, to Superior, Michigan, and Huron, skirting or crossing the waters, at Michilimackinac, Sault Ste. Marie, and the Detroit ...

halting, camping, to enjoy the fisheries: a resting place, a staging area, a secondary point of emigration ...

> ... and in the Eastern Land, the fish land, beside a body of water far from the buffalo country ...

... at the Coppermine River, the men's feet were worn out with walking ...

... south of Lake Superior, a culture center: the Woodland Pattern, with pottery but without agriculture, imported without loss from Lake Baikal, Siberia ...

To the southeast, the Creeks came from the northwest, penetrated as far as Florida, and fell back to the headwaters of the Alabama and Savannah Rivers ...

> *... others came from the Red River, crossed the Mississippi, to the Coosa, the Tallapoosa, and the Ocmulgee ...*

> *... from the Mississippi, the Muskogee and the Natchez moved southeastward ...*

> *... the Alabama came from northwest and southwest, the Tuskegee from the north ...*

> *... from the Great Lakes, tribes of Algonquin stock reached into Tennessee, then across the mountains to Virginia and the Carolinas ...*

> *the Calusa crossed the Mississippi, penetrated the Florida peninsula ...*

> *... the Cherokee were of Iroquoian stock, turned south from the upper reaches of the Ohio ...*

. . . the Tuscarora separated from the Iroquois at the Lakes, and, wandering and hunting, southeastward, crossed the Alleghanies to the Carolina Piedmont, and the Neuse . . .

. . . the areas of Tennessee and Kentucky were crossed and recrossed, there were movements east and west on the Tennessee River . . .

. . . Siouan tribes crossed the mountains, from the Ohio valley to the Piedmont . . .

. . . the Yuchi migrated from East Tennessee to Florida . . .

. . . Biloxi came from the Juniata River, or from eastern Ohio, to the Gulf Coast . . .

. . . in search of grains, edible roots, fish and game . . .

. . . the southernmost tip of the Florida peninsula was reached by tribes of Apalachee . . .

. . . the Chickasaws came from the west, across the Mississippi to the Alabama, and Chickasaw Old Fields . . .

. . . a tribe of Creeks lived anciently in the west, but they could find nothing pure in the world except the Sun, and they determined to travel eastward to find the place from whence it came . . .

. . . from the Lakes or from Mississippi headwaters, the Shawnee crossed to the Scioto, and then into western Kentucky . . .

. . . with the Nanticoke and Shawnee to land in the south.

. . the Catawha emigrated out of Canada to the sources of the Kentucky, thence eastward into Carolina . . .

. . . there was a continuous filtration southward from the northeast . . .

. . . and later, northeastward, from the south . . .

. . . in an extensive country; and there for a long time they were to remain in this eastern stony land . . .

. . . which did not belong to the Snakes: it was a good land and a rich land.

. . . from the Juaniata-Susquehanna pass, the Lenni Lenape moved to the Great Bay River—the Susquehanna—and thence to Chesapeake Bay . . .

. . . the Iroquois moved into New York, arriving, very early, from the region of the Ozarks . . . or they came from the north, from Canada . . .

The Snow Mountain men were now south of the lakes; and while their Iroquois friends were north of the lakes . . .

. . . arriving at the western end of Lake Erie, separating, flowing eastward north and south of the lake, rejoining at the Niagara River, again separating, flowing eastward . . .

. . . to proceed towards the sunrise . . . and come to a river . . . and going round a mountain . . . and went down the bank of the river and come to where it discharges into a great river running towards the midday sun . . .

The people were yet in one language; some of the people went to the banks of the great water towards the midday sun; but the main company returned as they came . . .

. . . diversifying, spreading along the Mohawk, at the falls of the Oswego, and westward . . .

. . . and tribes of the Algonquins, moving in from the west, separated, flowing eastward, north and south of the established Iroquois, filling the open spaces . . .

Earlier, a neolithic Siberian people, neither Eskimo nor Indian, arrived in Alaska, moved eastward, along the polar periphery, as far as Greenland . . .

. . . later, the caribou Eskimo crossed Bering Strait, spread to Greenland and south to the shores of Hudson Bay . . .

. . . driven by the Athapaskans who followed . . .

. . . and the Iroquois drove the Micmacs down the St. John valley, south of the Shick Shocks, into New Brunswick and Nova Scotia . . .

In the west, immigrants following the valleys of the Rockies and the Pacific littoral southward, reached Mexico and the southern hemisphere . . .

. . .discovered teosinte, *the tasseled grass, and developed maize . . .*

From the Huasteca region of coastal Tamaulipas, overland through Texas—or from south of the Yucatan peninsula—or from the Olmec cultures at La Venta and around Vera Cruz, thence by large canoe to Florida, the mouth of the Crystal River:

. . . a mesoamerican emigration northward, of corn culture and mound building, to the American Bottoms: the Mississippi valley, at the mouths of the Missouri and the Illinois . . .

. . . radiating thence northward to the limits of corn culture . . .

. . . southward to the Gulf . . .

. . . thence eastward and northward again—blending with Siberian Woodland—throughout Appalachian America, to the Atlantic shore . . .

All the hunters were approaching the large body of water where the sun rises from the water.

The Coweta made boats and crossed the Mississippi, and continued eastward until they reached the Big Water. They found that the water of the ocean would come up and go out again, enabling them to collect oysters and other good things to eat, so they remained here, being unable to pass beyond . . .

. . . and the Creeks, traveling eastward in search of the Sun, camped at the ocean shore. In the morning, they saw the Sun rise out of the water, and they concluded that that was why it was so pure and bright . . .

When Red Arrow was chief, they were so far downstream that tides could be felt.

When Red-Paint Soul was chief, they were at the mighty water.

. . . at the great–salt–water–lake . . .
. . . the Mohegans stated that their forefathers came out of the northwest, foresaking a tidewater country, and crossing over a great watery tract . . . they crossed many streams, but none in which the water ebbed and flowed, until they reached the Hudson, which reminded them of the tidal ocean of their nativity . . .
. . . and the Indians almost universally believed the dry land they knew, to be a part of a great island, everywhere surrounded by waters whose limits were unknown . . .

HERJOLF BARDARSON HAD LIVED FOR A TIME AT DREPSTOKK; HIS WIFE WAS CALLED THORGERD, AND THEY HAD A SON CALLED BJARNI.

BJARNI WAS A MAN OF MUCH PROMISE. FROM EARLY YOUTH HE HAD BEEN EAGER TO SAIL TO FOREIGN LANDS; HE EARNED HIMSELF BOTH WEALTH AND A GOOD REPUTATION, AND USED TO SPEND HIS WINTERS ALTERNATIVELY ABROAD AND IN ICELAND WITH HIS FATHER. HE SOON HAD A MERCHANT SHIP OF HIS OWN.

DURING THE LAST WINTER THAT BJARNI SPENT IN NORWAY, HIS FATHER, HERJOLF, SOLD UP THE FARM AND EMIGRATED TO GREENLAND WITH EIRIK THE RED . . .

BJARNI ARRIVED IN ICELAND AT EYRAR IN THE SUMMER OF THE YEAR THAT HIS FATHER HAD LEFT FOR GREENLAND. THE NEWS CAME AS A SHOCK TO BJARNI, AND HE REFUSED TO HAVE HIS SHIP UNLOADED. HIS CREW ASKED HIM WHAT HE HAD IN MIND; HE REPLIED THAT HE INTENDED TO KEEP HIS CUSTOM OF

ENJOYING HIS FATHER'S HOSPITALITY OVER THE WINTER— 'SO I WANT TO SAIL MY SHIP TO GREENLAND, IF YOU ARE WILLING TO COME WITH ME.'

THEY ALL REPLIED THAT THEY WOULD DO WHAT HE THOUGHT BEST. THEN BJARNI SAID, 'THIS VOYAGE OF OURS WILL BE CONSIDERED FOOLHARDY, FOR NOT ONE OF US HAS EVER SAILED THE GREENLAND SEA.'

HOWEVER, THEY PUT TO SEA AS SOON AS THEY WERE READY AND SAILED FOR THREE DAYS UNTIL LAND WAS LOST TO SIGHT BELOW THE HORIZON. THEN THE FAIR WIND FAILED AND NORTHERLY WINDS AND FOG SET IN, AND FOR MANY DAYS THEY HAD NO IDEA WHAT THEIR COURSE WAS. AFTER THAT THEY SAW THE SUN AGAIN AND WERE ABLE TO GET THEIR BEARINGS; THEY HOISTED SAIL AND AFTER A DAY'S SAILING THEY SIGHTED LAND.

THEY DISCUSSED AMONGST THEMSELVES WHAT COUNTRY THIS MIGHT BE. BJARNI SAID HE THOUGHT IT COULD NOT BE GREENLAND. THE CREW ASKED HIM IF HE WANTED TO LAND THERE OR NOT; BJARNI REPLIED, 'I THINK WE SHOULD SAIL IN CLOSE.'

THEY DID SO, AND SOON THEY COULD SEE THAT THE COUNTRY WAS NOT MOUNTAINOUS, BUT WAS WELL WOODED AND WITH LOW HILLS. SO THEY PUT TO SEA AGAIN, LEAVING THE LAND ON THE PORT QUARTER; AND AFTER SAILING FOR TWO DAYS THEY SIGHTED LAND ONCE MORE.

BJARNI'S MEN ASKED HIM IF HE THOUGHT THIS WAS GREEN-LAND YET; HE SAID HE DID NOT THINK THAT WAS GREENLAND, ANY MORE THAN THE PREVIOUS ONE—'FOR THERE ARE SAID TO BE HUGE GLACIERS IN GREENLAND.'

THEY CLOSED THE LAND QUICKLY AND SAW THAT THEY THOUGHT IT ADVISABLE TO LAND THERE, BUT BJARNI REFUSED. THEY CLAIMED THEY NEEDED BOTH FIREWOOD AND WATER; BUT BJARNI SAID, 'YOU HAVE NO SHORTAGE OF EITHER.' HE WAS CRITICIZED FOR THIS BY HIS MEN.

HE ORDERED THEM TO HOIST SAIL, AND THEY DID SO. THEY TURNED THE PROW OUT TO SEA AND SAILED BEFORE A SOUTH-WEST WIND FOR THREE DAYS BEFORE THEY SIGHTED A THIRD

LAND. THIS ONE WAS HIGH AND MOUNTAINOUS, AND TOPPED BY A GLACIER. AGAIN THEY ASKED BJARNI IF HE WISHED TO LAND THERE, BUT HE REPLIED, 'NO, FOR THIS COUNTRY SEEMS TO BE WORTHLESS.'

THEY DID NOT LOWER SAIL THIS TIME, BUT FOLLOWED THE COASTLINE AND SAW THAT IT WAS AN ISLAND. ONCE AGAIN THEY PUT THE LAND ASTERN AND SAILED OUT TO SEA BEFORE THE SAME FAIR WIND. BUT NOW IT BEGAN TO BLOW A GALE, AND BJARNI ORDERED HIS MEN TO SHORTEN SAIL AND NOT TO GO HARDER THAN SHIP AND RIGGING COULD STAND . . .

. . . persons floating in from the east: the Whites were coming.

SOME TIME LATER, BJARNI HERJOLFSSON SAILED FROM GREEN-LAND TO NORWAY AND VISITED EARL EIRIK, WHO RECEIVED HIM WELL. BJARNI TOLD THE EARL ABOUT HIS VOYAGE AND THE LANDS HE HAD SIGHTED. PEOPLE THOUGHT HE HAD SHOWN GREAT LACK OF CURIOSITY, SINCE HE COULD TELL THEM NOTH-ING ABOUT THESE COUNTRIES, AND HE WAS CRITICIZED FOR THIS . . .

THERE WAS NOW GREAT TALK OF DISCOVERING NEW COUN-TRIES. LIEF, THE SON OF EIRIK THE RED OF BRATTAHLID, WENT TO SEE BJARNI HERJOLFSSON AND BOUGHT IIIS SHIP FROM HIM, AND ENGAGED A CREW OF THIRTY-FIVE . . .

THEY MADE THEIR SHIP READY AND PUT OUT TO SEA. THE FIRST LANDFALL THEY MADE WAS THE COUNTRY THAT BJARNI HAD SIGHTED LAST. THEY SAILED RIGHT UP TO THE SHORE AND CAST ANCHOR, THEN LOWERED A BOAT AND LANDED. THERE WAS NO GRASS TO BE SEEN, AND THE HINTERLAND WAS COV-ERED WITH GREAT GLACIERS, AND BETWEEN GLACIERS AND SHORE THE LAND WAS LIKE ONE GREAT SLAB OF ROCK. IT SEEMED TO THEM A WORTHLESS COUNTRY.

THEN LEIF SAID, 'NOW WE HAVE DONE BETTER THAN BJARNI WHERE THIS COUNTRY IS CONCERNED—WE AT LEAST HAVE SET FOOT ON IT. I SHALL GIVE THIS COUNTRY A NAME AND CALL IT *HELLULAND*.'

THEY RETURNED TO THEIR SHIP AND PUT OUT TO SEA, AND SIGHTED A SECOND LAND. ONCE AGAIN THEY SAILED RIGHT UP TO IT AND CAST ANCHOR, LOWERED A BOAT, AND WENT ASHORE. THIS COUNTRY WAS FLAT AND WOODED, WITH WHITE SANDY BEACHES WHEREVER THEY WENT; AND THE LAND SLOPED GENTLY DOWN TO THE SEA.

LEIF SAID, 'THIS COUNTRY SHALL BE NAMED AFTER ITS NATURAL RESOURCES: IT SHALL BE CALLED *MARKLAND*.'

THEY HURRIED BACK TO THEIR SHIP AS QUICKLY AS POSSIBLE AND SAILED AWAY TO SEA IN A NORTHWEST WIND FOR TWO DAYS UNTIL THEY SIGHTED LAND AGAIN. THEY SAILED TOWARDS IT AND CAME TO AN ISLAND WHICH LAY TO THE NORTH OF IT.

THEY WENT ASHORE AND LOOKED ABOUT THEM. THE WEATHER WAS FINE. THERE WAS DEW ON THE GRASS, AND THE FIRST THING THEY DID WAS GET SOME OF IT ON THEIR HANDS AND PUT IT TO THEIR LIPS, AND TO THEM IT SEEMED THE SWEETEST THING THEY HAD EVER TASTED. THEN THEY WENT BACK TO THEIR SHIP AND SAILED INTO THE SOUND THAT LAY BETWEEN THE ISLAND AND THE HEADLAND JUTTING OUT TO THE NORTH.

THEY STEERED A WESTERLY COURSE ROUND THE HEADLAND. THERE WERE EXTENSIVE SHALLOWS THERE AND AT LOW TIDE THEIR SHIP WAS LEFT HIGH AND DRY, WITH THE SEA ALMOST OUT OF SIGHT. BUT THEY WERE SO IMPATIENT TO LAND THAT THEY COULD NOT BEAR TO WAIT FOR THE RISING TIDE TO FLOAT THE SHIP; THEY RAN ASHORE TO A PLACE WHERE A RIVER FLOWED OUT OF A LAKE. AS SOON AS THE TIDE HAD REFLOATED THE SHIP THEY TOOK A BOAT AND ROWED OUT TO IT AND BROUGHT IT UP THE RIVER INTO THE LAKE, WHERE THEY ANCHORED IT. THEY CARRIED THEIR HAMMOCKS ASHORE AND PUT UP BOOTHS. THEN THEY DECIDED TO WINTER THERE, AND BUILT SOME LARGE HOUSES.

THERE WAS NO LACK OF SALMON IN THE RIVER OR THE LAKE, BIGGER SALMON THAN THEY HAD EVER SEEN. THE COUNTRY SEEMED TO THEM SO KIND THAT NO WINTER FODDER WOULD BE NEEDED FOR LIVESTOCK: THERE WAS NEVER ANY FROST ALL WINTER AND THE GRASS HARDLY WITHERED AT ALL.

IN THIS COUNTRY, NIGHT AND DAY WERE OF MORE EVEN

LENGTH THAN IN EITHER GREENLAND OR ICELAND: ON THE SHORTEST DAY OF THE YEAR, THE SUN WAS ALREADY UP BY 9 A.M., AND DID NOT SET UNTIL AFTER 3 P.M.

WHEN THEY HAD FINISHED BUILDING THEIR HOUSES, LEIF SAID TO HIS COMPANIONS 'NOW I WANT TO DIVIDE OUR COMPANY INTO TWO PARTIES AND HAVE THE COUNTRY EXPLORED; HALF OF THE COMPANY ARE TO REMAIN HERE AT THE HOUSES WHILE THE OTHER HALF GO EXPLORING—BUT THEY MUST NOT GO SO FAR THAT THEY CANNOT RETURN THE SAME EVENING, AND THEY ARE NOT TO BECOME SEPARATED.'

THEY CARRIED OUT THESE INSTRUCTIONS FOR A TIME. LEIF HIMSELF TOOK TURNS AT GOING OUT WITH THE EXPLORING PARTY AND STAYING BEHIND AT THE BASE.

LEIF WAS TALL AND STRONG AND VERY IMPRESSIVE IN APPEARANCE. HE WAS A SHREWD MAN AND ALWAYS MODERATE IN HIS BEHAVIOR

ONE EVENING NEWS CAME THAT SOMEONE WAS MISSING: IT WAS TYRKIR THE SOUTHERNER. LEIF WAS VERY DISPLEASED AT THIS, FOR TYRKIR HAD BEEN WITH THE FAMILY FOR A LONG TIME, AND WHEN LEIF WAS A CHILD HAD BEEN DEVOTED TO HIM. LEIF REBUKED THE MEN SEVERELY, AND GOT READY TO MAKE A SEARCH WITH TWELVE MEN.

THEY HAD GONE ONLY A SHORT DISTANCE FROM THE HOUSES WHEN TYRKIR CAME WALKING TOWARDS THEM, AND THEY GAVE HIM A WARM WELCOME. LEIF QUICKLY REALIZED THAT TYRKIR WAS IN EXCELLENT HUMOUR.

TYRKIR HAD A PROMINENT FOREHEAD AND SHIFTY EYES, AND NOT MUCH MORE OF A FACE BESIDES; HE WAS SHORT AND PUNY-LOOKING BUT VERY CLEVER WITH HIS HANDS.

LEIF SAID TO HIM, 'WHY ARE YOU SO LATE, FOSTER-FATHER? HOW DID YOU GET SEPARATED FROM YOUR COMPANIONS?'

AT FIRST TYRKIR SPOKE FOR A LONG TIME IN GERMAN, ROLLING HIS EYES IN ALL DIRECTIONS AND PULLING FACES, AND NO ONE COULD UNDERSTAND WHAT HE WAS SAYING. AFTER A WHILE HE SPOKE IN ICELANDIC.

'I DID NOT GO MUCH FARTHER THAN YOU,' HE SAID. 'I HAVE SOME NEWS. I FOUND VINES AND GRAPES.'

AS THE VERY BEATING

'IS THAT TRUE, FOSTER-FATHER?' ASKED LEIF.

'OF COURSE IT IS TRUE,' HE REPLIED. 'WHERE I WAS BORN
THERE WERE PLENTY OF VINES AND GRAPES.'

AS THE VERY BEATING AND SURGE

THEY SLEPT FOR THE REST OF THE NIGHT, AND NEXT MORN-
ING LEIF SAID TO HIS MEN, 'NOW WE HAVE TWO TASKS ON OUR
HANDS. ON ALTERNATE DAYS WE MUST GATHER GRAPES AND
CUT VINES, AND THEN FELL TREES, TO MAKE A CARGO FOR MY
SHIP.'

THIS WAS DONE. IT IS SAID THAT THE TOW-BOAT WAS FILLED
WITH GRAPES.

AS THE VERY BEATING AND SURGE OF THE SEA

THEY TOOK ON A FULL CARGO OF TIMBER AND IN THE SPRING
THEY MADE READY TO LEAVE AND SAILED AWAY. LEIF NAMED
THE COUNTRY AFTER ITS NATURAL QUALITIES AND CALLED IT
VINLAND.

*AS THE VERY BEATING AND SURGE OF THE SEA OUER-
FLOWED THEM*

. . . where persons were floating in from the north and
from the south: the Whites . . .

BY GOD'S WILL, AFTER A LONG VOYAGE FROM THE ISLAND OF
GREENLAND TO THE SOUTH TOWARD THE MOST DISTANT
REMAINING PARTS OF THE WESTERN OCEAN SEA, SAILING
SOUTHWARD AMIDST THE ICE, THE COMPANIONS BJARNI AND
LEIF EIRIKSSON DISCOVERED A NEW LAND, EXTREMELY FERTILE
AND EVEN HAVING VINES, THE WHICH ISLAND THEY NAMED
VINLAND.

. . . THIS TRULY VAST AND VERY RICH LAND . . .

. . . friendly people with great possessions: who are
they?

COCOANUT INDIANS

ROSTER

OF THE OFFICERS OF THE ARMY OF THE UNITED COLONIES,
AS ORGANIZED FOR THE NARRAGANSETT CAMPAIGN,
AND MUSTERED AT PETTIQUAMSCOT,
DECEMBER 19, 1675

General Josiah Winslow, Governor of Plymouth Colony,
Commander-in-Chief.

General Staff.
Daniel Weld, of Salem, Chief Surgeon
Joseph Dudley, of Boston, Chaplain.
Benjamin Church, of Little Compton, R.I., Aid.

MASSACHUSETTS REGIMENT.
Samuel Appleton, of Ipswich, Major and Captain of First Company.

Regimental Staff.
Richard Knott, of Marblehead, Surgeon
Samuel Nowell, of Boston, Chaplain
John Morse, of Ipswich, Commissary.

Officers of the Line.
First Company: Jeremiah Swain, Lieutenant.
Ezekial Woodword, Sergeant (Acting Ensign).
Second Company: Samuel Mosely, Captain.
Perez Savage, Lieutenant.
Third Company: James Oliver, Captain.
Ephraim Turner, Lieutenant.
Peter Bennett, Sergeant (Acting Ensign).
Fourth Company: Isaac Johnson, Captain.
Phineas Upham, Lieutenant.
Henry Bowen, Ensign.

Fifth Company: Nathaniel Davenport, Captain.
Edward Tyng, Lieutenant.
John Drury, Ensign.
Sixth Company: Joseph Gardiner, Captain.
William Hathorne, Lieutenant.
Benjamin Sweet, Ensign (promoted Lieutenant).
Jeremiah Neal, Sergeant (promoted Ensign).
Cavalry Company ("Troop"): Thomas Prentice, Captain.
John Wyman, Cornet (promoted Lieutenant).

PLYMOUTH REGIMENT.
William Bradford, of Marshfield,
Major and Captain of First Company.

Regimental Staff.
Mathew Fuller, of Barnstable, Surgeon.
Thomas Huckins, of Barnstable, Commissary.

Officers of the Line.
First Company: Robert Barker, of Duxbury, Lieutenant.
Second Company: John Gorham, of Barnstable, Captain.
Jonathan Sparrow, of Eastham, Lieutenant.
William Wetherell, Sergeant.

CONNECTICUT REGIMENT.
Robert Treat, of Milford, Major.

Regimental Staff.
Gershom Bulkely, Surgeon.
Rev. Nicholas Noyes, Chaplain.
Stephen Barrett, Commissary.

Officers of the Line.
First Company: John Gallop, of Stonington, Captain.
Second Company: Samuel Marshall, of Windsor, Captain.
Third Company: Nathaniel Seely, of Stratford, Captain.
Fourth Company: Thomas Watts, of Hartford, Captain.
Fifth Company: John Mason, of Norwich, Captain.

To the First and Fifth Connecticut Companies were attached Indian
Scouting Companies, numbering seventy-five to each.

*a flicker in the palm frond, as the busboy held a match to find the socket
in the husk of cocoanut, for the yellow bulb . . .*

*a flicker, a glow, a
puff of light, a black hole in the draped blue satin of the ceiling*

*the flame
the black hole eating wider, down the satin puff, red at the edge*

the men of Massachusetts and Plymouth had left a garrison at
Smith's trading post in Wickford, and marched to Pettiquamscot,
to be joined by the Connecticut contingent, forming, thus, the
largest army ever assembled in New England

they were aimed at
the Narragansetts to the west, wintering in a swamp of cedars:

"their
great remove is from their Summer fields to warme and thicke
woodie bottomes where they winter"

General Winslow had hoped
to camp at Jireh Bull's garrison, but

"found the garrison house in
ruins. This is said to have been a very strong stone house, easily
defended by a small number, and its destruction must have been
accomplished by either surprise or treachery.

the armies mustered
in the snow, and

"that night was very stormy; we lay, one thousand,
in the open field"

"no Shelter left either for Officer or private Sol-
dier"

"no other Defence all that Night, fave upon the open Air, nor
other Covering than a cold and moift Fleece of Snow"

the men made
campfires, listened to the crackle of the trees in the frost, and
cleaned their guns

*one of the bartenders shouted, ran toward the palm with a bar towel,
where small flames nibbled the frond*

sleepless and frostbitten, the men stirred before dawn

                                  "In the morn-
ing, Dec. 19th, Lord's day, at 5 o'clock we marched."

    "without Fire to warm them, or Refpite to take any Food fave
what they could chew in their March"

                            the men

                                  "waded fourteen
or fifteen Mile through the Country of the old
Queen, or *Sunke Squaw of Narhaganfet*"

                           over Tower Hill, across
Chippuxet . . .

*T-formation, with flankers, slot backs, split ends, lonesome ends—
split-T, tight-T, wing-T, shotgun: the Eagles of Boston College (1942)
won 9 straight games*

                    *November 28th faced Holy Cross at Fenway Park,
the last game of the season. It was gray and drizzly, Mayor Tobin and
the Sugar Bowl committee were in the stands. But the Eagles never got
off the ground*

*"Holy Cross . . . romped, skipped, passed and lateraled its way to touch-
down after touchdown. The final score was a humiliating 55 to 12 in
favor of Holy Cross."*

                    *the victory celebration at the Cocoanut Grove was
called off, but most everybody showed up anyway*

guided by the renegade, Indian Peter,

                        "they came at one a Clock
upon the Edg of the Swamp, where their Guide affured them they
fhould find Indians enough before Night."

                         a swamp, a tangle—
"which by Reafons of the Froft all the Night before, they were capa-
ble of going over (which elfe they could not have done)"

                              Our Forces
chopping thus upon the Seat of the Enemy, upon the fudden, they
had no Time either to draw up in any order or form of Battel, nor
yet Opportunity to confult where or how to Affault."

"But the Fron-
tiers difcerning *Indians* in the Edg of the Swamp, fired immediate-
ly upon them, who anfwering our Men in the fame language, retired
prefently into the Swamp, our Men followed them in amain with-
out ftaying for the Word of Command, as if everyone were ambi-
tious who fhould go firft, never making any Stand till they came to
the Sides of the Fort, into which the Indians that firft fired upon
them betook themfelves."

The Cocoanut Grove, Piedmont Street, Boston, Massachusetts,
November 28, 1942: a sprawling structure of brick and glass brick, con-
crete and stucco, walls and false walls, satin, bamboo, rattan, and
leatherette

beyond the revolving door were the Foyer, and the Carica-
ture Bar (the longest bar in Boston) and beneath these, at the foot of a
narrow, steep stairway—the mysteries of prohibition carefully pre-
served by management—the Melody Lounge (drinks could be bought
only with tickets purchased upstairs)

beyond the Caricature Bar,
spreading to Shawmut Street, the Main Dining Room, with Terrace,
Villa, Dance Floor, and Rolling Stage

and East of this, opening to
Broadway, the New Lounge

"The Fort was raifed upon a Kind of Ifland of five or fix Acres of
rifing Land in the midft of a Swamp; the fides of it were made of
Palifadoes fet upright, the which was compaffed about with an
Hedg of almoft a rod Thicknefs, through which there was no paff-
ing, unlefs they could have fired a way through"

"within the cedar
swamp we found some hundreds of wigwams, forted in with a
breastwork and flankered, and many small blockhouses up and
down, round about"

"a stockade more than usually stout and strong
. . . reinforced with a hedge and inner rampart of rocks and clay"

"their bark wigwams were lined with skins and well stored
with their winter supplies of corn and dried fish"

it was in the Melody Lounge, downstairs:
                                   "Get a seltzer bottle!"
                                                          "Throw
some of that bar rye on it. That's mostly water!"
                                            waiters and bartenders
hustled among the tables throwing pitchers of water and rushing back
to the bar for refills
                      one swung wildly with a bar towel
                                                  the cocoanut
palm was pulled down, but almost without flame the fire danced in the
satin overhead
                         the busboy pulled down a handful of it and sparks
showered
                 people stood up, watched the fire, edged to the stairs, formed a
crowded crescent between fire and stairs
                                 spark showers fell, squeals
and shrieks arose
                   the crescent shifted, tables and chairs overturned
                                                            a man
tried to climb through a false window
                                 the lights went out, squeals
screamed, the crescent panicked to the stairs, jammed
                                          roiling black smoke
quilted down from the ceiling, the leatherette walls ignited
                                                 yellow-white,
blue-white, gaseous, the fire seared and hissed, phosphoresced without
illumination
                   at the stairwell, the hiss whiplashed, roared, chimneyed

"It feems that there was but one Entrance into the Fort, though the Enemy found many Ways to come out; but neither the Englifh nor their Guide well knew on which Side the Entrance lay, nor was it eafie to have made another; wherefore the good Providence of Almighty God is the more to be acknowledged, who as he led *Ifrael* fometime by the Pillar of Fire, and the Cloud of his Prefence a right Way through the Wildernefs; fo did he now direct our Forces upon that Side of the Fort, into which the Indians that firft fired upon them betook themfelves."

13 steps to the head of the stairs, 12 feet to the right, and 28 feet through the Foyer to the revolving door: smoke puffed and eddied around the corners, followed by a dart of flame followed by a rush of flames and fugitives

two men reached the door, landed in the same wedge, jammed it

"The Place where the *Indians* uſed ordinarily to enter themſelves, was over a long Tree, upon a Place of Water, where but one Man could enter at a time, and which was ſo waylaid that they could have been cut off that had ventured there"

at the head of the stairs was another door, a panic door, opening to Piedmont Street—welded shut against a possible exodus of deadbeats

"But at one corner there was a Gap made up only with a long Tree, about four or five feet from the Ground, over which Men might eaſily paſs"

the revolving door didn't revolve, the crowd surged, one man smashed the glass, another tried vainly to free his arms to put out the fire in his hair

"But they had placed a Kind of Block-houſe right over againſt the ſaid Tree, from whence they ſorely galled our Men that firſt entred; ſome going ſhot dead upon the Tree, as Capt. *Johnson,* and ſome as ſoon as they entred, as was Capt. *Davenport*"

the cables snapped, the door spun fugitives, cut, bleeding and burned, to the sidewalk

"ſo as they that firſt entred were forced preſently to retire and fall upon their Bellies till the Fury of the Enemies ſhot was pretty well ſpent, which ſome Companies that did not diſcern the Danger, not obſerving, left ſundry of their Men"

a Grove employee threw up his arms: "Nobody gets out of here till he pays the check!"

"but at the laſt, two Companies being brought up besides the four that firſt marched up, they animated one another to make another Aſſault, one of the Commanders crying out, *They run, they run;* which did ſo encourage the Soldiers that they preſently entred amain"

half-burned gases arched into the vaulted Foyer, sucked forward by a fan over the Caricature Bar, and into the spaces of the Dining Room
                                                                    a waiter shouted "Fire!" and the word was heard as "Fight!"—a busboy on the Terrace saw a flash of light, thought gangsters were shooting up the joint
            black smoke, a rosy tongue along the ceiling, a blast, a ball of flame
                a group in the Villa made for the double doors opening to Shawmut Street—found them bolted
                            the lights went out, many fell to the floor and slept, breathing the sweet noxious gases
                                        others hurled tables, chairs

"After a conſiderable Number were well entred, they preſently beat the Enemy out of a Flanker on the left Hand, which did a little ſhelter our Men from the Enemies Shot till more Company came up, and ſo by degrees made up higher, firſt into the Middle, and then into the upper End of the Fort, till at laſt they made the Enemy all retire from their Sconces and fortified Places, leaving Multitudes of their dead Bodies upon the Place."

the headwaiter slumped, tuxedo ablaze

"And by this time the English people in the fort had begun to set fire to wigwams and houses in the fort, which Mr. Church laboured hard to prevent. They told him that they had orders from the General to burn them. He begged them to forbear until he had discourse with the General. And hastening to him, he begged to spare the wigwams, &c., in the fort from fire. And told him that the wigwams were musket proof; being all lined with baskets and tubs of grain and other provisions, sufficient to supply the whole army until the spring of the year, and every wounded man might have a good warm house to lodge in, who otherwise would necessarily perish with the storms and cold; and moreover that the army had no other provisions to trust unto or depend upon; that he knew that the Plymouth forces had not so much as one biscake left, for he had seen their last dealt out, &c."

but the wigwams were fired

"in the which men, women and Children (no man knoweth how many hundreds of them) were burnt to death"

"by the firing of at least five or fix hundred of thofe fmoaky Cells"

from the point of origin to the top of the stairway, 43 feet, the fire spread in two to four minutes; down the 40-foot Foyer in seconds, and from the stairway to the New Lounge doorway on Broadway, 225 feet, five minutes at most

"within two to five minutes of the first appearance of the fire most of the possible exits, including all exits normally open to the public, were useless. Pouring fire through such exits made it impossible for humans to pass simultaneously through these exits safely. In the course of such pouring, the mass of burning gaseous material appears to have been depressed from its high elevation within the premises in order to pass through the exits. The finding of bodies piled up at many of the exits is attributable to this fact."

"the shrieks and cries of the women and children, the yelling of the warriors, exhibited a most horrible and appalling scene, so that it greatly moved some of the soldiers. They were in much doubt and they afterwards seriously inquired whether burning their enemies alive could be consistent with humanity and the benevolent principle of the gospel"

smoke reached the New Lounge door on Broadway, and striking cold air, exploded

"It is reported by them that firft entred the Indians Fort, that our Souldiers came upon them when they were ready to drefs their Din-

ner; but one ſudden and unexpected Aſſault put them beſides that
Work, making their Cookrooms too hot for them at that Time,
when they and their Mitchin fryed together"

a man climbed on the Caricature Bar, ran the length of it
                                        the drummer
slumped, trapping others of the orchestra behind him, when he tried to
salvage his drum, the goddam thing wedged in the corridor
                                        the cashier
died, guarding the cash
                    a woman screamed in a walk-in refrigerator
    a bus-boy tried to get in another refrigerator, "Get out of here, kid!"
he was told, "It's full. There's no room left!"

"though there might not be above three or four hundred at any time
within the Fort at once, yet the Reſt in their Turns came up to do
what the Exigence of the Service required in bringing off the dead
and wounded Men: The Major of the *Maſſachuſets* Regiment,
together with Capt. *Moſely*, was very ſerviceable; for by that Means
the Fort being clear of the dead Bodies, it ſtruck greater Terrour
into the Enemy, to ſee but eight or ten dead Bodies of the English
left, than to meet with ſo many hundreds of their own ſlain and
wounded Carkaſſes"

outside on the sidewalk, as they were removed, the bodies piled up,
neatly ranged, like stacks of cordwood
                            and inside, near the exits, simi-
lar piles were found, each a barrier to those behind

English fell not only to Indians, but to careless shooting from their
own men in the rear

on Piedmont, Shawmut, and Broadway, the cordwood corpses—and
chairs, stools, settees, handbags, blankets, coats, broken glassware, doors
and tables

the Indians that escaped were
                        "forced to hide themſelves in a Cedar

Swamp, not far off, where they had nothing to defend them from the Cold but Boughs of Spruce and Pine Trees"

cars, trucks, taxis were commandeered, until the ambulances arrived

a

garage was broken open, to make room for bodies off the sidewalk

evac-

uation routes to hospitals and morgues were sealed to traffic

when near-

by theatres let out, crowds gathered, watched

"after two or three Hours fight, the Englifh became Mafters of the Place; but not judging it tenable, after they had burned all they could set Fire upon, they were forced to retreat, after the Daylight was almost quite fpent, and were neceffitated to retire to their Quarters, full fifteen or fixteen Miles off, fome fey more, which with their dead and wounded Men they were to march, a Difficulty fcarce to be believed"

"That long snowy cold night we had about 18 miles to our quarters, with about 210 dead and wounded . . . Many died by the way, and as soon as they were brought in"

the retreat be-
ginning by the light of the still flaming wigwams . . .

the temperature fell below freezing, water from the hoses froze, litter bearers skidded

"the Night before the Fight was, and all that Day, and the Night after, there fell fuch an extraordinary Snow that the like hath not been known for many Years"

at Boston City, the yard filled with trucks, cars, taxis, ambulances, overflowing onto Albany Street

the accident floor filled, then the cor-
ridors, stretchers could not be brought in, doctors examined in the yard
so many were checked in DOA, the dispatcher was called, told not to
send any more dead

*but they kept on coming, even those without
burns dying from inhaled gases*

*there was no room in surgery, patients
went straight to the wards*

in the confusion dead bodies were put to bed

the men, bearing dead and wounded, staggered into Wickford at 2
in the morning—except for one group that became lost, stumbling
in the snow until 7

"The whole army . . . is much disabled and
unwilling to march, with tedious storms, and no lodgings, and
frozen and swollen limbs"

"our Lofs was very great, not only be-
caufe of the Defperatenefs of the Attempt it felf (in fuch a feafon of
the Year, and fuch a Diftance from our Quarters, whereby many of
our wounded Men Perifhed, which might otherwife have been pre-
ferved, if they had not been forced to march fo many Miles in a cold
and fnowy Night, before they could be dreffed)"

*at Mass General, CO's were sent onto Charles Street to flag down traffic
and beg for blood*

"But it mercifully came to pass that Captain Andrew Belcher
arrived at Mr. Smith's that very night from Boston with a vessel
laden with provisions for the army, which must otherwise have per-
ished for want"

*The Cocoanut Grove was licensed for 460 patrons, but that night there
were close to 200 in the Melody Lounge, another 200 in the New
Lounge and, with extra tables squeezed in, better than 600 in the
Main Dining Room*

"But, O! Sir, mine heart bleeds to give your honor an account of our
lost men"

"Dec. 20th we buried in a grave 34"

"wounded and Slain
in all — 207"

"490 deaths can be verified"

"What numbers of the Enemy were slain is uncertain"

———————

behind the rear wall of the Melody Lounge, firemen stumbled onto a huge storage vault, with a cache of liquor, better than 4000 cases, on which tax had never been paid

" . . . great piles of meat and heaps of corn, the ground not admitting burial of their store"
                              meat, corn, and dried fish—alewife, shad, eel, and scup

in 1945, more than 2 years after the fire, another secret vault was opened: safecrackers entered the walled-up shell of the building and in the basement—so cleverly hidden it had escaped all probers—they found and blasted it . . . nothing was left for police

"The island was cleared and plowed about 1775, and at that time many bullets were found deeply bedded in the large trees; quantities of charred corn were plowed up in different places"

"In August of 1945, the building was razed . . . workers tore down the fence, and entered the shell . . . they picked up a blackened wrist watch, an empty wallet, the stub of a football ticket

"Indian arrow-heads, etc., have been found here at different times"

BEOTHUK

ONE

a.
the earth an ocean. the earth ocean,
      panthalassa,
          pelagos,

and under this, the rockshell,
      crustal,
          brittle,
              the lithosphere,

footing and slipping on the
      fluid,
          molten
              asthenosphere . . .

—————

above the water's surface,
      supramarine:

pangaea!

—————

the continental core:
      veins of lava, distorted, then undisturbed

auriferous: the goldcentre

surrounded by gneisses, twisted and contorted in stress of
    spreading

at the outer limits:

    arcuate submarine fractures, vents and fissures for acid lavas,
    for thermal gases, alkaline and silaceous solutions, to create
    oceans and atmosphere

the auriferous core, the provenance area:
    greenstones, overlain by grits and slaty graywackes, by water-
    lain tuffs and young clastics

the arcuate offshore fractures growing . . .

———————

the order of orogenies:

    keewatin and yellowknife, athabasca, labrador, great bear,
    grenville, appalachian, cordillera

       the canadian shield

b.
pangaea,
    the one land

———————

narrow hot dikes, dilation fissures, opened along a network of
mobile belts, the world rift system, along mountains, major faults or
midocean ridges . . . outpourings and infillings of basalt, geothermal
flow, convection currents, the lithosphere brittle under tensional
stress . . .

pangaea split up, laurasia drifting from gondwana—south america
and africa from india, antarctica and australia—north america from
eurasia . . . the atlantic opened, as north america rafted northwest-
ward on the surface of the lithosphere

the atlantic opened, and closed again, leaving only canadian basin
and gulf of mexico . . . reclosed, and the continents collided, the one
overrode the other, producing great local uplifts, pushing taconic
and newfoundland klippen before it

(gliding taconic tectonics

the foldbelt of northwest africa lay with appalachia, georgia to new
england, and into nova scotia and newfoundland:

an afroamerican border:
afroappalachia

the atlantic opened, reclosed, and opened again

extrusion of flood basalts on the ocean floor, forming dikes,
flexures, and molten aprons, forcing the continents apart

(earth's magnetic field reversing, and turning again,
causing magnetic anomaly patterns in the lavas out-
pouring from midocean ridges

paleomagnetism locked in the rocks at the time of
hardening

shear-motions, half-shears, strike-slip faults, wrench-faults,
megashears

continental block drifts, blocks of crust slipping differentially
away from the crest of the rise-ridge system, the ocean inter-
posing between sundered continents, as the lands drifted on
the subcrustal plasticity, the viscous flow of the asthenos-
phere

TWO

a.

a snowdrift,
 blown onto a sheltered shelf
survived the summer

snow fell, failed
to melt,
the drift fattened,

>   (in what is now
>   hudson bay . . .

fattened & compressed,
compacted, re-
congealed, became

>   firn . . .

water, percolating from
the melting surface—
and from close compaction
of the crystals—refroze,
recrystallized, and
firn became ice . . .

fattening and thickening,
nourished by wet winds from the south,
the ice domed

>   (over what is now
>   hudson bay

lower layers
flowed outward
from the center,

growing, fattening,
down valleys and onto
elevations

          (leaving nunataks,
          as, the tongaks

snow
     to firn
        to ice,

domed, flowing outward,
over north appalachia:

the laurentide ice

———————

under the weight
of ice,
the brittle lithosphere

became plastic:

the crust subsided,
basinlike,

the younger sediments
compacted, fluid,

          (most deeply
          under what is now
          hudson bay . . .

———————

but, rooted,
antique and isostatic,

the laurentian shield
held,

the land
did not yield . . .

the land
held

---

the ice spread
southward, asymetrically,

more heavily southward
from the domecenter,

      (originally at
      the pole

producing a
centrifugal effect
on the spinning
earth

and the land beneath
dragged → southward

to what is now
hudson bay

b.
bosses of rock rising in the glacial bed raised corresponding ice-
domes at the surface: unborn nunataks, shattered or unbroken

sunpits marked the surface, & honeycombs: . . . suncups, spikes,
pinnacles, thumbprint ice, decapitated shafts, and

penitents:

regular & uniform,
elliptical & pyramidal,
occasionally acicular,
the apices
leaning
equatorwards . . .

———————

subglacial streams roared softly, their tunnels rising and falling, undulating irregularly, to appear at the snout as vaults . . .

———————

the glacier, plastic and fluid, debouching over plains or insinuating into fissures, grooving the sole in the lee of boulders, conforming to twisted and tortuous channels . . . sheets of hexagons, although puckered, gliding over one another, the grains slipping, and slip within the grains, the ice moving along slipplanes, glideplanes, faulting and dragging, twisting, distorting and fluting, clusters of crystals jerking, pulsing . . .

at the snout, live ice overrode the dead

———————

a flexible rasp, the glacier left the rock striated & grooved, quarried & fluted, polished into faultmirrors . . . lunoid furrows and lunate fractures, crescentic gouges and chattermarks, bedrock knobs with rockdrifts streaming from the lee . . . the rock brecciated, slicken-sided, crushed, and shattered . . .

———————

. . . pushed till beyond the shore: the continental shelf swathed with thick terrigenous drift . . .

———————

halting,

and retreating,

the ice first yielded at the peripheries: sudden outbursts of sub-
glacial lakes and rivers, great walls of water draining through
englacial fissures and subglacial chutes, forming transient lakes and
shortlived streams, shrinking, enlarging, rising, falling . . .

the shrinking icesheet ponded water in the deepsagged crustal
basins

and as the weight of ice lifted, the crust upwarped, doming, and the
water decanted:

the great lakes drained first to the mississippi, then to the mohawk
and hudson, and finally the st. lawrence

wasted at the peripheries, the glacier released at the center:

residual laurentide ice, in hudson bay, calved weakly into the intrud-
ing sea

---

the laurentian shield, now, a young land: drained by shallow rivers,
connected lakes, waterfalls

restigouche: the river which divides like the hand

c.

gaspé, percé, le rocher percé:

northeastern supramarine terminus of appalachia

appalachia, entering canada from new england, swings from its
northeast spine through an ogee arc, into an east and finally a
southeast curve, the peninsula a great sigmoid shape

a region of drowned mountains, out to the codbanks, the lost lands
of percesia, the folded cliffs, gnawed, broken and gnawed, by the
tooth of the sea

> pine, spruce,
> spine of rock,
> *insula,*
> *paene insula,*
> saline assaults,
> sun and fog

and the offshore islands crowned by fog scuds of cormorants and
gulls

d.
"sabla lieth to the seaward of cape breton"

sable island: 110 miles se of cape canso, in 43° 6' n. and 60° west

sable island, emerging out of the sea, out of the codbanks, after
glacial submergence

moonshaped, lunoid, crescentic . . . like a beothuk canoe

at the focus and meeting point of ocean currents: the gulf stream,
flowing from the south . . . the arctic current from the north, past
labrador, and dividing, part flowing around newfoundland, and part
passing through the strait of belle isle, to join the outflow of the st.
lawrence, thence through cabot strait, to sable

the currents meeting, conflicting, swirling, with a westerly wind, so
that an empty cask, or a man's body, may circumnavigate the island
many times, before landing

composed of pure sand, quartz, and tiny garnets, the island is
pushed eastward by the prevailing westerlies, the wind cutting in
the hills on the sea face, forcing the sand over the crest or up the

gullies, the island moving, rolling, sand engorged and re-exposed

and shrinking: now half as large as originally reported, as sand blown off the hills settles at sea

hurricane winds whip off the summits of the hummocks, wind-scoop the sand hollows, carry before them clouds of seadrift, altering overnight the face of the island

the old land, ponded with fresh water, diminishes, and the old lagoon alternately opens and closes to the sea, sandfilling and shrinking

earthquakes shift the coastline, throwing up reefs

the sea at night will blaze with phosphorescence, the waves breaking high, as in flames

THREE

a.

These Indians are the original inhabitants of the Island of Newfoundland, and though beyond a doubt descendants from some of the tribes upon the continent of America . . . yet it will be very difficult to trace their origin. They have been so long separated from their ancient stock, as well as from all mankind . . .

> *"The Voice" told them that they sprang from an arrow or arrows stuck in the ground.*

kamchatka, perhaps,
thence
across the strait

to alaska,
down the backbone of the earth,
down the colorado,
up the mississippi,
thence
eastward, northeastward:

the beothuk indians.

zigzagging,

driven from behind,

by abnaki and micmac,

to the penobscot river,

thence northward, northeastward,

to new brunswick, nova scotia, newfoundland,

arriving after the vikings, but found (1497) by cabot, fully set-
tled in *terra nova* of the codfish:

the people painted with red ocher,
the red indian,
the Naturall people of the country

---

in the fall migrations, they passed from the rugged mountains of the
north, to the low mossy and sheltered valleys, the woody parts of the
interior and south:

flat rattle
rangers river
river of exploits

thunder brook
bloody point
red indian lake

they had black hair, tied on top with a wooden pin . . . broad face, flat nose, and large eyes . . .

lived in conical lodges and low huts, made fire by striking sparks from iron pyrites into down of the canada jay . . .

enjoyed steam baths . . .

ate the inner bark of the balsam pine, drank seal oil, baked an egg cake in the sun, ate pudding of seal's fat, livers, and eggs

built deer fences along the river of exploits, hunted from a gaze . . .

and put to water in sharpkeeled birchbark canoes, *made in forme of a new Moone*

b.
sable island:

sighted, perhaps, by bjarni herjolfson, 986

. . . the Portingalls about thirty years past did put into the same Island both neat and swine to breed, which were since exceedingly multiplied

cattle and sheep introduced, 16th century, by portuguese or french

1598, the marquis de la roche landed 40 convicts, *tramps and able bodied beggars* . . . intending to return, he was driven off by storms . . . the convicts made shelters from boards of a wreck, clothed themselves in sealskin, ate a few sheep washed ashore, wild cattle and fish . . . 1603, only 11 survived to be rescued

1633, john winthrop reported walrus, red cattle and black foxes on
the island

wild horses appeared, 18th century, swimming ashore, perhaps, from
a french wreck, or introduced, of new england stock:

> 12 to 14 hands high,
> head large and ill set on,
> jowl thick,
> ear small,
> neck cock thrappled or swelling out in front,
> withers low,
> quarters short and sloping,
> legs robust,
> pasterns thick and upright,
> forelock and mane abundant,
> > reaching nearly to the ground

----

hogs were brought in, ran wild, became fierce, but failed to
survive a bad winter
                    english rabbits were landed, and prospered
    but rats landed from wrecks, ran wild, killed the rabbits
                                                            cats
were introduced, killed the rats, then finished the rabbits, ran wild,
became fierce
            dogs were landed, they killed the feral cats
                                                    once again,
rabbits were stocked, they thrived and multiplied, became a nui-
sance
        until the snowy owls appeared, exterminated the rabbits, and
left
        a third time, rabbits were released, they prospered, cats were
brought in to control them
                            seven red foxes were let loose, and in a
single season destroyed both rabbits and cats

----

the blown sand forms a mound, a dune, and the sandwort, the sand grass takes possession, *the growing point so hard and sharp that it might almost penetrate wood*

crowberry growing in the old land, the empetrum heaths, forms a green springy carpet

sand grass and wild pea: hay and fodder for the wild horses

cranberry growing in damp sand and thin humus

ponds with boggy marshes

wild rose, blue lily, goldenrod and china-aster

strawberry and blueberry, sorrel, everlasting and meadowrue

the nuthatch the ips

wich

sparrow

on the vanishing island

FOUR

a.

june 22, 1611,

in the southernmost part of hudson bay,

in the Ise in the partes of America:

. . . and Nicholas Sims, late of Wapping, sailor, to be indicted for having, on 22 June 9 James I, in a certain ship called The Discovery of the port of London, then being on the high sea near Hudson's Straits in the parts of America, pinioned the arms of Henry Hudson, late of the said precinct of St. Katherine, mariner, then master of the said ship The Discovery, and putting him thus bound, together with . . . mariners of the said ship, into a shallop, without food, drink, fire, clothing or any necessaries, and then maliciouly abandoning them . . .

Grene, with 11 or 12 more of the company, sailed away with the Discovery, leaving Hudson and the rest in the shallop in the month of June in the ice

What became of them he knows not.

There was no watchword given, but Grene, Wilson, Thomas and Bennett watched the master, when he came out of his cabin, and forced him over board into the shallop, and then they put out the rest, being sick men.

They were not victualled with rabbits or partridges before Hudson and the rest were turned into the shallop, nor after.

But, when they were in the shallop, Grene and the rest would not suffer them to come any more on board the ship, so Hudson and the rest in the shallop went away to the southward, and the ship came to the eastward, and the one never saw the other since.

What is otherwise become of them he knoweth not.

In the meane time, went Henry Greene *and another to the Carpenter, and held him talke until the Master came out of his Cabbin, which hee soone did. Then came* John Thomas *and* Bennet *before him, while* Wilson *bindes his armes behind him; he asked what they meant; they told him that he should know when hee was in the Shallop.*

Now were all the poore men in the Shallop . . . the Carpenter got of them a piece, and powder and shot, and some pikes, an Iron pot with some meale, and other things. They stoode out of the Ice, the Shallop being fast to the sterne of the Ship, and so when they were nigh out (for he cannot say they were cleane out), they cut the head-fest from the sterne of their ship, and then out went topsailes, and stood to the E. in cleare Sea, having lost sight of the Shallop.

Being asked what became of the said Hudson the Mr and the rest of the companie that were put into the shallopp saythe that they put out sayle and followed after them that were in the shipp the space of halfe an houre and when they saw the shipp put on more sayle and that they could not follow them then they putt in for the shoare and soe they lost sighte of them and never heard of them since . . .

. . . by reason of which they came to their death and miserably did perish . . .

(. . . and so . . . did kill and murder . . .)

———————

Men turned owte of the Ship, 23 June

Henry Hudson, Mr.
John Hudson, his Son
Arnold Ladley
John King, qrMr.
Michall Butt, Maried.
Thomas Woodhowse, a mathematition put away in great
distress.

Adame Moore.
Philip Staff, Carpenter.
Syracke ffanner, Maried.

b.

WHEREAS *it has been represented to the King, that the subjects residing
in the said Island of Newfoundland, instead of cultivating such a
friendly intercourse with the savages inhabiting that island as might be
for their mutual benefit and advantage, do treat the said savages with
the greatest inhumanity, and frequently destroy them without the least
provocation or remorse. In order, therefore, to put a stop to such inhu-
man barbarity, and that the perpetrators of such atrocious crimes may
be brought to due punishment, it is His Majesty's royal will and plea-
sure, that I do express his abhorrence of such inhuman barbarity, and I
do strictly enjoin and require all His Majesty's subjects to live in amity
and brotherly kindness with the native savages of the said island of
Newfoundland. I do also require and command all officers and magis-
trates to use their utmost diligence to discover and apprehend all persons
who may be guilty of murdering any of the said native Indians, in
order that such offenders may be sent over to England, to be tried for
such capital crimes . . .*

> (. . . *they secrete themselves in the woods,*
> *keep an unremitting watch*
> *and are seldom seen;*
> *a conduct which*
> *their defenceless condition*
> . . . *have compelled them to adopt.)*

1770, the beothuk quarrelled with the micmac, fought a dis-
astrous battle at grand pond . . .

> the french offered the micmac a reward
> for every head of a beothuk

I fear that the race will be totally extinct in a few years . . .

What number of these Indians may still be left, no person can even hazard a conjecture, but it must decrease annually: for our people murder all they can . . .

. . . at the East end of Badger Bay Great Lake, at a portage known as the Indian path we found traces made by the Red Indians . . .

> *. . . the chance of finding even a single family now . . . is very small indeed.*

> *. . . the native Indians have not been seen on the coast this year.*

The good work should be continued, until it becomes morally certain that none remain . . . The prospect of success seems clouded, but however late the effort, it will be a consolation to have done all that was now possible.

> *They had totally deserted their favorite Rendezvous . . .*

> *The banks of the noble River of Exploits we afterwards also found abandoned.*

1827, the beothuk institution for the civilization of the native savages sent out an expedition:

. . . but discovering nothing which indicated that any of the living tribe had recently been there, Mr. Cormack rafted about seventy miles down the river, touching at various places in his way, and again reached the mouth of the Exploits, after an absence of thirty days, and having traversed 200 miles of the interior, encompassing most of the country which is known to have been hitherto the favorite resort of the Indians.

> *. . . the race has emigrated, or become extinct.*

Although we may infer where the remnant of the Red Indians would most likely be found, yet from the certainty of the smallness of their number, if any really do exist, it would not be prudent again to send an armed ...... (the remainder of this MS. is torn off)

> on some of the old french charts
> of the north of the island,
> *le petit nord,*
> a track or path is shown,
> along the low flat shore
> forming the south side of
> the strait of belle isle,
> and facing the coast of labrador:
> it is called
> *chemin de sauvage,*
> and may mark the last of the beothuk,
> emigrating to the north . . .

> they feared
>
> a powerful monster,
>
> who was to appear
>
> from the sea . . .

> the micmacs
>
> thought them witches:
>
> they could raise
>
> a fog,
>
> through which
>
> to escape

BIBLIOGRAPHY

BASH BISH

Alvord, Clarence and Lee Bidgood. *The First Explorations of the Trans-Alleghany Region by the Virginians, 1650-1674.* Cleveland, Oh., 1912.

American Scenic and Historical Preservation Society, 15th Annual Proceedings. Albany, N.Y., 1910.

Arber, Edward. *The First Three English Books on America.* Edinburgh, 1885.

——. *The Story of the Pilgrim Fathers, 1606-1623* - (N.P.), 1897.

Archer, Gabriel. *Relation.* [Old South Leaflets, No. 120] Boston, Mass.

Atwood, Wallace W. *The Physiographic Provinces of North America.* New York, N.Y., 1964.

Beauchamp, W. M. *Aboriginal Place Names of New York.* Albany, N.Y., 1907.

——. *Indian Names in New York State.* Fayetteville, N.Y., 1894.

Beverley, Robert. *History and present state of Virginia.* Chapel Hill, N.C., 1947.

Boyd, S. G. *Indian Place Names.* York, Pa., 1885.

Braun, E. Lucy. *Deciduous Forest of Eastern North America.* Philadelphia, Pa., 1950.

Brown, Alexander. *The Genesis of the United States.* London, 1890.

Budd, T. *Good Order Established in Pennsilvania & New Jersey in America* ed. E. Armstrong. New York, N.Y., 1865.

Burnaby, Andrew. *Travels through the Middle Settlements.* London, 1904.

Burrage, Champlin, ed. *John Pory's Lost Description of Plymouth Colony.* Boston, Mass. 1918.

Burrage, H. S. *Early English & French Voyages.* New York, N.Y., 1906.

——. *The Beginnings of Colonial Maine.* Portland, Me., 1914.

Chadbourne, A. H. *Maine Place Names.* Portland, Me., 1955.

Chamberlain, B. B. *These Fragile Outposts.* New York, N.Y., 1964.

Chase, L. B. *Early Indian Trails.* Worcester Society of Antiquity Collections, vol. 14.

——. *The Bay Path.* Norwood, Mass., 1919.

Douglas, Marjory Stoneman. *The Everglades: River of Grass.* New York, N.Y., 1947.

Douglas-Lithgow, Robert A. *Dictionary of American Indian Place and Proper Names in New England.* Salem, Mass., 1909.

Dunaway, W. F. *A History of Pennsylvania.* New York, N.Y., 1935.

Dunlap, A. and Weslager C. A. *Indian Place-names in Delaware.* Wilmington, Del. 1950.

Espenshade, A. H. *Pennsylvania Place Names.* State College, Pa., 1929.

Fenneman, N. M. *Physiography of Eastern United States.* New York, N.Y., 1938.

Force, Peter. *Tracts and Other Papers* . . . Washington, D.C., 1836-46.

Georgia Historical Society, Historical Collections. 1840-42.

Grifone, Francis V. *The Middle Trails.* Auburn, N.Y., 1956.

Hakluyt, Richard. *Divers Voyages* . . . N.P., 1582.

——. *The Principal Navigations, Voyages, Traffiques and Discoveries of the English Nation.* Glasgow, 1903-05.

Hall, C. C., ed. *Narratives of Early Maryland, 1633-84.* New York, N.Y., 1910.

Hanna, C. A. *The Wilderness Trail.* 2 vol., New York, N.Y., 1911.

Harisse, Henry. *The Discovery of North America.* London, 1892.

Hart, A. B., ed. *American History Told by Contemporaries.* N.P., 1897-1929.

Higginson, Francis. *New England's Plantation.* N.P., 1630.

Horsford, E. N. *The Indian Names of Boston.* Cambridge, Mass., 1886.

Huden, J. C. *Indian Place Names of New England.* New York, N.Y., 1962.

Hulbert, A. B. *Historic Highways of America.* Cleveland, Oh., 1902-05.

James and Jameson, eds. *Journal of Jasper Danckaerts.* New York, N.Y., 1913.

James, Thomas. *The Strange and Dangerous Voyage* . . . N.P.), 1633.

Jameson, J. Franklin, ed. *Narratives of New Netherland.* New York, N.Y., 1909.

Johnson, Douglas. *Stream Sculpture on the Atlantic Slope.* New York, N.Y., 1931.

——. *New England Acadian Shoreline.* New York, N.Y., 1925.

Johnston, J. S., ed. *First Explorations of Kentucky.* Louisville, Ken., 1898.

Josselyn, John. *An Account of Two Voyages to New England.* Boston, Mass., 1865.

Kalm, Peter. *Travels into North America.* London, 1772.

Kenny, Hammill. *Origin and Meaning of Indian Place Names of Maryland.* Baltimore, Md., 1962.

King, Philip B. *The Evolution of North America.* Princeton, N.J., 1959.

Lawson, John. *History of North Carolina.* Richmond, Va., 1937.

Levermore, C. H., ed. *Forerunners and Competitors of the Puritans and Pilgrims.* Brooklyn, N.Y., 1912.

Lindestrom, P. *Geographia Americae* trans. A. Johnson. Philadelphia, Pa. 1925.

Lobeck, Armin K. *Things Maps Don't Tell Us.* New York, N.Y., 1956.

Lorant, S. *New World.* New York, N.Y., 1946.

Marye, Wm. B. *The old Indian Road.* Baltimore, Md., 1920.

Masta, H. L. *Abenaki Indian Legends, Grammar and Place Names* . Victoria-ville, Queb., 1932.

McKeen, John. *Remarks on the Voyage of George Waymouth.* Maine Historical Collections, vol. 5, series 1. Portland, Me., 1857.

Mereness, N. D., ed. *Travels in the American Colonies.* New York, N.Y., 1916.

Miller, W. D. *The Ancient Paths to Pequot.* Providence, R.I., 1937.

Moore, Ruth. *The Earth We Live On.* New York, N.Y., 1963.

Morgan, L. H. *League of the Iroquois.* Rochester, N.Y. 1851.

Myer, W. E. *Indian Trails of the Southeast.* 42nd Report, Bureau of American Ethnology, Washington, D.C., 1924-25.

Myers, A.C., ed. *Narratives of Early Pennsylvania, West New Jersey and Delaware, 1630-1707.* New York, N.Y., 1912.

Nelson, Wm. *The Indians of New Jersey.* Paterson,N.J., 1894.

New England Historical & Geneological Register, vol. 55.

Parsons, Usher. *Indian Names of Places in Rhode Island.* Providence, R.I., 1861.

Penn, William. *Description of Pennsylvania.* Boston, Mass., 1906.

Price, C. B. *Historic Indian Trails of New Hampshire.* Lowell, Mass., 1958.

Purchas, Samuel. *Hakluytas Posthumus, or Purchas his Pilgrimes.* Glasgow, 1905-07.

Quinn, David B. *The Roanoke Voyages, 1584-1590.* London, 1955.

Raesly, Ellis L. *Portrait of New Netherland.* New York, N.Y., 1945.

Read, Wm A. *Florida Place Names of Indian Origin.* Baton Rouge, La., 1934.

——. *Indian Place Names in Alabama.* Baton Rouge, La., 1937.

Ruttenber, E. M. *Footprints of the Red Men.* Newburgh, N.Y., 1906.

Salley, Alexander, S., ed. *Narratives of Early Carolina.* New York, N.Y., 1911.

Schoolcraft, H. R. *Report of Aboriginal Names* . . . New York, N.Y., 1845.

Sheafer, P. W. *Historical Map of Pennsylvania.* Philadelphia, Pa., 1875.

Shimer, John A. *This Sculptured Earth.* New York, N.Y., 1960.

Smith, John. *Travels and Works* (ed. by Edward Arber). Edinburgh, 1910.

Snyder, C. F. *The great Shamokin Path.* Sunbury, Pa., 1945.

Strachey, Wm. *History of Travaille into Virginia Britannia.* London, 1849.

Tooker, W. W. *The Indian Place-names on Long Island.* Port Washington, N.Y., 1962.

Trumbull, J. H. *Indian Names of Places, etc., In and On the Borders of Con-necticut.* Hartford, Ct., 1881.

Tyler, Lyon Gardiner, editor. *Narratives of Early Virginia, 1606-25.* New York, N.Y., 1907.

Wallace, Paul A. W. *Indian Highways of Pennsylvania.* Philadelphia, Pa., 1953.

Whitaker, Alexander. *Good Newes from Virginia.* N.P., 1613.

Wilson, Samuel. *Account of the Province of Carolina in America.* London, 1682.

Winsor, Justin. *Narrative and Critical History of America.* Boston & New York, 1889.

Winthrop, John. *Journal* ed. J. K. Hosmer. New York, N.Y., 1908.

THE FEAR IN YE BUTTOCKS

Anderson, Melville B., trans. *Relation of the Discovery of the Mississippi River* . . . Chicago, Il., 1898.

——. *Relation of the Discoveries and Voyages of Cavalier de la Salle from 1679 to 1681.* Chicago, Il., 1901.

Arber, Edward. *The First Three English Books on America.* Westminster, 1895.

Baxter, J. P. *A Memoir of Jacques Cartier.* New York, N.Y., 1906.

Bigger, H. P., ed. *The Voyages of Jacques Cartier.* Ottawa, 1924.

Christy, Miller. *The Voyages of Captain Luke Fox and Captain Thomas James.* London, 1894.

Collinson, Richard. *The Three Voyages of Martin Frobisher* . . . London, 1867.

Coyne, James H., ed. & trans. *Exploration of the Great Lakes, 1669-1670* . . . Toronto, 1903.

French, B. F. *Historical Collections of Louisiana.* New York, N.Y., 1846-53.

Gosch, C. C. A. *Danish Arctic Expeditions 1605 to 1620.* London, 1897.

Hakluyt, Richard. *Early English Voyages to America.* London, 1889.

——. *The Principal Navigations, Voyages, Traffiques and Discoveries of the English Nation.* London, 1927.

Hart, A. B., ed. *American History Told by Contemporaries.* New York, N.Y., 1897.

Hennepin, Louis. *A New Discovery of a Vast Country in America.* Chicago, Il., 1903.

Kellogg, Louise P. *Early Narratives of the Northwest, 1634-1699.* New York, N.Y., 1917.

LeClercq, C. *First Establishment of the Faith in New France.* New York, N.Y., 1881.

Lescarbot, Marc. *The History of New France.* Toronto, 1907-14.

Markham, A. H. *The Voyages and Works of John Davis.* London, 1880.

Markham, C. R. *The Voyages of Sir James Lancaster, Kt., to the East Indies.* London, 1877.

Parkman, Francis. *The Pioneers of France in the New World.* Boston, Mass., 1899.

Pease, T. C. and Warner, R. C. *The French Foundations, 1680-1693.* Springfield, Ill., 1934.

Purchas, Samuel. *Hakluytas Posthumus, or Purchas his Pilgrimes.* Glasgow, 1905-07.

Radisson, Pierre E. *The Voyages of Peter Esprit Radisson.* Boston, Mass., 1885.

Sagard, Gabriel. *Long Journey to the Country of the Hurons.* Toronto, 1939.

Shea, J. D. G. *Discovery and Exploration of the Mississippi Valley.* New York, N.Y., 1852.

——. ed. & trans. *The Jogues Papers.* New York, N.Y., 1857.

Steck, Francis B. *The Jolliet-Marquette Expedition, 1673.* Washington, D.C., 1927.

Thwaites, Reuben Gold. *The Jesuit Relations and Allied Documents.* Cleveland, Oh., 1896-1901.

Tyrrell, J. B., ed. *Documents Relating to the Early History of Hudson Bay.* Toronto, 1931.

Williamson, J. A. *The Voyages of the Cabots and the English Discovery of North America under, Henry VII and Henry VIII.* London, 1929.

SOUTH→

Amory, Thomas C. *William Blackstone.* Boston, Mass., 1877.

Carpenter, E. J. *Roger Williams.* New York, N.Y., 1909.

Chapin, H. M., ed. *Documentary History of Rhode Island.* 2 vols., 1916-19.

Covey, Cyclone. *The Gentle Radical.* New York, N.Y., 1966.

De Costa, B. F. *William Blackstone.* New York, N.Y., 1880.

Easton, Emily. *Roger Williams, Prophet and Pioneer.* Boston, Mass., 1930.

Elton, Romeo. *Life of Roger Williams.* London, 1852.

Ernst, James E. *Roger Williams, New England Firebrand.* New York, N.Y., 1932.

Gammell, Wm. *Life of Roger Williams.* Boston, Mass., 1846.

Haley, John W. "William Blackstone," *Old Time New England*, vol. 49, No. 1. Boston, Mass., 1958.

Hopkins, Stephen. *An Historical Account of the Planting and Growth of Providence.* Providence, R.I., 1885.

Knowles, James D. *Memoir of Roger Williams.* Boston, Mass., 1834.

Mather, Cotton. *Magnalia Christi Americana.* 2 vol., Hartford, Ct., 1820.

Strickland, Arthur B. *Roger Williams.* Boston, Mass., 1919.

Williams, Roger. *The Complete Writings.* 7 vol., New York, N.Y., 1963.

Winslow, Ola E. *Master Roger Williams.* New York, N.Y., 1957.

TELEMAQUE

The Robert Williams story is taken entirely from the files of the Charlotte Observer, on the dates indicated in the text.

The Denmark Vesey story is from the following sources:

Hamilton, James Jr. *Negro Plot. Account of the Late Intended Insurrection among a Portion of the Blacks of this City.* Boston, Mass., 1822.

Higginson, T. W. *Travellers and Outlaws.* Boston, Mass., 1889.

Homer. *The Odyssey.* Trans. Robert Fitzgerald, New York, N.Y., 1961.

Kennedy, Lionel H. and Parker, Thomas. *An Official Report of the Trials of Sundry Negroes.* Charleston, S.C., 1822.

Lofton, John. *Insurrection in South Carolina.* Yellow Springs, Ohio, 1964.

I would also like to acknowledge a personal letter—April 24, 1962—from the late Chalmers S. Murray of Edisto Island, South Carolina, who clarified for me a few points of early Charleston geography, and gave information on the plantation boats.

OKEFENOKEE.

Material for this chapter was gathered at the Museum at Okefenokee Swamp Park.

SHICK SHOCK

Adair, James. *The History of the American Indians.* New York, N.Y., 1968.

Antevs, Ernst. "The Spread of Aboriginal Man to North America." *Geographical Review,* vol. 25, no. 2. April, 1935.

Beach, W. W., ed. *Indian Miscellany.* Albany, N.Y., 1877.

Birkit-Smith, Kaj. Folk-wanderings and Culture Drifts in Northern North America. *Journal de la Societé des Americanistes de Paris.* vol. 22, Paris, 1930.

Brinton, D. G. *The Lenape and their Legends.* Philadelphia, Pa., 1885.

——"The Shawnees and their migrations." *Historical Magazine,* vol. 10, no. 1. New York, N.Y., 1866.

Bushnell, D. I. *Tribal Migrations East of the Mississippi.* Washington, D.C., 1934.

Caldwell, J. R. *Trend and Traditions in the Prehistory of the Eastern United States.* Memoir 88, American Anthropological Association, 1958.

Cusick, David. *Ancient History of the Six Nations.* Fayetteville, N.Y., (no date).

Dixon, Roland B. "The Early Migrations of the Indians of New England and the Maritime Provinces." *Proceedings,* American Antiquarian Society, 1914.

Gatschet, A. S. *A Migration Legend of the Creek Indians.* Philadelphia, Pa., 1884.

Griffiin, J. B. "Some Prehistoric Connections Between Siberia and America." *Science,* vol. 131, no. 3403. March 18, 1960, Washington, D.C.

Haywood, John. *Natural and Aboriginal History of Tennessee.* Nashville, Tenn., 1823.

Hulbert, A. B. *Historic Highways of America,* vol. 2. Cleveland, Oh., 1902-05.

Jenness, Diamond. *Prehistoric Culture Waves.* Washington, D.C., 1941.

Jennings, J. D. *The Native Americans.* New York, N.Y., 1965.

—— and Norbeck, Edward. *Prehistoric Man in the New World.* Chicago, Il., 1964.

Lilly, Eli. "Tentative Speculations . . .", *Proceedings, 54.* Indiana Academy of Science, 1945.

Magnusson, Magnus, and Palsson, Herman. *The Vinland Sagas: the Norse Discovery of America.* Baltimore, Md., 1966.

McGowan, Kenneth, and Hester, J. A. Jr. *Early Man in the New World.* Garden City, N.J., 1962.

McKern, W. C. "An Hypothesis for the Asiatic Origin of the Woodland Culture." *American Antiquity,* vol. 3, 1937.

Mooney, James. *Myths of the Cherokees.* U.S. Bureau of American Ethnology, Annual Report, Washington, D.C., 1900.

Mowat, Farley. *West Viking.* Boston, Mass., 1965.

Neuman, George. "The Migration and the Origin of the Woodland Culture." *Proceedings 54,* Indiana Academy of Science, 1945.

Sauer, Carl. "Geographic Sketch of Early Man in America." *Geographical Review,* vol. 34, 1944.

Schoolcraft, H. R. *Notes on the Iroquois.* Albany, N.Y., 1847.

Silverberg, Robert. *Mound Builders of Ancient America.* Greenwich, Conn., 1968.

Skelton, R. A., Marston, T. E. and Painter, G. D. *The Vinland Map and the Tartar Relation.* New Haven, Conn., 1965.

Swanton, J. R. *Social Organization and Social Usages . . .* 42nd Annual Report, Bureau of American Ethnology, Washington, D.C., 1924-25.

——. "The Indians of the Southeastern United States." *Bulletin 137,* Bureau of American Ethnology, Washington, D.C., 1946.

Thomas, Cyrus. "Prehistoric Migrations in the Atlantic Slope of North America." *American Antiquarian and Oriental Journal,* vol., 18-19, 1896-1897.

——. *Some Suggestions in Regard to Primary Indian Migrations . . .*

——. *Proceedings*, Fifteenth International Congress of Americanists.

Wallace, A. F. C. and Reyburn, W. D. "Crossing the Ice: A Migration Legend of the Tuscarora Indians." *International Journal of American Linguistics*, vol. 17, no. 1, 1951.

Walum Olum or Red Score. *The Migration Legend of the Lenni Lenape or Delaware Indians*. Indianapolis, In. 1954.

COCOANUT INDIANS

The account of the Cocoanut Grove fire is derived from:.

Benzaquin, Paul. *Holocaust!*. New York, N.Y., 1959.

The facts of the Great Swamp Fight are selected from the following:

Abbott, J. S. C. *History of King Philip*. New York, N.Y., 1859.

Bennett, M. K. "The Food Economy of the New England Indians, 1605- 75". *Journal of Political Economy*, vol. 43, no. 5, October, 1955.

Bodge, G. M. *Soldiers in King Philip's War*. Boston, Mass., 1906.

Church, Thomas. *The History of King Philip's War*. ed. H. M. Dexter, N.P., 1865.

Drake, S. G., ed. *The Old Indian Chronicle*. Boston, Mass., 1867.

Ellis, George W. and Morris, John E. *King Phillip's War*. New York, N.Y., 1906.

Hubbard, William. *The History of the Indian Wars in New England*. ed. S. G. Drake. N.P. , 1865.

Leach, D. E. *Flintlock and Tomahawk*. New York, N.Y., 1958.

Lincoln, Charles H., ed. *Narratives of the Indian Wars*. New York, N.Y., 1913.

Mather, Increase. *A Brief History of the War with the Indians in New-England*. ed. S. G. Drake. N.P., 1862.

Tompkins, Hamilton B. *The Great Swamp Fight*. N.P., 1906.

BEOTHUK

Blackett, P. M. S., Bullard, E. and Runcorn, S. K. *A symposium on Continental Drift*. London, 1965.

Bonnycastle, Richard H. *Newfoundland in 1842*. London, 1842.

Charlesworth, J. K. *The Quaternary Era*. London, 1957.

Christy, Miller. *The Voyages of Captain Luke Fox and Captain Thomas James*. London, 1894.

Clarke, John M. *L'Ile Perce'e*. New Haven, Ct., 1923.

——. *Perce: a Brief Sketch of its Geology*. Albany, N.Y., 1904.

——. *Sketches of Gaspe*. Albany, N.Y., 1908.

Dawson, George M. *Summary Report.* Annual Report (1899), vol. 12, Geological Survey of Canada, Ottawa, 1902.

Des Barres, J. F. W. *The Isle of Sable.* Atlantic Neptune, i, 68—1777 and 1779.

Dietz, Robert S. & John C. Holden. "The Breakup of Pangaea." *Scientific American,* October, 1970.

Dixon, R. B. "The Early Migrations of the Indians of New England and the Maritime Provinces". *Proceedings.* American Antiquarian Society, April, 1914.

Dyson, James L. *The World of Ice.* New York, N.Y., 1962.

Encyclopedia Britannica, 11th Edition. New York, N.Y., 1911.

England, G. A. *Isles of Romance.* New York & London, 1929.

Ewen, C. E. *The North-West Passage.* London, 1938.

Flint, Richard F. *Glacial and Pleistocene Geology.* New York, N.Y., 1957.

Hapgood, C. H. *Earth's Shifting Crust.* New York, N.Y., 1958.

Hodge, F. W., ed. *Handbook of American Indians North of Mexico.* Washington, D.C., 1907.

Howley, J. P. *The Beothuks or Red Indians.* Cambridge, Mass., 1915.

Janvier, Thomas A. *Henry Hudson.* New York, N.Y., 1909.

Kirke, H. *The first English Conquest of Canada.* London, 1871.

Kuiper, Gerard P., ed. *The Earth as a Planet.* Chicago, Il., 1954.

Lanctot, Gustave. *A History of Canada.* Cambridge, Mass., 1963.

Lloyd, T. G. B. "On the Beothuks of Newfoundland." *Journal of the Anthropological Institute,* vol. 5, 1876.

Martin, Alan. "Journal of the Late Captain J. A. Farquhar." *Collections,* vol. 27, Nova Scotia Historical Society, Halifax, 1947.

Moore, Ruth. *The Earth We Live On.* New York, N.Y., 1956.

Oxley, J. M. *"Historic Aspects of Sable Island." Magazine of American History,* vol. 15, 1886.

Patterson, George. "Sable Island: Its History and Phenomena." Transactions of the Royal Society of Canada, 1894 & 1897.

Prowse, D. W. *History of Newfoundland.* London, 1895.

Sanderson, Ivan T. *The Continent We Live On.* New York, N.Y., 1961.

Selwyn-Brown, Arthur. "People Without Relatives." *Newfoundland Quarterly,* December, 1928.

Speck, F. G. "Montagnais-Naskapi bands and early Eskimo distribution." *American Athropologist,* vol. 33, 1931.

St. John, Harold. *"Sable Island." Proceedings, Boston Society of Natural History,* vol. 36, no. 1, March, 1921.

Stokes, W. L. *Essentials of Earth History.* Englewood Cliffs, N.J., 1960.

Swanton, John R. *The Indian Tribes of North America.* Washington, D.C., 1952.

Wilson, J. T. *A New Class of Faults and their Bearing on Continental Drift* Nature, 207, 1965.

——. "Did the Atlantic Ocean Close and Re-open?" *Nature*, vol. 211, 1966.

——. "Some Implications of New Ideas on Ocean-floor Spreading Upon the Geology of the Appalachians." *Royal Society of Canada.* Special Publications, no. 10. Toronto, 1967.

ADH-0271

11/18/97

PS
3563
E83
1996

V.1

Middlebury College

0 00 02 0685639 5